A

MW00810158

The Netherlands is known among foreigners today for its cheese and its windmills, its Golden Age paintings and its experimentation in social policies, for example around cannabis and euthanasia. Yet the historical background for any of these quintessentially Dutch achievements is often unfamiliar to outsiders. This concise history offers an overview of this surprisingly little-known but fascinating country. Beginning with the first humanoid settlers, the book follows the most important contours of Dutch history, from Roman times through to the Habsburgs and the Dutch Republic and the Golden Age. The author, a modernist, pays particularly close attention to recent developments, including the signature features of contemporary Dutch society. In addition to being a political history, this overview also gives systematic attention to social and economic developments, as well as in religion, the arts and the Dutch struggle against the water. The Dutch Caribbean is also included in the narrative.

JAMES C. KENNEDY, an American, is an expert in recent Dutch history. He has published widely in this field, including books on the cultural revolution of the 1960s and Dutch euthanasia policy. For eight years he was Professor of Dutch History from the Middle Ages at the University of Amsterdam before becoming Dean of University College Utrecht.

CAMBRIDGE CONCISE HISTORIES

This is a series of illustrated "concise histories" of selected individual countries, intended both as university and college textbooks and as general historical introductions for general readers, travelers, and members of the business community.

A full list of titles in the series can be found at:
www.cambridge.org/concisehistories

A Concise History of
the Netherlands

JAMES C. KENNEDY

University College Utrecht

CAMBRIDGE
UNIVERSITY PRESS

CAMBRIDGE
UNIVERSITY PRESS

University Printing House, Cambridge CB2 8BS, United Kingdom

One Liberty Plaza, 20th Floor, New York, NY 10006, USA

477 Williamstown Road, Port Melbourne, VIC 3207, Australia

4843/24, 2nd Floor, Ansari Road, Daryaganj, Delhi – 110002, India

79 Anson Road, #06-04/06, Singapore 079906

Cambridge University Press is part of the University of Cambridge.

It furthers the University's mission by disseminating knowledge in the pursuit of education, learning and research at the highest international levels of excellence.

www.cambridge.org
Information on this title: www.cambridge.org/9780521875882
DOI: 10.1017/9781139025447

First published 2017

Printed in the United Kingdom by TJ International Ltd. Padstow Cornwall

A catalog record for this publication is available from the British Library.

Library of Congress Cataloging-in-Publication Data
Names: Kennedy, James C., 1963– author.
Title: A concise history of the Netherlands / James C. Kennedy
(Vrije Universiteit, Amsterdam).
Description: Cambridge, United Kingdom; New York, NY: Cambridge
University Press, 2017. | Series: Cambridge concise histories |
Includes bibliographical references and index.
Identifiers: LCCN 2017003654 | ISBN 9780521875882 (hardback) |
ISBN 9780521699174 (paperback)
Subjects: LCSH: Netherlands – History.
Classification: LCC DJ109 .K46 2017 | DDC 949.2–dc23
LC record available at https://lccn.loc.gov/2017003654

ISBN 978-0-521-87588-2 Hardback
ISBN 978-0-521-69917-4 Paperback

CONTENTS

v

FIGURES

MAPS

ACKNOWLEDGMENTS

I was educated as an historian in modern European history, but my advisor, David Schoenbam, thought that due to my background, I ought to try Dutch history, given that the Netherlands was an undervalued and little-known country. It was good counsel, for which I am grateful, and it resulted in my dissertation on the Netherlands in the 1960s. This specialization also led, after teaching Dutch history at Hope College in Holland, Michigan, to be asked to become professor of contemporary history at the Free University of Amsterdam before being asked to become professor of Dutch history since the Middle Ages at the University of Amsterdam. It was also about that time – in 2007 – that I was invited to write this book, though many projects got in the way of a timely completion of the work. The course I offered in Dutch history, along with my colleagues Peter van Dam and Paul Knevel, did serve as a basis for this book and for my own reflection on Dutch history, and without that experience the writing of this book would have been much more difficult. All of my colleagues at the section of Dutch history, which I had the privilege of leading, served as important inspiration for this work.

The book would not have been possible without several leaves of absence, including from the University of Amsterdam in 2013 and Utrecht University, my new employer, in 2015. Although I bear all responsibility for any errors, I have been tremendously aided by readers who helped spare me from worse: Peter van Dam, Mario Damen, Joost Jonker, Paul Knevel, Mart Rutjes, Catrien Santing and student assistant Kiki Varekamp.

Last of all I would like to thank my parents. As the son of a Dutch mother and American father, who traveled frequently during the summer months to the Netherlands from the United

States, I had the great advantage of experiencing two sides of the Atlantic. Their reflections, their observations and their experiences as a Dutch-American couple have been seminal to my own understanding of the Netherlands and in the deepest sense, then, the book could not have been written without them.

CHRONOLOGY OF EVENTS
IN DUTCH HISTORY

c. 5,550 BC	First agricultural settlements in the Netherlands.
c. 3,000 BC	Dolmens constructed in Drenthe.
c. 750 BC	First *terpen*, or *wierden* (mounds), constructed in Frisia.
57 BC	Julius Caesar invades the southern Netherlands.
12 BC	Roman rule established in many parts of the Netherlands.
AD 69–70	Batavians revolt unsuccessfully against Roman rule.
270s	Franks penetrate far below the old Roman boundaries.
c. 400	Roman rule comes to an end in the Netherlands.
600s	Rise of Dorestad as leading trade center of the region.
695	Missionary Willibrord becomes "archbishop of the Frisians."
754	Missionary Boniface murdered in Frisia (Dokkum).
785	Charlemagne defeats the Saxons under Widukind
843	Treaty of Verdun divides Carolingian Empire into three parts.
1018	Dirck III defeats the emperor, helping to define the future county of Holland.
1227	Battle of Ane ensures eastern areas of the Sticht are free from Utrecht.
1288	Battle of Woeringen confirms Brabant's leading regional role over Guelders.

1346	Beginning of the long-term clan conflicts in Holland between Cods and Hooks.
1356	"Joyous Entry" agreement compels dukes of Brabant to respect existing privileges.
c. 1407	First windmill.
1421	Great St. Elizabeth's Day Flood, destroying the Grote Waard.
1428	"Kiss of Delft" between Jacqueline (Jacoba) of Hainaut and her rival cousin Philip the Good.
1464	First meeting of the States-General after being called together by Philip the Good.
1477	Great Privilege concedes historical rights privileges and limits power of ruler.
✗ 1525	First Protestant martyr to be burned at the stake in the Netherlands.
1548	Burgundian Circle established, containing almost all of the Low Countries.
1566	The Great Iconoclasm, in which Protestants destroy "idols" across the region.
1568	Battle of Heiligerlee, now seen as start of the struggle for Dutch independence.
1572	Sea Beggars seize Den Briel, catalyzing revolt against Spain in Holland and Zeeland.
1573–1574	Alkmaar and Leiden withstand the sieges of the Spanish.
1579	Union of Utrecht signed, effectively the constitution of the future Dutch Republic.
1581	"Plakkaat van Verlatinghe" repudiates King Philip II and his "tyranny."
1584	Murder of Willem the Silent.
1588	Defeat of the Spanish Armada.
✗ 1618–1619	Synod of Dordrecht, establishing Calvinist doctrine internationally.

1619	Establishment of Batavia on Java, the chief Dutch base in the East Indies.
1634	Dutch seize Curaçao, to become their most important base in the Caribbean.
1642	Rembrandt completes *The Night Watch*.
1648	Peace of Münster, which ends eighty-year war with Spain, recognizes Republic.
1650–1672	First period without a *stadhouder*, called the "True Freedom."
1672	"Year of Disaster," in which the Republic is attacked by France, England and others.
1688	*Stadhouder* Willem and his wife Mary seize power in Great Britain.
1702–1747	Second period without a *stadhouder*, after death of Willem III.
1713	Peace of Utrecht brings an end to long war with France.
1747–1748	Revolutionary tumult across the Netherlands brings the House of Orange back into power.
1787	Patriots' Movement seeking restoration of old rights is suppressed by Prussian army.
1794–1795	French armies invade the Netherlands, ushering in revolutionary regimes.
1798	The first modern constitution promulgated, creating a unitary state.
1806	Louis Napoleon becomes the first king of the Netherlands.
1810–1813	The Netherlands in its entirety annexed to France.
1813	Return of Prince Willem Frederik of Orange to become head of new regime.
1814	Unification of the Netherlands and Belgium under guidance of the Great Powers.

1815	Napoleon defeated at Waterloo, in part through role of Dutch forces.
1830	Cultural system introduced on Java – a financial windfall for the Dutch government.
1830	Belgian revolt puts an end to the United Kingdom of the Netherlands.
1848	A new liberal constitution is penned by J. R. Thorbecke.
1873	Beginning of the Aceh Wars, signaling expansion of Dutch power in the East Indies.
1878	Opposition to the liberal School Law sparks political mobilization of religious groups.
1903	Great Railway Strike, forcefully put down by the confessional government.
1914–1918	The Netherlands, with occasional difficulties, stays neutral during World War I.
1917	Pacification of 1917 grants universal franchise and publicly funds religious schools.
1932	Completion of the causeway (Afsluitdijk) cuts Zuyder Zee off from the sea.
1935–1936	Dutch economy at its lowest point during the Great Depression.
1940–1945	The Netherlands invaded and occupied by Nazi Germany.
1942–1944	Jews systematically deported to their deaths in eastern Europe.
1944–1945	"Hunger Winter" in the Netherlands, resulting in over 50,000 deaths.
1948	Marshall Aid, including $1 billion in grants, offered to the Netherlands.
1949	Netherlands recognizes Indonesian independence.

1953	Great North Sea Flood hits the southwestern part of the country.
1959	Natural gas tapped in Groningen, financing Dutch welfare state.
1965	Provo launches activities in Amsterdam; advent of Dutch counterculture.
1973	Oil Crisis emblematic of start of slowing economy and higher unemployment.
1975	Independence of Surinam triggers widespread migration from that country.
1979–1985	Large protest movements delay decision about stationing NATO cruise missiles.
1980	Squatters demanding better housing disrupt inauguration of Queen Beatrix.
1982	Wassenaar Accord revitalizes Dutch economic "polder model."
1995	Dutch UN troops fail to prevent fall of Srebrenica and ensuing massacre.
2000	Dutch Parliament legalizes same-sex marriage, the first to do so.
2002	Murder of Pim Fortuyn is the catalyst for political turmoil in Dutch politics.
2005	Dutch voters reject the European Constitution by a wide margin.
2010	Dissolution of Dutch Antilles, with each island choosing its own form of government.
2013	Government begins decentralization of the once extensive welfare state.

Introduction

~

The Significance of Dutch History

"The Dutch are quite small and can never be top nation really," the famous English parody *1066 and All That* (1930) concluded after acknowledging their successful Golden Age naval exploits. Though intended as anything but a judicious assessment of Dutch history, the mock appraisal is amusing precisely because many do think of the Netherlands as too small to be a big factor in European or world history. Even modern Dutch historians tend to think disparagingly of their own national history. The modest size of the Netherlands, in the context of larger nations or mammoth transnational processes, seems to doom the country's past to the historical dustbin.

This book, in contrast, is committed to the idea that Dutch history is "big" enough to be of great interest to many readers. In the first place, the history of the Netherlands has been chiefly characterized by intense and quick adaptation to new situations that have had wider consequences. For the last six centuries at least – if not longer – the country has been at the forefront of human change, playing a central and leading role in the development of the modern economy; in the development of technical innovation, most famously but hardly exclusively related to water management; at times in defining artistic and intellectual expressions of creativity. In doing these things, the Netherlands has punched above its weight and size in the last six centuries, becoming in the course of these centuries prosperous and well educated, all the while being governed, for the most part, by the rule of law that offered a stabilizing context for these achievements. One could argue, if one is interested in such comical distinctions, that the Dutch Republic did get very close to becoming "top nation" in the seventeenth century, and even as it settled to the status of a small country in Europe and mid-sized colonial power it continued to play a role in continental and global affairs beyond what its size would suggest.

Perhaps another way of putting it is that the Netherlands stands out in its extensive and intricate involvement in long-term globalization processes. Ancient migrations and subjugation to Roman and Frankish rule exposed the country early on to new influences. Dutch participation in the flow of people, ideas and goods in the later Middle Ages eventually made them the middlemen of Europe, and later, during the Dutch Republic, the world. Since that time, the Dutch have been deeply influenced by, and dependent upon, these larger transnational dynamics, just as they continued their own significant role in shaping the modern world. Given its small size, which depended so much on interactions with the outside world, there is no better country than the Netherlands to study the history of globalization.

The second reason why Dutch history is important is that it is a fascinating study in how a perennially fractured and highly differentiated society managed not only to survive but to thrive. No lord exercised absolute rule for long over their Dutch subjects. From the Middle Ages power was widely diffused among many players, and the expansion of religious diversity – more extensive for a long time than practically anywhere else in Europe – after the Reformation only made the country more fractured. That this situation did not lead to endemic chaos – despite serious periods of dislocation and violence – is one important reason to study the history of the Netherlands. The Dutch frequently needed to find common cause in tackling shared problems or in facing common enemies, creating over time the practices of consultative government and citizen participation that have by now characterized Dutch society for a long time. This success has perhaps made the Dutch and Dutch history dull to some, lacking the exciting instability that has characterized more colorful – and bloodier – regions of Europe or the world. Yet that success is just as important and as compelling for those wanting to see how diverse societies manage to hold together – which in the Dutch case also involves many turbulent and violent episodes.

The abiding themes of this book, in summary, are the Dutch historic ability to adapt to their continually changing situation, often effectively so, whether against their environment; their economic rivals; or their mortal enemies, foreign or domestic; as well as their sustained ability to create a relatively tranquil commonwealth that necessarily took account of the fractured nature of power in Dutch society. These are human and not uniquely Dutch themes, but the striking contours of the Netherlands' past offers particularly compelling insights into each.

Seen this way, the history of the Netherlands is an improbable success story, of how the residents of a soggy wasteland made for themselves a free, secure and prosperous society. But the paths to that success were uneven and paved with difficulties, and for that reason this history cannot be a facile onwards-and-upwards narrative. Violence, inequality, divisions, instability and deprivation – all of these things accompanied Dutch achievement, even in its recent history, perhaps even to the present day. Dutch trading talent, for example, was – to put it mildly – not always a win–win outcome for all parties, and Dutch freedoms, stubbornly defended and deeply cherished, were not freedoms meant for everyone in equal measure. This history, then, is at pains also to recognize the complexities and the shadow sides of a past that for so long has been marked by signal successes and triumphs.

Defining the Netherlands

In order to offer this history, this book looks chiefly at historical developments within the *territory* that *at present* constitutes the Kingdom of the Netherlands. That is in itself something of a challenge, and for several different reasons.

The first challenge has to do with Holland. For many English speakers, Holland is synonymous with the whole of the Netherlands. The reason for this conflation is historical: since the sixteenth century Holland has been the most populated and the most economically powerful part of the country. Down to the present day, it is where most of the country's political, economic and cultural elites live and work. It is the part that still attracts the most tourists and visitors to its cities, including Amsterdam, Rotterdam and The Hague, and still offers the stranger the country's most quintessential landscapes: the dikes, the polders, the windmills. For this reason, it is tempting to fold the history of the Netherlands into the history of Holland. Yet in reality the two modern provinces of North and South Holland constitute only about a sixth of the total size of the country. Moreover, their decisive dominance over what is the Netherlands might be restricted to the time of the Dutch Republic, in the seventeenth and eighteenth centuries. Prior to this, Holland was not the most important force in the region, and the creation of the unitary state in 1798 diffused its influence thereafter. My work here attempts to correct an overly Hollando-centric view of Dutch history by pointing to telling developments and events elsewhere, all the while taking account of Holland's significance.

Another conundrum is "the south," and the fact that the Netherlands is tied so closely to other parts of the Low Countries. Dutch society owes much in language and culture to developments in Flanders and Brabant, the Dutch-speaking parts of Belgium, where for a long time everything seemed to happen earlier than in "the north." Until the unforeseen outcome of the war between Spain and the young Dutch Republic divided "north" and "south" they were for several decades joined together as the Burgundian Circle, and commercial and cultural synergy between them had been more or less unfettered for centuries. Seen from this perspective, it is difficult to ignore southern developments, at least before the seventeenth century. Complicating this picture is that a large part of the southern provinces of the Netherlands – Limburg, North Brabant and Zeeland – were once part of Brabant or Flanders, underscoring the point that from a territorial point of view the history of the Netherlands is also the history of Brabant and Flanders, and not just of Holland or the other northern and eastern provinces.

To this might be added that some southeastern parts of the Netherlands became "Dutch" only in the early nineteenth century, having constituted until then parts of the Holy Roman Empire. And if one considers that almost all of the Netherlands was once part of the Holy Roman or German Empire, one could conclude that "Dutch" history must be considered part of "German" history. Indeed, the designation "Dutch" (*deutsch*) is a reminder that centuries ago English speakers regarded the Dutch and the Germans as a single people.

However tempting it might be to tell the history of Belgium and Germany along with the Netherlands, and however refreshing it might be to offer a perspective that transcends national boundaries, a "concise" national history such as this does not allow for it. What I have attempted to do is to pay significant but not extensive attention to developments in Flanders and Brabant, especially in relevant periods, with more attention to the parts of these old provinces that are now part of the Netherlands. Keeping the history of "the south" and (to a much lesser extent) Germany obliquely within the boundaries of this story might be seen as a marginalization of these pasts, but I see their slanted inclusion precisely as a way to emphasize that there are other historical strands of Dutch history than a "northern" or Hollando-centric vision alone would allow.

Tricky, too, is the issue of the country's colonial past and present. The Dutch once had an extensive "seaborne empire" that at present has been reduced to six Caribbean islands: Aruba, Bonaire, Curaçao, Saba, St. Eustatius and St. Maarten, all formally part of the Kingdom of the Netherlands. Since Sri Lanka, Surinam,

South Africa and especially (given its longstanding importance) Indonesia no longer constitute part of this kingdom, they fall by definition outside the confines of this book. And yet here, too, a studied avoidance of the intensive Dutch interactions with these places seems a distortion even of a history that defines itself by the territorial boundaries of the present. I have thus felt the need to give some very modest attention to the Dutch imperium as it historically developed.

Because the Dutch Caribbean remains part of the Netherlands, its islands receive relatively much attention in this history compared to the former colonies, even as I continue to take account of their rather small size (only about 2 percent of the kingdom's total current population live there). The importance of slavery to most of these islands accounts for the multiple references to it in this book, a focus that exceeds that which some Dutch histories have given the phenomenon. And it also explains the focus on Atlantic slavery in contrast to slavery in the East Indies, which, though differently constituted, was at least as widespread as it was in "the West."

A final word on "territory" is less problematic but still worth saying, and that has to do with the relationship between the Dutch and the water. Simply put, the Netherlands historically has been a shapeshifter, taking on new forms as the sea made its claims on the land and as the Dutch fought back. Some lands once subject to human habitation have sunk irretrievably beneath the seas; the western coastline, for instance, was at points kilometers further west than it now is, and this is only one of many examples. Other areas have been claimed or reclaimed from the water, most successfully and extensively in the twentieth century – a campaign that continues into this century through the expansion of Rotterdam harbor. This history, in thinking territorially, pays attention to the changing boundaries between land and water as the Dutch experienced it in the course of centuries.

Coverage and Periodization

This book is the only one that covers the whole history of the Netherlands in a few hundred pages, a size that allows enough room to lay out the most important developments without being too abbreviated. The book in its style aspires to be comprehensive by paying attention to a range of different developments in Dutch history, so that a reader might get a taste of the breadth of it. And yet my background and specialization reveal certain emphases. In the first place, it will be clear that I am a modernist, privileging the period from the late sixteenth century onwards. Those familiar with Dutch history may further distill that I am particularly at home in the two most recent chapters, covering the period after 1870. Nevertheless, I believe it important to offer a comprehensive overview of all of Dutch history. Two of the seven chapters are thus devoted to the period before 1588 and the establishment of an independent Dutch state. A national history without this early history would be a truncated one.

My choice of topics reveal my commitment both to "coverage" and to a hierarchy of interests that I hope is only subtly evident. Political history, the tried-and-true way of structuring national histories, is the leading framework here as well, giving as it does considerable attention to important domestic and international developments in the realm of politics. Religious history, so important a part in the Dutch story of managing (or failing to manage) difference, is also highlighted – a choice made easier by my own expertise in this field. Economic and social developments, vital as they are, also receive systematic focus. Cultural and intellectual advancements receive less systematic attention, though I diligently attempt to point to the "highlights" of Dutch cultural life that are an indispensable part of this country's heritage. Some attention is also paid to the military history of the Netherlands, as recognition that the boundaries of the Dutch state and its predecessors have often been violently contested.

This last point has bearing on a final one: the periodization of the chapters. All chapters, except for the very end, which culminates in the present day, start and conclude with some kind of foreign intervention. This underscores a basic pattern of Dutch history: that the country's past has been shaped by numerous interfaces with external developments that intruded into the affairs of the Dutch. These expressions of outside influences are not only – or are even most importantly – defined by armed invasion, but more by long-term economic and cultural processes. Still, the choice of periodization, and the discontinuities in Dutch history that they suggest, have been chosen to illustrate how much external actors – including outright invaders – have determined the historical direction of this country.

Nevertheless, as I have stressed, the Dutch were not simply the passive objects of such interventions. No nation, group or individual is ever simply that. The Dutch, as I have argued above, have proved adaptive and inventive in the face of new external challenges: whether the water, or machinations of the Great Powers. Without stooping to clichés about "brave little Holland" or avoiding the darker sides of Dutch history, I hope to offer readers a portrait of a country that will elicit some sympathy for the way the Dutch tried to rise above difficult circumstances and create, in ways however circuitous and unpredictable, the enviable country that it is today.

From the Margins to the Mainstream

Dutch History to 1384

∽

(For most of human history, the territory that now constitutes the Netherlands lay at the edges of human activity.) Its climate and geography were not conducive to early or easy settlement. Even as empires expanded across parts of northwestern Europe – first the Romans, then the Franks – the Netherlands remained at the edges. By the beginning of the Middle Ages, this allowed local rulers and, increasingly, local residents, to create their own spaces. By the time of the High Middle Ages, effective duchies and counties had emerged with a productive agricultural system and a heightened measure of urbanization, even if they could not match in size the great cities of Flanders. By the late fourteenth century the region's wealth and strategic importance made it increasingly coveted by Europe's dynastic houses, who now strove for control over it. The Netherlands was no longer at the edges of Europe.

Pre-Roman Times

The Earliest Human Inhabitants

Continuous human habitation came late to what is now the Netherlands. It came later than it did in the Americas, where the first identified settlements date from roughly 15,000 years ago. To be sure, *Homo heidelbergensis*, predecessors of modern humans, lived as hunters and especially gatherers in the southern parts of the Netherlands perhaps a quarter of a million years ago, when most of the country was covered by ice sheets. No skeletons of these peoples remain, but the discovery of tools near Maastricht and Rhenen, dating roughly, if not unproblematically, from that period, suggest their presence. Their stay, in relative terms, was also late; *Homo heidelbergensis* had lived in southern Europe for tens of thousands of years before migrating to the Netherlands. Later these people were joined by other, competing types of humans. The stay of these peoples, however, was not permanent; the last indications of their presence ended about 35,000 years ago. As a result of extended ice ages, and the fact that the Netherlands lay far away from the warmer zones of more extensive human habitation, the land would not again witness humans until after 10,000 BC, when the last ice age ended. As the sea level dramatically rose and the once-dry North Sea filled from melting glaciers, the region became wetter, more subject to flooding and also more suited to human habitation, full of vegetation and wildlife.

It was a hesitant population process – the first of these people may not have settled permanently – and it was, even by global population levels of the time, a modest migration. The groups who lived in the present-day Netherlands were small in size, perhaps averaging twenty or so individuals, and in the first years of their presence may not have numbered more than 1,000 – a number that grew slowly over time. Their archaeological record is more extensive than for the very first inhabitants, but establishing the contours of their lives remains elusive. Some startling finds have pointed to some details. The so-called Pesse Canoe, named after the town in Drenthe where it was found, is a 10-foot dugout dating back to no later than 7,500 BC, making it the oldest extant boat in the world. It was a suitable vehicle for inhabitants who spent much of their time hunting and fishing in a watery landscape of marshes, creeks and lakes. This is confirmed by another even more arresting discovery in the region of the great rivers Maas, Rhine and Waal: one of the very oldest graves in the Netherlands, dating back to between 5,500 and 5,000 BC, containing the remains of a woman between forty and sixty years of age.

Her own small group, judging by the food remains near her grave, lived on the safe heights of river dunes while using their canoes to catch pike in the river, in addition to using flint arrows to shoot birds while gathering fruits, vegetables and nuts.

These initial inhabitants did not erect permanent buildings or settle down to a farm life – let alone build towns or cities, as was then being begun far to the south and east. But this, too, would gradually change, as new technologies encouraged more people to settle in the region.

A More Settled Existence

The first signs in the Netherlands of the Neolithic age, in which farming and more sophisticated stone instruments were the key components, began about 5,500 BC on the plateaus of southern Limburg, a region with a loam soil that is well suited to agriculture, and with the closest proximity to the Neolithic technologies then spreading across Europe. In fact, it is likely, judging by their ceramics, that these first farmers were themselves migrants from central Europe. They domesticated cattle and pigs and cultivated legumes, wheat, and flax, made possible on an extensive scale through the adoption of the plough. The first producers of earthenware in the region, possibly through the use of ovens, these farmers' most impressive achievements were their long wooden houses. These were up to 40 meters in length, likely built in part to accommodate their animals. Their farmsteads seldom grew to become settlements of any size, but the more reliable way of life they created boosted the population of the region.

Agriculture may have been the wave of the future, but its advance was fitful in the Netherlands. It was less evidently suited to the more watery regions of the country, where hunting and fishing continued to predominate for a long time, and where farming, even late in the Neolithic period, was often more of a secondary and small-scale activity. It also depended on patterns of migration. It was a different group of hunter-farmers from northern Europe, for instance, that came to settle and farm in the northern Netherlands, some 2,000 years after the Limburg farms first appeared. These people of the so-called Funnel-Beaker Culture, so named for the shape of their distinctive pottery, established their own small-scale settlements in this part of the country. That their society had become both more sedentary and more socially complex and hierarchical is evidenced in the most enduring testament to their culture: dolmens, or stone burial chambers, of which several dozen have partially survived in the province of Drenthe. Making use of stones weighing in excess of 20,000 lb each, these settlers likely built the impressive tombs not for everyone but for their elite. The creation of the stone tombs was discontinued by about 2,800 BC in favor of a practice that found widespread emulation in the region: the earthen burial mound.

1 Older than fabled Stonehenge, the 5,000-year-old dolmens are by far the oldest extant structures in the Netherlands. Their makers and their purposes remain shrouded in mystery.

The continued isolated position of the region is underscored by the fact that the Iron Age, too, was slow to make its entry into this part of the world. By about 700 BC, about five centuries after they appeared in the Mediterranean, the first iron artifacts began to be used in the southern Netherlands, and it would take another century or two before these technologies penetrated into the northern parts of the region.

The peoples initially producing these Iron Age instruments were the Celts, whose origins stemmed from central Europe, and it is likely that these new inhabitants of the southern and western Netherlands kept close cultural and economic contacts with their kinfolk of the so-called La Tène Culture across large portions of western Europe. The Netherlands was the northern continental boundary of Celtic settlement, and from the northeast, Germanic groups began to move into the region. In a gradual process that may largely have been completed by the arrival of the Romans, it may be that the Germanic languages supplanted the Celtic across all or most of what is now the Netherlands, although it seems likely that the people of this sparsely populated region spoke differing language mixtures and drew from different cultures.

No one knows with any certainty how many people lived in the Netherlands on the eve of Roman invasion; it has been estimated that anywhere between 10,000 and 100,000 people lived there. In western and northern parts of the country life continued to be characterized by accommodation of the water. The first *wierden*, or *terpen* – artificial mounds that afforded their inhabitants protection from the water – were built about 2,750 years ago in Groningen and Friesland, the lower-lying land around these mounds being used for grazing and farming at times of low water. These activities, in addition to fishing and trading, made this region perhaps one of the most prosperous of the Netherlands by about the time the Romans arrived.

Although the inhabitants of the Low Countries may have settled down to cattle-tending, fishing and farming, late Iron

Age culture was anything but pacific. In a society with no central authority, winning glory through martial feats of arms – including making war on rival groups and looting their possessions – was a key activity of the Germanic Batavians who came to reside in the Betuwe region in the center of the contemporary Netherlands. The Romans would have to take account of these warrior traditions when they first made active acquaintance with the region, and the Romans' ability to pacify or combat these "barbarians" would become a major challenge to their rule.

The Roman Netherlands

The Establishment of Roman Power

Seeking military prestige and needing money that could be attained by demanding tribute of the defeated, Julius Caesar, as governor of Gaul, aimed to pacify restless northern Gaul. By 57 BC, with as many as eight legions at his disposal, this possibly brought him near the southern boundaries of the present-day Netherlands. Caesar's own histories, the very first extensive written source on the region, identified two of his chief antagonists, who may have inhabited the southern parts of the present-day Netherlands: the Menapii in the west and the Eburones in the east. For the next several years, they were at war against Rome. Unable to defeat Caesar on the battlefield, they withdrew into the forests and swamps, prompting the Romans to burn down their farms and, in the case of the Eburones, despoil as much as they could of their tribal lands. The Menapii submitted in 53 BC; it may be that the Eburones eventually did as well. But the Roman grip on the region was itself fleeting.

It was only a full generation after Julius Caesar's first foray that Rome, after a long period of civil war and political consolidation, had the focus and the resources to establish itself in the region. Determined to pacify the Germanic tribes that were raiding their territories, the Romans, led by the talented general Nero Claudius

2 Brother and father to future Roman emperors, it was Nero Claudius
Drusus Germanicus, and not Julius Caesar, who ushered in a longstanding
Roman presence in the Netherlands.

Drusus Germanicus, set out to pacify areas east of the Rhine. To
this end, they made use of the Batavians by exempting them from
tribute in exchange for the use of their troops. In an effective
show of force in 12 BC they easily subdued the Frisians in the
north and west of the current Netherlands and moved far east of
the Rhine. Not all of these gains were permanent, however. The
complete decimation of three Roman legions at the Teutoburg
Forest (about 100 km east of the current Dutch border) in AD 9
forced the Romans back, for the most part, to the west side of the
Rhine. In AD 28 the Frisians rose up against the Roman military
authorities – who had enslaved a number of Frisians after a dispute over the quality of the cowhides the Frisians had to deliver as
tribute – and managed to slaughter hundreds of Roman soldiers as

they chased them from the area. Twenty years later the Romans, in one last, abortive attempt to invade Germania, made an alliance with the Frisians, which facilitated the extensive trade between them, but the lands north and east of the Rhine remained, for the most part, free of direct Roman rule.

Even then, the Rhine was not always a stable boundary, and the occasion for its breach in AD 69 was, as it had been with the Frisians, a revolt against Roman injustice. The Batavians, who provided Rome with large numbers of auxiliary soldiers, some of whom had helped to conquer Britain, were at the center of the revolt. Two of its leaders, Julius Civilis and his brother Paulus, both Roman citizens, were wrongly accused of treason, with the latter executed for it, prompting the former to seek vengeance. That opportunity arose during the brief civil war in Rome in the wake of the Emperor Nero's death, in which one of Nero's fleeting successors demanded that the Batavians be conscripted into the Roman army instead of volunteering as they had always done. This led to a full-scale revolt by the Batavians, aided by other Germanic tribes on the far side of the Rhine. Initially successful, the revolt pushed the Roman legions far away from the Rhine, endangering much of Roman Gaul.

The end of the civil war, though, enabled its winner, the new Emperor Vespasian, to send a large Roman force to retake the lost provinces. By the end of AD 70, as Rome made use of its superior military power, he forced a negotiated peace on his opponents. What happened to Julius Civilis himself is unknown, but after ransacking the Batavians' territory Rome made peace with them and other Germanic tribes, whose cooperation remained an essential element of the Roman defense structure. The Batavians, in any event, were restored in their role as auxiliary soldiers for the empire. The revolt, in short, achieved little, though it became the basis of a later popular myth that the Dutch were descendants of the freedom-loving Batavians (a myth made highly questionable by the probability that the Batavians eventually migrated out of the Netherlands).

These disruptions notwithstanding, the frontier – the *limes* – on the Rhine, protected by the Roman navy, the Roman legions and their Germanic auxiliaries, enabled the stable development of Germania Inferior – as the region became known by the end of the first century – as a Roman province. It was in the first century, too, that the first real towns of the region were built, perhaps on the basis of earlier pre-Roman settlements, perhaps on the basis of Roman military needs. Of these towns, now in the Netherlands, the first was possibly Maastricht (Mosae Trajectum), its name indicating that this is where the Maas could be forded. On the Rhine and its tributaries, in addition to many forts, a number of towns were erected, including Nijmegen, the first town to receive a Roman city charter (part of its original name, Novio Magus, is rooted in the Celtic for "new field"); the initially secondary Rhine fortress settlement of Utrecht (Traiectum ad Rhenum); and, near the sea, Voorburg (Forum Hadriani), the only town in present-day Holland with a Roman municipal charter. By the early second century the frontier was quiet enough that the Romans could substantially reduce their military presence around Nijmegen, the central settlement of the Batavians. Roman rule was – at least for a time – unchallenged south and west of the Rhine.

Life in the Empire

The Roman Netherlands, or the lands north of it, never became heavily settled, harboring a population that can only be numbered, and then with great uncertainty, in the tens of thousands. Its biggest towns, Heerlen, Maastricht and Nijmegen, probably each had at least a few thousand residents. Although the considerable presence of Roman artifacts suggests that Roman culture came to penetrate the lives of the Batavians deeply at their capital, Novio Magus, the most extensively Romanized parts of the present-day Netherlands lay in southern Limburg. It was there that the all-important military road between Roman Gaul and

17

3   This may have been what the first Dutch settlement with city rights, Ulpia Novio Magus, or Nijmegen, looked like in its first years. It was also the chief settlement of the Batavians.

the German frontier ran, which in time also encouraged commerce. Romans built a bridge in Maastricht in the first century as a link in this road. It was there that settlement from the south, from Gaul, was likely the most extensive. And it was there, in the loam soil, that landed estates arose, where farming techniques varied little from those in the Roman heartland of northern Italy. The work on these largely wheat-growing estates, which also dotted Belgium and northern France, was probably performed by tenant farmers in the service of the landowner: either a local luminary or a former legionnaire rewarded for his services. The size of these larger farms grew over time, and the wealthiest of the *villae* offered its owners all of the creature comforts of Roman culture and technology, including frescoes, mosaics, tile-warmed central heating and extensive baths. The sizeable settlement of Coriovallum (Heerlen) also offered baths to the public, attested to by the most extensive Roman ruins discovered in the Netherlands. It was in these southern areas that Roman industry such as pottery-making was most extensive. Here, too, the absence of stationed troops suggests that it was a safe part of the empire.

If less Romanized, the areas further north were nevertheless significant to the economic life of the empire. The Rhine and its tributaries not only formed the *limes* of the empire but, just as importantly, were major trading arteries on which the empire relied. The whole river region was important as a transit area, helping to enable seafaring trade with Roman Britain, from which grain was imported, and the Romans built a couple of canals to make the Rhine more navigable. Trade with the Frisians, either through money or barter, continued, as indicated by the numerous Roman artifacts found on the *terpen* of Friesland or what is now North Holland. The river region and the sandy grounds of Brabant were also developed agriculturally, though the emphasis there was less on crops and more on the tending of cattle and horses.

Over time, too, the *Pax Romana* did foster new expressions of cultural and religious life across the region. Only a small group of either Romans or non-Romans read and wrote well in the region's first written language, Latin, but a broader group, including some beyond the *limes*, possessed a level of practical literacy necessary for daily business. Roman law became the norm and, even where not dominant, influenced, over time, the legal traditions of the regional tribes. Religious life, too, changed. Though the Romans themselves were hardly averse to violent spectacle, practices upon which they expressly frowned – such as human sacrifice, practiced by Germanic tribes, or druidic rituals – probably faded away. More certain is that local populations began to supplicate their own gods in ways that increasingly resembled Roman custom, illustrated in the new temples, altars and consecrated stones that marked the landscape. The temple at Elst in Gelderland, built around 2,000 years ago, was dedicated to Hercules Magusanus, the chief god of the Batavians. The Romans encouraged local populations, with some success, to synchronize their own gods with

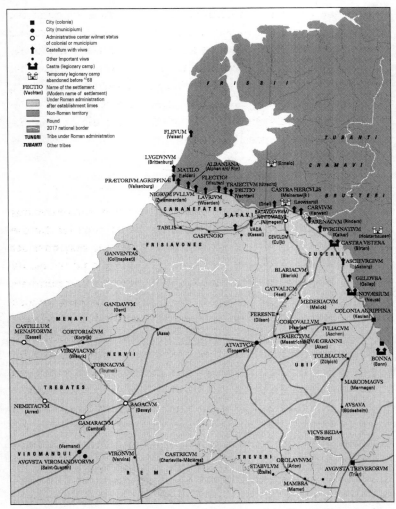

1   The Rhine served as the *limes*, or boundary, of the Roman Empire, but despite Roman forts the boundary was often porous, and trade across the river was extensive.

those of the Romans, but distinctly non-Roman gods persisted as well. Over time "imported" religions such as Mithraism and Christianity were introduced to the Low Countries. Like many parts of the empire, Germania Inferior was home to a culturally mixed population, partially Roman, partially Germanic or Celt, with a different mix in each locale. Seen this way, the Roman Netherlands was a microcosm of the diversity that characterized most of the empire.

Roman Decline, Migration and Depopulation

By the end of the second century this settled existence was threatened. The first serious "barbarian" raids, repelled by the Romans, took place in the 170s. Economic decline may have set in before any large-scale migrations of the Germanic tribes. By the beginning of the third century, at any rate, many settlements in the rivers region were already abandoned. The climate also became colder and wetter, the sea more dominant; large portions of Frisia were washed away, forcing its inhabitants – the first Frisians – eventually to seek a new home, likely in Britain. The Roman fort at Aardenburg on the southwest coast was abandoned early in the third century, to be temporarily garrisoned again in the 260s and 270s before the climate became too wet for it to be maintained. By the middle of the third century – with Rome wracked by continual political instability – the *limes* had been breached by peoples called the Franks, a designation used by Roman writers from the late third century to describe disparate tribes such as the Chamavi and Salians who had begun to federate together. Their push southward after the year 270 had a chilling effect on the region; farms and settlements were abandoned on a widespread scale, with most or all of the population likely fleeing southwards. One settlement that proved durable was Maastricht, which was sacked in the late third century but held on as a town in the early fourth century through the construction of a formidable fortress, whose perimeter was much smaller than that of the original town. Hundreds, not thousands, lived in what was now left of such settlements. More tellingly, most of the once-cultivated countryside, no longer used for agriculture, became wild again, its forests larger.

After the stabilization of its empire at the very end of the third century Rome attempted, if rather fitfully, to restore its authority up to the *limes*, replacing the old wooden forts with stone ones. The reassertion of a heavily militarized Roman presence in the fourth century made some resettlement possible, though the *villae* had long been replaced by simpler wooden farmhouses, the wheat crops with the easier-to-grow barley and rye. In the long run the stability depended on the willingness of various Frankish groups to settle down and swear allegiance to Rome – and the ability of Rome to enforce such pledges. The Salian Franks, though initially resistant to Rome's effort at taming them, were allowed to move later in the fourth century from the present-day Salland region (so named after them) in Overijssel, and to settle well behind the *limes*. There the Salians did, for a time, defend Roman interests. Such arrangements, however, were unstable in a time of great migratory pressure; by the beginning of the fifth century the Roman government had lost its remaining ability to direct or stem movements in Germanic migration into the empire. The collapse of the Rhine frontier and the retreat from Britain in order to defend the Roman capital conclusively sealed the fate of the province.

Thus, the last Roman authority came to an end in the Netherlands, and it seems likely that many civilians left with the soldiers for the relative safety of the south. The Salian Franks themselves remained on the move, many or most migrating further south by the mid fifth century. The Chamavi probably migrated to and settled in the river region where the Batavians had once lived. Unlike the coasts, this river region remained settled after the Romans had left for good. But the groups who continued to live in the Netherlands did not have large populations to start with, and the poorer weather, wetter landscape and decreased agricultural productivity probably helped further to reduce the region's population. In the fifth century the Netherlands is likely to have been as empty of humans as it had been for centuries, its wilderness attracting few permanent settlers among the tribes passing through its territory.

The Merovingian and Carolingian Periods

Society in the Early Middle Ages

New migrants from Germania and southern Scandinavia slowly moved into the Low Countries in the decades and centuries after the Roman retreat. This was seldom the movement of large tribes moving lock, stock and barrel to a new home, but smaller groups splitting off from older settlements in search of new prospects. The Franks may have thought of themselves as belonging to a single bond of kinship – they were, after all, descendants of the semi-mythical King Merovech, through whom their "Merovingian" leaders claimed legitimacy – but the fact that the Franks lived in small, autonomous communities meant that political life was initially quite decentralized. A local figure with enough personal authority might become the equivalent of what sixth-century writers called a *grafio*, but in a context of sparsely populated settlements with little hierarchy that position would have been a far cry from the elevated title of "count" (*graaf*) in a later age.

Contrary to public perception, these groups were hardly models of ethnic purity or political unity, nor were the "tribes" always hostile toward each other. The Franks intermingled with what was left of the local population in the old empire, even if Frankish ways and language came to dominate much of the present-day Netherlands, as Gallo-Roman influences were weaker than in France. The Angles and Saxons who moved into Frisia and parts of

Holland by about 600 may have intermarried with possible remnants of the old Frisian population; in any event, the new inhabitants, too, became known as Frisians. The Saxons, moving into the eastern Netherlands somewhat later, also lived next to, and mixed with, the indigenous inhabitants. These Germanic groups initially shared a similarity of language that made it possible, if not necessarily easy, for them to understand each other. In time, more modern forms of the Dutch language stemmed from a long-term interaction among Frankish, Frisian and Saxon. The inhabitants, moreover, shared a common material culture that extended over much of northwestern Europe and held many of the same cultural practices, such as the extensive use of burial mounds that now constitute the best-preserved testaments to their presence. The new residents of the Netherlands were thus not highly coherent and distinct tribes, but shifting conglomerations of associated

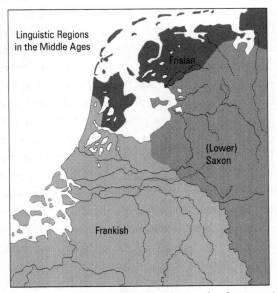

Linguistic Regions
in the Middle Ages

Frisian

(Lower)
Saxon

Frankish

2   Dutch as a distinctive language was the result of a centuries-long interaction among the Frankish, Frisian and Saxon languages that would long determine regional variations.

24

communities. Franks, Frisians and Saxons fought turf battles among themselves and with each other when deemed necessary, but as their common culture confirms they also actively traded with each other across distances both long and short, making use of the old Roman roads, and building their own sea- and river-going vessels.

Eventually, by the seventh and eighth centuries, the population began to grow again, as evidenced in the resumed reduction of the forests during those centuries, and in the building of new settlements. The weather also began to become warmer in the sixth century. Perhaps about 50,000 people lived in what is now the Netherlands in the year 700, almost all of them within short distance of a navigable river, the economic lifeline of every community. The 'new' Frisians began to recultivate, with great success, the coastal regions, and traded across much of Europe; most of the recently uncovered rare valuables in the Netherlands appear to have had Frisian owners. The chief settlement, established in the seventh century by the Frisians at the site of an old Roman fort and strategically situated on the fork of the Lek and the Rhine, was Dorestad. For about two centuries it was the leading trading center of the region, its ships traveling down the rivers of Europe or across the sea, utilizing its networks with merchants in the Baltic and Mediterranean. Situated on the swampiest of land, Dorestad relied on an extensive row of wooden piers, eventually some 3 km long, for its commercial existence. It was home in its heyday to perhaps as many as 10,000 inhabitants. Warehouses ensured that all kinds of goods could be stored there. It minted its own coinage, an indication of its economic importance. It seems likely that not only wine and olive oil or other non-native products were sold there but also Frisian cloth or fine iron from the Veluwe. Slaves from the British Isles or eastern Europe were probably also purchased there. Dorestad embodied the restoration of urban life and the resumption of extensive trade in the region.

4 Crafted in late eighth-century Burgundy, this striking fibula, found in an old Dorestad well, reveals the trade-generated wealth of the Netherlands' leading "Dark Age" settlement.

The Advance of Frankish Christendom

As its population and trade grew, the seventh century witnessed the beginning of new conflict over political control, religious belief and economic power; Dorestad lay near Frankish territory. A more cohesive Frankish kingdom began to coalesce around the Salian Franks, headed by the Merovingians, a Christian dynasty after its king, Clovis, had converted to Catholicism at the end of the fifth century. In geographical contrast with the Frankish Chamaves of the eastern river region, the locus of power of the Salian Franks lay as far south as Metz in eastern France. It took time before these Frankish kings, in a slow process of expanding their authority, made their weight felt in the present-day Netherlands. By the early seventh century they were casting their eyes on the prosperous river region, and the Merovingian King Dagobert seized Utrecht in 630. Though twenty years later the town would again fall into Frisian hands, this move was but the first step in an ultimately successful expansion of Frankish power into the northern Low Countries.

Closely allied with them was the Roman Catholic Church, which by the mid seventh century took the first systematic steps to Christianize the area that now comprises northern Belgium and the southern Netherlands. It is possible that Christianity in the Netherlands had survived the collapse of Roman authority, but then only very locally, and most likely around Maastricht, which had had its own bishop (the Armenian-born Servatius) in the late fourth century, and where a small Christian community may have persisted into the fifth and early sixth centuries. In any event, the country's earliest known church was erected in Maastricht around 570. The establishment or re-establishment of several bishoprics and abbeys in the northern Frankish kingdom, supported by the Frankish leaders (who themselves took leading positions in the Church) strengthened the presence of the Church in the southern part of the Netherlands. Nijmegen's first known church was built in the seventh century. All this notwithstanding, the widespread acceptance of Christian ritual and belief in this still scantly populated area was a gradual and uneven process. In Frisian and Saxon territory, Christian conversion was more difficult, likely in part because of Christianity's association with Frankish aims of conquest. Crucial to the Church's eventual success, indeed, was the work not of Frankish missionaries but of English ones, who stemmed from the recently converted Angles and Saxons and whose language was so close to their kinfolk, the Frisians. The first successful if short-lived mission took place in the 670s.

Further Christianization would not take place, however, without military pressure on the Frisians, particularly given the stance of Radbod, the Frisian king, who resisted the encroachments of the Franks and the Church. Taking the lead in the campaign against the Frisians was the energetic Mayor of the Palace for the Merovingians, Pepin of Herstal, born in the town of that name just south of Maastricht. Around 690 Pepin defeated Radbod at Dorestad, taking both it and nearby Utrecht, the town that Radbod had regarded as his residence. Pepin then forced Radbod into an alliance. In 695 Pope Sergius I consecrated another English missionary, Willibrord, "archbishop of the Frisians," and for most of the next four decades he used Utrecht as his missionary base, a base that for a long time would serve as the springboard for English mission work into northern Europe. Willibrord himself apparently met with success around Utrecht and in the west, including present-day Holland, where the first churches began to appear in the early eighth century. These churches supplanted the old mounds as sites of Christian burial in subsequent decades. But the large tracts of Frisia north and east of Utrecht remained outside Willibrord's reach.

Pepin of Herstal's death in 714 and the political chaos that followed allowed Radbod temporarily to drive Archbishop Willibrord out of Utrecht, but a new Frankish offensive under Charles Martel (known for his victory at the Battle of Tours some years later) after Radbod's own death in 719 was part of a military push that would place all of Frisia, at least nominally, within the Frankish orbit by the 730s. Nevertheless, it took many additional decades before Frisians in the north definitively accepted the Christian religion, an outcome that depended on the cooperation or at least forbearance of local elites. That this support did not always exist in Frisia's fragmented political landscape is evidenced by the fate of yet another English missionary, Boniface, a former co-worker of Willibrord, who had spent much of his long life as an evangelist and bishop in central Germany. In 754, during an infamous confrontation that may simply have been a violent robbery, the eighty-year-old churchman was killed by a hostile crowd near what is now Dokkum in northern Frisia. The Franks responded with an expedition to avenge the death of the missionary, but many parts of Frisia remained on the fringes of Frankish and ecclesiastical authority. A cycle of impelled conversion and rebellious de-conversion would persist there well into the ninth century. Almost a century passed after Boniface's death before the region became reliably Christian, illustrating just how slow and uneven the Christianization process could be in the early Middle Ages.

The Carolingian Legacy

The Merovingian kings lost power over time to the Mayors of the Palace, a post ultimately filled by Charles Martel and his descendants, whose traditional family base was rooted in the triangle between Aachen, Liège and Maastricht. In 751 his son Pepin the Short deposed the last of these kings, having himself crowned instead by Boniface, then archbishop of Mainz, marking the advent of the Carolingian dynasty. It was under his son, Charlemagne, who succeeded him in 768, that the Frankish kingdom would reach its zenith.

Carolingian achievements could be marked by territorial expansion that eventually came to encompass much of western Europe, a feat that was literally crowned by the pope in making Charlemagne Holy Roman Emperor in 800. Charlemagne's initial military adventures began closer to home, however. In 772 he launched a campaign against the pagan Saxons, who had recently destroyed the church in Deventer erected by the English missionary Liafwin. Using Nijmegen as his strategic base, Charlemagne subdued all of the eastern Netherlands that was Saxon territory, including present-day Overijssel and Drenthe. Although this brutal war would last three decades, Charlemagne's control over all the present-day Netherlands was reached in 785, when he defeated a Saxon–Frisian revolt led by the Saxon leader Widukind, who then converted to Christianity.

The amount of time that Charlemagne personally spent in the present-day Netherlands – Frankish kings moved about frequently to secure personally the loyalty of their subjects – is uncertain. Charlemagne may have used an already existing Frankish *palts* (fortified palace) at Meerssen near Maastricht, in addition to his stay at Nijmegen while fighting the Saxons. The last years of his life (807–814) he chose to spend at the soothing hot springs of Aachen, just a few kilometers east of the current border. But the Low Countries was not his chief focus; he had to direct almost all of his military and political attention eastwards and southwards. Moreover, the "renaissance" associated with his name – including his promotion of scholarship and the introduction of an easy-to-read minuscule – found its deepest cultural response not in the Netherlands but in the more populated areas of western Germany and France. Some traces of this renaissance do remain, such as the so-called Wachtendonck Psalms, written after 850 in East Lower Frankish, dialect of the eastern Netherlands, and often regarded as the first extant "Dutch" text.

It seems at the same time that a more disputable legacy of Charlemagne's rule, the development of great aristocratic estates at the expense of the poorer farmer-freedmen, did not occur in the northern and western parts of the Netherlands. Whatever the case, the region benefited from the peace and stability that Frankish rule brought; Dorestad seems to have reached the high point of its prosperity and importance as an economic center in the late eighth and early ninth centuries. Its silver coinage became a popular unit of exchange across many parts of Europe.

The political legacy of the Carolingians was more complex, and would have long-lasting consequences for the Netherlands and other parts of western Europe. As long as Charlemagne lived, his political system functioned well. He appointed non-hereditary counts to oversee his counties (*pagi*), of which there were before Charlemagne's time already several dozen in the Low Countries, and which in many cases formed the basis for later regional units, such as Texla (Texel, then one of the most populated areas in the Netherlands and not yet an island) and Threanti (Drenthe). Building on an older tradition, he also sent *missi dominici*, typically from his trusted circle, to inspect and report on the situation in each county. This arrangement was sustainable only through a kind of patronage that could and eventually did weaken central authority. In securing their service Charlemagne often rewarded nobility and counts with the spoils of war, and the spoils of war enabled him more easily to command their loyalty. This meant that local nobility, probably including some counts, held the king's land as a fief in exchange for services rendered, and that the Church, too, was granted tax exemptions and land by the emperor in order to advance its work. The end of Frankish military expansion and its reward system, as well as the death of the revered Charlemagne, however, would tempt many local rulers to treat these concessions as their own property, with far-reaching implications for the future.

Incursions and Fragmentation

In the decades after Charlemagne's death political fragmentation and conflict in fact became the norm. Only one legitimate son survived Charlemagne, Louis the Pious, but Louis's sons fought with their father in the 830s over their own inheritance, which according to Frankish tradition was divided among all sons. This infighting empowered local power-brokers to choose sides on the basis of their own interests, further fragmenting the political field. The conflict abated temporarily after Louis's death in the Treaty of Verdun (843), in which most of the Netherlands became part of the Middle Frankish Kingdom under Louis's son Lothair, between what later became France (Western Kingdom) and Germany (Eastern Kingdom). But the Middle Kingdom, which stretched from Italy to the North Sea, was not a viable political entity, and when the Emperor Lothair died in 855 it was once again divided among his sons, with Lothair II becoming king of what came (in

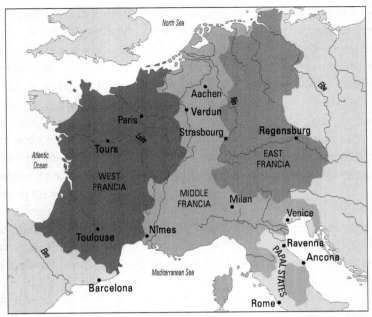

3   The short-lived Middle Kingdom persisted as an idea through the late
Middle Ages, but in practice all but the extreme southwest
Netherlands was subsumed into the German Empire.

his honor) to be known as Lotharingia, or (in French) Lorraine.
This territory included most of the Low Countries.

   This fragmentation occurred as threats from abroad increased.
The empire became prey to different invaders, including the
Danes, known as the Vikings, who first attacked, without success, the Frisian coast around 810. Conquest was not the Vikings'
sole aim, though the difference between trade and pillage was not
always very great. To the Christian inhabitants of the region the
Viking threat could be severe enough. Dorestad was first attacked
in 834, and written (as opposed to archaeological) sources suggest that it was attacked multiple times for the next thirty years.
The bishop of Utrecht felt compelled to flee his see in 857 under
pressure from the pagan Vikings, leaving for the safety of far-off

St. Odiliënberg in Limburg, and later moving to Deventer. It was not until 925 that the bishop ventured to return to Utrecht. Serious raids by different groups of Vikings continued through the ninth century. Maastricht, situated well up the Maas and thought secure, was sacked around 881; a year later the Vikings encamped at Nijmegen, once the proud site of Charlemagne's *palts*.

The increased political infighting among the Frankish kings made effective defense more difficult. It could be added that in the Netherlands, already a relatively unimportant corner of the empire, there was also less to defend: in December of 838 a catastrophic flood washed away many settlements on the western coast, the foreboding of a new period of bad weather and resurgent seas that would last for a century and make low-lying habitation additionally difficult. The island of Walcheren in Zeeland, hitherto the site of significant settlement, was inundated, its population sharply reduced. Dorestad itself went into decline in this period as its rivers began to silt up, and it disappeared as a trading post by the end of the ninth century.

Various Frankish overlords attempted to make the Vikings vassals and allies against their rivals, giving them land to hold in exchange for recognition of their sovereignty and their right to collect taxes. This seems to have been the case with Rorik the Dane, who held large parts of Frisia, including parts of Holland and Utrecht, from the 840s to the 870s, and who eventually, it seems, let himself be baptized. Seen this way, Rorik did not so much destroy the Carolingian order as become an integral part of its admittedly disintegrating political system. The Dane Godfried, having established a base on the western coast, was killed in 885 after demanding additional territory in exchange for his continued fealty to Frankish overlordship. His death came partially through the connivance of the West Frisian nobleman Gerulf, possibly also of Viking descent, who was rewarded with Godfried's coastal lands, creating an embryonic county that – two centuries later – would come to be called Holland.

33

Meanwhile, the margrave of Flanders, Baldwin I, erected fortifications against the Vikings as far north as the Zeeland coast –
including a fortress that served as foundation for the town of
Middelburg. In 891 Viking forces suffered a decisive defeat near
Leuven at the hands of the East Francian king, Arnulf of Carinthia.
The Viking threat was thus effectively checked. It is striking that –
in contrast to England – no permanent Viking settlements seem to
have been established in the Netherlands; perhaps the prospects
were more attractive to them elsewhere. Some Vikings undoubtedly did, however, stay, settle and mix with the local population. In
any event, it was not until 1007 that the last known Viking incur-
sion took place in what is now the Netherlands.

Deflecting the Viking threat did not bring a return to a strong
and united empire – quite the contrary. After a struggle for power
in the decades after Lothair II's death in 869, and the very brief
reunification of the empire under Charles the Fat (884–887), most
of the Middle Kingdom was effectively annexed into East Francia
by King Henry the Fowler in 925. A duke of Lower Lorraine, a
vassal of the king nominally in charge of the Low Countries, continued formally to exist until the early twelfth century, suggesting
that, notionally at least, political elites saw the region as a single entity. (It was an identity that centuries later the Burgundians
would attempt to revive.) From that time on, Lower Lorraine,
including the present-day Netherlands, would constitute a part
of the Germany-centered East Kingdom, and not, like Flanders,
part of the West Kingdom, which became the kingdom of France.
Boundary disputes between the German and the French kingdoms did effect the region, however, as the border between the
two ran across present-day Zeeland, precipitating intrigues and
wars for centuries to come.

Rather than becoming a part of a kingdom of France that later
showed strong centralizing tendencies, the Netherlandic parts
of the German kingdom remained for a long time, as they had
in Roman and Carolingian times, at the political and economic

periphery of an already fragmented German kingdom. The German kings (who after 962 had themselves crowned emperors), had enough difficulties maintaining control of the lands over which they were formally sovereign –not least their vital holdings in Italy – and they did not typically have the resources or focus to intervene in the region. Though most of the Netherlands would formally remain a part of the Holy Roman Empire until 1648 (and in a few eastern principalities until 1795), the falling apart of the Carolingian Empire in the course of the ninth century created above all a fragmented political space that would continue until at least the rise of the Burgundians in the late fourteenth century. The chronic instability that accompanied this situation led to nearly constant tension and warfare, but in the long run it also created room for new local actors to assert their own freedom.

New States, New Lands, New Cities

Creation of the Prince-Bishoprics, Holland and Flanders

It was precisely in the absence of an effective central authority, then, that new political units began to coalesce amidst a patchwork of local jurisdictions. Local lords and their clans built fortresses across the landscape to protect their own fiefs – and offer protection to an insecure population in exchange for their services. Although slavery largely disappeared during this period, serfdom, in which free persons were bound to work the land or offer services to their masters, became an extensive practice. A more tightly hierarchical society, organized at the local level, emerged as a result of the disruptions of the ninth century. The creation of villages around or near a fortified place, or *burg*, often testifies to this arrangement of a lord offering security for service from his bound tenants. This manorial system was not everywhere as strong; it was most established in the southern Netherlands, where the power of local nobility, enabled by

35

landed estates requiring agricultural workers, was greatest. In the Netherlands north of the great rivers, where the nobility was initially weaker and agriculture less developed, this was much less the model, with far-reaching social consequences, as shall be shown.

In this context, kings and emperors, counts and bishops, tried, frequently with limited success, to regain control over local lords, often vassals who held the lands of the great lords in exchange for their military or financial support. Although these lesser nobility, as vassals, owed their holdings to the higher lord, their loyalty or obedience could not always be counted upon, as they increasingly regarded, as noted, the land they held in fealty to their lord as their own permanent, hereditary possession. One early way in which the German emperors sought to retake some control over their expansive imperium was to appoint bishops as temporal rulers over territories. Bishoprics were by definition non-hereditary territories, and appointing bishops was a way for the emperor to appoint men from his own family to do his own bidding. These bishops were often also better administrators because they were among the few who could read. Notger, the powerful and influential bishop of Liège, and as such responsible for the spiritual life of the Low Countries south of the great rivers, began ruling in the 980s as a secular ruler in the nearby town of Huy – a position that he had inherited – and began to expand his episcopal lands after that. It was the beginning of a process that elevated the bishop to the title of prince within the empire, transformed Liège into a center of learning and led to the accumulation of a large principality that would extend up into a few portions of present-day Dutch Limburg.

A generation later, in 1024, the emperor granted the same temporal rights to the bishop of Utrecht, whose spiritual authority had covered most of what is now the Netherlands, when he gave the county of Drenthe to him. Long before this, though, the bishop had become a significant landowner in his own right, and his direct control began to extend westward toward the coast, lands that had once been occupied by the Vikings. In the course of that century the nobility who became bishops in Utrecht would inherit multiple territories that then, with imperial support, became a permanent part of the prince-bishopric, or *Sticht*, of Utrecht. In this way, the secular authority of the bishop extended far beyond the Utrecht region to reach into most of the northeastern Netherlands: the Veluwe, Overijssel, Drenthe and the town of Groningen. Even far-flung Friesland came formally under the joint authority of the count of Holland and the bishop of Utrecht. Around half of the land now part of the Netherlands formally came under the bishop's nominal authority.

Imperial recognition of the bishop as a temporal ruler constituted an arrangement that would make both prince-bishoprics wealthy landowners and important power-brokers in the region. Utrecht, moreover, had become the most important city in what is now the Netherlands, as the center of ecclesiastical government north of the great rivers. The eleventh century witnessed an expansive church-building program in the city of Utrecht as it became the nerve center of a growing number of Church functionaries, ensuring that the city remained the largest of all the northern Netherlandic towns until the thirteenth century. Utrecht's power, incidentally, made it vulnerable to the criticism that it had become worldly and unspiritual, as popular preachers such as the cleric Tanchelm apparently claimed around 1100.

In the long run, though, the power of the bishop of Utrecht was limited, compared to his wealthier counterpart in Liège, whose strategic position between France and Germany additionally allowed him to become a vital, long-term power-broker between the two larger states. From his seat in Utrecht, in contrast, the bishop very frequently struggled to establish effective control over his thinly populated territory. He was moreover dependent on the loyalty of castellanies to hold in his name far-flung fortified outposts, from Leiden in the west to Coevorden in the east. The power of the bishop further declined after the international resolution of the so-called Investiture Controversy in 1122, which allowed emperors to select bishops but only the pope to consecrate them. After that, it was Church authorities, the local canons and, of course, the pope himself who had the most decisive say. The canons of Utrecht, however, were sons of prominent families from the region, who came under heavy pressure from their kinfolk to make the selection of a bishop serve their own familial interests. Too many opposing parties, then, had a stake in the bishop's seat for the transfer of authority to occur harmoniously or, as the reforms of 1122 intended, to place spiritual criteria first in the selection process. This development undermined the ability of both the emperor and the bishop to steer an autonomous course, and it would subject Utrecht, with its competing factions, to squabbling or violence over most new episcopal appointments.

Local lords could and did contest Utrecht's expansion from their fortified homes. Future powerhouses such as Brabant to the south and Guelders to the east would emerge as significant forces only in the course of the twelfth century, and only in the thirteenth would Utrecht's power be seriously challenged by others. The bishop's earliest threat came from the west, from the Frisians led by Gerulf's descendants. These counts modestly but steadily expanded their power from their base, where the Rhine then flowed into the sea, near present-day Valkenburg and Rijnsburg in South Holland. They re-established the ruined abbey near Egmond in the early tenth century, in time making it one of the most influential spiritual centers in the northern Netherlands, as well as the administrative heart of the counts. At the end of the tenth century, Count Dirck II donated to the St. Adelbert Abbey the Evangeliarium of Egmond, a richly illustrated book of the gospels that includes the first extant depictions of early medieval Dutch architecture and people. Until about 1200, Egmond was also the only place in the Netherlands where books were produced.

38

5 Count Dirck II and his wife Hildegard are depicted here in two
tenth-century miniatures, dedicating a gospel manuscript to Egmond
Abbey, an early center of what became Holland.

By around the year 1000 the counts in Gerulf's line controlled
a strip of land that stretched from Texel in the north to the islands
south of the Maas. Their growth was initially supported by the
emperor, who apparently recognized the importance of a strong
vassal at the river mouths. The bishops of Utrecht viewed with
dismay the rising strategic importance of these counts, and ultimately the ambitions of these counts ran foul of both the emperor
and his allies, the bishops. In the early eleventh century Count
Dirck III built a stronghold at Vlaardingen along the Maas and
imposed tolls on all passing ships. The count had no legal right to

impose tolls – that was the prerogative of the emperor – and skippers from Tiel and other inland ports complained at his intervention. Led by the count of Lower Lorraine and supported by the bishop of Utrecht, an imperial army in 1018 advanced on Dirck with the intention of reducing his power. That army suffered an ignominious defeat at the hands of the count and his Frisian allies, and Dirck triumphantly continued to exact tolls on the ships passing through his territory, gaining grudging recognition from his erstwhile enemies.

These counts continued to expand their territories in the eleventh and twelfth centuries, funded in no small part by the shipping tolls they exacted. By around 1100 – roughly the time that Leiden had fallen to them – their lands were referred to as "Holland," derived from "Holtland" or "Woodland," for reasons unclear today. (Holland now became a distinguishing marker of identity, both in contrast to the Frisian lands to the east and north, and as a mark of autonomy over and against imperial and episcopal authority.)

The fortunes of Utrecht and Holland may have been rising from the tenth century, but in importance they were both dwarfed by another regional power: Flanders. The greatest regional winners of the political shake-up of the ninth century were not the West Frisian counts but the margraves and their successors, the counts of Flanders. Central authority in France, to whom Flemish counts formally owed their allegiance, was for a time even weaker than in Germany. The early count of Flanders, Baldwin II, exploited this weakness in the years around 900, and ultimately the county of Flanders would take Artois and penetrate deep into French territory. Later on, in the eleventh century, his successors Baldwin IV and V would again make Flanders a contending power and substantially increase its size and influence. Militarily Flanders came to overshadow its rivals; in 1100, the count could rely on 1,000 mounted knights in his service, whereas the French king – his nominal lord – had only half this number at his own disposal. The effective use of castellanies through a centralized military and civilian authority increased the count's grip on the administration of his lands. As shall be shown below, the counts' early and active promotion of commerce and of cities soon made the region the trendsetter for the whole region.

Only a small part of the current Netherlands – Zeeland–Flanders and some of the Zeeland islands – ever constituted a part of Flanders. But for over 500 years, from the tenth to the fifteenth century, it was Flanders that constituted the chief power in the Low Countries. It was more thoroughly urbanized and economically specialized than anywhere else in the region, as well as the most culturally creative. It was substantially wealthier and, at least for a long time, better administered than any of its neighbors. The northern regions looked to Flanders as their standard. One example of this influence was the Southern Netherlandic language of the Flemings, which came to predominate in Holland, supplanting Frisian in this part of the country. But if the Flemings and Flemish were becoming the standard, Flanders remained largely uninterested in what was going on north of the rivers, leaving local and regional actors to develop economic life as they saw fit.

New Economic Initiatives

What is now the Netherlands remained a still fairly sparsely populated country; perhaps 250,000 to 300,000 persons lived there at the turn of the second millennium. Frisia remained, as in the old days, relatively well populated, its people the chief traders of the region and, as in the days of the Romans, fisherfolk and breeders of cattle. It was they who for the next few centuries arguably remained the most successful traders, with their extensive North Sea networks.

In general, trade began to revive in the tenth century, chiefly along the great rivers, where fortresses erected against the Vikings, such as Zutphen along the IJssel River, served as secure bases for the recovering river trade that increasingly linked England with the Rhineland and with northern France. Starting at roughly this time, the Netherlands took part in a series of European innovations that transformed agriculture by making it more efficient and sustainable: the introduction of the heavy plough ideal for the clay soil; the halter for the deployment of horses instead of oxen in tilling; and the three-field system, which rotated crops and thus spared the land from exhaustion. It also helped that the climate again became warmer, enhancing agricultural production until the early fourteenth century.

Yet most of the Netherlands remained devoid of extensive human habitation. In addition to the unproductive sandy territory in the eastern part of the country, most parts along the western coast, or the countryside between Utrecht and Holland, were wilderness. Much of it was watery fenland, perhaps as much as 4 or 5 meters above sea level, unused by the region's few inhabitants, except for the gathering of wood and turf, or for fishing.

The first initiatives to drain and farm parts of Holland and Utrecht began as early as the late tenth century, but it was in Flanders that the most systematic efforts were undertaken to develop the land further. In the tenth century sheep-grazing – one of the few ways for humans to make use of the soggy Flemish coastal area – was systematically encouraged and developed, with an eye to the sale of wool to France and Germany. The fortresses built by Margrave Baldwin against the Vikings, Ghent and Bruges, became important centers of this economy. By the eleventh century, western Flanders did not have enough sheep to meet the demand for wool – it began to import wool from England – but it continued to grow in importance as a central marketplace for an increasingly international wool trade and as an industrial center for cloth production, which in turn spurred a further diversification of the economy.

The take-off of the wool industry, as well as the sharp rise of a population who enjoyed a better economic basis for existence but who also required more food, was an important factor in the further intensification of agriculture. Lands that had lain undeveloped as too difficult to bring into cultivation now came under the plough. The most fertile of these lands – and therefore the next to be exploited – were the extensive fens dominating large portions of Flanders, Zeeland, Holland and Friesland that lay behind the sea dunes. Dikes, laboriously created by human hand from the heavy clay that was adjoined to natural sea barriers, had been constructed long before the year 1000 along the Dutch coastlines, allowing cattle and residents a greater measure of reasonably secured land than their elevated *terpen* afforded. Efforts to tame the fenlands for agricultural use began in Utrecht as early as the tenth century, and also along the northern Frisian coast.

Large-scale, systematic efforts, however, began in the eleventh century, with Flanders again taking a leading role. Count Baldwin V actively stimulated in the mid eleventh century the creation of colonies expressly for the purpose of cultivating new lands. Setting a trend for the future across the Low Countries and, later, other parts of northern Europe, he offered the settlers fiscal and legal advantages superior to the terms of servitude on the manorial estates. Later, monastic houses would play a large role in the cultivation of the landscape, including the vulnerable Flemish coast. Still later, private entrepreneurs would risk their own capital on the development of new agricultural estates. These initiatives included efforts by Flemish abbeys, begun in the eleventh century, to drain their marshy and watery lands in Zeeland by creating "polders" there – a term first used around 1150 to denote low-lying fields protected by dikes.

In the eleventh century, too, systematic efforts to reclaim land began in Utrecht. It was a process that was at once more extensive – involving more land – and more intensive – requiring more human and capital investment in a more demanding geography – than had been the case in Flanders. Land clearance was also a process that, as shall be shown, was often characterized by setbacks.

In the fenlands between the city of Utrecht and the dunes of Holland, the drive for new agricultural land would prove particularly and permanently transformative, turning what had been mostly wilderness into an extensive landscape of fields, dikes and canals.

This process could be top-down. In 1085, when the bishop of Utrecht and his canons endeavored with success to drain the swamps near Abcoude for agricultural purposes, all was executed along the lines of an efficient grid. These efforts necessitated over time an increasing measure of cooperation among local officials and landowners. The earliest known example of such cooperation took place in the 1120s, when the bishop of Utrecht, his functionaries and many local communities dammed the so-called Crooked Rhine, and redirected the water into the artificial Lek. This at once improved river navigability and drained new areas of land for reclamation. In exchange for goods, the bishop and his canons issued contracts for the exploitation of these new lands that resembled the established manorial relationships. This was also true in eastern areas, where land clearance involved clearing sandy grounds more than clay fenlands. Building on the existing social system, the twelfth-century counts of Guelders imposed the same manorial system on colonists they encouraged to settle in the new lands of Montferland along the present-day German border.

Further west, in contrast, the process seems to have been much more bottom-up. As early as the late tenth century it seems that in what became Holland, settlers – many of them from northern Frisia in search of a better life – launched their own initiatives to drain and cultivate the fenland, an effort that was facilitated by a drier climate. In West Friesland just to the east of Holland, land reclamation, too, was executed by local leaders and residents, who methodically diked and drained their lands without direction or incentives from above. The manorial relationship barely existed in these regions. When they did intervene, the counts of Holland offered generous terms to prosperous farmers, regarding them as free and not –as elsewhere – bound to the land or the lord. Having little to offer, the upstart counts could ask for little in return, but in their encouraging stance hoped to foster new networks of loyalty with the settlers. Whatever the motivation, the creation of a free farming class would have long-term effects on the political and social contours of western Holland, creating a free farming class less beholden to the counts, or the Church, for their positions.

Despite these very significant successes, the available water management techniques ran against their limits in the course of the twelfth century. Reliably dry land was in limited supply, prompting many settlers to up stakes and accept invitations to start colonies in more promising, still empty regions of Germany. Just as crucially, it proved difficult to defend the reclaimed land from the ravages of the water. Part of the problem – one that continued to plague the Dutch for centuries thereafter – was that land that had been drained tended to shrink and sink at a rate of about a centimeter a year, causing already low-lying lands to sink below sea level. Extracting peat from the fen for fuel significantly accelerated this process. In this respect, the region's below-sea-level-landscape was the doing of the Dutch themselves.

The problems, though, were not only artificial; Dutch dikes and dams, and the quality of their water management, were simply not sufficient to resist powerful storm surges, likely made more powerful by warmer weather and higher sea levels. Big storms had a devastating impact: the storm surge of 1134 reduced Zeeland to a set of islands; the storm of 1163 blocked the Rhine at the sea, thus causing Holland's polders to flood. Four powerful storms between 1170 and 1219 struck the northern coasts particularly hard, drowning (particularly during the last of these storms) thousands of people and permanently flooding large areas of reclaimed fen. The mysterious Creiler Woods, an extensive thicket that probably lay in northern Holland, disappeared beneath the waves.

45

The later storm of 1287 transformed an expanse of fenland into the shallow Waddenzee, definitively separating the West Frisian islands from the mainland. The sea also struck deeply inland, carving out the large cavity that became known as the Zuyder Zee, an expanse of water that now divided West Friesland from the rest of Frisia. This body of water, subject to the influences of the North Sea, was gradually salinated in the course of subsequent decades and centuries.

None of these disasters, which would recur in subsequent decades, seems to have deterred local residents from again reclaiming land when it was lost. This would, however, require future generations to invent ever more ingenious techniques – and ever closer cooperation – to defend their gains or take new ground.

The Rise of Cities

At the beginning of the second millennium, the Netherlands was a country of farms and small villages. Perhaps only 5 percent of the population lived in a municipality that could be classified as a city, and even these never exceeded 5,000 inhabitants. Initially it was in relatively densely populated Frisia that the existence of towns, and with them a money economy, may have been strongest. It was there that the North Sea trade went hand-in-hand with the existence of small trading towns such as Dokkum, Leeuwarden and Stavoren. The largest and most important towns continued to be those founded in Roman times – Maastricht, Nijmegen and Utrecht. In addition to them, there was the IJssel town of Deventer, an important religious, political and economic center since the days of Charlemagne. It received city rights very early on, in 1123. A relative latecomer but quickly important was Groningen, founded in 1040 as the northernmost outpost of the bishop of Utrecht's domains, which was subsequently accorded the right to impose tolls, mint coins and hold markets (full city rights came in 1227). There were small merchant towns such as

46

Tiel (near old Dorestad) in the great river regions that did a brisk business, and by the eleventh century fortresses such as Zutphen were rebuilt in stone, a sign of their rising economic significance. Cities in what became Holland also began to emerge as centers of trade in the eleventh century, notably Leiden, Haarlem, Alkmaar and Delft; most of them had become important as sites where the count held his itinerant court. Dordrecht, mentioned for the first time in 1050, was then no more than a line of dwellings at the edge of a land clearance project, but developed into a real town in the course of the twelfth century.

With the stone-built, spired churches that began to dot the land-scape around 1150, religious life also became more central to life in the towns and in the villages. The twelfth-century reintroduction of ovens that baked clay into bricks would gradually transform Dutch churchscapes, and indeed all of the country's architecture. For the time being, though, the northern Netherlands continued to host few of the monasteries and abbeys that had characterized the social geography in the southern Netherlands since the seventh century. This began to change in the twelfth century; the Rolduc Abbey in Limburg, founded in 1104, was an early example. A couple of key religious houses were founded to support the new, ascetically minded monasticism, both made possible through the land donations of wealthy nobility. The Premonstratensian abbey Mariënwaerdt, in what was then in the bishopric of Utrecht, was granted land in 1129, and in Frisia the Cistercian monastery Klaarkamp around 1164. The wealth (and arguably, the piety) that made such monasteries possible continued to lag behind the southern Netherlands.

In this light it must be emphasized that all the towns of the northern Netherlands at this time paled in significance compared with the great cities of Europe and also of Flanders – Bruges, Ghent and Ypres – which burgeoned into places ultimately harboring tens of thousands of residents each by the thirteenth century, making the southern Low Countries with northern Italy the most densely urban area of Europe. As the center of the cloth trade, these Flemish cities engaged in extensive commerce with their partners in Germany and Russia, France and England. Over time, they developed close ties with Italy, giving it access to luxury dyestuffs and to spices from the Levant previously unavailable in northern Europe, opening up Flanders in time to its banking institutions. As a result, these cities also impacted the economies of what is now the Netherlands as they drew much of the whole region into their economic web in the search for new goods and markets. Already by the late twelfth century, the economic activity of these cities spilled into northern Flanders and into Zeeland. Many towns in what is now Flemish Zeeland, such as Axel, Hulst and Aardenburg, flourished as the result of trade generated by the urban centers of Flanders. Several of them were accorded city rights at the end of the twelfth century: early for the Low Countries and a sign of their economic importance. Around 1200, Dordrecht became the first of the Holland cities to be recognized as an *opidum* (city) and receive corresponding rights that were formally granted by its own count.

The urbanization of the south also constituted a model for the northern parts of the Netherlands. It encouraged its own counts, dukes and bishops to charter towns as a way to enrich themselves and thus to expand their influence. In this process new political and cultural norms were established. Many Flemish cities were accorded charters in the twelfth century, which substantially reduced, if not eliminated, the obligations of their residents to the local lord. These agreements tended to confirm the cities' role as refuges where people were free from manorial and feudal bonds, and as places administered by self-government. Property rights, so essential for trading and commerce, were widely respected in these towns. By the late twelfth century the counts routinely consulted the cities on policy, a sign of their new clout.

Edifices that exuded civic pride, including the building of impressive churches and chapels, became an important focus, as

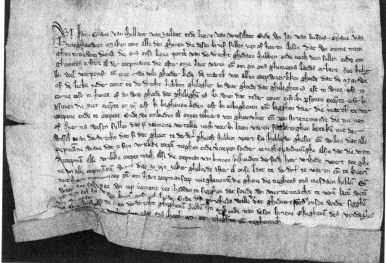

6   These documents suggest that Dordrecht had already been granted a
city charter in 1220, rendering it Holland's first city. The document below
confirmed its staple rights in 1299.

did a vernacular literature, including poetry. This included the
socially trenchant mock epic *Ysengrimus*, featuring the adventures of Reynard the Fox, who outwits clergy and nobility alike.
Economically prosperous, politically assertive and sometimes literate, city people could be increasingly critical of the institutional

49

Church as a mere defender of its own powerful interests or as an organization that had strayed from its spiritual purpose. Reform movements that began to impact the region, such as the Cistercians or Premonstratensians, found support among these urban critics. The cities were also places were new forms of inequality arose, city government lying chiefly in the hands of a patrician class that became more tightly defined and exclusive over time. The Flemish cities were, for these reasons, not only centers of wealth and freedom but cauldrons of political and social tensions. The rise of a highly urbanized culture would have long-term consequences for the future of the whole region, creating new centers of economic power, and with it, political influence.

⚜ The Prosperous Thirteenth Century

Toward the end of the twelfth century, crucial parts of the territories constituting the contemporary Netherlands began to exhibit many of the features that had characterized Flanders a century before: the growth of substantial towns with their own charters, the arrival of mendicant and other reform-minded orders that impacted both city life and land management, and the rise of fairly efficient and powerful secular principalities that included not only Holland but now Brabant (in its push northward) and Guelders as well. Further initiatives to reclaim land not only improved the agricultural production of the country but also changed social relations, creating unprecedented new opportunities for a wider range of people.

New Civic Bodies

It has often been remarked upon that places such as Holland and Frisia were largely free from the feudal structures that imposed themselves more on the more settled southern territories, or those in the eastern Netherlands. By the thirteenth century the feudal structures were breaking down in many places – in Flanders they virtually disappeared – as cities drew peasants away and landed lords developed a different, more business-like relationship with the agrarian population. Nevertheless, the early rise of an independent farming class that emerged in parts of the northern Netherlands created a more pluralistic political culture where power was more diffuse than it was in districts further south.

The most striking example of the free farmers stemmed from Frisia, which in the Middle Ages prided itself on its liberties, and where the nobility were only modest property-holders. "Frisian freedom," as it became known in the medieval period, meant being free from the rule of foreign potentates. Until the sixteenth century the Frisians – at least those living east of the new Zuyder Zee – for the most part successfully resisted a host of invaders from all directions, including their most insistent antagonists, the counts of Holland. Famed and feared for their feats of arms, the Frisians found protection by living in a treacherous, watery environment that made incursions difficult. Frisians of modest status and means may have had more say than their southern counterparts in their relatively egalitarian society. But as was more frequently the case in the medieval Netherlands, freedom from a strong-arm lord went hand-in-hand with greater lawlessness. The Frisians created and maintained their own body of shared law, as evidenced in their annual meeting at the Upstals, the holy oak tree near Aurich in East Frisia. But in practice interpretation of this law was left to local landed farmers and to village communities, and laws elaborately defining punishments for killing and maiming did not halt the enduring vendettas. No local count, either, succeeded in opposing his rule over the Frisians. This fragmented political picture made it more difficult for the *zijlen*, water management boards, to extend into a broader, regional network of cooperation, though in eastern Frisia, present-day Groningen, this was more successful through the influence of the great landed abbey at Aduard.

Further south, where centralized authority around the count, bishop, duke – or, on occasion, the emperor – was better established, these water local authorities proved better able to extend their influence and, in the course of the thirteenth century, achieve a superior level of water management that demanded a much greater degree of cooperation. The need for such forms of cooperation was acutely felt at the local level, in part because of the experience with the great storms, but also through the growing realization that the effective control of water required many parties to work together – even over the established political boundaries. An early case in point was Holland's decision in 1165 to place a dam on the Rhine near Zwammerdam, protecting low-lying areas, but creating flooding above the dam and hampering shipping. It took more than half a century before this conflict was effectively resolved, when Holland and Utrecht together rechanneled the water flowing to the sea northward: a project completed in 1226.

Such projects, however, usually demanded new solutions to new problems, crucially reconciling the need for protection from the water with the need of skippers to sail unencumbered through the rivers. In response to local demands and the advice of his newly formed council, Count Willem II oversaw the completion in 1253 of an expensive and innovative sluice-gate at Spaarndam near Haarlem. This sluice altered the water level for ships passing through and enabled travel between the Zuyder Zee and ports to the south. In the late thirteenth century water boards were formalized and given authority to address water problems, the first of which, established by Willem, was the *hoogheemraadschap* of the Rhineland (1255). Crucial to the success of these boards were the cooperation and support of the count, whose representative typically headed these water boards, and who had the authority of enforcement. Just as important was the commitment of local property owners, whose own willingness to contribute to the maintenance or expansion of the water management system – typically

52

on the basis of proportionality – was essential to the labor and funding required. These water boards were not democratic in the modern sense – those with the most land had the most say – but they were in the first instance the initiatives of many different residents who came to share responsibility for the common good. Soon the boards found their application outside Holland as well.

Changing the political balance of power in the Netherlands was the strong rise of the cities in the thirteenth century. Hendrik I, duke of Brabant, founded Den Bosch in the late twelfth century, inviting merchants to reside there and to establish a prosperous trading center near the Maas. Cities' rights were also granted as a way of building loyalty among a town's political elite. Strategic considerations – bolstering the prince's authority in a key area – were also important. A city's rights typically included the right to hold markets, to exact tolls on roads and waterways that ran through it, and to build its own defensive fortifications. Many medieval city walls, first often earthen fortifications and later made of stone or brick, began to be erected wherever cities had been recognized. It might be added that not all places granted city rights in the thirteenth and fourteenth centuries succeeded as cities. Particularly in the eastern parts of the country, further from the trade routes or built on less fertile ground, cities failed to grow or sustain themselves, however much the lord or local elites might have wished otherwise. The terms of the city charter could also be less generous; when the count of Guelders accorded city rights to Harderwijk in 1231, he stipulated that none in his own service could become free burghers there without his express consent.

Particularly in the west, though, these cities were successful and made their mark politically as well. This was especially true of Holland cities such as Gouda and Delft, with Amsterdam, a modest trading town at the confluence of the Amstel and IJ rivers and a relative latecomer, receiving city rights around 1300. With city rights came also, as in Flanders and elsewhere in Europe, a city's right to its own representation. Typically, as in Flanders, this was manifested in the office of the aldermen, whose tasks included both the dispensing of justice and overseeing important public dossiers, such as the state of the city walls. Aldermen typically stemmed from the patrician class. Over time, however, participation in the town's affairs became an increasingly contentious issue. In particular, in some towns many artisans and craftspeople felt that they, too, ought to have a voice. The rise of their organizations, the guilds, began to make an impact only later in the thirteenth century, though the first mention of a merchant's guild dates from 1020 in the town of Tiel. The guilds, a wider European phenomenon, first manifested themselves and were most successful in older towns of the Low Countries, with bakers and weavers among the first to organize in this way. This pattern was certainly true in the great Flemish cities, where social tensions were greatest, but also in Deventer and in Utrecht, where uncommonly fractious politics generated bad blood between the various antagonists. In 1274, the guilds of Utrecht rose up against the city government, temporarily taking it over before being crushed. They would bide their time before again asserting their rights. This revolt did not quickly repeat itself in the northern Netherlands, but the issue of representation remained a perennial one in many municipalities.

Representation within towns was one issue; another was the representation of towns in the affairs of the principality. The cities of Flanders took advantage of the weak counts of the thirteenth century to assert themselves. But everywhere it became increasingly difficult for the dukes and the counts to ignore the central concerns of cities. Holland, where many of the new cities sprang up, was a case in point, as the counts increasingly had to consult with them and reckon with their interests. Already striking was a different urban pattern in Holland than in Flanders. Whereas, in the latter, three cities (Bruges, Ghent and Ypres) dominated, Holland was characterized by a larger number of smaller cities, which had the effect of further diffusing power among many groups, making the region harder to rule and control. It was perhaps Brabant, however, where cities, starting in the mid thirteenth century, began with their new power to demand "constitutional" pledges of its dukes, a sign of an urban strength that would last a century and a half.

In general, by the thirteenth century the population in the Netherlands was able to engage in organizing itself into representative bodies and other institutions that advanced its interests. This was clearly true in the cities, but also in the countryside, where villagers and farmers, as was the case in Drenthe, organized their own commons for shared use. It was also true, as shall be shown, in the way that the laity, out of religious motivations, organized their own charities, in cooperation with Church and civic authorities. This pattern of local decision-making by a host of different authorities was hardly unique to the Netherlands, but it was nevertheless important for its future, making it more difficult for a single ruler or oligarchy unilaterally to assert their own power. The rise of cities was thus important for the diffusion of power that came to characterize much of the Low Countries.

Jockeying Principalities

This diffusion of power had consequences also for the great lords, whose own dynastic considerations had to take account of such factors. This was true for the often hapless bishops of Utrecht. In an attempt to reassert control over all of the Upper Sticht, Bishop Otto von Lippe marched an army against his insubordinate castellan in Drenthe in 1227, only to be killed and have his forces annihilated at the Battle of Ane. Although his successor quickly avenged him, Drenthe and Groningen remained permanently outside the real reach of the bishop. Its bishops weakened by internal dissent and a chronic lack of money, the bishopric was perennially subject to the intrigues of its neighbors, particularly Brabant, Guelders and Holland. This was not difficult; nearly all of its bishops were brothers or cousins of the high nobility in the Low Countries or in the empire, who contended with each other for the bishop's miter.

This contention for titles and for territory, conducted through strategic marriages; opportunistic, shifting alliances; and military incursions, characterized the abiding rivalry among the princes of Holland, Guelders and Brabant, and their other neighbors. This kind of rivalry, as in many other parts of western Europe, had typified dynastic politics since the dismemberment of the Carolingian Empire, but the simultaneous rise of these three principalities would have far-reaching consequences for the long-term territorial contours of the present-day Netherlands.

Guelders had become a force of note in the late twelfth century, and the success of Otto I in combining the counties of Zutphen and Guelders in his person provided a strong basis for the expansion of his territories. The forested Veluwe, once belonging to Utrecht, came under the sway of these counts, who also came to possess large areas of eastern river region between the key towns of Arnhem and Nijmegen – crucially giving the county a major stake in trade between Germany and the coast. Guelders's greatest and internationally respected count was Otto II (1229–1271), who solidified its position through generally cordial relations with the emperor, further territorial expansion and the granting of many city rights. It remained a sprawling, non-contiguous territory, divided between northern quarters more or less equivalent to the current province of Gelderland, and some of its oldest territories to the south, including the (now German) town of Geldern from which it derived its name, hugging the east bank of the Maas. Guelders reached its territorial limits in 1288, when it was defeated by a Brabant-led coalition at the Battle of Woeringen for control over the duchy of Limburg and its strategic – and lucrative – trade roads. Although elevated to dukes in the 1330s, Guelders's ineffective rulers, as well as competing noble clans, would stymie greater internal cohesion.

7 Reinoud of Guelders stands defeated after the Battle of Woeringen in 1288, as painted by De Keyser 550 years later. Woeringen decisively expanded the size and power of Brabant.

Brabant, with its original base far to the south in Leuven and Brussels, was, as a power, a relative latecomer to the territory of what is now the Netherlands, and in its politics remained oriented in other directions: toward its opponents eastward in Germany, and westward in its rivalry with Flanders. Its assertive duke, Hendrik I, did not exercise control over most areas of northern Brabant until around 1200. From this time on, though, the dukes of Brabant were keen to expand their influence over territories along the wealth-generating Rhine and Maas. This ambition precipitated military confrontations with the archbishop of Cologne, and in time also with Holland and Guelders, as both expanded southward. Brabant's signature duke was Jan I (1267–1294), a magnetic and energetic personality who inspired epic poems. He was the first to build up an alluring court culture in Brabant. He linked his dynastic ambitions with the success of Brabant's cities and their economic interests, giving them many privileges in exchange for a

57

generous portion of their rising incomes and their willingness to finance his military campaigns. Jan was a popular figure who did much to tighten an enduring sense of Brabançon identity, which in turn emboldened the cities in their demands to help run the duchy.

A near contemporary of Jan was Holland's most famous count, Floris V (1256–1296). Holland faced many enemies in the thirteenth century, the most abiding of which were the Frisians. In fact, Floris's father, the elected king of Germany Willem II, had lost his life attacking the Frisians in 1256, after his horse sank through the ice and he was butchered by his foes. Only two years old at the time of his father's death, it took Floris some time before he was successful in securing his own county and in launching military and diplomatic initiatives from his new county seat at The Hague. By 1289 he had decisively conquered West Friesland, putting all territory west of the Zuyder Zee under Holland's control. Taking advantage of the bishop of Utrecht's lack of money, Floris lent to him in exchange for having himself enfeoffed with the bishop's western lands, preparing the way, as it turned out, for Amsterdam and the whole of Amstelland to become effectively attached to Holland in the 1280s, to be formally annexed in 1323. For a long time an ally of England against France for reasons of trade, Floris suddenly joined hands with France in 1296, in the hope of obtaining better support for his longstanding efforts to wrest the Zeeland islands from another adversary, Flanders. This was too much for Floris's internal enemies – Holland nobles who had lost power under the count – who kidnapped him, possibly at the behest of the English King Edward I. Floris was killed by his captors when local farmers attempted to rescue him, sending the county into chaos. By the time of his death, though, Holland's cohesion as a county and as a regional power had substantially increased. Its rivalry with other principalities of the region would, however, continue.

By the thirteenth century, then, powerful principalities that would help shape the political contours of the Netherlands were well established. Internal struggles made them vulnerable to external enemies, but weak centralized power also gave urban elites much leeway to determine their own affairs, a development that would long characterize Dutch political life.

Religious Life

The thirteenth century witnessed a blossoming of religious life in the Netherlands, and as before, most religious trends came first through Germany, France or the southern Netherlands. Not all of these trends had a great impact on the Netherlands. The advent of the university and the parallel development of theology as a discipline, as well as the rise of "heretical" movements such as the Waldensians and Albigenses, arguably had greater impact further south. Religious culture as reading culture, so characteristic of Dutch religion later on, was on the rise, but was as yet in an early phase. Faith, for most inhabitants at that time, was less a matter of theological doctrine than of in an intense identification with the Host, the sacred body of Christ offered by the priest during the Eucharist. The procession of the Eucharist, begun as a feast day in Liège, was one of the most exuberantly celebrated among the fifty feast days (in addition to Sundays) the regional Church offered.

Faith was also increasingly a matter of doing. The laity, particularly in the larger towns, engaged in acts of charity such as erecting kitchens for the poor, or alms-houses for the destitute or for the elderly. The first mention of a hospital dates from 1252 in the town of Delft. Dutch burghers in these ways set up their own organizations, chiefly run by themselves. Increasingly, too, active believers went on pilgrimages, mostly to local sites. Few people had the means to travel to the Holy Land, though the failed Fifth Crusade, led by Count Willem I of Holland in 1217, offered some warriors from Flanders, Frisia and Holland one such, albeit disappointing, opportunity.

A different sign of lay spirituality lay in the rise of the beguine movement, another from the south and also sometimes suspected by the Church of heresy. Possibly named for their grayish, uncolored clothing, beguines attempted to live simply as imitators of Christ, often holding a more mystical faith, inspired by mystics such as the Flemish woman Hadewijch. They forswore convent life, favoring a more informal community within the towns, often spinning to make a living. Unusually well represented in the towns of the Low Countries, the beguine movement spread northwards, first reaching Breda around 1240. Though not nuns themselves, they were influenced by the rise of the mendicant orders, the monks who forswore the material security of the established orders and abbeys in favor of begging for alms. The Franciscans, the most famous of these orders, first established themselves in what is now the Netherlands in 1228, in Den Bosch, ultimately establishing nine monasteries before 1300. The women Franciscans, the Poor Clares, also made their presence known. Though the older orders of monks also grew strongly in the course of the thirteenth century, it was even more the Cistercian nuns who succeeded in establishing many chapters in the Netherlands during this period, exceeding the number of men in monastic life.

The role of these monasteries as landed estates, especially in Zeeland and on the northern coast, was sometimes crucial to the further process of land reclamation, though their power could lead to new conflicts, particularly with the tenants of their land. These conflicts were emblematic of a theme that the religious orders themselves had signaled: the tension between the Church as powerful and wealthy institution and a faith that demanded personal identification with "the Man of Sorrows," the way in which Jesus was increasingly depicted in art and in theology of the period. Over time, the deepening of religious faith would paradoxically come to challenge the authority of religious institutions.

Economic Developments

Although Christian devotion may have become more intense than ever before, this hardly meant that all prescriptions, increasingly spelled out by the Church in Rome, were obeyed. One prohibition imposed on Christians that was openly flaunted in the thirteenth century was the lending of money with interest, condemned by the Church as usury. Flemish cloth merchants, however, seeking ways to invest their earnings, began to offer short-term credits at interest, and the historically Flemish city of Arras became the regional hub of this financial activity. This lending of money was part of a much wider European pattern centered in the wealthy cities of Italy with their emerging banking houses. Soon many different parties were availing themselves of this credit, from merchants to monarchs, including the dukes of Brabant and counts of Holland. These capitalistic money markets would, in the long term, further commodify society, notably in the purchase and exploitation of land for profit. By around 1300 this development, already long evident in Flanders, was beginning to impact the economy north of the great rivers.

This went hand-in-hand with the accumulation of wealth and of capital made possible by the mushrooming of cities, partly the result of local push factors, partly through the encouragement of the great lords. But of course these towns could only profit if they were themselves part of an international trading network. In Holland, extensive participation in this international network began only in the last half of the thirteenth century, aided by an international trend in which more advanced shipping made the Atlantic trade more profitable, moving commerce toward the coasts. Even more important for Holland was the creation of new waterways, making a north–south route possible through the region, including the new locks at Spaarndam. Now ships could travel safely from the newly formed Zuyder Zee through to the Merwede and Maas rivers. This placed cities such as Haarlem, Gouda, Leiden and Delft – all on or near these waterways – in a much stronger strategic position than before. It placed Dordrecht, where the Maas and Merwede meet, at the center of this new trade. For that reason, Dordrecht was accorded staple rights in 1299, which required all passing ships to offload their cargoes for possible sale at Dordrecht before moving on – a privilege that would make it (the leading town in Holland for the better part of two centuries.)

The growing strength of Holland's economy in the late thirteenth century may be considered the most dramatic and – with much hindsight – the most important factor for the later development of a northern Netherlandic state. But this economic growth was evident across the region, especially along the all-important rivers. The cities along or near the IJssel benefited from the creation of the Zuyder Zee, making the sea approaches to their river more easily navigable. And towns along the Maas, most notably Maastricht, also grew sizeably in this period. Still, the economy of Flanders, though it had peaked by around 1270, remained much larger. This can be seen in the size of the cities: Dordrecht housed perhaps 5,000 people in 1300, Utrecht a few more, and Maastricht as many as 10,000, compared with up to 65,000 in Ghent. The thirteenth century had been a landmark century, but its share in the flourishing economy of western Europe during this period remained as yet very modest.

Fourteenth-Century Crisis

In the course of the fourteenth century the Low Countries faced new and in some cases unprecedented challenges. The reasons for what some have called a "crisis" were divergent if often related. Some stemmed precisely from the past successes, which generated new inequalities and social tensions, and which made the region attractive to the newly powerful dynastic houses of Europe. Some of the problems stemmed from natural factors – a worsening climate and vicious plagues – for which these societies had but limited answers.

Declining Economic Fortunes and Political Tensions

Several factors contributed to a stagnation or even decline of the region at the end of the thirteenth century. Flanders, with the most sophisticated economy and largest cities, likely suffered the most, and less affluent newcomers such as Brabant and Holland may have fared relatively well at Flanders's expense. Nevertheless, several long-term factors negatively affected many regions.

Famine and widespread hunger had been banished from the Low Countries in the thirteenth century, owing to the expansion of land under cultivation. By around 1300 these projects had reached a point of exhaustion; there was no more land that could productively be brought under cultivation, evidenced by the fact that forests reached their smallest size around that time. Or, as probably was the case in Holland, gains from the winning of new lowlands for agriculture were wholly negated by the loss of existing farmland to the waters, as they were slowly submerged below sea level. Indeed, from the 1370s Holland would lose considerable amounts of land during half a century of wet weather. Moreover, the cultivation of less productive land to feed more mouths brought diminishing returns and lower average yields. All this happened as the population continued to grow, resulting in rising food prices and, as an additional result, rising hunger.

Added to this were the growing political instability and its consequences for trade. Chronic war in the Mediterranean Sea, from a newly assertive Ottoman Empire to the wars in southern Italy, frequently disrupted trade for several decades. The increasingly sharp confrontation between France and England, which ultimately culminated in the Hundred Years' War in 1337, forced the Low Countries' regional powers to choose sides, lest they be excluded from trade. These political conflicts affected Flanders the most, which between the 1320s and the 1340s was wracked by a civil war between a pro-French count and mostly pro-English cities dependent on English wool. All of this was bad news for the Flemish economy, though Brabant in particular benefited from being able to sell its own cloth to countries with which Flanders was at war.

These developments, as well as longstanding grievances held by the population against the closed oligarchies that governed them, led in some places to popular unrest and revolt. In Flanders and in Utrecht this led, as it had in some Italian cities, to the participation of the guilds in the municipal administration, including the creation of civic militias to defend both the town and their own interests. In 1304 the guilds of Utrecht, supported by a Flemish army moving against the bishop tied to their rivals in Hainaut, forced the patricians and the bishop to accept a new charter that squarely placed the guilds at the center of power. For the next two centuries they would lead a city government that carefully regulated the interests of some forty different guilds. The same demands were successfully made in Dordrecht. In Liège and in Brabant the ruling prince was forced to grant charters that formally gave cities a say in the administration. The Charter of Kortenberg (1312) made provision for a permanent council of nobility and cities to assist the duke in running Brabant, including control over its finances – an effort that anticipated the provincial "States" that would be later organized.

Elsewhere such reforms were not formally realized. In Zeeland and most of Holland guilds remained weak and the influence of cities informal. Nowhere, in any event, did these reforms – despite the protectionist economic measures of the guilds – effectively check what were to be long-term trends after 1300: the further accumulation of capital in the hands of relatively few, or stagnant or declining real wages, which would, time and again, precipitate new unrest.

Unprecedented Natural Disasters

To make the food crisis worse, the so-called medieval warm period came to an end; the climate again turned colder by the turn of the new century. The first serious indication of this for all of northwestern Europe came in the spring of 1315, when it

The Low Countries in the
Early Fourteenth Century

4   A political map of the Low Countries in the fourteenth century shows
a highly fragmented situation, but this would slowly change as power
consolidated in the hands of a few families.

began to rain incessantly. The following fall and winter it rained daily for months, and it was not until the summer of 1317 that the weather returned to normal. After the first winter the majority of the population had depleted their reserves, and grain prices skyrocketed – if grain could be had at all. Only the desperate search for new foodstuffs, including the slaughter of horses and cattle, saved some from starvation. The famine was accompanied by reports of a dysentery-like disease that struck a particularly vulnerable populace. No one knows how many people died, but some estimate that between a tenth and a quarter of the total population died in this part of Europe. This disaster was lengthened in 1318 by the arrival of cattle pest from England, which diminished society's capacity to recover. Only in 1322 did the yields return to roughly the old levels.

A quarter of a century later a new, deadly threat appeared. The Black Death seems to have hit Flanders in the summer of 1349 and moved north in the course of the following year. It has been a matter of some discussion whether the plague in the Low Countries, about which relatively little is known, was as lethal as it had been in southern Europe, where between one in two and one in two people died, but the limited statistics are inconclusive. The pandemic, though striking deeply into all segments of the population, struck at the poor with their worse diets more than the rich, and people in the countryside more than in towns. The severity of the visitation varied very widely; some districts may have been largely or wholly spared. That the plague could be devastating is, however, clear enough at the abbey of Aduard in Groningen, forty-four of the ninety monks died during the plague and there are other evidences of massive death rates. Nor did the threat dissipate once the first wave of sickness and death ended around 1352; the plague returned, on average once a decade, until the turn of the next century, preventing the population from making any recovery. It has been estimated that Holland in 1400 had up to 10 percent fewer people than half a century before.

No one at the time knew the cause of the disease, and panicked reactions of local populations in search of culprits frequently focused on the Jews in those places where they had settled. Moving from the Rhineland, sometimes as money-lenders, or possibly from England, from where they had been expelled, the first Jews in the region seem to have settled mostly in the river towns of the eastern Netherlands such as Maastricht in the course of the thirteenth century. Frequently condemned as the killers of Christ, the Jews were easily regarded with suspicion; in 1309 over 100 of them were reportedly killed by a mob near Born in Limburg as they sought protection from the local lord in his castle. In 1349 the need to identify and punish scapegoats during the Black Death led to the extinction of many of these communities, especially in Brabant. Their members were robbed of their property, imprisoned or expelled; hundreds were killed. For a generation this inhibited further Jewish settlement in the Netherlands.

The Black Death had this and a myriad of negative effects; some institutions, for example, simply broke down because of the lack of people to run them. In the long run, though, the plague also brought about positive benefits, and arguably encouraged the tendency toward capital and property accumulation that had already begun. Although declining agricultural output made grain more expensive, labor shortages, caused by the plague, often had the effect of increasing real wages. As the standard of living rose, so did the demand for luxury goods, stimulating trade. More expensive labor in turn prompted new cost-cutting measures, such as larger ships that improved profit margins, and larger, more efficient farms that made use of contract labor. This also reduced the share of people working in agriculture, and the relatively small percentage of people working in this sector became a lasting characteristic of the region. Seen this way, the plague both facilitated and enabled a social and economic development that had already begun.

8 Manuscript from 1349 depicting the burning of the Jews, at the height of the Black Death. Anti-Jewish sentiments could suddenly emerge, by a variety of actors and motives.

Political Instability

The murder of Floris V in 1296 showed how much the politics of Holland were intertwined in the strategic interests of larger powers such as France and England. The instability of the dynastic system, so dependent on the unpredictability of dynastic births and deaths, however, played itself out differently depending on the strength of other forces. In Flanders, the enormous size of the cities ensured that they could obtain a say in the Flemish political system. Even after the advent of a powerful count, Louis of Male, restored political stability to Flanders around 1350, the duke was realistic enough to share power with representatives of the cities on which he was dependent. Much of the political energy in Flanders was spent by various city factions contending with each other for municipal power. In Brabant, the cities were smaller and could assert their power only at moments of ducal weakness (as evidenced in the Charter of Kortenberg) or of invasion. In 1356 they determined that each new duke swear by a charter that recognized the rights of the key cities, the great abbeys and the nobility. The duke also had to promise not to declare war or make treaties without their consent. This pledge would in later decades be embodied in a so-called "Joyous Entry" of the duke into each of Brabant's cities. However, this initial effort – undertaken to ensure that the new Duchess Joanna and her husband Wenceslaus would keep Brabant both united and free – failed when Louis of Male demanded, on the basis of his wife's inheritance, his own share of Brabant. The Joyous Entry charter of freedoms and promises became a nearly mythic ideal of shared, representative government in the Low Countries, but future dukes, even as they pledged good faith during their joyous entries, did not always feel bound by its letter or spirit.

The situation was different again in Guelders, Holland and Zeeland, where the cities, if much grown and enjoying increasing clout, were still relatively small and without formal political representation. The Church, a force to be reckoned with in southern territories and of course in the Sticht, was relatively weak institutionally in these regions. This meant that the nobility of Holland and Guelders remained, for the time being, the most important power-brokers. Their power increased when, as was often the case, the count of Holland or duke of Guelders was a weak or absent figure. Count Willem III of Avesnes, who as count of Hainaut inherited Holland after Floris's line died out, was effective in permanently attaching Zeeland to Holland, but spent little time there, freeing the nobility to do as they chose. The real crisis came after 1345, when Willem's namesake son was killed in another failed effort to take Frisia. Willem IV's death without issue ultimately led to conflict between his sister, who had inherited his lands, and her son, also Willem. Both were supported by different factions of the nobility who vied for power with each other: the so-called Cods, possibly named after the coat of arms of the House of Bavaria from which both mother and son stemmed, and the Hooks, a reference to the hooks used to catch cod. By 1351 the Cods, the supporters of Willem, had won. But the factional conflict would continue on and off for a century and a half, and the deep enmity between these factions would go a long way to account for why any instability in the ruling dynasty could have such explosive effects.

In Guelders, a similar conflict for headship of the duchy was fought out in the 1340s by supporters of two young brothers, named after the two noblemen who led the opposing parties: the faction of the lord of Bronkhorst against the party led by the Van Heeckeren family. Again in the 1370s, with both brothers dead, this factionalism again reared its head, resulting in new instability. In Groningen and in Frisia similar factions rose up in the fourteenth century. All of these internal fights were additionally fueled by outside parties: kings, bishops and dukes of surrounding regions all had a stake in the outcome of these struggles.

No one could know it – the vicissitudes of dynastic fortunes were too great – but this picture of fragmentation would begin to change in the 1380s, as new dynastic houses would begin to consolidate the various territories of the Netherlands. That scions of the House of Bavaria would become counts of three counties at once – Hainaut, Zeeland and Holland – in the 1340s was one early sign of this shift, but only one read in hindsight. Seen from this perspective, the rise of the Burgundian dynasty after 1384 would bring about an additional and even more important shift that further integrated the Netherlands into a wider European politics.

Enviable Morsels

The further integration of what became the Netherlands into the broader European picture had much to do, of course, with the changing contours of the region. With the important exception of Flanders most of the Low Countries, and certainly the areas north of the great rivers, had been areas on the political and economic periphery of Europe. Its participation in the religious and cultural life of the continent had been modest, and was influenced more by cultural forces coming out of Flanders and Germany than by any movement in the opposite direction. The difficult-to-tame wetness of the countryside and the sandiness of its eastern marches had not sustained many people until the eleventh or twelfth centuries. Economic activity picked up at the beginning of the second millennium, but in contrast with many other places that development was modest and slow, with a clear breakthrough in the expansion of cities and extensions of waterways in the thirteenth century.

By the late fourteenth century, the regions north of Flanders were no longer at the periphery, as shall be shown in the next chapter. Brabant – including its northern parts, which are now part of the Netherlands – was becoming a political and economic powerhouse in its own right. The eastern river towns were becoming a thoroughly integrated part of the German-based Hanseatic League. And Holland began systematically to export cheese and other dairy products in the 1350s, the first sign of a specialized economy that would eventually make it an economic contender of the first order. All of these developments were sustained by an expanding European economy that progressively availed itself of the markets, products and services of the region. For this reason, the Netherlands was increasingly eyed by European princes eager to expand their own power by exercising control over these promising territories. In this sense the "crisis" of the fourteenth century entailed not only disaster but, as it its original meaning suggests, a turning point.

2

Rise of the Northern Netherlands, 1384–1588

~

Starting in the late fourteenth century, then, the northern Netherlands began to become important in a wider economic and political context. The IJssel towns and Holland had become important economic centers by the fourteenth century, but they both continued to be dwarfed by the great Flemish cities of the southern Netherlands. In the course of the fifteenth centuries, all of Brabant, with its emerging metropolis of Antwerp, became much more important, transforming Zeeland and Holland as well, which were fast becoming players in their own right. The growing synergy among the regions – and with other parts of Europe – was facilitated by the rising dominance of European dynasties, first the House of Burgundy and later the Habsburg family, which tried to rule its new provinces in a single administrative regime and which in time gave the region a leading role in the European economy and culture. If dynastic ambitions initially brought both greater dynamism and stability to the region, rising taxation and – in response to the Protestant Reformation – religious repression triggered increasing resistance to centralized rule, which finally resulted in massive revolt. Only in the more easily defensible northern provinces – led by Holland – was this revolt ultimately successful, resulting there in a republic that repudiated monarchical rule and struck out on its own into the unknown.

Rise and Fall of the Burgundians, 1384–1477

Dynastic Politics and the Triumph of the Burgundians, 1384–1435

By the 1380s two important European dynasties ruled over large parts of the Low Countries. Holland–Zeeland and Hainaut were ruled by Albert I, duke of Bavaria, who formally became count in each of these lands when his insane older brother, Willem V, died in 1389. Albert was frequently in Holland, and confirmed The Hague as the permanent residency of the count, making it the center of an increasingly extravagant court life. With Albert the father of seven legitimate children who reached adulthood, including three sons, his house seemed well positioned further to embellish its excellent dynastic position. Yet the Bavarian house would be supplanted by the other dynasty – the House of Burgundy – which would come to dominate much of the Low Countries by the 1430s.

Philip the Bold, so called by his chroniclers, was the first duke of Burgundy. He sprang from the reigning dynasty of France, the House of Valois, being a son of the French king. He married Margaret of Dampierre, daughter and heir of the count of Flanders, and in 1384 himself became count of the most important region of the Low Countries after both of his in-laws had died. What is more, this was part of a double marriage: a year later their son Jan (John the Fearless) married Albert's daughter Margaret. This set the stage – though no one could know it at the time – for a Burgundian accumulation of titles and concentration of power unprecedented in the region.

As the marriage of Margaret and John indicates, dynastic houses were deeply interrelated, and who emerged victorious depended on children: whether any were born, what their sex was, whether they lived to adulthood and who they managed to marry – all in all a largely unpredictable calculus. The Burgundian House benefited from the fact that Johanna of Brabant, the respected

74

but childless duchess, willed first Luxembourg and then Brabant to her niece Margaret of Dampierre in 1404. Philip the Bold's son Anton and grandsons would be installed as dukes of Brabant – all, it must be added, with the support of Brabant's influential towns, who hoped that economic stability would be the result of having so powerful a duke. The duke of Guelders's own ambitions to take over Brabant were thus thwarted.

Brabant's relatively stable internal politics therefore smoothed its entry into the Burgundian camp. In contrast, it was precisely decades of feuding – particularly in Holland – that preceded the unforeseen triumph of the House of Burgundy in Holland–Zeeland–Hainaut. "Hook" and "Cod" were notoriously unstable identities where switching sides was common, and where families were frequently divided against each other. This enduring rivalry was almost always motivated by quarrels over succession rights. Duke Albert navigated a tortuous path between the two factions, but the murder of his chief servant and his mistress in 1392 – by actors and for motives that are now unclear – revived the old vendettas between Cod and Hook. After Hook leaders were accused of the murders, Albert vented his fury against them and against his son Willem, who sided with the Hooks, forcing him to flee abroad for a time. Although father and son soon reconciled, the destruction and seizure of Hook property in the 1390s had deepened the antagonisms.

Willem's own position as count was strengthened by the defeat of his mortal enemy, Jan, lord of Arkel, who had once been his father's right-hand man in the Cod–Hook feud of the early 1390s and whose own base around Gorinchem threatened Holland's river economy. His last years as count were peaceful, but his early demise in 1417 – he died of complications from an infected dog bite – left his fifteen-year-old daughter Jacqueline of Hainaut, known in Dutch history as Jacoba, to rule over his lands. For centuries Jacoba has captured the Dutch historical imagination for her plucky but completely luckless effort to maintain her rights as countess. Willem's

9　That countess Jacqueline of Hainaut, pictured here, could be cast aside
by her cousin, Philip the Good, was only possible through longstanding
factionalism between Hooks and Cods.

death had revived again the clannish enmities between Hooks and
Cods, and Jacoba's uncle Jan (John the Pitiless), brother of her dead
father, contested her right to succeed Willem on the grounds that
she was a woman. With the support of the Cods, he took up court
in The Hague as the effectual count. Jacoba's first husband had
already died, and her next spouse, the weak-willed teenage duke
of Brabant, John IV, consorted with her uncle against her. Holland
in particular suffered from the warfare between these two parties.

Following John the Pitiless's death in 1425 – Jacoba may have
had a hand in his fatal poisoning – a new nemesis challenged
the countess: her cousin, the young duke of Burgundy, Philip the

Good. Like John, Philip contrived reasons to delegitimize Jacoba, in this case by contesting her marriage. In doing so, he could count on the anti-Jacoba Cods in many Holland towns, as well as the very same nobility who had supported John the Pitiless. The countess, escaping from Philip's imprisonment, marshaled a handful of Hook towns to her side, and waged war against Philip and his Cod allies between 1425 and 1428. This struggle did not go well for Jacoba; in the Battle of Brouwershaven in January of 1426, her Zeeland followers, supplemented by English soldiers sent by her third husband, the duke of Gloucester, were annihilated by Burgundian-led forces. Gloucester abandoned his wife for one of her ladies-in-waiting as her military situation further deteriorated, and she was forced to surrender when Philip besieged her at Gouda. Tired of war, the Holland towns put pressure on the two cousins to reach an accord. In the now famous Kiss of Delft of 1428 – a "kiss" (*zoen*) was a medieval metaphor for reconciliation between two parties – the childless and now unmarried Jacoba formally kept her titles but designated Philip as her regent and heir, and promised not to remarry without his permission. In 1434 she did marry one last time, to a powerful Zeeland nobleman. Now Philip ensured that she renounced all her rights to rule. She died, disinherited, of tuberculosis two years later. Making clever use of internal divisions within Holland–Zeeland, Philip had succeeded in incorporating these lands into his domains.

Philip seldom visited these northern regions, though; the primary focus was on Burgundy and on the richer lands such as Flanders and Brabant. Soon after the Kiss of Delft, Philip became duke of Brabant and Limburg, after both sons of his uncle Anton, including the hapless Jan IV, died young and without issue. Here, again, it was the States of Brabant that were crucial in choosing which of the ten claimants they wanted to become duke. As head of wealthy Flanders, Philip seemed to offer Brabant financial security, placing him in the States' eyes above his competitors. By the time he was in his thirties, then, Philip was master of not only large portions of what is now eastern France, but most of the Low Countries, including its most key territories of Flanders, Brabant and Holland. Breaking with the Paris-focused policies of his grandfather and father – the latter had been murdered by the French king's men – Philip eventually made peace with France in 1435, focusing instead on strengthening his territories within the Low Countries.

Effectively free from subservience to either the French king or the German emperor, Philip began to title himself "Grand Duke of the West" after 1435, and began creating the most sumptuous court of Europe, designed to prove that he was, in effect, equal to any king. His lavish patronage of painters such as Jan van Eyck is just one small piece of evidence for this. Philip's last three decades of rule were fairly peaceful, setting the stage for a more effective administration of his far-flung domains as well as new economic activity. It would be the Low Countries' first extensive experience with a single powerful ruler in a long time, one with far-reaching consequences.

Economic Developments

The fifteenth century witnessed difficult economic times for much of Europe. The return of the plague (in the late 1430s and late 1450s), as well as economic and political conflict, including increasing taxes, kept population growth low. Nevertheless, many parts of the Netherlands did not fare badly in the period; in fact trade volume doubled in the Low Countries between 1400 and 1475. Some areas, though, clearly did better than others. No new towns were established after 1400, and the recently established outposts built on the sandy grounds in the east stagnated, while in contrast the mostly older settlements on the more fruitful clay-and-peat soil, typically in the west of the country, grew.

Throughout the Burgundian period Flanders remained the leading territory in the whole region; in population and economic activity it easily surpassed any other single principality. By the end of the fourteenth century the Flemish city of Bruges, however, outpaced Ghent as the most economically flourishing city and most important trading center. The great banking houses of Europe, then mostly Italian in origin, established permanent offices in Bruges. The growing wealth of Bruges offered the harbor towns on the Schelde, in what is now Zeeland, new opportunities to make money from trade with it.

Despite the success of this Flemish city, Brabant became more important under the Burgundians. Its central location and booming cities led the Burgundian regime to prefer its capital of Brussels as an important seat of its own authority. At the same time, Brabant – not least its northern parts, which included Bergen op Zoom and Den Bosch – was rising in economic importance. With its pastures full of sheep, this part of Brabant sold wool both to its own weavers and to Flanders, remaining a textile powerhouse in the early fifteenth century. It also benefited from buying and selling English linens that had been banned from Flemish markets. Its northwestern region around Breda made money by selling its turf to the energy-hungry cities. The region's annual fairs linked the economies of Flanders with those of Germany, and increasingly cities such as Antwerp and Bergen op Zoom became an important locus in traffic among England, northern France and the Baltic as well, including Skåne, where they traded their textiles for Scandinavian herring. The Maas River was, for Den Bosch, a main artery of trade that connected it with both the sea and the Rhineland. If Brabançon textiles lost ground to cheaper competitors in the course of the fifteenth century, the region became a center of artisanal expertise, producing luxury goods for not only the duke and his court but the wealthy urban bourgeoisie as well.

At the height of their economic and political powers in the first half of the fifteenth century were the trading towns in the eastern Netherlands, such as Nijmegen and Zutphen in the duchy of Guelders, and Deventer, Kampen and Zwolle in the Oversticht.

Utrecht and Maastricht, always important, remained so. All of these cities dominated their respective regions, which were thinly settled and subject to relatively weak rule. In Guelders the nobility and the dukes – who with near regularity died without legitimate children, precipitating multiple crises of succession – accepted the political say of the cities in ducal affairs. The generally weak reach of the bishop of Utrecht across the empty expanses of the Oversticht gave the cities along the IJssel River a large measure of autonomy, and even a relatively successful bishop such as Frederik van Blankenheim (1393–1423) more or less left the local church and civil authorities alone. Cities and the bishop were, when the times dictated it, united in common cause against marauding nobility, often from Guelders, who threatened trade within the region.

What made all of these river towns prosperous was their membership of the Hanseatic League, the extensive trading network of cities that held a near-monopoly of trade on the North and Baltic Seas by the mid fourteenth century. With easy access to the goods for sale in these towns across the North Sea and the Baltic these eastern towns were able to boost their already important economic position. Deventer, probably the most important of them, possessed the oldest annual fairs in the northern Netherlands, with fairs being held to ensure supply at precise times in an age of uncertain transport, trading in turf, lime, herring, rye, butter, wine and wood. The towns were an important link among the Baltic, England and Holland on the one hand, and the Rhine towns further inland on the other. In addition to sitting on the river they were, just as the Brabançon cities, strategically situated along key east–west roads.

By the mid 1400s, however, these cities were slowly losing ground to the towns along the North Sea: in Zeeland and in Frisia, but especially in Holland, which had become a trading power in its own right by the end of the fourteenth century. This shift stemmed only in small part from the gradual silting up of the Zuyder Zee, which made maritime trade more difficult, and far more from the fact that the Dutch western coastal towns were producing and not merely transporting goods, as was largely the case in the eastern towns. Without any significant home trades of their own these towns ceased to grow much further – in contrast, then, to the dynamic economies further to the west.

Production in Holland was in the first instance driven by necessity. Since the beginning of cultivation, the fruitful, peaty soil along the coast, eroded by oxidation and heavy crop use, began to sink in the span of a few years, in many cases rotting the crops and, in the worst cases, forming inland lakes. Dutch water management, though continuing to make ingenious use of sluices and dikes, was not fully able to contain this problem; the windmill, though introduced for the first time in 1407, was decades away from full utilization. In fact, western parts of the country were periodically subject to catastrophic flooding. The worst was the St. Elizabeth's Day flood of November 1421 (only one of three large floods to take place on this saint's day in the early fifteenth century), which inundated the productive Grote Waard near Dordrecht and swept away its sixteen villages. A growing sea arm put too much pressure on the dikes and sluices, causing them to fail at one crucial point. Perhaps 2,000 died, though many residents escaped as it took the water months to swallow up the last of the Grote Waard. The event was a great trauma to local residents: the church towers that continued to stick out of the water of what became known as the Biesbosch a reminder of their irretrievable loss. Developing better defense techniques against nature and deriving other sources of income than farming were now more essential than ever.

Since crop cultivation hastened the sinking of farmland, its owners sought alternative uses. By turning their land into pasture Dutch farmers spared it, and as a result began to specialize in the production of butter and cheese, and cattle-farming, soon exporting across the wider region. And because they now grew less grain, the Hollanders in particular were forced to import more of it, further stimulating their participation in trade. Holland's merchant fleet grew strongly in the course of the fifteenth century, becoming well positioned to carry the goods produced and sold in Flanders and in Brabant, whose fleets they numerically exceeded. The regional economy got a boost from the fortuitous migration of herring from Scandinavia to the western North Sea, and the development of fish-processing techniques while the herring buss was at sea was an innovation that enabled sailors to process and barrel the fish efficiently on board, making fishing far more efficient and more profitable for export. Borrowing from the newest German techniques, Holland also specialized in the production of hopped beer, which it primarily sold to the southern Netherlands. More than elsewhere, the cities and countryside of Holland thus started to become sites of intensive specialization, where products were not made for subsistence but were carefully tailored for the wider market, now being expanded by Holland's fast-rising shipping sector.

In hindsight, the strong economic rise of the Holland coastal regions would have profound consequences over time, creating a northern economic powerhouse that would eclipse Flanders and Brabant, and make Holland the center of a European and later global economy. The Frisians, who long had been competitors of the Hollanders for trading on the North Sea, were the first to suffer from Holland's rise. But the north German cities of the Hanseatic League certainly also noticed Holland's competitive edge, and in 1430 it closed the Danish Sound to Dutch ships, effectively blocking their passage to the Baltic and to the granaries of pro-Dutch Hanseatic towns such as Danzig. It was 1438 before Philip the Good, long attentive to the concerns of Flanders, which had good relations with the Germans, permitted the aggrieved Hollanders and Zeelanders to wage war formally against the League. Although the war amounted to little more than piracy against each other's ships (and often against neutral vessels), the Holland-led coalition ultimately wreaked enough damage on the German Hanseatic cities to secure, for modest payment, its access to the Sound. Though armed clashes would periodically break out after the Treaty of Copenhagen in 1441 – three wars would follow in the next century – the Dutch presence in the Sound would only grow stronger over time. Telling, too, was the strong financial cooperation within Holland in its first war against the League; most if not all of the towns soon found the money to wage war against a common enemy, a sign of both their financial means and their ability to work together – and giving them an important shared experience.

Urban Ferment

Holland's cities may have effectively cooperated with each other in their fight against the Hanseatic League, and in contrast with the mighty cities of Flanders – who were used to getting their way – they mostly avoided direct conflict with their lord, Philip the Good. Internally, however, the towns of the northern Netherlands, both inside and outside Holland, were hardly models of peace and quiet. There were many divisions within almost every city. Sometimes, as in Holland, the old vendettas between Cods and Hooks surfaced in open conflict, as they did in 1444 when the appointed lieutenant of the duke – the *stadhouder* (in English, stadholder), as he was locally known – appointed many Hooks, breaking with the pattern of selecting chiefly Cods. In Utrecht, acrimonious conflict continued, as it long had, between the cathedral canons and the city council over control of the town. Selecting a new bishop, with rival candidates supported by competing neighboring states, often threw the city into intense turmoil.

Just how much political power the guilds should retain in city government persisted as a crucial issue in many cities during the fourteenth and fifteenth centuries. All cities had historic privileges, and each had recognized groups with their own rights.

Every ruler had to take account of these arrangements, if only to undermine them better. Philip the Good knew that effective rule meant making enduring alliances with local power-brokers, and he selected the patricians of the towns as his partners, at the expense of the lesser bourgeoisie or the guilds. In the western provinces this resulted in the creation of the *vroedschap* for each city, an administrative council of leading burghers who served for life and who nominated all officers to city government, including the mayors. In this way the power of the guilds, and thus of a broader representative government, were curtailed in most western towns. Local leaders continued to be alert to the demands of the guilds and city inhabitants in order to prevent unrest, but city government in the Low Countries, especially in the west, tended to become less, and not more, representative over time.

The old corporatist model of civic government, with greater power granted to guilds and to citizen entities, persisted best where it had been established early: in the south and the east of the region, and in the Holland town of Dordrecht. Even in the eastern towns not under Burgundian rule, though, the influence of the guilds was sometimes hotly contested. In 1413, a pro-guild government swept into power in the Hanseatic town of Zwolle, threatening the interests of the bishop and of city patricians. In 1416 they struck back, toppling the government, executing ten guild leaders and restricting guild privileges. And even in relatively open Brabant representative government was anything but democratic; sixty wealthy families, for instance, effectively ran Den Bosch, and even that was a wider representation than was present in other towns.

In addition to this it might be added that the towns of the region were often held bitter rivalries with each other, or with the countryside around them. Dordrecht, having attained the right in 1299 to sell all goods that came along its rivers, insisted on its privileges, to the great irritation of competing towns. The loss of the Grote Waard in 1421 made Dordrecht virtually an

10   Utrecht's cathedral as pictured prior to the destruction of the nave through a 1674 tornado. (The size of church and tower confirmed Utrecht as the Dutch center of religious authority.)

island, making it harder for the city to enforce its staple right, as passing ships could now more easily skirt the town by sailing over what had been land. This led to more conflict, as Dordrecht went to war in the mid fifteenth century against rival river towns such as Gorinchem and Schoonhoven, which each sought to circumvent the staple requirement in their own favor. In any event, the growing significance of other Holland cities effectively began to reduce the Dordrecht's importance. Further north the city of Groningen, in its isolation virtually a state unto itself, demanded (in a manner parallel to the practice of the great Flemish cities) that local villages deliver all of their products to its market, generating a mutual animosity that would last decades, even centuries.

This urban conflict does not even address the persistent conflicts that afflicted the countryside. The internecine border conflicts among, for example, Guelders, Holland and Utrecht, added a measure of uncertainty and misery to the areas and towns affected. Frisia, though it remained largely and fiercely free of the direct control of foreign overlords, was increasingly wracked by violent factional fighting. Like other parts of the Holy Roman Empire, the Low Countries was a region fractured by the competing interests of and violent disputes among many towns and rural communities.

Precisely because they were so competitive, the towns attempted wherever possible to project their own greatness. The glory of urban life, however, was precarious in a time when most of the buildings were still made of wood and thatch and when most cities were afflicted by devastating fires. Only four houses were reportedly left standing when Gouda burned to the ground in 1438; some 4,000 buildings were reported destroyed in the great fire that destroyed Den Bosch in 1463. In response to a large fire, Amsterdam began reconstruction in stone in 1452 – though the heavier buildings required underground stilts to keep them above ground – and other cities, too, began rebuilding with more durable materials. Churches traditionally had been the way in which towns manifested both their piety and their civic pride, and great churches continued to be built; the highest spire of the northern Netherlands, the Dom of Utrecht, was completed in 1382, and perhaps the region's most majestic cathedral – St. Jan's in Den Bosch, an inspiring example of Brabançon Gothic – was completed in 1530, after a century and a half of painstaking effort.

But the shift toward more durable materials would have its most profound effects on civic buildings. Taking their cue from the southern Netherlands and from architects active there, Dutch towns began to develop a more alluring public face. The striking late Gothic city halls of Gouda (finished in the 1450s) and Middelburg (begun in the same decade) were designed by the same Brabançon family of architects – the Keldermans – and rivaled the achievements of their southern neighbors. The arts, too, flourished in many of the region's towns. The best artists, such as the cutting-edge miniatures of the Nijmegen-born Limbourg brothers, would find service among the nobility further south. Van Eyck's use of oil paint on panels, and his crisp portraitures and church painting, paved the way for new generations of artists active not only in the service of the count but also the cities. Less tangible forms of cultural expression also became

86

increasingly exuberant in the cities: civic festivals and saints' feast days became ever more elaborate. By the 1460s chambers of rhetoric, convivial clubs that engaged in public debate, sprouted in the northern Netherlands, and sought to add to the luster of their towns by composing odes in honor to them. Civic paintings and histories retold the glories of each town, further strengthening citizens' identification with their respective cities, and their willingness, when the time came, to defend the rights and interests of their home towns.

Religious Reflection

Religious devotion remained a mainstay of life for many. The crusade – the ultimate military expression of piety – did, however, come to an end. The last great western European effort (under the Burgundian leadership of John the Fearless) was smashed by the Turks in 1396, and the Knights of the Teutonic Order, initially established to fight the heathen in the Baltic, and to which Dutch and Frisian nobility belonged, were obliterated on the Polish battlefield (Grunwald) in 1410. Philip the Good's aspirations to go on a crusade himself like his father John had come to nothing. But devotion in everyday life continued unabated. Ordinary people continued to venerate deeply the mystery of the Eucharist; became more than ever devotees of the Virgin Mary; and took inspiration from living saints such as Sister Bertken, who in 1461 had herself bricked up in a local Utrecht church, spending more than half a century (she died at eighty-seven) praying for and talking to the poor. Pageantry, processions and ritual were also part of religious life, which in turn largely determined the rhythm of daily life. In places such as Utrecht locals additionally held church consecration festivals that were little more than popular carnivals. The splendor of the more formal celebrations was a way for the Church to demonstrate both its spiritual and its worldly importance.

By the late fourteenth century the Church's "worldly" habits, however, triggered criticism across some parts of Catholic Europe. In the Low Countries it took the form of a religious movement that stressed the inward dimensions of faith instead of external and "empty" forms. An early pioneer of this movement was Geert Groote (1340–1384), an academically trained, Deventer-born cleric, who ten years before his death underwent a deep conversion experience, rejecting what he saw as the vanity and materialism of his past life. Partially drawing his new inspiration from the Flemish mystic Jan van Ruysbroeck, Groote advanced a particular kind of spirituality known as the *Devotio moderna*, which called the Christian to an intense and silent reflection on the Cross and on her own mortality. Groote criticized merely outward forms of religiosity – he thought the recently finished Dom tower in Utrecht empty pride – and called the faithful inward.

Groote's message had great appeal, perhaps all the more in an uncertain age that had undergone plague, crop failures owing to a colder climate, and social and political instability (Groote would himself die of the plague while tending to the sick). Groote's message resonated not least with women, and he used his home in Deventer to shelter poor female disciples. These women became part of a wider movement, the Brethren and Sisters of the Common Life, where participants took up a form of monastic life together without swearing permanent vows. The Brethren's stronghold remained the eastern Netherlands from where it stemmed, but its message quickly traveled down the rivers to the Rhineland, and westward and southward to the great population centers of the region. Ultimately about 100 chapters were established across the Low Countries and Germany. Its most famous member was Thomas à Kempis (he was born in Kampen), whose *Imitation of Christ* (c. 1418) became a classic of Christian spirituality.

Neither Groote nor Kempis contemplated any break with the Catholic Church, and it is problematic to label them forerunners of the Reformation. But their distinction between inner and outer forms of religion constituted a strong critique of the institutional Church, feeding an already existing alienation from the official Church and its perceived excesses. Speaking to the relatively literate population, they helped create a reading-centered spirituality that was at once critical of the self and of the feigned spirituality of public institutions and persons, stimulating what some scholars have argued was a distinctive Netherlandic religiosity. In any event, the *Devotio moderna* would subsequently impact Dutch humanism and its most famous practitioner, Erasmus, in his criticism of ecclesiastical practice.

Growing Centralization and Regional Cooperation

Life among the Brethren in Deventer was a world away from the Burgundian court, although many of its key members were eager to have themselves painted by the era's great artists in acts of devotion. Their rule very much depended on demonstrating their glory as a dynasty, though the unwilling Holy Roman Emperors steadfastly refused to grant kingship to the dangerous upstart family on the empire's western borders. But Burgundian power rested not only on external recognition but in further integrating the rather diverse and diffuse set of territories into a coherent administrative whole. Patterning this ambition on the Kingdom of France, from which the family stemmed, Philip set out to coordinate his disparate lands more closely through centralizing the administration, standardizing the rules and integrating local elites into the Burgundian power structures. A truly centralized state, though, was beyond his ambitions and his powers.

Some of Philip's efforts eased economic life. In the early 1430s he issued the "Fourlander" currency, which stabilized and simplified financial traffic across his realms. Over time, representatives of the various regions met frequently to discuss tolls, taxes and trade policies, developing a shared policy toward neighboring states. More controversially, Philip introduced a Grand Council that served as the highest court across all of his lands, using Roman law sometimes to override the common-law jurisprudence of his various domains, to the unhappiness of local jurists. He attempted to bring about uniformity in taxation by expanding the authority of his exchequers; in addition to the offices already established in Dijon, Lille and Brussels he set one up in The Hague in 1447 in response to local authorities who wanted a more efficient tax system. He typically appointed close bilingual associates from francophone regions to rule over the Dutch-speaking areas with the view that these "foreigners" would both rule with greater impartiality and be more loyal to him. These men were the first *stadhouders* – lieutenants who governed for the ruler during his physical absence – an office that became important over time.

The quality of Philip's Burgundian administrators, however, could not be guaranteed. Tax revenues frequently disappeared into the pockets of his civil servants, and the Burgundian tendency in the later years of the dynasty to sell public offices to the highest bidder further undermined the effectiveness of government. This practice, as well as tax hikes, caused some discontentment among local officials and the population.

At the same time, though, Burgundian efforts at greater coordination created new possibilities for the different regions to join together in common cause. Joint military resistance to central authority was still a century away – all revolts against the duke, chiefly in Flanders, remained local – but Philip's creation of the States-General in 1464 – where all the different states of his domains had representation – created a formal podium for the discussion of Burgundian tax policies and related issues. Philip had introduced the States-General to make his requests for money easier, but it was also an important impetus for a new and wider regional identity among provincial elites – as well as a realization of their shared rights.

The Sudden Collapse of Burgundian Fortunes

Perhaps in time the Burgundian state would have gelled into a coherent state that rivaled France. But if dynastic vicissitudes had aided the sudden rise of the House of Burgundy earlier in the century, they now gravitated against it. Philip had sired many children out of wedlock; one of them, David, he imposed on Utrecht as bishop in 1455. But Philip and his wife, Isabella of Portugal, produced only one son who lived to adulthood: Charles. Father and son, not uncommonly for the dynasties of the day, were on bad terms, and Charles was effectively banished from court for a time, holed up for several years in the Blue Tower near Gorinchem before taking the reins from his sick father in 1465.

The new duke, who unlike Philip regarded himself mainly as a warrior – he sought to emulate Alexander the Great – became known as Charles the Bold, pursuing a visibly more aggressive policy than his more prudent father had. He was perennially at war, continually demanding new grants from his subjects to pay for it. Resentment against Charles rose, all the more so because he showed little regard for the historical privileges of his different lands. Initially, though, his strategy was successful; he seized both Liège and Guelders through a combination of brute force and intrigue. His opponents in these states were supported by the French, with whom he was now in open conflict by actively seeking an alliance with the English, a conflict his father had spent the last decades of his rule avoiding.

In the 1470s, however, Charles abruptly made peace with France, focusing instead on his obsessive aim – as many observers of the time thought – of connecting his ancestral lands of Burgundy with the more recently acquired Low Countries. This ambition required him to subdue Alsace and Lorraine, an aim that earned him new enemies. These included the German emperor – who at the last moment reneged on a pledge to crown him king – and the Swiss Confederation, who saw his encroachments as a threat to their own regional ambitions. The Swiss defeated him

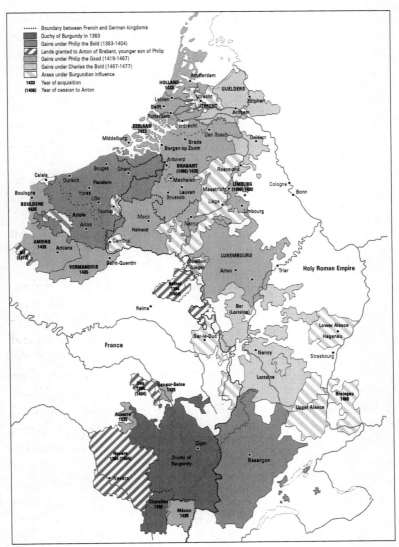

5 Charles the Bold rapidly expanded Burgundian rule, but after
his death the gains were quickly undone, soon putting most of
the Low Countries in the hands of the Habsburg dynasty.

three times in battle, in the first seizing his encampment (including his silver bathtub), in the second annihilating his army and in the third – at Nancy in January 1477 – taking his life. His naked and disfigured body was identified three days after his death. He was forty-three years old.

The death of the duke immediately transformed the political situation for his lands. His only child, Mary, almost twenty years of age and not yet married to her betrothed, Maximilian of Habsburg, had been left untutored in the affairs of state and was unprepared for the power vacuum her father's death had caused. Soon Liège, Utrecht and Guelders rebelled, attaining their former independence, and the French king, sensing his opportunity, seized Burgundy, decisively breaking – permanently as it turned out – the administrative ties between that region and the Low Countries.

In many places, rebellion broke out against the ducal regime, in which some of Charles's most hated local representatives were killed. Most importantly, the change of fortunes led to a meeting of the States-General in February of 1477. The States-General had already asserted themselves against Charles, denying the embattled duke additional war credits in 1476, and now their representatives saw an unprecedented opportunity, with Mary's position under assault internationally, to roll back the unwanted centralization policies of the past years. Claiming the old rights of the past Brabançon charters of 1312 and 1356, the assembly drew up the Great Privilege, forcing Mary to accept a series of reforms intended to limit ducal rule and restore the power and rights of each sovereign principality. The reforms determined that the duchess could not tax her subjects nor go to war without the permission of the States, had to appoint officials for each region from within that region, and must respect the common law of each region.

The Great Privilege was an historical moment, and it would remain etched in the memory of the region's elites for the decades

11   The Great Privilege of 1477 built on a longer tradition of self-government in the Low Countries. Though soon abrogated by Maximilian, its vision remained an important ideal.

to come. It powerfully confirmed a tradition of the right to resist princely power, and its precedent would help fuel, a century later, the Dutch Revolt. It bound the Burgundian lands of the Low Countries in a shared sense of political community and it set the standard for representative government over and against the arbitrary demands of the sovereign. But as an actual basis for government it would prove short-lived. In the end, most regional leaders did not want the Burgundian state to collapse, or the end of interregional cooperation that that might entail. As a result, many proved unwilling to challenge Charles the Bold's successors, even though new political conflicts would soon arise.

Habsburg Rule and Further Centralization, 1477–1555

The Habsburg lands before the marriage of Maximilian to Mary in August of 1477 were still largely confined to Austria, and the young Maximilian, born and raised far away in a rural setting, had little knowledge of – or respect for – the traditions and rights of city-dwellers. Yet at the time of his death in 1519 the House of Habsburg would become the largest and most powerful dynasty in Europe; his successor and grandson, the Emperor Charles V, would rule over one out of every three Europeans as well as a world empire. The Low Countries became during this period an important part of this expanding empire, creating unprecedented new opportunities for the exchange of goods and of ideas. Brabant and increasingly Holland would be the greatest beneficiaries of these changes. At the same time, the drawbacks of an increasingly centralized and autocratic state – exponentially higher taxes, wars and revolts and, over time, the brutal repression of religious dissent – put new stresses and strains on Netherlandic society.

A Rough Start

Maximilian solidified Mary's position, but their marriage hardly put an end to their political troubles. Proclaiming his own right to the Burgundian legacy, the French king continued to contest the Habsburg claims. The inheritance dispute over the Low Countries (and rival interests in Italy) triggered a struggle of power between France and the Habsburgs, and would foment nearly constant hostilities lasting down to the Peace of Cateau-Cambrésis in 1559. Making the situation even more contentious was that France was able to capitalize on, and make common cause with, strong anti-Habsburg forces in the Low Countries, such as the towns and nobility in Guelders, who were determined to maintain their independence in the face of Habsburg claims to their duchy.

The legitimacy of the new dynasty was not helped when Duchess Mary, an avid equestrian, suffered a fatal fall from her horse at the age of twenty-five, leaving a three-year-old son, Philip, as heir. Maximilian now ruled the Low Countries directly as Philip's guardian, and pursued a war against France in the 1480s that went against the wishes of the Flemish states and required substantial additional taxation. Open revolt broke out in Flanders twice, and was twice quelled by Maximilian's armies, who made cities such as Bruges pay dearly for their disloyalty. In the northern Netherlands, too, revolts broke out against Habsburg rule. Disaffected Hooks in Holland, long chafing at their lack of representation, rose up and joined forces with Utrecht dissenters against their bishop, David of Burgundy. Pro-Habsburg forces in support of David crushed supporters of the revolt in December 1481, massacring hundreds of Utrecht civilians in the process. Later, in 1488, the Hooks would make a last effort to restore their fortunes, seizing, among other towns, Rotterdam, and pirating along the Maas before being defeated by Maximilian in 1490. Maximilian's access to international armies of mercenaries, as well as a lack of popular support, doomed the Hooks, who now vanished, after a century and a half, as a political force in Holland.

War and the disruption of trade had caused bread prices to sky-rocket in the early 1490s, and northern Holland witnessed its own popular uprising against burdensome war taxes. In 1492 stricken commoners, calling themselves the "bread and cheesepeople," rose up against tax officials, taking Alkmaar, Hoorn and Haarlem, where they killed the hated sheriff. Plundering the countryside themselves, their makeshift army quickly proved easy sport on the battlefield for the government's trained mercenaries and they were brutally cut down. Popular revolts such as this against the ruling prince almost always lost, but they were a looming, potential danger to authorities, who raised taxes further in order to pay soldiers for additional security. The measure may have had an effect: the "Bread and Cheese Revolt" was the last large-scale uprising in Holland before the Dutch Revolt of the 1560s. At any rate, Habsburg rule was now solidified in the once-restive counties of Flanders and Holland.

The Gradual Triumph of the Habsburgs

Initially, dynastic misfortunes continued to dog the Habsburgs, despite Maximilian's ambitious marriage policy. Philip the Fair, the son of Mary and Maximilian, was by most accounts an ideal prince, well acquainted with and well disposed toward the Low Countries, but he died of fever at the age of twenty-eight and

12   Charles V, depicted here in middle age, was born in the Low Countries and well-acquainted with its institutions, but used its resources primarily to finance his empire's many wars.

his surviving wife, Joanna – daughter of Ferdinand of Aragon and Isabella of Castile – was shunted aside as mentally unhinged. The male successor was, again, a very young boy, Charles, who was six when his father died – his aunt Margaret of Austria ruling for him as governor of the Netherlands until he was fifteen. The Ghent-born Charles, though, benefited from other unexpected deaths in the family, becoming king of Spain in 1516 and the Holy Roman Emperor in 1519. With the addition of Spain's conquered territories in the Caribbean and South America, Charles V, as he became known, had become lord of a massive world empire before he was twenty.

Under Charles's rule, too, the parts of the Netherlands outside the grip of his dynasty finally fell to the Habsburgs. That process was not easy or predetermined, and took several decades to complete. It was the final result of a longstanding conflict, begun in 1502, between the Habsburgs and the French-supported dukes of Guelders, especially its long-ruling Karel of Egmond. Guelders understandably felt threatened by Habsburg power to the south, and the Habsburgs in turn felt stymied by Guelders whenever the dynasty sought to expand its influence northwards. For this reason both battled with each other, sometimes through allies in places such as Frisia and the Sticht of Utrecht, which were themselves chronically divided by opposing coalitions.

Habsburg might was far greater than anything Guelders and its local allies were able to muster, but the Habsburgs also had many enemies, not least France, which hampered their ability to make a concerted effort in the northern Netherlands strong enough to knock out Guelders once and for all. As a result, for many years parts of the countryside in the northern Netherlands were subject to raiding parties that plundered with wild abandon. In initial phases of this ongoing warfare, it appeared that the duke of Guelders, having made an alliance with France, had the upper hand. By 1522 Karel of Egmond had substantially expanded his territory, controlling most of Frisia and the Oversticht. For a time, too, he could count on the popular support of the local population in the fight against the Habsburgs. The Frisian folk hero Grutte Pier Donia fought the Habsburg enemy, terrorizing the Zuyder Zee coast by preying on Holland's ships and harbor towns; his name became so infamous that the Hollander Erasmus depicted him as the archetype of violence. This situation was shortlived; by 1524, Guelders's forces were defeated by the Habsburg armies. The triumphant emperor created the Lordship of Frisia, roughly corresponding to the current province, effectively putting an end to both the political chaos in Friesland and its autonomy. With few recognized historical privileges, Friesland could be ruled more tightly by Karel than most of his other territories.

Habsburg advances continued, with Charles V achieving complete control over Utrecht and the Oversticht only a few years later. Rescuing the bishop, who had been ejected by angry residents from Utrecht for imposing high taxes, Charles demanded, in return for the restoration of his spiritual position, that the bishop yield his temporal authority to him. In 1528, after 500 years, the prince-bishopric of Utrecht came to an end. The Oversticht now became separate from Utrecht, the Lordship of Overijssel being formally used as a name for the first time in that year. Karel of Egmond did his best to prevent this direct control of Utrecht by the Habsburgs, sending his infamous field marshal Maarten van Rossum to burn and pillage his way into Habsburg-held Holland. The formal seat of that county, The Hague, was unprotected by any city walls and ransacked by Van Rossum before he was paid off by the citizenry to leave. This brazen and frightening attack mobilized the towns of Holland and Brabant to pay for an effective regional army, which forced Guelders to sue for peace later that year.

Holland's increasing financial ability to give military support to its regional interests served as the basis for the subsequent Habsburg seizure of Groningen and Drenthe. The preparation of a Holland-led fleet to support the beleaguered Catholic Danish King Christian II, who was allied to the Habsburg House (and supportive of Holland's maritime interests), triggered an invasion of the Low Countries by Danish opponents of this king, supported by Guelders. Here, too, the Habsburg armies handily defeated the Danish–Guelders army, and Drenthe and Groningen came under the rule of Charles V in 1536 after the duke of Guelders renounced his claim to these lands.

Guelders itself was the last prize to fall. Its inveterate Duke Karel of Egmond had died in 1538. Four years later his successor, Willem V of Cleves, encouraged by Denmark and above all by a powerful French invasion of the Low Countries, ordered Van Rossum to attack Brabant, who pillaged his way across the north of the duchy all the way to the gates of Antwerp. This, too, generated a powerful if late response from Charles V, whose financial ability to raise armies was much greater than that of the now-bankrupt duchy of Guelders. Charles's soldiers put the population of the Jülich city of Düren to the sword, intimidating the rest of the duke's cities into surrender. In the Treaty of Venlo of September 1543 Willem surrendered the duchy to Charles V, who now formally became its duke.

Thus Habsburg might triumphed in the northern Netherlands. Almost all of the Low Countries – the prince-bishopric of Liège remained the only large principality outside Habsburg rule – were now bound together under the same overlord. Enabled by the growing economic muscle of Holland and Brabant, Charles V effectively had annexed the six "provinces" of Friesland, Groningen, Utrecht, Drenthe, Overijssel and Guelders (the future Gelderland) between 1524 and 1543. Together these territories constituted about half the land mass of the current Netherlands. These mostly inland provinces more closely resembled in culture and economics the landlocked provinces to their south than the economically dominant western maritime regions of Holland and Zeeland. All of these provinces, though, now had to heed the wishes of Brussels, the permanent capital of the region from 1531. And increasingly, despite their differences, they would face some of the same choices and dilemmas that Habsburg rule posed for all of them.

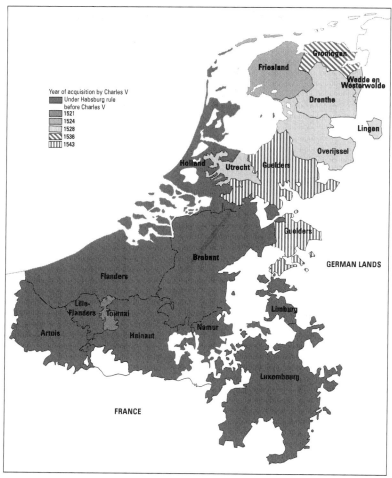

Year of acquisition by Charles V
- Under Habsburg rule before Charles V
- 1521
- 1524
- 1528
- 1536
- 1543

Groningen

Friesland

Wedde en Westerwolde

Drenthe

Lingen

Overijssel

Holland · Utrecht · Guelders

Guelders

GERMAN LANDS

Brabant

Flanders

Limburg

Lille-Flanders · Tournai

Namur

Artois · Hainaut

Luxembourg

FRANCE

6 The early sixteenth century witnessed a remarkable expansion of Habsburg power across Europe and the world. The Netherlands was a part of this larger trend.

The Contours of Habsburg Rule

More intensely than the Burgundians before them, the Habsburgs launched a drive toward centralization, standardizing the laws of their realms, so that policies and (in the case of courts) verdicts could more effectively be imposed from above. The aim was to streamline the administration of Charles's different territories and thus to gain more effective control over his subjects. Sixteenth-century states, some of them more powerful than ever, were increasingly, in a time of social upheaval, concerned about public order. They progressively made laws more strictly regulating the behavior of people – such as reducing drunken and rowdy behavior at carnivals (which might induce rioting); controlling vagrancy (with its threat of violence); censoring the growing printing press; and demanding, as we shall see, religious conformity. The Habsburg state was as keen as any other in western Europe to discipline its population, and this tendency became more pronounced as the century wore on, issuing more and more laws stipulating the boundaries of behavior.

Accordingly, Charles's territories were, as much as possible, ruled as a single entity from the Brabant towns of first Mechelen and then Brussels, and run through appointed governors-general, from 1507 to 1567 all close relatives of the ruling monarch. They did not have a mandate to rule as they saw fit, but received instructions from their sovereign lord. The same was true at the regional level. In Holland, for instance, the *stadhouder* functioned as head of the judicial court. All of them were important nobility with close personal ties to the monarch. One of them was Henry III of Nassau-Breda, uncle of the future Willem the Silent, who was *stadhouder* of Holland–Zeeland from 1515 to 1521. Though bound by the instructions of their sovereign, the high nobility kept a measure of autonomy for themselves, relying as they could on their own network of patronage. Charles, however, being determined to implement his own policies, made increasing use of university-trained civil servants who were loyal to him alone, reducing the political operating room of these nobility.

Following Burgundian precedent, but with more success, Charles called into life three different councils that worked closely together in Brussels – one a Council of State made up of the high nobility he had appointed to rule under him, one a Council for Finance to coordinate fiscal policy across the whole region, and a Privy Council that increasingly functioned as the highest court. These new administrative councils, established in 1531, much reduced the power of local nobility, and of the city guilds and magistracy. The Council for Finance imposed new taxes that doubled the income of the emperor and thus reduced financial dependence on the States-General. Local common law increasingly was made to conform to centralized applications of Roman law – and to the wishes of the monarch. A full-scale, centralized codification was still decades off, to be implemented only after the Dutch Revolt, owing in part to the foot-dragging of local jurists, but local magistrates lost much of their autonomy under Charles. A good example of this is Charles's stipulation in 1529 that all local courts uniformly punish heresy with the death penalty, a measure many towns and provincial courts had been reluctant to implement. And since the high court acted as an appeals court to local parties unhappy with the verdict, it was in the interest of local jurists to conform their laws closely to what the court in Brussels wanted. In this way, legal reform centralized the Habsburg Netherlands more than anything else.

Even as these centralizing measures increased Habsburg influence over their subjects, there were countervailing tendencies, embodied especially in the Habsburg failure fully to centralize and to control their own finances. The central government continued to be dependent on its subjects' willingness to be taxed, or – increasingly – to grant it loans. The Habsburgs' nearly uninterrupted wars with the French kings from the 1520s through the 1550s severely strained the ability of both dynasties to raise enough money to pay for the conflict. This was due in large part to the fact that waging war was simply becoming more expensive in the sixteenth century. The advent of effective cannon changed the military quotient; they required a better-trained army and they required more solid fortifications than the old medieval walls. As a result, taxes went up sharply; Holland at mid century, for example, paid ten to fifteen times more in taxes than had been the case in 1520.

Throughout these developments, the various States of the Low Countries refused to approve permanent taxes, forcing Charles to remain dependent on temporary grants, and making it difficult to finance and thus wage long wars. Sometimes regional officials, especially if they felt imminent danger, were willing to offer grants to pay for the emperor's armies, causing taxes to spike in those years. This often caused hardship to the poorer classes, as food prices accordingly rose sharply in price. But for all the suffering it brought about this method did not solve the money problem. The States-General resisted Charles's appeals for grants, and so he preferred to negotiate with each of the regional states individually, especially the wealthy western ones. Getting taxes from the states of Holland and Flanders often meant making concessions to them, in which the states paid less than their formal quota or wrung other concessions from Charles. The wealthy burghers of Brabant and Holland could also make money from the Habsburgs by financing his wars through loans – the money markets of Antwerp lent sixty times as much money to Charles at the end of his reign than they had at the beginning. In Holland, leaders of the states authorized debt, and then, with wealthy merchants, bought it up, ensuring interest payments for themselves and reducing risks of default by keeping the loans within bounds. In this way, a financial and administrative elite was created in Holland that served as the nucleus for a future independent state. The common people were heavily taxed, but the oligarchic elites benefited financially from this arrangement while at the same time maintaining their financial autonomy from Brussels.

Additionally and in relation to this, Habsburg centralization efforts did not break the power of the cities or diminish civic life. Throughout this period the quality of the city government improved, increasingly directed by competent jurists and highly educated "pensionaries" (municipal secretaries). Guilds and the city militias – manned by men of some means and charged with the defense and order of the towns – continued to assert their place in local life. A host of charitable institutions, often established by wealthy burghers, were important as ways both to assist the poor and to demonstrate the self-worth and self-government of the citizenry. Northern cities may not have had the same tradition of militant independence that the larger Flemish cities had vainly tried to maintain against their overlords, but they, too, remained fiercely proud of their town and of their own rights and privileges.

Habsburg rule brought high taxation and imposed repressive laws – faults that in the long run would help trigger massive revolt. But it also promoted the streamlining of government and encouraged a greater measure of coordination and cooperation. That was true too at the regional level. Guelders, which while autonomous had been a loose collection of "quarters," now exhibited more administrative coherence than ever before, and Holland's cities, sharing many of the same financial concerns and economic interests, also worked together more intensively, precisely because they were in the Habsburg orbit. Indeed, the cities of Holland cooperated in order to stymie or reduce the grants desired by the emperor. At the interregional level, ruled from Brussels, leaders from the different provinces and larger towns of the Low Countries met together frequently to discuss tax, trade and other matters, both while the States-General were in session and when they were not. Seen this way, Habsburg promoted regional government, giving members of the states valuable experience in complex fiscal and administrative affairs.

Through all of these changes and continuities, it had become clear that the Habsburg government regarded the region as administratively distinct, and it created the "Burgundian" Circle in 1512, which was expanded in 1548 to include the newly won territories. With their new status as one of the ten "circles" of the Holy Roman Empire, the States-General of the region were no longer directly under the authority of the Imperial Reichstag, and now enjoyed a status that made them all but autonomous from the rest of the empire. As it turned out, the boundaries between the Burgundian Circle and the empire proper would determine much of the border between the Netherlands and Germany up to the present day. The Circle, furthermore, was proclaimed indivisible, and in 1549 all the relevant states made uniform their rules of succession in the so-called Pragmatic Sanction, ensuring that the same ruler would rule over them all in the future. In the first instance that was to be Charles V's son Philip, who succeeded his father in 1555. For the first time in its history, the Low Countries now became a single, autonomous unit under a single ruler. For the time being, the Habsburg grip on power was secure, but the countervailing local and regional powers that had also been empowered by imperial policies were also, more than ever, ready to defend their own interests.

Antwerp, Holland and a Globalizing Economy

By 1500 Antwerp had surpassed Bruges as the most important commercial center of the Low Countries and as the most important port in western Europe. Much of the economy of the whole region centered around the magnet of Antwerp, which, after Paris, would become the largest city of Europe by the middle of the century. Spanish and Portuguese colonies in the Americas further shifted the focus of trade from the Mediterranean to the Atlantic, to the benefit of Antwerp and the whole region. Brabant towns such as Den Bosch and Bergen op Zoom were satellite trading towns for Antwerp, and Middelburg, center of the maritime wine trade, and the neighboring port of Arnemuiden offered important harbor facilities for the city. Other Zeeland towns also became prosperous in the shadow of Antwerp in the early sixteenth century. But even Amsterdam, well to the north of Antwerp, depended on that city for its economic livelihood by selling its goods there. Amsterdam also became an important port in connecting the Baltic with Antwerp; grain and wood would travel from Amsterdam via the inland waterways to Antwerp. Holland's growth depended to a very large degree on its role as a satellite of Antwerp, and Antwerp, though still by far the largest export center, depended increasingly on the services and goods, notably shipping, provided by Holland in an ever more integrated economy.

Thus Holland further expanded in the first half of the sixteenth century, as did its now heavily urbanized population; in 1514 some 45 percent of its population lived in cities. The early sixteenth century was not in all respects good to Holland; the wars against Guelders and against the French, which also had consequences for its access to the Baltic, seriously dampened trade. Its beer and textile industries lost ground to cheaper competitors. But its highly diversified, commercialized and innovative economy – only 15 percent of the population was engaged in agriculture – had numerous strong points. Textile producers in Leiden lost market share when they stuck to expensive English wool for their materials, but Haarlem and Amsterdam cloth-makers switched on time to cheaper, high-quality wool to continue prospering. Fishing continued to be a healthy mainstay of the Zeeland–Holland economy, but perhaps the dynamism was most evident in ship-making and cargo-hauling. Shipwrights were building some 175 to 250 vessels a year in the Haarlem area around 1500, and successfully made the shift from building primarily river-going ships to the larger sea-going vessels a few decades later. Even more decisive was the size of Holland's maritime shipping, the dangers at sea from many enemies notwithstanding. By 1500 the number of ships hailing from Holland exceeded those of the whole Hanseatic League, and half the ships entering the Danish Sound came from there. Already by the late fifteenth century, Amsterdam was the biggest motor of Holland, and by the early sixteenth century it easily eclipsed Dordrecht and the other Holland towns in importance. The eastern cities along the IJssel and the Maas continued to be vital trade centers, but were now clearly outpaced by their western counterparts. The shift can be seen in the decline in importance of annual fairs after 1530. Fairs were markets that sold goods at particular places and particular times to ensure enough supply and demand. But now goods, supplied by innumerable ships from all over the continent and the world, could be bought and sold perennially, often at any time of year, reducing the need for fairs. Antwerp in particular was a place where goods could be bought from all around the world.

The empire made trading easier than ever, and commerce intensified across much of Europe and beyond. Increasingly Holland, Brabant and other western regions of the Low Countries were being drawn into a strongly globalizing economy with a relatively modern capitalist market strongly shaped by international supply and demand. This capitalist economy was also seen in the increasing use of mortgages and property shares to ensure long-term income, even among people of fairly modest means. The ability to read and write, together with some facility in mathematics, had already been strong in this increasingly urban culture, but the new economy placed even more emphasis on these capabilities. A sophisticated and capitalized economy created new markets that offered unprecedented opportunities for investment and consumption.

There was a downside to these economic changes, at least for many ordinary people, as they went hand-in-hand with an extended price revolution; the cost of living rose from the late fifteenth century into the beginning of the seventeenth century. New demands for food from a rise in population and urbanization, the emergence of a wealthy class eager to buy property, and perhaps especially the glut of silver that was now being imported from Latin America, all helped to boost prices. Wages had a hard time keeping pace. This pressure on wages impacted growing regions such as the western Netherlands the least, and they avoided much of the decline in living standards witnessed in other parts of western Europe. But even in relatively prosperous Brabant it was only Antwerp that possessed an economy strong enough to boost wages for all. Growing income inequalities between those, such as well-established merchants, who profited handsomely from the new economy and those who did not widened, and economic life became more precarious. Brabanders of modest means had had enough to eat in the good times of the late fifteenth century, which in addition to dairy and varied breads included about 30 kg of meat a year (which included about two herring a day). But in real terms they paid twice as much for the same consumer goods in the early 1540s as they had half a century before, and by the late 1550s they paid three times as much. Tax spikes, when they occurred, could be ruinous for families. For many of the poor, this meant a reduction in the standard of living: more rye than wheat bread and thinner, cheaper garments. More than before, families began relying on their children to bring in additional income. These were indications of social distress and need that would only grow in subsequent decades as religious and political tensions increased.

Netherlandic Culture at the Center of Europe

The Low Countries under Charles V were a wealthy and important part of his wider empire, and it cannot be surprising that the talent and artistic traditions of the region influenced and interacted with wider European developments. Many of these contributions came from the southern Netherlands, where court life was centered and where the great and uncommonly wealthy cities of Flanders and Brabant, with their unsurpassably extravagant traditions of civic pride, played an enormous role in cultivating the arts. This was particularly true in music and the visual arts.

But artistic work was becoming more important in the northern Netherlands, and attracting more international attention.

The most celebrated of these artists today is the painter Hieronymus Bosch, who spent most of his life in or near Den Bosch. Little is known about his life, and the meaning of his often arresting paintings has been frequently debated. Though stylistically in a league of his own, Bosch was hardly the only important artist in the northern Netherlands; versatile artists such as Jan van Scorel, Lucas van Leyden and Maarten van Heemskerk (whose surnames, like Bosch's, stemmed from their place of birth) were especially admired in their day and since for their high-quality engravings. (Rembrandt would later cherish his full collection of Van Leyden's work.) Though religious themes were hardly absent, everyday life became the focus of Holland painters, and by around the mid sixteenth century they also began to paint collective portraits of city magistrates, guilds and militias, a sign of the rise of a new political and social elite as well as of a self-confident civic culture. That civic culture also encouraged the development of all kinds of skilled artisans, including goldsmiths, tapestry weavers and glassmakers. Gouda became the center for colored glass, most impressively after the arrival of the Crabeth family in 1540, soon to responsible for the renowned stained-glass windows of the St. Jan's Church in that city.

Netherlandish art enjoyed a growing reputation in the early sixteenth century, but its most famous cultural figure stemmed from the region's rich humanist tradition: Desiderius Erasmus. Already in the late fifteenth century, humanist scholars such as Rudolf Agricola and Wessel Gansfort (both from Groningen) had emphasized both the scholarly and spiritual importance of studying the ancient texts of antiquity. The spiritual concerns of the *Devotio moderna* and the new humanist scholarship were an important focus of the recently invented printing press and the publishing houses that came with it. It is not coincidental that Deventer, as the historical center of the *Devotio moderna* and home

13   Famed for his erudition, and Europe's leading intellectual figure,
Erasmus combined an acid wit with an irenic piety that would continue to
inspire Dutch religious life for centuries.

to an important Latin school, became the leading publishing center in the northern Netherlands; 610 books were published there
in the last decades of the fifteenth century, though this number
was only one-sixth of what the market leader, Venice, published.

Erasmus, who was born in Holland but studied in Deventer, was
heavily influenced by this tradition. Disliking his work as a monk, he
first dreamed of becoming a Latin poet, perfecting his knowledge of
this language before mastering New Testament Greek, a language
still little known in northern Europe. He would soon play an important role in using the ancient languages to publish more accurate
versions of the Bible so that it might be studied better. Hailed by

his readers as a brilliant stylist, this priest won fame for his sharp criticism of ecclesiastical abuses and eloquent pleas for a simpler, inwardly motivated spirituality and ethics, a concern most famously articulated in his satirical *In Praise of Folly*, Erasmus's great fame across much of Europe would not have been possible without the printing press, which disseminated his works, and he was an influential player in the European publishing world, expanding the network of a new kind of international scholarship that was now able to discuss and debate emerging new ideas that had become increasingly accessible.

The Early Protestant Reformation

Erasmus's reputation and career, however, would be seriously troubled in the last fifteen years of his life (he died in 1536) by the decisive break in the Catholic world: the Protestant Reformation, a movement that was both deeply influenced by Erasmus but that in the radicality of its criticism went further than he himself was prepared to go. Initially, Erasmus hoped and believed that the theological conflict between Martin Luther and the Catholic Church leadership could be resolved, but by the early 1520s it was clear this would not happen. Erasmus's efforts at a middle way proved untenable.

Some German princes, in their support of Luther, ensured early successes in their principalities for his Protestant cause, but this was most certainly not the case in the Low Countries. To be sure, key Catholic clergy of the Low Countries wanted, like Luther, to curb certain Church excesses; the only Dutch pope, Adrian VI, born in Utrecht and a close advisor to Charles V, wanted some reform but his tenure at the Vatican (1522–1523) was too short to achieve anything. The emperor himself quickly condemned all forms of Protestantism as heresy, and the Habsburg government in the Low Countries moved swiftly to stamp it out. The first person to be executed in the northern Netherlands for the Protestant faith (in 1525) was Jan de Bakker – so named for the profession that he adopted after having rejected, as a priest, the Catholic doctrine of the Eucharist. In 1527, Wendelmoet Claesdochter of Monnickendam – dubbed "Lutherdam" for the sympathies of its residents to the reformer's ideas – was also prosecuted for maintaining that the sacrament of the Eucharist was mere bread and wine and not the body and blood of Christ as the Church taught. She was strangled and then burned for maintaining these views. Heretics who recanted their heresies might still save their lives in these early years, but later, as the problem became more widespread, authorities were less forgiving.

For the time being, expressions of "Protestant" conviction in the Netherlands were very diffuse, with individuals and small groups coming into contact with religious ideas that mostly came from Germany in the form of publications or through itinerant preachers. Though there was considerable alienation from the Catholic Church – legacies and other forms of giving dropped substantially from the 1520s – many people, even those deeply interested in the matter, remained unsure of where they actually stood with respect to the urgent theological issues of the day. In any event, organizing a public alternative to Catholicism, as implemented in the newly Lutheran states of Germany and Scandinavia, Anglican England, or the Reformed Church cantons of Switzerland, was not immediately possible in the face of virulent Habsburg opposition. High literacy rates made people aware of the new religious ideas and often excited their interest in them, but people with much to lose, such as the burghers and the nobility, chiefly kept their views to themselves. They did so for understandable reasons; two high-born ladies in Twente were executed in 1544 after revealing their Protestant convictions to family members.

It was the working-class artisans, suffering under eroding economic prospects, who took the greatest risks. This was most evident in their support of the Anabaptist movement, which held that only "born-again" adults should be baptized, and which believed – at least in these early years – that rich and poor alike should share all property. They also held that the end of the world was near, the old order rapidly passing away. Inspired by the Anabaptist seizure of Münster to the east, Anabaptists in Amsterdam – where they had many adherents – launched their own protest. Heralding the coming of a new egalitarian order, forty of them ran naked through the streets early in 1535. Hoping for popular support that never came, a group of them later attempted to take over the city, seizing the city hall and killing a mayor in the process. The authorities brutally suppressed them, placing their heads publicly on stakes as a warning to other would-be rebels. At about the same time, armed Anabaptists in Friesland, in their bid to take over the whole province, were wiped out by soldiers of the Habsburg *stadhouder*.

The Anabaptist movement would survive, influenced in the Low Countries by the (in contrast to his predecessors) convinced pacifist Menno Simons, a former priest from Friesland who soon lent his name to the "Mennonite" church. This movement would continue to inspire many from the working classes in the cities and countryside of the west as well as its base in Friesland. Persecution remained, of course, a very real threat to these and other Protestants. In 1545 Charles V introduced a special inquisition to root out heresy, largely aimed at printers and booksellers who might spread such ideas. Many local magistrates, as well as Charles V's sister and governor of the Netherlands, Mary of Hungary, were unenthusiastic about this hard-line policy. Sometimes these leaders sympathized with the Protestant Reformation, sometimes they simply had little appetite to prosecute town residents for their beliefs. The policy was nevertheless implemented in most of the larger towns, even if grudgingly and relatively sparingly. All in all, between 1523 and 1565 about 1,300 people were executed for heresy in the whole region, most of them from the northern Netherlands. The policy, however, remained ineffective, as familiarity with the new theological ideas, as well as disaffection with both the Church and the state, fed religious dissent. By the time King Philip II came to the throne in

1555, he faced a region that was rife with heretical ideas, but not, as yet, a tinderbox for widespread revolt.

Crisis and Revolt, 1555–1588

The First Confrontations

Philip would stay as sovereign in the Low Countries for four years, before spending, as it turned out, the last four decades of his life in Spain, the nerve center of his far-flung global empire. His elevation to office was lavishly celebrated in the region, and the professions of love and loyalty to his person profusely expressed. The great lords of the region, led by Willem, the young prince of Orange, were eager to curry favor with the new monarch. Political impasse, however, soon soured relations between Philip and his subjects.

In the short term, this impasse was not about religion but about finances. By the time Philip became king, the Habsburgs and the French kings had been battling each other half a century for domination in western Europe – most of the time in Italy, sometimes in the Low Countries. Increasingly, the wealthy Low Countries had been the cash cow of the Habsburg war machine, paying far beyond what their direct security needs required. French military action on the Netherlandic border after Philip's succession made it urgent that the king raise new money – and a lot of it. Yet it took the States-General two years before they acceded to most of the king's request. Grievances over the high and inequitable tax burden prompted the States-General, led by a wealthy Flanders, fearful of being fleeced again, to resist his demands. But also the northern provinces, further from France, and the new eastern provinces, alienated by the usurpation of their cherished and once extensive local privileges, chafed at paying for this war.

Only in 1558 did they all approve a plan for financing it, and then only on the condition that they raise the revenues under their own authority. Philip, whose Spanish lands had declared bankruptcy the year before in trying to defend his world empire, had no choice but to accept. The war, finally well financed in its last year, was something of a modest victory for Philip, who could rely on the skills of local high nobility such as Lamoral, the count of Egmond (scion of the once-ruling house of Guelders) to defeat the French. But the whole confrontation over money left a bad taste on both sides. Philip did not have the necessary control over the finances of his empire, which was subject to attack on many sides, and the states and their representatives resisted the perennially high tax requests that grew greater with each passing year. In 1558–1559, the military budget of the Habsburg Low Countries was in real terms almost two-and-a-half times higher than it had been in the early 1540s, when it had last faced French invasion.

The end of war temporarily reduced the tax crisis, but the jockeying for power continued. The next large confrontation was religious in nature, and about patronage. In 1559 Philip began a large-scale campaign to reform the structures of the Roman Catholic Church in the Low Countries, introducing three archbishoprics (there had been none) and fourteen bishoprics. As an organizational reform it was long overdue; the existing Church administration, stemming from the early Middle Ages, had hardly taken account of shifts in either political boundaries or populations. But opponents found its intentions and its effects threatening. First, it put an end to the old system of ecclesiastical patronage; the regional nobility had viewed for centuries higher Church offices as sinecures for their own sons. Now, however, in a time of widespread heresy, bishops were to be selected by the king and by Rome, who together would choose devout, dedicated and competent candidates to do exactly what their superiors demanded. This reduction of noble control over Church patronage was thus highly unwelcome to those with a stake to lose.

The second way in which Philip's reforms were controversial was that each bishopric would now come with its own inquisitional tribunal, intended to prosecute heretics more effectively across the Low Countries. This would essentially put an end to foot-dragging in hunting down heretics; Amsterdam, the largest town of the north, had last sentenced a heretic to death in 1553, and by 1560 prosecutions against them had ceased altogether in Holland. The prospect of new bishops was thus widely regarded as chilling. The plans were unpopular not only among crypto-Protestants but also among Catholics who saw them as either too severe or as a further erosion of local privileges and decision-making. Several towns such as Deventer, Haarlem and Roermond simply refused to admit their newly appointed bishops. The anticipated upswing in heresy prosecution created a new basis for unrest.

The political focal point of these reforms – and the hatred and fear they engendered – was Antoine Perrenot de Granvelle, a man of Burgundian origins whose family had long served the Habsburgs. Not from a noble family himself, Granvelle's considerable talents and services were dictated not by dynastic interests but by his loyalty to his master, and he attempted to implement Philip's Church reforms without too much attention to the opposition they created. His elevation to archbishop of Mechelen (1560) and to cardinal (1561) confirmed his special mandate and offered the means to achieve his mission – and to circumvent the most important regional nobility whose power was still considerable. For high nobility such as the prince of Orange; the count of Egmond; and the influential Philip de Montmorency, count of Horne, Granvelle was an upstart and foreign bureaucrat who meant to usurp power from them. Perhaps even worse, he was the central figure of a dangerous and unpopular policy that the nobility would, to their own political detriment, have to enforce. These great nobles did everything they could to whip up opposition to the cardinal and his plans.

Granvelle's opulent and ostentatious lifestyle (he was one of the most avid art collectors of Europe) probably did not add to the popularity of a prelate whose religious policies were roundly detested throughout much of the region. Reactions against this policy could be ugly; in early 1563 a nunnery near Leiden was ransacked by an angry mob. Thus Orange, Egmond and other members of the nobility were able to make a successful case to Philip that they would resign from the ruling Council of State if Granvelle continued in office, since they, as nobility in charge of the army, could no longer guarantee public order if he remained. The king thus shunted the churchman out of sight, to be put into royal service at a later time. Granvelle's sudden absence strengthened the power of the nobility led by Orange. But the primary points of conflict – the desirability of administrative centralization and the future of anti-heresy policy – were not in any structural way resolved by his departure.

Indeed, the problem of what to do with the Protestant population had only grown more intense since Philip's accession to the throne in 1555. Specifically, the rise of organized Calvinist churches presented the authorities with a new challenge. Inspired by the church model developed by John Calvin in Geneva and his vision for the reform of both Church and society, tightly disciplined local churches began to develop among Dutch followers in the Netherlands and those who were refugees abroad. More intellectual in its theology and more systematic in its plans to purify Church and society than the Mennonites, Calvinism appealed more to the better-educated classes of society (whose prestige and money were to be of importance to its staying power) than the former group, while it was successful in reaching artisans as well. Its influence initially strongest in the French-speaking cities of the southern Netherlands, Calvinism found great appeal across many parts of Flanders and Brabant, though it was slower to penetrate the northern provinces. By the early 1560s, the Calvinists' presence in some southern towns was only barely under the surface. City magistrates could hardly suppress them, even if they so wished. It is striking, then, that Protestant support was strongest in the south, even though in the long run (and contrary to any expectation) it was only in the north that the Protestant-led revolt would succeed.

Thus the will of magistrates to prosecute heretics, already lagging in most towns, declined still further. To the east in Germany, Roman Catholics and Protestants had divided up the empire by principality, letting each local ruler decide the territorial religion, effectively acknowledging religious pluralism within the empire. The advent of the French Wars of Religion in the early 1560s had the effect, at least in the short term, of giving Calvinists some measure of religious toleration. Indeed, Willem of Orange, as a Catholic ruler, had in 1563 granted toleration to the many Protestants in his own principality of Orange, a sovereign enclave surrounded by France, justifying it as a necessary concession to maintain his rule. Philip's policies in the context of this wider development seemed only to invite open revolt, and making at least some allowance for the religious conscience of the king's subjects increasingly seemed the most politically prudent, if not the most just, option. This was certainly the view of Willem of Orange; though this gregarious man was called "the Silent" for keeping his own views and, in particular, his religious convictions to himself, he took some risk in standing for freedom of conscience. Under his leadership, most nobles in the Council of State concluded by the end of 1564 that the systematic prosecution of Protestants – and its violation of the religious conscience – must be abandoned as government policy. This stance seriously risked a conflict with Philip, but there was still hope he might be persuaded to set a new course.

The Showdowns of 1566

The Council of State duly sent the count of Egmond to Spain to entreat the king to give the Council more authority to deal with the complex situation in the region and to relax his anti-heresy policy. The king offered no clear response for months, but in the fall of 1565 he responded to similar requests from his half-sister and governor-general of the Low Countries, Margaret of Parma, to soften his religious policies. In his so-called "letters from the Segovia woods," written at his favorite retreat, Philip underscored that there would be no compromise on this issue. Though cautious by nature, he believed, more than ever from the distance of devoutly Catholic Spain, that only the most resolute stance could save the Catholic Church from ruin in the Low Countries.

Philip's unwillingness to make concessions elicited an unprecedented response from the region's nobility, who were in agreement with each other that heresy prosecution must stop. Deeper down, though, they were hardly of one accord; while some remained convinced Catholics and wholly loyal to the king, others had already come into negotiations with, or converted to, the Protestants, and a few, such as Willem of Orange's brother Lodewijk, had become convinced, inspired by the French Calvinist example, that only armed resistance could resolve the crisis. Among the lower nobility the idea of a petition to the king emerged, which some higher nobility, initially wary, chose to tolerate in the winter of 1566. Several hundred of the more critical nobles walked to the palace of Margaret

14   Pieter Brueghel the Elder titled this 1566 painting as *The Preaching of St. John the Baptist*, but it clearly depicts the hedge preaching of that year that would soon lead to open revolt.

of Parma on April 5, forced their way into it and presented to her a Petition of Compromise. Avoiding criticism of the king and the Church, it denounced the inquisition as antithetical to the traditional freedoms of the realm, and demanded that it be dismantled and that the placards against heresy be withdrawn, darkly implying the need for armed revolt should the petition be rejected.

Though her chief advisor, the high nobleman Charles de Berlaymont, urged her to dismiss the demands of these "beggars" (*gueux*), Margaret, less than a decisive administrator, was swayed by the demands of her uninvited guests and agreed to suspend the anti-heresy measures until Philip himself had answered the petition. Her decision, or rather the delay of one, emboldened the long-suffering Protestants to come out of hiding and to begin to worship openly by May of 1566. The spring and summer of 1566 were marked by the rise of "hedge-preaching" – Protestant open-air sermons, necessitated by the fact that few if any churches were then available to the group. Calvinists, the best organized group, made the most of the new openness, their clergy drawing tens of thousands of listeners, with many joining their cause. Clearly there was great interest in the message of the hedge-preachers, perhaps enhanced in part by the high price of bread and high unemployment that had hit the Low Countries in the mid 1560s. Whatever the reason, Protestants, sensing their rising power, started making demands that they be given churches at the expense of the Catholics.

The stakes rose even higher in early August, when artisans in West Flanders, inspired by a hedge-preacher, destroyed the religious art of the local monastery in Steenvoorde, believing that its images were perverse idols that drew people away from the true worship of God. From there the "Iconoclasm," as it became known, spread mostly northward, first across Flanders and Brabant and then to Holland and Utrecht, before reaching Friesland and Groningen in the north about six weeks after it had begun. In towns under its full force no image, art treasure or vestment in any church, chapel or cloister was safe; Catholic clergy too were often a target of violent mobs. Though the Iconoclasm was in one sense a single movement, it was differently motivated and differently executed. In some cases, as on the Zeeland island of Walcheren, fury against the authority of the Catholic Church was unbridled, ignoring the opposition of even Calvinist leaders to these wild expressions of vandalism and violence. In other places, particularly in its latter weeks and in the north, it was a more regulated affair, with local authorities directing the fate of churches and their objects; in Leeuwarden, municipal direction of the Iconoclasm was conducted with the aim of giving a couple of the town's churches to the Protestants, whose worship needs would require a sanctuary free of idols. In some towns, where city authorities and especially the city militias held firm, there was no smashing of images at all.

The sudden rise of a militant Protestantism further radicalized the region's politics and effectively ended the search for a compromise settlement. Many Catholics, including the nobility, were appalled at the destruction of sacred objects and feared what now seemed to be an unlimited Protestant lust for total control. By November of 1566 Margaret's government made the first moves to check the Protestant surge. Once close allies in the compromise coalition, Orange and Egmond now parted ways. The former, perhaps influenced by his German Lutheran family ties, remained resistant to the king's policies; the latter, a devout Catholic, now used his military skills to restore royal order. In the short run, at least, it was the Catholic party that prevailed. Being able to rely on professional soldiers, Margaret of Parma's government easily routed the badly trained Calvinist forces in early 1567. Towns that had countenanced Protestant worship now forbade it again. The restoration of a Catholic order and advance news of the arrival of 10,000 Habsburg soldiers under the leading Castilian nobleman, the duke of Alba, in the summer of 1567 prompted about 50,000 people, including most signatories of the Compromise, to flee the anticipated vengeance. Willem of Orange, too, prudently left Brussels for the safety of his German estates. The search for religious compromise, popular Protestant revolt and the full restoration of royal Catholic authority had succeeded each other in barely more than a year.

The Duke of Alba and the First Years of the Revolt

Alba's first task was to dispense with those who had been complicit in the revolt. To this end he established a special body charged with the prosecution of treason and heresy cases called the Council of Troubles, or, as it was infamously known in the Low Countries, the Council of Blood. All in all, about 9,000 people were condemned to death by the Council, of whom only about 1,000 were actually executed, the rest having been convicted in absentia after having fled. Its most famous victims – despite the furious protests of Margaret of Parma – were the counts of Egmond and Horne, whose pro-toleration stance before the Iconoclasm had raised the wrath of Alba. Regarding themselves as loyal to Church and king, they were surprised at their arrest, and their supporters were estranged by the fact that Alba denied these noblemen the right to be tried by their peers, bringing them before the Council of Troubles instead. The Council's prosecution of heresy, incidentally, was selective, hitting the more heretical southern Netherlands harder than the North.

Alba's repression of rebellion was not merely relegated to dealing with past sins. By 1568, he faced an armed insurgency led by Willem of Orange, who had raised enough money from Protestant German nobility to hire armies to invade the Netherlands from the east. Willem's incursions have been seen as the start of the Eighty Years' War, which culminated in formal Spanish recognition of the Dutch Republic. But from the rebel standpoint the first campaigns of this war were hardly a success. A French Protestant army was easily driven off, and the two German-based

armies were crushed – not, however before one of them, led by
Lodewijk of Orange, had won the Battle of Heiligerlee near
Groningen in May of 1568. However, that battle – later commemorated as the start of the war of independence against Spain
in Dutch national history – would be the last land victory of the
rebels for some time. Willem was only very partially successful
in inducing German Lutheran princes to support the Calvinist
rebels. He was soon out of money and besieged by angry creditors, reduced to churning out propaganda for his flagging cause. In
the several years after 1568 he received strikingly little tangible
support from within the Netherlands itself, and at no time was
he in a position seriously to challenge Alba's power. This is not to
say that the opponents of the regime remained entirely still; exiles
organized the Calvinistic Dutch Reformed Church in the safety
of German Emden, providing, as it would turn out, an important
basis for an effective church organization within the Netherlands
after the tide turned in their favor. For the moment, however, they
would have to bide their time.

Meanwhile, Alba, unconcerned with the objections of an unruly
population whom he held in scant regard, pursued a rigorous policy that served – again – to generate rising opposition to royal
rule. He did this by seeking to achieve two goals that had been
longstanding aims of the government of Madrid: enabling the
Catholic Church to ensure religious conformity, and giving the
Habsburgs a reliable tax base in the region. He pushed through
the new bishoprics and the inquisitional apparatus that came with
them, and standardized the criminal code so as to ensure the
effective prosecution of heresy. Alba had less success, though, with
even more controversial plans – in particular those to introduce
what amounted to a permanent 5 percent tax on real estate sales
(the so-called twentieth penny) and a 10 percent tax on all other
transactions (the so-called tenth penny). The States-General were
loath to surrender to the royal government a permanent (and
substantial) set of sales taxes, and merchants were alarmed by the

prospect of taxes that might be ruinous to their trade. By 1571 there was a political impasse with little prospect of a harmonious resolution. Indeed, Alba's failure to secure the support of moderates led to widespread hostility against Spanish "tyranny," and heightened the chances for revolt – when the chances for success seemed real.

Holland and Zeeland: New Bases of Rebellion

Opposition to Alba's policies may have been intense, then, but in itself it was insufficient to ignite open revolt. That it did happen in the spring of 1572 had to do with developments in France and in England. French Huguenots, at the height of their influence, pushed for war against Spain, prompting Alba to redeploy his soldiers to the French border and away from the northern provinces. And Elizabeth I of England, in order to improve relations with Spain, ordered that a fleet of Dutch rebels, affixing to themselves the name of *gueux* ("beggars") as a badge of honor, be evicted from the safety of English harbors.

These "Sea Beggars," mostly militant Calvinists, had been from the start the most militarily successful of the revolt led by Orange. Licensed by him as privateers and sometimes just as interested in attacking neutral shipping as Spanish, they made a living by raiding the Holland coast. Now in search of a new sanctuary, they stumbled upon the Holland town of Den Briel, now without a Spanish garrison, which they seized after the town's population had hesitated to let them in. From there they were able to seize a much more important prize, the port of Vlissingen. Plying their way across Holland's inland waterways, relatively small numbers of Beggars were able to persuade many Holland towns to go over to the revolt. These cities included most of its crucial towns, including Haarlem, Gouda and Dordrecht, where the States of Holland met in the summer of 1572 to recognize Willem of Orange as *stadhouder* of Holland, a position he had held for the king until 1567. By this time, then, not only most of Holland but also Zeeland had been won for the revolt, a surprising turn of events for both Orange and for Alba, who each had expected the main body of action to lie elsewhere.

Yet the revolt could not count on universal support. The radicalization begun in 1566 had eliminated much of the ground for religious consensus, rendering the region a house divided against itself, an arena for civil war. The Beggars, eager to exact vengeance for the wrongs done to them and other Protestants, tortured and killed nineteen Catholic clergy in Den Briel for not recanting their faith, and Willem of Orange's own soldiers committed similar excesses in Roermond during his abortive effort to invade the Low Countries once again from the east. Some wondered whether a Protestant government would be any better than Catholic rule had been. Amsterdam, the most important town in Holland, remained Catholic and loyal to the king, and the eastern provinces remained for the time being largely loyal as well. And many towns were simply divided in loyalties; a vote by the burghers of Hoorn in 1572 revealed that two-thirds wanted to join the revolt while one-third did not. The inhabitants of the Low Countries remained bitterly divided among themselves about the merits of the rebellion. The polarization could be intense.

To be sure, many people took no side. The relatively weak support for the Catholic Church in northern provinces such as Holland – in contrast to much of the south – indicates much uncertainty about, or outright indifference to, religious affairs. Additionally there were religious moderates, resistant to choosing sides. The famous humanist writer and theologian Dirck Volkertsz. Coornhert found an appreciative and lasting following among a Dutch readership who valued his rejection of dogma. But his attempts to stake out a theologically middle position met with failure in the radicalized atmosphere of revolt. Towns such as Haarlem that attempted formally to allow two faiths to be recognized could not sustain this position over time. There was a large measure of support for freedom of conscience among the rebels, but that was not necessarily the same as the freedom to practice one's religion publicly. In any event it was perhaps not surprising that it was the Calvinists, well organized and highly motivated (they had the most to lose with the return of Spanish rule) who came to dominate the religious direction of the revolt. It was their Reformed Church that now supplanted Catholic worship in many of the towns in revolt, sometimes quickly, sometimes in the span of a few years. Willem of Orange, born Lutheran and much of his life a Catholic prince, now joined the Reformed Church himself, expecting that all Catholics over time would do the same as he had. The religious divide, contrary to his expectations, was not overcome.

Meanwhile, the Spanish military planned a counteroffensive to take back rebel-held territory. Spanish vengeance while retaking rebellious cities – almost all the population of Naarden was slaughtered in December of 1572 – stiffened the resolve of the rebels. At first the Spanish seemed well on their way to retaking Holland; after an extensive siege they took Haarlem when the city agreed to pay a huge indemnity in order to prevent a sack. Spain's sieges of Alkmaar and Leiden, however, failed. In both cases, rebels opened the sluices and breached the walls of the dikes to put a decisive end to the sieges through flooding. In the case of Leiden final triumph came at a terrible price; the siege that lasted from late May to early October of 1574 claimed a third of the population of 18,000, mostly through famine and disease, and it was only after two months of breaking the dikes that a fortuitous northwesterly storm pushed the water in the direction of Leiden, allowing the rebels' inland fleet to chase the Spanish away. Two years later Woerden, after being besieged for over a year, was also relieved by dike breaches.

Despite an initially successful attack by the Spanish in 1575, by November of 1576 most of Holland and Zeeland were free of royal forces, with Catholic-led Amsterdam a major exception.

The Oranges' own military forays from Germany, the last in 1574 in which Lodewijk was killed, had done relatively little to bring this about, though Willem the Silent remained the rebellion's leader, his effective political skills giving direction to the revolt. The deployment of water as a weapon had certainly helped, and would continue to shield these provinces from new military dangers. But it was the difference in financial capabilities between the two parties that proved decisive. The self-financing of the war by the rebellious regions of Zeeland and Holland had ensured, for the most part, that their cities were well defended, and that the mercenaries in service of the revolt (whom the fearful local population would have preferred to keep outside the city walls) were regularly paid. In contrast, Philip II, faced with severe liquidity problems, was forced to declare bankruptcy in 1575, and he was unable to pay his troops. His highly trained soldiers, who might have ensured victory for the king, now undermined his ability to wage war by engaging in mutiny. Suffering the most from their mutiny was the rich city of Antwerp, where some 7,000 civilians were killed by rioting Spanish soldiers in November of 1576. Their actions gave the rebels the necessary breathing room to strengthen their defenses.

Convergence and Divergence

The "Spanish Fury" in Antwerp was, however, more than a reprieve; it changed the political equation in the Low Countries, causing, for the moment, a convergence of opinion. The shocking excesses of the mutiny led both Catholics and Protestants to demand that Spanish troops leave the region, and it hastened negotiations between regional leaders on both sides. The result was the Pacification of Ghent of November 1576, signed by the rebellious provinces with the States-General, which released prisoners; restored property; and, above all, though not breaking with Philip, created a defensive union against Spanish troops. It proclaimed freedom of conscience for all. For Willem of Orange, who had sought religious toleration, it was the high point of his career. As the hero against Spanish tyranny he was acclaimed by the population when he returned to Antwerp and Brussels in 1577.

In reality, though, the political situation was extremely unstable and the anti-Spanish consensus very shallow. Though freedom of conscience had been proclaimed, the question of which faith had the right to practice its religion publicly had not been decided, with Protestants and Catholics jockeying for power, each at the same time fearful of what would happen should the other side prevail. Hostilities between the armies of the States-General and Spanish troops continued through 1577 and 1578 while in many localities the situation was anything but stable. Amsterdam, which had increasingly suffered economically as an isolated Catholic city in a Protestant-led Holland, pushed through the "Alteration" in May of 1578, in which Protestants successfully orchestrated a bloodless coup against the Catholic town council, forcing them out of town on a boat. Though Catholics were initially accorded their own public places of worship, within months this right, too, was withdrawn. In Gelderland, the new *stadhouder*, Jan of Orange-Nassau, brother of Willem, successfully schemed against the mostly Catholic leadership to find men more amenable to the Protestant cause. In the south, Ghent established itself as a virtually autonomous Calvinist republic. Philip responded to the States-General's decision also to allow Protestants to worship alongside Catholics with a dismissal of that body. The Pacification brought anything but stability.

In this context, it was not surprising that two camps came to oppose each other only two years after the Pacification. In January 1579 the Union of Arras, signed by several French-speaking provinces of the Low Countries, pledged loyalty to the king and the exclusive rights of the Catholic Church. Later that month, a competing Union of Utrecht was signed by Holland, Zeeland, Gelderland and Zutphen, Utrecht, and the Groningen countryside or *Ommelanden*. In subsequent weeks and months it would encompass more signatories, most importantly the great southern cities such as Ghent and Antwerp. Crucially, then, the Union of Utrecht enjoyed wider support than from Holland and Zeeland alone, as central as they remained in the struggle against Philip. It is important to note, too, that the Union of Utrecht was not, although inspired by Calvinist leaders such as Jan of Orange-Nassau and eventually effectively becoming one, a Protestant union as such. It proclaimed freedom of conscience and later stipulated that each signatory decide its own religious affairs. In its self-description it was an alliance against Spanish tyranny and a defender of the Pacification. To this end it pledged, even as it respected the sovereignty of each signatory territory, to act as a single entity toward all external powers, to create a common army and to share the costs of a joint defense.

The Union of Utrecht, in effectively outlining a loose confederation that would act together in military and foreign affairs, came as close to a constitution as the Dutch Republic would ever get. But the Republic was still years off, and the future of the Union was anything but certain. Spanish power had been broken by mutiny and chaotic leadership, but the king could be expected to strike back when he could. Indeed, in the spring of 1580 Philip II declared his former *stadhouder* Willem of Orange an outlaw whose death he would financially reward, underscoring his low regard for the Union as a mere rebellion to be crushed.

The Search for New Leadership amidst Spanish Resurgence

Philip's denunciation of Willem as an outlaw was the first step in a formal break between the Union and the Spanish monarchy. Willem's *Apology*, written in response, included assertions that it was not he but the king who had been untrue to his oath, had refused to recognize his errors and had persisted in his tyranny.

Orange then began to look for a new sovereign to replace Philip, homing in on Francis, duke of Anjou, brother of the French king. Extending sovereignty to Francis had the attraction that it would bring French troops and resources to bear in the struggle against Spain, but distrust of this foreign Catholic prince was strong within the Union, with several provinces refusing to accept him as lord. What the States-General of the Union did agree to, however, was to depose Philip II as king in July of 1581 in the Act of Abjuration (*Plakkaat van Verlatinghe*), which condemned Philip as a reckless and lawless breaker of oaths and a scourge to the conscience of his subjects. The Act of Abjuration, often hailed as a revolutionary document for its deposition of the monarchy, also reached back to the Great Privilege of 1477 in asserting traditional rights over arbitrary princely power. In any event, it was now the representatives of the population, the States-General, who determined who was fit and not fit to rule over them, rather than any divine right of kings.

As important a landmark as the Act would in time prove to be, it did not immediately solve the problem of who should succeed Philip. Anjou proved to be a bad choice, after he sought more power than the States-General had accorded him by attempting – and failing – to seize Antwerp by force. This eliminated all credibility he had as sovereign, and he fled to France. Attempts to make Willem of Orange count of Holland (a title that the Spanish king had hitherto held) also ran into resistance from republicans in Holland who, confident in their own ability to govern themselves, felt that no sovereign was entitled to rule over them. In any event, discussion over Willem's status ended when a Catholic assassin, posing as a Calvinist refugee, killed him at his headquarters in Delft on July 10, 1584.

Willem's last years had been difficult. Groningen had come again under Spanish control after the defection of its *stadhouder* to the Spanish side. After 1582 the position of the rebels steadily declined in the South. This was largely the work of Alexander Farnese, the

15 William the Silent's murder in 1584 was a serious setback for the Dutch rebels, but his value as martyr to the cause would lead to the dramatization and mythologization of his death.

duke of Parma, a successor of his mother as the king's governor-general in the region. A superb general, by the early 1580s he possessed the money and the troops necessary to defeat the lesser-trained rebels. Gradually, he retook the cities where Calvinist opposition and enthusiasm for the revolt had been greatest, including

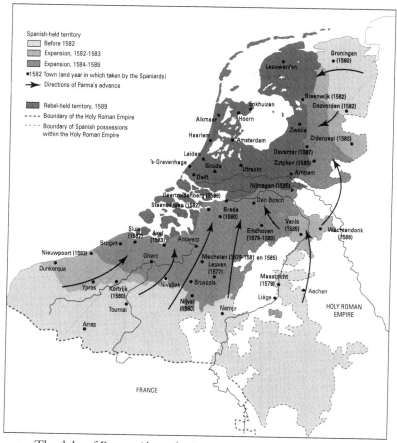

7   The duke of Parma, Alexander Farnese, reconquered many parts of
the Low Countries, including all of Flanders and Brabant, the
heartland of the Protestant revolt.

Ghent in 1584 and, a year later, after an extensive siege, Antwerp.
Farnese was more pragmatic and more lenient than his predecessor
Alba had been fifteen years before; he did not prosecute heretics
immediately, giving them two years to convert or to leave the city.
Some 100,000 persons chose to leave the southern Netherlands in
the late 1580s, many of them fleeing to the north.

No one in 1585 could have anticipated that the fall of Flanders and Brabant to Parma would result in an enduring political and religious boundary between the northern and southern Netherlands. But this development did have short-term effects on the rebels' government. It quickly confirmed the clear and unrivaled ascendance of Holland as the dominant force in the rebellion. As early as 1586 Holland saw to it that the vanquished Flemish and Brabançon cities, signatories to the Union of Utrecht, were denied continued representation in the States-General. The closing of the Schelde River to traffic, now imposed by the rebels, would further ensure Holland's economic growth at Antwerp's expense. In the second place it meant that the rebels needed desperately to find new allies in the fight against a resurgent Spanish army. They turned to England, where relations with Spain had deteriorated.

The sought alliance with England was, however, anything but a success. Queen Elizabeth I was too wary to accept claims of sovereignty over the rebels for herself, and she was angry to hear that her favorite, Robert Dudley, first earl of Leicester, had allowed himself to be appointed governor-general, implicitly in her stead. Leicester had been sent to the Netherlands by the queen to help shore rebels up against the Spanish, but her disclaimers about Leicester as her representative, her reluctance to engage the Spanish directly in battle and her only meager financial support doomed the English venture to ineffectiveness. Leicester himself ran foul of Holland's elites by courting Calvinist pastors, whose power the Holland magistrates were trying to limit, and by colluding with the lesser provinces such as Friesland, which had begun to chafe against the dominance of Holland. His visit to England in 1586 was used by Holland to consolidate opposition to him, and his efforts to seize power in several Holland cities in 1587 failed. By the end of that year he left permanently for England, having accomplished little politically, or militarily.

Quite the contrary, two of his English commanders deserted to the Spanish, placing Deventer and Zutphen into Parma's hands.

By this time, though, the experience with Philip, with Anjou and with Leicester had consolidated the position of Dutch republicans: whatever the future might hold, the country was in essence to be ruled by the representative nobility and cities in the States-General. In the "Justification or Deduction," supported by the States-General in April of 1588, both the divine right of kings and a more popular representative system sought by the Calvinists of Utrecht were rejected in favor of placing sovereignty with the historical representatives of the respective states. The document contemplated in theory a future monarch, but only with very limited powers, and one that would serve at the pleasure of the States. Though they did not yet call it a republic, the leaders of this new confederacy would, from now on, regard themselves as wholly autonomous, looking to no other to vindicate the rights that they had claimed for themselves.

Under the Burgundians and the Habsburgs, Holland, benefiting from the economic interplay in the region, had very gradually come to challenge Flanders and then Brabant as regional leader. Though not initially the center of the Protestant-led revolt, Holland became in effect its major beneficiary, functioning as the core of a wholly new northern Netherlandic state that was born in the 1580s. From the perspective of the Spanish advance, though, the success of that new state seemed anything but certain.

3

A Young Republic's Golden Age, 1588–1672

~

The decision in April of 1588 by the States-General to forswear, for all purposes, sovereign lords in favor of a self-governing Republic was hardly in itself enough to reverse the tenuous position of the revolt. The Spanish reconquest of the Low Countries seemed set in mid 1588 to continue apace, and morale among Dutch soldiers and citizenry was low. In hindsight, the prospects of the revolt were about to improve dramatically, and within a short time the new Republic would become one of the leading powers of Europe and a dominant force in global commerce. This stunning success went hand-in-hand with the sustained growth of the Dutch economy that began in the 1580s and lasted until the 1660s. The unprecedented accumulation of wealth, and a well-ordered and relatively open society, generated a cultural "golden age" in the arts and in the sciences. It is the achievements of this short century on which the Netherlands' international reputation, then and since, as a country of singular achievement is largely based, and from which the Dutch continue to draw their self-identity.

And yet, as is the case with all "golden ages," the period had its own difficulties. Throughout most of this period the Republic was at war with enemies near and far, with the high personal and financial costs that came with war. These rivals would, over time, become more and more powerful. The Republic's political structures, mostly through benign neglect, gave its residents of the much freedom to say and do what they wanted, but the Dutch struggled to find an equilibrium by which the country might be governed.

Establishment of a New Economic and Political Order, 1588–1621

The Republic Strikes Back

A change in Spanish strategic thinking offered the young Republic breathing room. English open support of the revolt after 1585, as well as their attacks on Spanish ports across the Atlantic, prompted King Philip II to assemble a huge fleet, an Armada, calculated to knock England out of the war. The warships of the Armada were to escort a large portion of the duke of Parma's Flemish army by barge to England. This invasion, however, was severely hampered by unrealistic planning. Bereft of suitable harbors, many of the Armada's deep-water warships themselves could not reach Parma's soldiers. Instead, the vulnerable barges were to make their way out to open sea with insufficient protection. The soldiers were thus easily bottled up by Dutch armed fly-boats that, unlike most ships of the Armada, could make use of the shallow waters of the Flemish coast. Even without the soldiers, the Armada presented a serious danger to England, but the naval battle off Gravelines at the end of July 1588 scattered the Spanish fleet, and subsequent adverse winds forced the Armada to sail around the British Isles on the way back to Spain, in the process losing perhaps half of its ships. The failed Spanish gambit not only spared England from invasion, but had tied up Parma's troops for weeks in the abortive venture, giving their Dutch opponents time further to strengthen their defenses.

The young Republic thus benefited from Philip II's decision to marshal – and ultimately squander – his resources against enemies he considered more dangerous than the Dutch. That had been England, but the king was soon enough forced to fix his attention on an even greater strategic threat: France. The powerful French Protestant minority, emboldened by the Armada's loss, seized the initiative, and their standard-bearer Henry of Navarre, a Calvinist, unexpectedly became king of France when Henry

III died at the hands of an assassin in 1589. Philip considered it paramount that Spain do all it could to support French Catholic opposition to the new monarch, lest a powerful France become the permanent enemy of Spain. He accordingly ordered Parma to deploy a significant portion of his forces southward for operations inside France, and after April of 1590 Parma's forces pivoted fully southwards to meet the new threat. To make things worse for the Spanish, lack of money and mutinies by ill-paid soldiers would continue to hobble their war-making capabilities for the rest of the 1590s.

Spanish problems, as well as the help of English and French allies, show that a long string of rebel military successes that would follow, beginning in 1590 and lasting through 1597, did not depend on Dutch efforts alone. Just as crucial, though, was the fact that the Republic enjoyed effective political and military leadership. The departure of the earl of Leicester definitively placed the most important political decision-making in the hands of the highly competent Johan van Oldenbarnevelt, an Amersfoort-born jurist who had served as pensionary of Rotterdam before becoming a close associate of Willem of Orange and a central figure in politics of The Hague. Oldenbarnevelt's rising influence, built as it was on Holland's growing power, generated friction and resentment in the lesser provinces. Decision-making in the Republic was, as a consequence of the subsequent bickering, slow to capitalize on Spanish troubles after the Armada's debacle, arguably throwing away the chance to regain lost territory in the south. Within a few short years, though, Oldenbarnevelt cobbled together a functioning state apparatus. Through consultations, bribes and military shows of force, Oldenbarnevelt managed within a few years to cajole wayward provinces such as Friesland and Utrecht back into the fold. In this way, he forged the political cooperation that was essential in the war against Spain. At the same time, he was particularly attentive to commercial interests in Holland, working actively to advance its trade. More than simply a consummate and ruthless politician, though, Oldenbarnevelt was a tireless administrator, accompanying the Republic's armies on the battlefield to assess their needs, and helping to ensure that soldiers were regularly paid, an important reform to ensure troop reliability and public trust in the Republic's cause. An accomplished and trusted diplomat, he traveled to France and England to ensure continuation of the alliance against Spain. His political stature, recognized internationally, enhanced the reputation of the young Republic.

At the same time, the Republic was aided by an effective military leadership. Willem of Orange had already done much to discipline riotous rebels into a well-regulated force that was no longer the scourge of the local population. It was his son Maurits, however, who further shaped the States Army into one of the best-trained armies in Europe, drilling soldiers constantly when they were not off on campaign, instead of sending them home until they were needed again. Together with his co-commander, Willem Lodewijk of Nassau-Dillenburg, his cousin and fellow *stadhouder* in the northern provinces, Maurits effectively turned the States Army into a force that knew how to capture fortified towns and cities – the chief aim of land warfare in the late sixteenth century. The engineering skills of the Dutch army were additionally crucial to this end. These factors made the Republic's military reversal of fortune possible.

Military Advances

One of the Republic's earliest successes on this front was both improbable and dramatic: the seizure of the town of Breda in March of 1590, held by an Italian garrison for Parma. No engineering feats were necessary in this case, but merely an ingenious plan for subterfuge: some seventy soldiers of the States Army were smuggled into the town by means of a peat ship, which as a rule were never inspected. These soldiers quickly infiltrated the

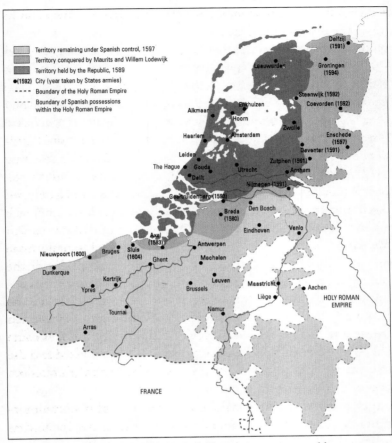

Territory remaining under Spanish control, 1597
Territory conquered by Maurits and Willem Lodewijk
Territory held by the Republic, 1589
●(1592) City (year taken by States armies)
- - - - Boundary of the Holy Roman Empire
- - - - Boundary of Spanish possessions
within the Holy Roman Empire

8   The young Republic, seizing the offensive in 1590, was able to recover
some of the lands seized by Parma. But the divide between "north" and
"south" would remain permanent.

city, sending the local garrison into a panic, and the gates were
soon open to Maurits's force waiting outside. The States Army
was thus able to use Breda as a base for the subsequent siege and
capture of nearby towns. This included the important fortress at
Geertruidenberg, which fell in 1593 after the States Army used

state-of-the-art siege techniques both surround the town and to hold off a Spanish relief army.

These successes took the States armies years to achieve. Emblematic in this case was Groningen, a city that under its *stadhouder*, Rennenberg, had defected from the rebel cause in 1580 and remained in Spanish hands. Willem Lodewijk spent five long years carrying out a systematic strategy meant eventually to seize Groningen by first taking other towns across the area, and building new fortifications to prevent food and supplies from reaching the city. Having been completely isolated from the outside world, and Spanish efforts to relieve it having been defeated, Groningen fell to the States Army under the leadership of Willem Lodewijk and Maurits after a two-month siege in July of 1594, in which the use of cannon and the construction of a tunnel to undermine the fortifications were employed. Groningen, merged with the surrounding *Ommelanden*, with which the city had always had a conflictual relationship, now became an integral region of the Republic, with representation in the States-General. As was often the case in the captured towns, the Reformed Church became the only public church; Catholic worship was suppressed and the inhabitants of the monasteries ordered to leave, though freedom of conscience was observed.

The successful campaigns of the 1590s brought important territorial gains for the Republic: a strip of Flanders under the vital Schelde Estuary and large sections of northwest Brabant to the south, and to the east not only Groningen and Drenthe but extensive parts of Gelderland and Overijssel that lay far beyond the IJssel River, the starting point of their offensive. The States Army also seized key territories outside the present-day Netherlands, specifically the county of Lingen and a number of fortified towns further up the Rhine. These newly acquired lands were hardly immune to further attacks in subsequent years and decades, and in the eastern sections of the Republic continued fighting seriously hampered economic life, in some places for several decades to come. But the territorial expansion provided the Republic with a considerably greater security buffer; the cities and towns of economically important Holland would be virtually untouched by warfare.

After Philip II's death in 1598 the governments in Madrid and Brussels sought to explore some kind of peace with the Republic. But war would continue on and off for another decade, in part because the Dutch were not keen to conclude peace when they seemed well positioned to benefit from further hostilities. A decade of inconclusive warfare was, however, the result. The bloody but indecisive Battle of Nieuwpoort (1600), stemming from Oldenbarnevelt's insistence that the States Army attack pirate outposts on the Flemish coast, had the chief effect of causing permanent alienation between himself and captain-general and *stadhouder* Maurits, who had opposed the adventure because of the considerable risk to his forces. New Spanish attacks, the high financial costs of warfare, and the fact that the Republic's English and French allies had made peace with Spain prompted the Dutch to reconsider a truce. The Republic's refusal to end its trade in the East Indies prevented the Spanish government from offering it full diplomatic recognition, and the most that could be reached between them was a twelve-year truce, which began in April of 1609. Until 1621, then, the Republic would be at peace.

Factors in the Success of the New Republic

Peace gave the young Republic breathing space, but by the time it came the Dutch were already benefiting from a host of factors that helped it not only to survive but to thrive. The political skills of Oldenbarnevelt, and the military exploits of the Nassau cousins, ensured that the Republic's economy was largely unhindered by the dislocations of war. Free from ruinous taxation and the repression of absolutist politics, the Dutch were able to launch new economic initiatives that would soon propel them to the forefront of the global economy. The strong state of the Republic's finances also guaranteed a secure economic climate. Conversely, Dutch political and military achievements could not have come to fruition without the sound financial footing that a booming economy, then taking place, provided. Depressed by the depredations of the 1560s and 1570s, the economy of Holland in particular improved dramatically in the course of the 1580s, and would by and large show sustained growth into the late seventeenth century. For almost a century, the Dutch Republic – and especially Holland – was Europe's economic powerhouse, dominating trade across the continent and indeed large parts of the world.

Thus, at the inception of the Republic its port cities were already well positioned to take a leading economic role. The Republic's permanent blockade of Antwerp harbor – which was to last two centuries – certainly played an important role in shifting the heart of the region northward. But even without this blockade the north was ascendant. Amsterdam in the course of the sixteenth century had become the leading port in the Baltic Sea trade, which traded grain and wood from eastern Europe in exchange for Dutch specialized goods, or increasingly goods from other parts of Europe and the rest of the world. Dutch shipping would dominate the Baltic for most of the following century, and it was the single most important source of Dutch prosperity during the seventeenth century. Already in 1583 some 84 percent of the exports and 73 percent of the imports of Danzig – the most important harbor in the eastern Baltic – were transported by Dutch skippers. Dutch commercial shipping was also strong along the European Atlantic coast, extending as far as Portugal and southern Spain. The Dutch chokehold on northwestern European trade was so strong that Spain – its own naval power diminished – was forced to end its embargo of Dutch goods in 1590, the Spanish being too dependent on the grain and wood supplied by Dutch merchants. Amsterdam again was the chief center of this trade, but the city's commerce with smaller towns inland along well-developed waterways made these towns, too, increasingly part of the international trade. Important also to the strong economic position of the Dutch was its increasing dominance in the herring trade, selling the pickled fish across Europe from ports such as Enkhuizen.

The Dutch built their Golden Age on importing goods, refining or refinishing them for sale, and then exporting them again. But why were they so successful in this respect? The reasons for this sudden and sustained economic surge have been much debated by historians. Much has been made of the economic impact of the at least 100,000 immigrants who, whether out of religious or economic motivation, left Brabant and Flanders in favor of German and especially Dutch cities, particularly Amsterdam, as the economy rapidly diversified. Perhaps 10 percent of the Republic's population in 1600 hailed from the south. A third of Amsterdam's residents could claim Flemish roots at the turn of the seventeenth century; about half the grooms marrying in Leiden in the decade after 1585 were southerners. Many of these migrants were wealthy or skilled, and their migration helps explain the economic dynamism that was brought from the southern Netherlands to the north. Antwerp merchants were specialized in the so-called "rich trades" that focused on luxury goods such as silk and spices. Flemings established for the first time sugar refineries and paper factories in the north. Flemish textile production resettled to a large extent in the north, in old cloth towns such as Leiden and Haarlem, which through superior Flemish techniques resuscitated these faltering towns and provided the young Republic with an important industrial base for its economy. Leiden doubled in population during the 1580s and 1590s, reaching 26,000 inhabitants at the end of the century. Southern knowledge, money and networks from the banks and from the financial markets of Antwerp also found their way to the north, again particularly to the benefit of Amsterdam, the Republic's growing financial center.

These mostly Protestant southerners were soon joined by other merchants. Portuguese Jews, fleeing policies that had forced their outward conversion to Christianity, first began to settle in Amsterdam in the 1590s, bringing with them their own valuable trading webs from Portuguese settlements on both sides of the Atlantic. As a result of this economic convergence, Amsterdam grew from about 30,000 persons in 1570 to some 105,000 in 1622, and that number would double again by 1670, making it, after Paris and London (which were each far bigger), the largest city in Europe. The Republic in its early years was already the most urbanized part of Europe, and by 1675 some 42 percent of its population lived in cities (rising to 61 percent in Holland alone).

This demographic statistic emphasizes that economic boom could only be sustained by the new sources of labor, supplied in the seventeenth century by tens of thousands of immigrants from the southern Netherlands, from eastern parts of the Republic as well as from Germany and Scandinavia. Many of them were impoverished and without skills, and were drawn to the economies of the western cities, which offered them job opportunities and relatively generous real wages – between 30 and 60 percent higher than in surrounding regions of Europe – even if the cost of living, including a considerable tax burden, was at equally high levels. In the seventeenth century immigrants constituted half the paid labor force in the Republic, far more than anywhere else. At the same time there was a strong influx of skilled labor, which supplemented an already expanding field of well-trained and literate craftspeople in the Republic, even though guilds were typically restricted to the native-born. Guilds remained important, and most were ecumenically open, but in Holland's towns they did not determine the full range of artisanal talent. This solidified Amsterdam's importance not just as a center of trade, but as a producer of finished goods.

"Foreign" and "native" economic strengths thus complemented each other and increasingly intertwined as they mutually intensified the country's commercial capabilities. The new trading possibilities beckoned new financial investments in the Dutch economy, permitting Dutch merchants to outstrip their rivals. The new commercial ethos centered around Amsterdam, furthermore, was different from that of Antwerp: cut free from both the protections and restraints of Habsburg rule and more oriented to the open seas, Amsterdam's business climate was more free-wheeling and more individualized, more likely to start new enterprises and to take new risks.

New technological innovations, developed at the end of the century, substantially bolstered this maritime-driven commerce. The first of these was the wind-powered sawmill, first patented in the 1590s, which drastically reduced the time and manpower necessary to construct houses, sluices, and of course ships. Many of these new sawmills – there were hundreds by the end of the seventeenth century – sprang up along the Zaan River just north-west of Amsterdam, which together with that city became the most important ship-building center in the Republic. At almost the same time, Dutch shipbuilders, after decades of experimenta-tion, engineered what became known as the *fluyt,* an inexpensive and easy-to-build merchant ship that was designed to store a max-imum load and to sail with a minimal crew. This type of ship was decisively more economically efficient than either its predecessors or its rivals in other countries. Difficult to convert into a warship, the *fluyt* was vulnerable to enemies, but with hundreds produced each year in Dutch shipyards it helped ensure the Republic's com-mercial dominance on the seas.

All of these factors, then, made it possible within a very short frame of time for a tiny upstart republic to become the leading economy of Europe and a world power of significance. Long-term factors, long evident in Holland, were now part of a larger dynamic that powered the country's startlingly successful economy.

Dutch Overseas Expansion

The Dutch were thus rapidly developing a capability for engaging in world trade, but it was shortages caused by the conflict with Spain that prompted them to strike out beyond European waters. Sugar, salt, pepper and spices had been imported to the region by other traders from Antwerp and from Portugal. The forced annexation of Portugal into Spain in 1580 largely closed off the market there and, with the fall of Antwerp, its refugee merchants in the Republic were looking for new trading possibilities. The result was an active search, starting in the mid 1590s, for new trading routes in the Atlantic, the Arctic Sea and the Indian Ocean, some of these more successful than others. The first Dutch trading post began in 1581 on the Pomeroon River in present-day Guyana, but this enterprise, later relocated to Essequibo, remained small. Attempting to avoid the Portuguese, several expeditions explored the mythical Northeast Passage, hoping to reach Cathay via the Russian Arctic. Aside from discovering the possibilities of whale-hunting around Spitsbergen and inspiring a famous account of Willem Barentsz.'s stranded crew surviving a winter on Nova Zembla, these efforts

16   Willem Barentsz.'s disastrous time on Nova Zembla, which he personally did not survive, reveals that Dutch "discovery" of the world was a trial-and-error process that could end badly.

came to nothing. Later the English captain Henry Hudson, then in Dutch service, abandoned his search for the Northeast Passage in 1609 and set off across the Atlantic, seeking an alternative north-westerly route to Asia. Here, too, he failed in his aim, but in the process "discovered" the river that now bears his name and laid the basis for Dutch claims to settle New Netherland.

Far more successful and more important were the Dutch forays down the western coast of Africa and across the Indian Ocean. Aided by the knowledge of Jan Huygen van Linschoten, who had worked for the Portuguese, the first fleet of Dutch ships completed the two-year return voyage in 1597. Focusing on the trading city of Banten in the Javanese sultanate of the same name, the first trip, faced with local and Portuguese opposition, managed just to break even with its modest cargo. The second trip, launched a year later, was far more successful, bringing back pepper, cloves and nutmeg. It was the beginning of the lucrative spice trade for the Dutch, stretching from Ceylon to Japan. And it was the beginning of a sustained Dutch presence in the Indonesian archipelago, not just on Java but on Sumatra and in the Moluccas. In 1605 the Dutch made their first military conquest, seizing the clove-rich island of Ambon from the Portuguese, and making it the first administrative center of the Dutch in the region.

In order to share the considerable risks of this trade and to control prices, leading merchants, with Oldenbarnevelt's encouragement, established the Dutch East India Company, the Vereenigde Oostindische Compagnie (VOC) in 1602. The first publicly traded joint-stock company in history, it was the joint venture of six "chambers" – Amsterdam, Zeeland, Delft, Enkhuizen, Hoorn and Rotterdam. Initially a loose and uncoordinated consortium of local economic interests, the VOC initially mirrored the strongly decentralized Dutch state. Over time, though, it became an efficient organization that shared liability across the chambers that by the 1630s was turning out annual cash dividends. The Republic's government granted it wide powers: it was not only given a trading monopoly east of the Cape of Good Hope but the power to make treaties, build forts and conduct war. From the outset it was understood that the growth of the company could only come at the expense of other European powers and, if they stood in the way, of local rulers and populations. An Anglo-Dutch agreement to divide trading spheres between them (present-day India to the English, present-day Indonesia to the Dutch) did not eliminate armed conflict between the two powers in Asia. In this respect, the commercial success of the world's first multinational corporation and the Republic's largest employer was predicated on the systematic use of violence against perennial enemies.

The commercial innovation of VOC points to another strength of the burgeoning Republic: its financial institutions. The financial administration of Holland in particular had long been efficient, and the Republic continued to be well funded by private financiers, mostly Hollanders, who were able to ensure that, in contrast to the banking houses serving the Spanish kings, they were paid back with interest for the credits they offered to the state. Soldiers and sailors in service of the Republic were thus paid regularly and on time, making them much less of a danger to the towns in which they were garrisoned. From the standpoint of the Republic's security, its superior ability to raise money and thus finance its military – the chief expenditure of all early modern states – enabled it to compete with its military rivals. The Amsterdam Wisschelbank, founded in 1609, offered a measure of financial stability, guaranteeing deposits and enabling large financial transfers. Advanced accounting techniques such as double-entry bookkeeping, used in banks and other public institutions, made it more difficult to steal or to commit fraud in a money-oriented culture where fraud and other forms of malfeasance were serious temptations. Taking its cues from Antwerp, London and Venice, Amsterdam established its own commodities exchange in 1611, where stocks, too, were bought and sold. This turned Amsterdam into a hub of news and secret information – and of any rumors that might have bearing on the markets. All this, along with the gigantic sums of money made by business, helped to transform the Republic, and Amsterdam in particular, into the financial center of the world.

Political Crisis

Away from its violence-ridden border regions, the Republic was a haven of political and religious stability, compared to either the violence of the late sixteenth century or the wars that wracked the British Isles, Germany and France in the early seventeenth century. The improvised alliance against Habsburg rule had managed to transform itself into a functioning confederation of sovereign states. But this hardly meant an absence of serious, unresolved issues about how that state should be constituted.

Chief among these was the relation between the whole and the parts of the Republic, and the extent to which all parties felt they were part of a common cause. The Republic was not only an association of seven states (Friesland, Gelderland, Groningen, Holland, Overijssel, Utrecht and Zeeland) each of which insisted on its own sovereignty, but these in turn were divided into "quarters" and towns that each had their own say in the governing of the Republic. The newly constituted States of Groningen, for example, were divided between the city and the surrounding "Ommelanden," parties that for centuries had been living in conflict with each other. It has been estimated that roughly fifty municipalities had a real say in The Hague, rendering policy-making fractious and time-consuming. Without the leadership of Holland – which accounted for well over half the population and wealth of the Republic – the Republic would have imploded. But Holland's natural dominance of the Republic's affairs also created resentments, manifested in arguments about how much precisely each region should pay. In the first half of the seventeenth century Holland paid roughly 58 percent of the total budget of the Generality, with

Amsterdam alone good for about half that amount. In contrast, Gelderland or Utrecht each gave only a tenth of what Holland paid – and even with such lopsided ratios Holland probably paid a bit less than its fair share. At the same time, Holland's leadership could be insistent that others pay their own way; Oldenbarnevelt had the city of Groningen occupied by States troops in 1599 when they resisted paying their allotted share of taxes. The necessity of both following Holland's lead and respecting regional sovereignty was a tension that the Republic never succeeded in effectively resolving.

This tension set the stage for potential conflict between Oldenbarnevelt, the Land's Advocate – a kind of secretary-general for the States of Holland – and the *stadhouder* Maurits. The two initially had divided powers between them – Oldenbarnevelt as the political leader, Maurits as the military man – but after Nieuwpoort their relationship had soured. In theory, the *stadhouder* was a servant of the province, but the *stadhouder*, as commander-in-chief, was at the same time the only officeholder in the Republic who transcended the provinces. Like most princes of his time, Maurits was eager to expand his dynasty's prestige and power, as much as the constraints of republican government would allow. Oldenbarnevelt in turn was wary of any office that would undermine the primacy of Holland's leadership. Here, too, the stage was set for an enduring conflict between the House of Orange-Nassau and the so-called States party, led by Holland's political elites, of whom Oldenbarnevelt was only the first.

Religious Crisis

The second issue was the place of the Church in state and society. The experience with violent religious repression under Habsburg rule prompted many Dutch – not least local officials – to conclude that it was counterproductive if not outright wrong to prosecute persons on grounds of their conscience, a principle already articulated in the Union of Utrecht. The Republic contained a potpourri of religious convictions, where no one was forced to join the Reformed Church, though as a rule only its members could hold public office. It was moreover the church with the only right, in most towns, to conduct public worship. This "public Church" had no formal role in the Republic's government, and at the same time it was relatively free at the local level to arrange its own affairs. It could count perhaps a sixth of the population as members in the early seventeenth century. Many Dutch remained Catholic – especially in places where the local Catholic clergy had stayed put despite persecution – and a substantial number of Protestants were Mennonite or Lutheran. A very large segment of the population was unaffiliated, sometimes out of indifference, sometimes because they were unsure where they belonged, sometimes because they found the demands of membership in the Reformed Church, with its emphasis on right belief and irreproachable lifestyle, too stringent. This religious pluralism would continue to characterize the Republic, a pluralism stimulating a pragmatic tolerance toward non-Reformed faiths that allowed them to worship according to their conscience, even if that often meant worshiping in private houses, or sometimes paying off the local sheriff for the privilege. But this fluid situation left the relationship between the public Church and the state unregulated, an unacceptable state of affairs in early modern times where religious and political authority were expected to go hand-in-hand. Efforts to decide this issue would lead to a sharp conflict.

For many Church leaders and laity in the Netherlands (as elsewhere in Europe), the task ahead lay in what modern researchers have called the "confessionalization" of society, in which the government actively prevented "false" doctrine from being proclaimed and in which the state-approved Church directed the population toward right belief and behavior. Though they encouraged the government to bear down hard on Catholics and other heretical groups, the Dutch Reformed clergy also believed that this mission

predestination

could only be accomplished if government refrained from meddling in the Church's self-government and in theological issues.

For Calvinism, one of the key theological issues in the early seventeenth century was whether a person had a role to play in her own salvation, or whether the person's saving faith was decreed exclusively by God. In a society where life expectancy was short, especially for infants, this existential theological issue – did one need to do good to be assured eternal salvation? – found broad resonance. In contrast to Jacob Arminius, a professor of Reformed theology at Leiden, who placed some emphasis on human agency in this process, most clergy and probably most members of the Dutch Reformed Church thought that it was God's wholly unbound will that determined who would be saved and who would be damned. Increasingly, they began to see Arminius's views as intolerable error. In some towns, the anti-Arminians were a genuinely popular force who let their weight count, demonstrably walking out of churches served by Arminian preachers, or by 1617, as in Amsterdam, forming mobs and plundering the homes of leading Arminians.

In contrast to this vision, many of the Republic's political elites thought that the Church needed to be brought under their effective control, in order to make the Church a harmonious part of the political order, instead of an autonomous and destabilizing force that might polarize society and challenge their own grip on power. To this end they demanded a decisive say in preaching appointments within the Church. They tended to be religious moderates, preferring an inclusive and irenic Church over a pure and theologically unified one. Many high-placed town leaders sympathized with Arminius's theological views, but a more widely shared belief among them was that the "public Church" ought to accommodate a wide range of theological convictions and be brought under the firm oversight of local government. These incompatible visions of the relationship between Church and state were bound to lead to trouble.

Showdown

From the start, then, the theological debate possessed a political dimension, and this political dimension would only intensify during the Twelve Years' Truce (1609–1621). Efforts by both parties to gain public support, starting with the pro-Arminian "Remonstrance" of 1610, which set out their theological and ecclesiastical agenda, only added fuel to the fire, leading to unrest – even riots – in some cities after the States of Holland responded positively to it. In this setting, efforts by, among others, the Arminian jurist Hugo Grotius, the internationally acclaimed intellectual, to find common ground proved futile. Both parties intensified their hostility toward each other by disagreeing over foreign policy. "Remonstrants," as they were called, tended to support Oldenbarnevelt's close relations with Catholic France and his preference for an extension of the truce with Spain, while "Contraremonstrants" were suspicious of Oldenbarnevelt and of his ostensibly pro-Catholic politics. Families once hailing from the south, typically more radical in theology than Hollanders, supported the Contraremonstrant cause, and regions such as Zeeland or cities such as Amsterdam, which saw their chance to expand their commerce at the expense of Spanish interests if war were resumed, also took a Contraremonstrant position.

Not noted for his piety but raised as a staunch Calvinist, Maurits, whose own glory as military commander had been stymied by the truce, openly chose the Contraremonstrant side in the summer of 1617, emboldening its partisans to make further demands. In response, Oldenbarnevelt determined that the towns of Holland could arm mercenaries to put down any unrest caused by anti-Arminian demonstrations, and this measure was adopted by several other provinces. In doing so, he encroached on Maurits's authority as military commander, a usurpation that the *stadhouder* found wholly unacceptable. In the course of 1618 Maurits, using threat of force, removed his political opponents, first outside Holland and then in the Holland towns themselves, replacing them with reliable Contraremonstrants. In a final dramatic move to seize all power in the Republic, Maurits had Oldenbarnevelt and Grotius arrested in August of 1618. Much to his surprise, the former was tried and convicted for treason, and consequently beheaded in May of 1619, while Grotius was sentenced to life in prison at the remote castle of Loevestein (from which he famously managed to escape in a book chest two years later). The Contraremonstrant party had won, and Holland's influence, at least for now, was weakened by Maurits's triumph.

In the long run, though, the results of the conflict were more mixed. The Synod of Dordrecht (1618–1619), an international council of Calvinist theologians, formally and emphatically rejected Arminius's teachings, setting a lasting standard for Reformed orthodoxy. It also determined Church policy on other issues, such as its judgment that baptized slaves could no longer be considered slaves – a policy routinely ignored in the East Indies. Inspired by the example of the King James Bible (1611), the Synod also launched the first scholarly translation of the Bible into Dutch. Authorized and funded by the States-General, its completion in 1637 had a fundamental impact – half a million copies were sold in the first twenty years – on the country's religious life and on the Dutch language. It was, however, the last time that a national synod – in itself a sign of the Church's independence – was ever held in the Republic, as political authorities were quite keen to prevent a powerful national church from asserting itself again. Though the Church maintained a doctrinal independence greater than elsewhere in Protestant Europe, local government authorities frequently continued to determine who would preach. Sometimes less than enthusiastic supporters of Calvinist orthodoxy, they were at best selective in listening to the Church's stringent demands for a more godly society. Emblematic of this situation is that in many towns, especially in Holland, the public Church had to accept, much against its will, that the small

Remonstrant church was effectively tolerated and allowed to worship quietly, at the edges of the law.

Politically, Maurits reaped little from his coup. His policies, to be sure, had weakened Holland, which was no longer directed by someone as formidable as Oldenbarnevelt. But his control over Holland was limited; he was unable to prevent the return in some towns of powerful elites who had embraced the Arminian position. As a result, Holland was wracked by serious internal divisions down into the 1630s. Maurits, less politically adroit than Oldenbarnevelt and increasingly in poor health, was thus unable to capitalize on his coup before dying at the age of fifty-seven in 1625. He failed either to implement political reforms that solidified the power of the *stadhouder* or to find a durable way to share power with his rivals. Frederik Hendrik, who succeeded his half-brother Maurits as *stadhouder*, was more theologically flexible and a more accomplished statesman, and generally succeeded in making the existing system work. But the structural weaknesses of the Republic would come to the forefront again after his death.

The Achievements of a Merchant Republic, 1621–1648

New Military Successes

War with Spain resumed in 1621 with the end of the Twelve Years' Truce. Both Maurits and the new Spanish King Philip IV – influenced by his chief advisor Count Olivares – thought that they could take military advantage of the war then being fought in Germany – later known as the Thirty Years' War. Dynastic considerations were important on both sides in the decision to resume war; the leader of German Protestants, the Palatinate elector Frederik V, was a full cousin of Maurits, and Spanish Habsburgs were keen to support the new Habsburg emperor in his determination to unify the empire by eliminating Protestantism. Spanish aims toward the Republic were less far-reaching; rather than reconquering the region they sought to end Dutch trade with Asia and reduce its naval presence in the Atlantic.

That the Dutch had high hopes of winning the conflict can be seen in the creation of the West India Company (WIC) in 1621, a kind of venture that expressly had been forbidden by the Truce and that the Dutch now used to undermine Spanish-Portuguese interests in the Atlantic and establish their own trading zone. In the short run, however, it was the Habsburgs who were more successful. They crushed the Protestant armies in Germany, driving Frederik from his possessions. They drove the defeated remnants of these armies into the Republic, and they took the military initiative, in 1625 seizing Breda, the town States soldiers had taken with so much verve in 1590. They imposed a blockade of the seas and rivers, severely hampering Dutch commerce, and even began building a canal in Brabant to bypass the Republic's control of the great rivers. Dutch financial support to European Protestants seriously threatened the government's solvency. As a result of these troubles, the Dutch economy suffered from a serious economic depression that would last more than a decade. Bereft of powerful allies, the Republic was as isolated and vulnerable as it had been in a generation.

As in the late 1580s, however, the Republic's military fortunes swiftly rebounded after 1625. The presence of Danish and later more successful Swedish Protestant armies in Germany reduced pressure on the Republic. Under Frederik Hendrik, the Dutch put their military house in order. Able to exploit the temporary weakness of Holland, the young *stadhouder*, at least in his younger years, was able to assert himself politically in The Hague, arranging the money and the men necessary for new military initiatives.

In subsequent years, Frederik Hendrik, a master strategist in his own right, won a series of important victories. The first of these was Groenlo in the far east of Gelderland, an imposing and strategic fortress from which the Spanish levied taxes over the region and from which their forces could strike key defenses of the Republic within hours. It fell to the *stadhouder*'s armies in 1627. A far more impressive victory came two years later when Frederik Hendrik seized Den Bosch after an extensive siege that lasted half a year. Den Bosch was the administrative center of northern Brabant and seat of a bishopric, called "little Rome" for the dozens of chapels, churches and monasteries as well as hundreds of nuns, monks and priests within its walls. There was no city in the region more critical to the interests of the Habsburgs or to the Catholic Church. Den Bosch was a fortress so well protected by marshes that it was thought impregnable, but Frederik Hendrik's engineers managed nevertheless to build siege fortifications in the surrounding swamps by using windmills, and eventually battered its walls into submission. When Den Bosch fell its convents and monasteries were forcibly closed, its clergy expelled from the city, and all of northeastern Brabant, including a large part of the Meijerij, came under control of the Republic. The Meijerij, especially the strategic but impoverished sandy grounds of the Kempen, did remain a militarily contested region, though later opposing forces slightly lightened the burden of the population by eventually agreeing not to despoil the territory they had just seized.

Three years later, in 1632, the *stadhouder*'s armies marched down to besiege Maastricht and, despite bloody attempts by Spanish forces to relieve the town, took it. Taking Maastricht gave the Republic, as it turned out, a permanent outpost far to the south of its main territories, creating a perennial threat to the Spanish Netherlands from the east. Meanwhile, at sea, the Dutch scored important victories. In 1628, under Admiral Piet Hein, WIC ships seized an entire Spanish silver fleet off Cuba. This feat deprived the Spanish of necessary funds for their armies and offered WIC shareholders an unprecedented dividend of 50 percent. And in 1639, a Dutch fleet largely destroyed a second Spanish "armada" off the English coast that had been transporting troops to Flanders. Spanish resources spent in Germany and in the Low Countries were now exhausted.

Further, mostly minor victories would follow for the Republic into the 1640s, including the recapture of Breda, and thus of western Brabant, in 1637. Frederik Hendrik's own ambitions to take more territory – even dividing the southern Netherlands between the Republic and France – foundered on the opposition of a revived Holland. Cities such as Amsterdam had little appetite for continuing to fund expensive armies on the scale needed for reconquest, and even less appetite for restoring the old rival city of Antwerp, now permanently hobbled by a Dutch blockade. What mattered to them was that the Republic, no longer seriously threatened, could continue its own pursuits unhindered, and be released from the taxes and wars that impeded their commerce.

New Accomplishments: Canal Houses and Polders

Political and religious conflicts at home did not seriously impede the cultural dynamism of the Republic; on the contrary, it has been argued that these uncertainties created new spaces where the Dutch could explore new ways of acting and thinking that broke with old conventions. And it was the cities of the Republic, particularly the towering presence of Amsterdam, where this new culture was most evident.

The face of the greatest city of the Republic, driven by the need to accommodate thousands and thousands of new residents and new businesses, began in the early seventeenth century to alter radically. The expanding city required larger harbor facilities and also a better separation of the functions that divided noisy and polluting industries from residential areas. With new walls built to accommodate a larger city, in 1613 Amsterdam began the monumental task of constructing three concentric canals around the city center, which was bounded on the north by the River IJ, all of it intended for upper-end housing. Between 1614 and 1619 the first neighborhood was completed, though it took nearly half a century to construct before the city completed the west and south sides of these concentric circles, the eastern part of the project ultimately being abandoned for lack of funds and interest. Though unfinished, the expansion was a remarkable achievement; executed with precision, it created exclusively residential areas alongside the new canals, which, with its trees and relatively clean waters, attracted the wealthiest residents of the town. In the course of seventeenth century the most affluent citizens of the Republic built large homes along these canals, particularly the most inner and prestigious of them, the Herengracht. The whole project was a financial spectacle from beginning to end; speculators – some from the city government – had grown fabulously wealthy from the buying and selling of land that had been set aside for the canals. And the builders of the houses along

17   Amsterdam's wealth generated many stately houses, such as those built on the Golden Bend on the Herengracht, as depicted in their partial completion just before the Year of Disaster.

the canals were eager to display their own wealth and prestige, even as they made some attempt to show some respect for more frugal Calvinist and bourgeois values.

Amsterdam money made possible not only the reconstruction of the city but the transformation of the countryside to the direct north of the city. The middle of present-day North Holland was a tangle of land slivers and shallow lakes (with depths of about 4 meters) that constituted a danger to the drier areas surrounding it. It was also known that the clay at the bottom of these waters would make for fertile farmland – precisely at a time when a growing city required more food. Investors flocked to support efforts to pump out the Beemster lake, making use of a row of windmills, each placed higher than the other. Reclaimed between 1609 and 1612, in part through the work of Jan Adriaensz Leeghwater, the Beemster was a polder exemplifying the latest technical insights, with a controlled water level regulated by symmetrical canals. Constituting some 70 km², the Beemster was the largest of North Holland's lakes to be tamed, but it was not the last: the Purmer (1622) and the Schermer (1635) were among the larger remaining lakes pumped dry into polders. Over 100 lakes were reclaimed in the region, totaling 840 km² and adding a third to its land size. The new farmlands brought a nice return on the money invested. The wealth generated chiefly in Amsterdam thus had an impact not only on city architecture but on agricultural development, as well as other ventures.

The Arts

Markets, houses and polders were not the only focus of the Dutch with excess money in the bank. The building spree in Amsterdam and other western cities also stimulated an unparalleled art market. Millions of paintings of all kinds of quality were sold in the Golden Age, and the flush of money drove up demand for high-quality works. Here, too, the new urban culture, less defined by conventional taste or by patterns of patronage dominated by

Church and nobility, stimulated artists to reinvent the way they worked. These artists included those who had fled from the south as well as an already well-developed network of artists born in the north. The extent of artistic talent and the strong demand for art from the 1590s onward encouraged an unprecedented specialization in painting, which in turn encouraged a high degree of innovation. Nor was this an Amsterdam-centered development, even though the city functioned as Europe's leading center where art was bought and sold. Utrecht and especially Haarlem were important sites of innovation, evidenced in the work of the famous Haarlem painter Frans Hals, who specialized in portraiture. Paulus Potter, famous for a large and extremely naturalistic study of a bull, specialized in animal "portraits." Characteristic of cityscape painting was the "Delft School," which soon included Jan Vermeer. Sometimes, provincial towns could be too small for aspiring artists: Govert Flinck, Jacob Backer and Abraham van den Tempel all left the provincial capital of Leeuwarden for Holland's greener pastures. The most famous painter of them all, Rembrandt van Rijn, moved from his home town of Leiden to Amsterdam in order to get closer to the big commissions, and achieved his greatest financial successes there in the 1630s and early 1640s, of which of course *The Night Watch* (1642), a group portrait of Amsterdam militia company officers, is the paramount example. The works of seventeenth-century masters were often, not surprisingly, oriented toward the world of the bourgeoisie who bought their work, as evidenced in the land-, sea- and cityscapes of the period, and many paintings were infused with deeper meaning. Reimaginings of the worlds of mythology or the Bible were also common themes undertaken by these artists.

The Bible was also an important if not exclusive theme of Joost van den Vondel, often to this day considered the greatest poet-playwright of the Netherlands. A prodigious spirit, he wrote twenty-six tragedies, of which the most famous was *Gijsbrecht van Aemstel*, its subject the ostensible enemy of Count Floris V and hero of Amsterdam. Vondel was part of the so-called Muider Circle, a group of artists and writers centered around the historian and poet P. C. Hooft, scion of a prominent regent family from Amsterdam. This "circle" of friends was just one informal expression of interactions between Dutch artists and literary luminaries, and also included the diplomat-musician Constantijn Huygens and the poet-jurist Jacob Cats, who topped out his career as pensionary of Holland. The poetry of both Cats and Huygens was often moralistic, though Cats had a less refined and more popular style intended to convey common-sense wisdom to ordinary people. Cats's *Marriage*, a popular volume from 1625, sought through verse to give a wide readership moral and religious instruction in matters of love and matrimony. Parallel to the arts, Dutch literature was bought and sold in great quantities and in all measures of quality, which together contributed to the distinctly literary voice of the northern Netherlands. Though the flourishing of painting in this period is best known abroad, Dutch literature, too, had its golden age.

Intellectual Developments and the Press

Intellectual life also thrived in the relatively free climate of the Republic. Because it had become a trade magnet and global emporium, it also became the center of new knowledge about the wider world, benefiting from the networks of knowledge that came through the VOC. The free climate also encouraged deeper reflection about the moral and political order. One theme that preoccupied intellectuals such as Grotius and Hooft was how to find, in the context of the impasse between disputing theological parties, a more reliable basis for knowledge. Combined with an enthusiasm in the Republic for technical innovation, this resulted in an emerging interest in rigorously scientific and mathematical modes of thinking. Copernican science, still controversial in the early seventeenth century, made good headway in the

Republic, and over time this would also prove to be true of the even more controversial ideas of the French mathematician and philosopher René Descartes, who spent most of his active intellectual life (1628–1649) in the Republic as it was politically safer than his own country. Though he denied it, Descartes came to his mechanistic understanding of matter through the influence of the Dutch intellectual Isaac Beeckman, and in turn it was in the Republic that his ideas quickly made inroads when they were published in the late 1630s. His work was vociferously opposed by Calvinist ministers and condemned by the University of Utrecht in 1641, and Descartes himself was badgered by local officials, compelling him to conclude that the Republic was not as free as he once thought. Nevertheless, his ideas found fruitful ground among many Dutch intellectuals in subsequent years.

This was made possible by the founding of universities in the northern Netherlands, which until 1575 – in contrast to surrounding regions – had had none of its own. Leiden, founded in that year, became the largest of Europe's Protestant universities, attracting many international students – roughly half of the total – not just for the traditional fields of theology and law but also the new sciences. Universities at Franeker (1585), Groningen (1614), Utrecht (1636) and Harderwijk (1648) added to the Republic's intellectual reputation, and this does not even count the so-called "Athenaea Illustre," institutions of higher learning that employed noted scholars and that were founded in cities such as Deventer and Amsterdam in the 1630s. And it should be added that the Dutch interest in practical science and knowledge was a passion that far exceeded the walls of these institutions.

Sustaining this cultural activity was a press that – within very wide margins – was free to publish all manner of content. Unlike the case in surrounding countries, there was no pre-censoring of books, prints or pamphlets, as there was no central authority to determine what could or could not be published. The availability of scores of printing presses in various towns – though nearly half of them were in Amsterdam – made it easy for motivated writers to publish their ideas. This freedom quickened the dissemination of scholarly thinking and made possible the discussion of serious issues, but it also made possible innumerable screeds and impudent broadsheets meant to name and shame enemies. Sometimes the free press of the Republic stimulated discussion and debate in the form of, for example, fictionalized dialogue, but the press could be used just as well to express the most unrestrained invective. The Republic may have made free discussion possible, but it was sometimes little more than a shouting contest. There were, at any rate, bounds to what the authorities would tolerate, for example disputing core Christian teachings such as the Trinity, or insulting political leaders; Vondel's play *Palamedes* (1625) ran foul of the censor and was banned for its barely concealed condemnation of Maurits for wrongly beheading Oldenbarnevelt, and later the Catholic playwright's *Lucifer* (1654) was prohibited for portraying angels and heaven onstage.

Open inquiry and the open exchange of ideas nevertheless characterized life in the Republic. And this generated, in the cities at least, a freethinking ethos that was not particularly fearful of authority, religious or secular.

Tolerance

A crucial part of this cultural dynamic, too, was the "everyday ecumenism" that characterized much of life in the Republic. In the large towns people lived and worked side by side, even as they knew who among their neighbors and fellow workers belonged to another faith. Though marriage to a person of another faith was widely condemned on all sides, conducting business with people of another persuasion was a common occurrence in a marketplace with strong interregional and international dimensions. Dutch artists for the most part painted whatever subject their patrons wanted, and oftentimes it mattered neither to the patron nor to the artist what the faith of the other was. Guilds or militias, at least in many towns, did not require membership of a particular church. *The Night Watch* depicted a militia with members of various religious backgrounds – painted, incidentally, by an artist with no known church affiliation. Though heartfelt commitment to toleration or emphatic religious indifference may account for this ecumenism – Descartes had believed the Dutch too focused on making money to care what he thought – it should be stressed that the degree of toleration depended on the local situation. The places where religious minorities were most numerous, and where commercial ties with diverse religious communities were most intense, were likely to be where religious tolerance, or outright religious indifference, was strongest, though there were exceptions to this rule.

It is not a coincidence that it was Amsterdam where both Lutherans – owing to migration from Germany and Scandinavia perhaps a sixth of Amsterdam's population by the end of the seventeenth century – and Jews were allowed publicly to build their own houses of worship. Neither group of "foreigners" was considered a threat to the public Church. These were concessions not typically granted elsewhere, or only considerably later, although Alkmaar, Haarlem and Rotterdam competed from the start with Amsterdam in offering residency to Jews, keen to take advantage of their lucrative trading networks. It might be added that freedom for Jews was at the same time not unlimited; in Amsterdam they could not marry Christians or have sexual relations with them (including prostitutes), and they could not proselytize, for example. Nevertheless, they might become citizens (*poorters*); as early as 1597 Emanuel Rodrigues Vega achieved this status. And Jews of influence and means often mingled freely with Christians, in trading relationships and in intellectual friendship. The Talmudic scholar Menasseh ben Israël was consulted and esteemed by Christian scholars for his knowledge of the Hebrew scriptures. There were no ghettoes in the Republic, as there were in other Jewish centers, such as Venice.

The limits of everyday ecumenism are well illustrated by the plight of the Catholics. Only in parts of Holland – most importantly in the larger towns – and the province of Utrecht, where Catholics were particularly numerous, was there a willingness among local magistrates to let them practice their faith just beneath the surface of public life. Here priests could celebrate mass in ornate robes in richly decorated house churches and travel freely from place to place. It was also in Holland and Utrecht that the Catholic population thrived in the early seventeenth century, benefiting in some cities from disaffected Remonstrants joining their ranks; from wealthy and influential patrons; and from the efforts of the Holland Mission orchestrated in the southern Netherlands, who sent priests and published devotional works for the population. Nevertheless, the number of available priests was small, and Catholic women known as *kloppen*, or "spiritual virgins," played an increasingly important role in organizing Catholic parochial life and pastoral care. In most parts of the remaining five provinces the Catholic population contracted, however, despite efforts by the Holland Mission to alter this situation. The maritime provinces of Friesland and Zeeland were particularly severe in their policies toward Catholics, and in the latter province they virtually disappeared as a community. The religious toleration of the Republic could be strikingly open, but it was not wholly unique – other regions in Europe developed parallel practices – and it was not evenly applied.

A Bourgeois Confidence

The vibrant cultural life of the Republic both reflected and further advanced the self-confidence of the Republic's middle class, and more particularly the well-to-do burghers who formed the ruling class of the towns. This self-confidence was obvious in the exuberant commercial culture of the Republic, which was only modestly restrained by religious injunctions against greed and speculation. The spectacular high point of this exuberance was the so-called "tulip mania" in the mid 1630s, when a single bulb could be sold for a few thousand guilders – the price of a fine house. In 1637 the tulip bubble suddenly burst, but zeal for money-making continued unabated. At the same time, they put their earned money to good use, and not only in the construction of canal houses or grand estates in the countryside. They financed public architecture to add luster to their well-run municipalities, and commissioned group portraits to highlight the fact that they took a collective responsibility for society. In contrast to surrounding countries, they were strikingly attentive to the needs of the poor and needy; not only did the municipalities and churches take care of the poor, but also hundreds of wealthy benefactors established almshouses, some with characteristic courtyards, where the worthy elderly might live out their lives with some modicum of comfort, or the mentally disabled find a home. Most charity came from voluntary gifts. This impulse was motivated by a felt responsibility for the poor, and at the same time by a desire to prevent the indigent from committing crimes and undermining the order and safety of the city. It also enhanced, as the great group portraits of the age did, the self-identity of the patrician elite as persons who were committed to the welfare of the city.

18   The Dutch created many institutions intended to help the poor. Just as men presided over men's almshouses, so, too, might women exercise authority over women's almshouses.

This confidence was not just felt by the men but by the women, who were also given some responsibilities in the running of institutions for orphans or widows. Foreign observers remarked on the equality of the sexes in the Republic, evidenced for example in the emphasis on a companionate marriage of two consenting parties. Dutch women seemed unfettered, as evidenced in their

19 Anna Maria van Schurman could only study at the university if a curtain shielded her off from the male students. But Dutch intellectuals widely and often praised her for her many talents.

literacy, in their direct manner toward men – they were sometimes portrayed as bossy – and in the social disapproval of violence toward women. Widows and daughters also sometimes took
over the businesses of their deceased husbands and fathers, and
like their English counterparts had strongly established economic
rights. Particularly noted was the control that women exercised
over household affairs, which gave them wide prerogatives but
was at the same time constraining. Anna Maria van Schurman,
accomplished artist and writer with command of ten languages,
made an eloquent public case for the ability and right of women
to study. But as the first woman in all of Europe to study at a
university (Utrecht) she remained an oddity and maintained her
own autonomous position only by rejecting the prospect of marriage. Though women's responsibilities were typically defined by
this single sphere of life, their apparent commitment to domestic
cleanliness and an ordered household advanced the pride and self-
esteem of the Republic's middle class. It was part of a wider self-
confidence that the propertied bourgeoisie of the Republic had
in their ability to manage their own affairs and their own institutions, without having to play second fiddle to Church or nobility.

The Darker Side of Life in the Golden Age

Seen from many angles, the seventeenth-century United
Netherlands, and Holland especially, was a wonder – a tiny
Republic that had pulled itself out of the morass and had become
the envy of Europe. Violent crime, though high by contemporary standards, was relatively low, with foreign visitors comment-
ing on the safety of both the countryside and the towns. Life was
well ordered, with canals offering comfortable hourly services to
towns across Holland. The Republic as a whole, and Holland in
particular, was decidedly the most prosperous region in Europe,
where every known commodity could be purchased and where
even the poor had enough to eat. Hunger riots were rare.

Life could, however, be anything but easy. Residents living through the first decades of the Republic endured exceptionally cold weather and short growing seasons, though the late 1630s brought a respite with warmer temperatures. Water management techniques had certainly improved, but after the 1630s the great land reclamation projects came mostly to an end, with additional bodies of water either too expensive or too difficult to polderize. The water was thus hardly vanquished as an enemy; the town of Reimerswaal, once one of Zeeland's most prominent towns but exposed and battered over the decades by fierce storms, was wholly evacuated by the 1630s before gradually disappearing under the waves. Some troublesome waters, such as the Biesbosch in southern Holland, lost to floods in the early fifteenth century, were too deep to be reclaimed, and continued in bad weather to threaten nearby towns such as Sliedrecht, where in winter the amassed ice floes easily punched holes in its dikes. Keeping Dutch feet dry thus remained a challenge, and death by drowning – children were frequent victims – was a common fate in a living environment surrounded by water.

Nearly everyone worked in the Republic, and this meant that hard physical work was a fact of life for most men, women and children, through which they aged rapidly. Food, though generally plentiful, was monotonous fare for the lower classes, and its lack of nutritional value rendered people vulnerable to disease. Plague would visit the country once every decade or two; towns might lose 15 to 20 percent of their populations when it did. Although Amsterdam's new canals may have been more healthful than the teeming streets and stinking waters of the Jordaan – such working-class areas of town were disproportionately afflicted by infectious diseases – no one was really safe from epidemics in the cities, where the lack of clean water and effective sanitation was a serious problem. Indeed, without a constant stream of immigrants to Dutch cities their high mortality rates would have caused them to lose population. As was the case across Europe, child mortality was high – less than half of all children born would live to become adults – and because of this fact average life expectancy in the Republic did not exceed forty years of age. Parents who witnessed the burial of all their children, and children who were orphaned at an early age, were common in all classes of society. Widows with children were the most numerous recipients of charity at Amsterdam's almshouses. In this world, where personal loss was common, people were expected to hold themselves together and not give in to emotions too long or too much, as difficult as everyone knew this was.

Death was the great equalizer in a society marked by economic contrast. The Golden Age was an age of plenty, but the wealth was also more unequally divided than ever before. Historical research indicates that the standard of living for a majority of the population in the Republic actually declined in early modern times, even if this lower standard was still high enough to attract masses of immigrants to the western towns. It is important to stress that urban elite sitting for individual or group portraits constituted only a very small segment of the city population. In Amsterdam, the well-to-do bourgeois, the shopkeepers and the craftspeople of the guilds were outnumbered by a majority of the population that lived in, or not far above, poverty. Even in good times the indigent in Amsterdam and other cities might constitute as much as 15 to 20 percent of the population. Many residents eked out a living as day-laborers for wages that offered no basis for financial security. Most of the immigrants to the towns of the western Netherlands were not well-connected merchants who made fortunes but bitterly poor laborers from the eastern parts of the Republic, or from Germany and Scandinavia. Many of them were not permanent residents but were seasonal laborers or sojourners who moved back home after a number of years. Though without their active presence the Republic's economy would have ground to a halt, they benefited little from the wealth generated. The same might be said of those who worked on board the ships from which the Republic grew rich; of the 300,000 who signed on for service on board the VOC's ships to the East Indies only 100,000 returned alive. One could fairly easily earn a living in the Republic, but living to a ripe old age was an entirely different proposition.

The Inland Provinces

It is impossible to write about the Dutch Republic in the seventeenth century without placing a good deal of emphasis on Holland and on Amsterdam. Both served as a magnet for trade in surrounding regions, and Holland's influence made itself felt across the expanse of the Republic – and beyond. For example, northern parts of Brabant became an integrated part of the Republic's economy, where workers, paid much less than in Holland, spun and weaved wool for the Leiden market. In return, Holland's goods, such as butter and salted fish, as well as overseas products, such as spices, entered Brabant. Vollenhove in western Overijssel stably provided peat for the ovens of Holland, thus becoming integrated into the trade and prosperity of the Republic's economy. Yet the Republic was not a unified whole economically or politically, and in crucial respects politics and society outside the Holland towns, or even the countryside, could be very different from the situation further south and east.

Compared to Holland, all of the remaining sovereign states were less urban – in some cases much less so. Friesland and Zeeland, with their maritime economies, were relatively prosperous, and their cities grew in the seventeenth century. This was not true of the inland provinces, where city life, including in the once dominant IJssel towns, stagnated or declined. By far the poorest of the provinces was Drenthe, which, because it possessed no towns of any significance and its population numbered perhaps no more than 20,000 of the Republic's estimated population of 1.8 million, was excluded from representation in the States-General. The political character of the inland states was different than in the West and in Friesland. The nobility played a more decisive role in politics in provinces such as Overijssel, where to be recognized as such they had to own an expansive estate replete with a house of sufficient allure – the so-called *havezaath*. Checked less by an assertive citizenry, the nobility could literally ride roughshod over the interests of local farmers. In some areas, such as Twente, serfdom persisted, though for want of labor the terms of perpetual servitude were relatively mild, and afforded protections not available to the free farmers of the region.

Without maritime dynamism urban society in the inland provinces was less open; in contrast to Amsterdam, the guilds of Utrecht were closed to newcomers, and the city forbade Jews to reside there, as was also true of the IJssel city of Deventer. At the same time, guilds in the east could be more insistent on asserting the traditional rights of its member-citizens, a legacy from medieval times that long had been weaker in Holland. Most of the inland provinces also became more thoroughly "confessionalized" by the Reformed Church. The public Church had more success in these areas where Catholics were more socially and economically isolated, and were more systematically excluded from the guilds in the towns. From Zeeland to Groningen, across most of Gelderland and Overijssel, the Reformed Church became the faith of the vast majority in the course of the seventeenth century, though the eastern parts of Gelderland and Overijssel that had long been under Spanish rule remained strongly Catholic. There the Catholic Reformation regained the loyalty of most inhabitants, with the Protestants unable to make more than a handful of converts.

The Generality Lands and the Catholic States of the Southeast

The strength of the Catholic Church was also evident in parts of Brabant brought under the control of the States-General. In the States of Brabant, too, the population remained under the influence of the Catholic Reformation, which had effectively reconnected with the population in the early seventeenth century. The

Republic, however, refused to allow public Catholic worship in this region, but here too there were variations. In lands held by the tolerant *stadhouders* Maurits and Frederik Hendrik, such as the barony of Breda, Catholics were given more latitude to practice their faith. The newly conquered Meijerij authorities, however, were stricter in cracking down on the Catholic population; as elsewhere, the bishop was barred from working in the area, though local priests were often allowed to say mass if Catholics paid authorities a fee. Nevertheless, Reformed congregations sprouted only in the larger towns, and the opening of Reformed churches was often actively resisted in the villages by a hostile Catholic population.

Variations in tolerance within the Republic can also be seen in the example of Protestant-run Limburg, where Catholics had more freedom, guaranteed as they were by international treaty to be allowed to practice their faith. In Maastricht, where the Republic formally shared power with the prince-bishop of Liège, Protestant and Catholic public worship were both allowed. Putting two faiths on the same formal footing as occurred in these parts of Limburg – a practice developed in a few other European cities – thus went further than the famed tolerance of Holland. And it was of course different from the religious situation in the Spanish Netherlands, where no tolerance existed for non-Catholics.

Even after the substantial expansion of the Republic under Frederik Hendrik, areas in the southeast part of the contemporary Netherlands continued to remain outside the formal bounds the Republic. Much of Limburg remained under direct control of the Habsburgs. But there were also Catholic principalities within the Holy Roman Empire that had never been swallowed by the Burgundians, the Habsburgs, or the Republic, and they maintained a fragile independence at the edges of the Republic. The most substantial of these was the land of Ravenstein, its chief town situated strategically along the Maas. States troops occupied it in 1621 and remained there even after the Catholic House of Palatinate-Zweibrücken-Neuburg took title to Ravenstein. Though a

Reformed church was built and put to use by the garrison, Catholics after 1630 had full freedom of worship, and multiple religious orders flourished there. A similar situation existed in the contested county of Megen, which, despite claims of the Republic, remained outside its jurisdiction. There, Franciscans who had been forced to leave Den Bosch founded a new monastery. The Free Imperial Lordship of Gemert remained an overwhelmingly Catholic part of the Holy Roman Empire, but after States troops temporarily occupied it in the years following 1647 it also had to allow Protestant worship. Other territories were wholly Catholic principalities. The smallest of these was the Imperial Abbey of Thorn; though little more than 50 km², this effectively autonomous state within the Holy Roman Empire was ruled by a collegiate order of noble-women who answered only to the emperor.

In short, the southeast of the current Netherlands in the mid seventeenth century was a patchwork of different regions and principalities, some directly ruled by the Republic, some by Spain and some remaining within the Holy Roman Empire, under the direct rule of local nobility. This made the region vulnerable to the conflicts among its various rulers, and the populations of some areas would suffer periodically through war.

The Atlantic and the Dutch Caribbean Islands

The Republic during this period, meanwhile, expanded its influence overseas. Building on the establishment of Fort Orange at present-day Albany in 1615, the WIC established New Netherland in 1624 when a handful of families settled at the mouth of the Hudson. Though the colony would continue to settle the Hudson Valley, the WIC never found enough colonists to settle there, in contrast to neighboring New England. A trade network that stretched from Europe to the Great Lakes was disrupted by the Dutch–Munsee wars, launched by eleven Munsee bands against Dutch expansion, which cost both sides hundreds of lives in the years after 1642. The colony's most famous governor, Pieter

Stuyvesant, appointed in 1647, did his best in New Amsterdam to restrict as much as possible the religious freedom of Jews, Lutherans and Quakers, despite public protest.

The most important of these Atlantic initiatives, however, was not New Netherland but the seizure from the Portuguese of Recife in Brazil in 1630. At a single stroke the Dutch monopolized Europe's sugar market. The Brazil conquest also made the Dutch interested, for the first time, in the African slave trade, since these slaves had long worked the sugar plantations for the Portuguese. Initially, the Dutch had opposed the enslavement of Christians – scores of baptized slaves from a Portuguese ship were freed in the harbor of Middelburg back in 1596 – but the new possibilities proved too lucrative for them to withstand. Having seized Elmina on the Gold Coast from the Portuguese in 1637, the WIC used this fortress as the center of its African slave trade.

20   Elmina, in what is now Ghana, is the oldest of the many slave forts along the African coast. Slaves would be held in impossibly small cells in the fort before they crossed the Atlantic.

In search of transit harbors between the Republic and Brazil, the Dutch scouted the Caribbean for new bases, seizing, between 1631 and 1648, the six Caribbean islands that are now part of the Kingdom of the Netherlands. All of them were sparsely populated: the Caiquetios had inhabited the arid Leeward Antillian Islands (Aruba, Bonaire and Curaçao) – at the closest point just 25 km off the South American coast – from about the year 1000. By the time the Spanish arrived around 1500 the Carib had displaced the Arawak in the more northerly and wetter Leeward Islands (which include the islands of Saba, St. Eustatius and St. Maarten). In the sixteenth century the Spanish had largely deported the remaining Native Americans, already reduced by disease and slavery, from these islands, though a few remained, particularly on Aruba. The Spanish, unable to turn a profit on these islands, did not, for the most part, heavily contest the Dutch seizure of them. St. Maarten, with its salt pans, was the only one over which they fought; Stuyvesant lost his right leg to a Spanish cannon ball in a 1644 Dutch effort to retake the island. The salt pans of St. Maarten and Bonaire gave the Dutch a new supply with which to preserve their fish. An island such as tiny Saba attracted few settlers, few slaves and only a handful of plantations. It was Curaçao that would turn out to be the most important of the six; it possessed an excellent deep-water harbor, and later in the century it became a vital link in the Dutch slave trade. Sephardic Jewish families, initially from Iberia, then moving to the Republic and later to Dutch Brazil, established themselves on Curaçao in the 1650s, the beginning of a small but significant Jewish presence in the Dutch Caribbean.

Asian Developments

In Asia, the story of Dutch success was more marked than in the Atlantic. As noted above, the Dutch quickly dominated the

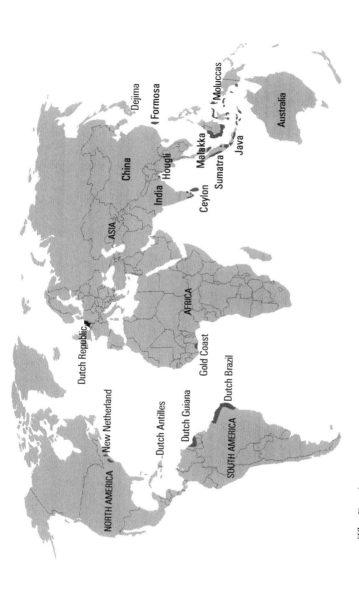

9 The Dutch overseas empire, as imposed on a modern map. Though often using force to assert their trading emporium, the Dutch also depended on local rulers, as at Dejima in Japan.

Moluccan spice trade. Initially, however, the VOC was at a disadvantage, because though Europeans eagerly bought Asian spices, there was little, other than precious metals, that Asian traders wanted in return. Since carrying bullion to the East Indies had serious drawbacks, the only other option was for the Dutch to develop their own intra-Asia trade network. In 1619 Jan Pietersz. Coen of the VOC established the trading center christened "Batavia" on the northwest tip of Java to serve as the center of this trading network. From this center the Dutch further expanded their commercial network to Sumatra, and across the Indian Ocean to Bengal and Ceylon. Though Chinese ports remained closed to their ships, the VOC developed a strong presence on the island of Taiwan, from where they traded intensively with the Chinese mainland. Exporting Japanese silver was the chief way to pay for Chinese goods such as silk, for example, and so developed a complex intra-Asia market that included some twenty chief ports. This network expanded in size and profitability in the first decades of the seventeenth century and made the VOC the leading trading power in the region. That position was cemented by special privileges and outright monopolies; after 1641, for example, the Dutch were the only trading power, albeit under the tightest of restrictions, allowed to trade with Japan and its xenophobic government.

As in the first years of Dutch trade in Asia, the VOC's continued commercial success depended on the ruthless marginalization or elimination of the competition. Dutch relations with the Bandanese, begun to obtain their nutmeg, had been bad from the start, with other European powers such as the English offering the inhabitants more than the Dutch could. After a series of escalating massacres on both sides Coen put an end to Bandanese resistance in 1621, butchering, enslaving or expelling from the Banda islands most of the population of perhaps 15,000. Dutch military efforts sometimes aimed at driving out rival European powers, but in the process drew in local populations, as in the drive to expel the

Portuguese from Ceylon. The Dutch also placed restrictions on trade with other Asian or European powers, forcing their ships to buy their products in Batavia. Some Asian trading networks, such as those run by the Chinese – who themselves became the chief residents of Batavia – maintained their own autonomy, but the VOC had rapidly become a dominant trading force in the region. Newcomers to the scene only shortly before, the Dutch eclipsed the Spanish and the Portuguese in East Asia and, for the time being, kept the French and English at bay. Until the mid eighteenth century, the Dutch would be the most important players in the region.

Toward a European Peace

With their power declining, and facing revolts in Italy and in Iberia, by the 1640s the Habsburgs had little interest in continuing the war against the Dutch Republic. In alliance with France against Spain since 1635, the Republic scored modest successes, in its last victory seizing the walled town of Hulst in 1645, solidifying its presence in the States-Flanders, on the south side of the Schelde River. If the Spanish were now resolved to make peace, the Republic was less sure. Most of the provinces and most of the cities of Holland were, to be sure, in favor of peace, given the costs of the war. Frederik Hendrik, once keen to conquer large swaths of the Habsburg Netherlands, associated himself with the peace party. But Zeeland, Utrecht, and the Holland towns of Haarlem and Leiden – all Calvinist bulwarks at the time – were afraid that Catholicism would again become a threat if peace came. They slowed the process toward a settlement. Bogging down the negotiations, too, was the fact that not only Spain and the Republic but multiple powers were seeking a comprehensive peace for the wars being fought in the Holy Roman Empire. Making peace thus involved many parties with widely divergent interests – the Spanish king; many German princes; the Swedes; and not least the French, who had benefited most from the warfare of the past thirty years and were particularly keen to press their advantage. For this reason negotiations, begun in the early 1640s, took years to bear fruit. Only in 1648 did several treaties in the Westphalian towns of Münster and Osnabrück formally bring an end to a range of conflicts, the first of these being the Peace of Münster between Spain and the Dutch Republic.

In this treaty the Spanish recognized the Dutch Republic as a sovereign state, as well as its trading companies, the East and West India Companies. It also confirmed the Republic as a Calvinist state, and its right to pursue its own religious policies. This mattered for domestic policy: only after the treaty did the Republic move decisively to Protestantize regions such as the Meijerij, confiscating and closing the 300 churches and cloisters in the region.

21   The Treaty of Münster of 1648, celebrated here, was part of a broader Westphalian peace that established longstanding rules for respecting the sovereignty of independent states.

Through the treaty the Republic thus made use of the principles of territorial integrity and the non-interference in the internal affairs of other states that were established in this Westphalian settlement. It also brought peace that was, in hindsight, but a brief reprieve. Spain may have been vanquished as a dangerous foe, and the Republic's right to exist may no longer have been questioned, but old allies would soon threaten the Republic again.

"True Freedom" at Home, Rising Troubles Abroad, 1648–1672

Constitutional Crisis

Just as the Twelve Year's Truce had given space for internal conflicts within the Republic, the Peace of Münster triggered a new political crisis in the Dutch body politic. Frederik Hendrik had been an able statesman, but his formal say in the appointment of many town and provincial officers was a substantial check on local autonomy. Many leaders of Holland, moreover, had viewed his increasingly dynastic pretensions with unease. He expensively refurbished several of his estates, began building the splendid summer palace Huis ten Bosch just outside The Hague, and entertained as lavishly as a king might. Though arranged to serve the Republic's interests in keeping England friendly, the 1641 marriage of his son Willem to the ten-year-old Mary Stuart, daughter of King Charles I, further enhanced the Oranges' status to that of near-monarchs. When Frederik Hendrik died in 1647, his son, Willem II, as he now became known, was determined to further the family's dynastic ambitions. And in decided contrast with his father, he meant to fulfill this mission by taking the Republic to war, preferably against Spain.

Willem found fertile ground for his plans. Some Dutch had reason to be discontent with the peace. In addition to the strongly anti-Catholic agenda of the Calvinists, discontent stemmed from economic malaise; the end of the war had damaged Zeeland economically by opening up the Flemish ports, and the reduction of the army in eastern garrison towns hit the local economies hard. Bad harvests made the population additionally restive. But it was military policy and not economics that lay at the root of a new constitutional crisis. Most but not all cities in Holland wanted further troop reductions, and proponents of Holland's sovereign rights believed that when it stopped paying the bills, which the States of Holland did in the summer of 1650, the troops in its pay should be disbanded. Proponents of the *stadhouder* believed, in contrast, that the Republic required a military leader who stood above the provinces and made the chief military decisions, including troop levels. The Dutch pamphlet press furiously debated this issue.

Despite the power in Holland of Amsterdam, Dordrecht and other opponents of a strong *stadhouder*, Willem II had considerable influence in most of the other provinces, in some of the Holland towns and among the orthodox Calvinist population, and he made secret plans with his cousin, the *stadhouder* of Friesland, Willem Frederik van Nassau-Dietz, for a coup d'état. Taking power into his own hands, he intimidated the Holland towns that had voted for troop reductions, arrested six of his most prominent opponents and imprisoned them in Loevestein, and – most spectacularly – sent a 10,000-man army to take Amsterdam by stealth. Dense fog caused his army to lose its way, and Amsterdam, alerted to its coming, closed the city gates on time. Though Amsterdam had escaped occupation, Willem's military posturing forced Holland to reconsider its troop position. When Holland conceded to maintain the levels he wanted it looked as if he had won the contest for power. His success, and that of the Orangist cause, were, however, short-lived; Willem II died of smallpox in November of 1650. And though his wife Mary Stuart gave birth to a son eight days after his death, a sudden power vacuum at the center of the Republic had opened up.

Ruling without a Stadhouder

Holland was not slow in taking every advantage from this wholly unexpected situation. It quickly decided that the position of *stadhouder* for the province of Holland would remain indefinitely open. Though Willem Frederik of Friesland managed now to become additionally *stadhouder* of Groningen and Drenthe as well, Holland worked behind the scenes to check further Orangist influences. Ultimately, all of the remaining provinces followed Holland in not appointing a *stadhouder*. At the Great Assembly held in 1651 – a special meeting of the States-General along with other provincial delegates to decide crucial constitutional questions – it was Holland's agenda that prevailed in other areas as well. Holland blocked admittance of Drenthe and Brabant to the States-General in order to maintain its own preponderance. The Assembly further determined, in line with Holland's wishes, that each province was to finance its own share of the army and that the Reformed Church was to continue to be organized along provincial and not national lines, thus denying it additional status and power. Provinces – and each of the quarters and larger towns within them – could thus enjoy "true freedom," as it was called, to manage their own affairs. In practice, this arrangement most benefited Holland and its chief city, Amsterdam, whose economic dominance could now freely translate itself into more political influence over the Republic.

More than ever, then, the successful functioning of the Republic depended on strongly decentralized political arrangements, which in the mid seventeenth century was contrary to the strongly centralizing tendencies that led to absolutist states in France and in Scandinavia. And at the local level, at least in the towns, the Republic was generally well ruled. In some towns, perhaps half of those in the various city councils possessed law degrees, a sign of their professional commitment to administration. Local magistrates, in dispensing justice, though informed by the class justice of the day, could be strikingly judicious in their decisions. The effective running of municipal institutions such as orphanages and schools was considered a badge of honor – and a stepping stone to a higher position if done well. Needless to say, the local water boards were considered an important task that could not be neglected. A whole host of local citizens, some of them unpaid, oversaw the administration of local government. Living in close proximity to residents, officials usually took the many petitions of the common people seriously. Moreover, guilds and militias, proud of their own contribution to the wealth and prestige of the city, were an important civic force, taking care of their own members, defending the city and organizing town festivals. In these crucial respects, many towns in the Republic enjoyed high standards of government and civic participation.

Yet the merits of local republican government, aspiring to harmony and serving the common good as it was, should not be idealized and be held to contemporary standards. Bribery and extortion were illegal and considered unethical, but local officials also saw their offices as a way to make money from fees and excises they were authorized to collect, to help get their friends and family members ahead, and to increase their influence at the expense of their rivals. Sheriffs, for example, could easily pocket money from detained persons in exchange for not hauling them into court. The most important councils of government, moreover, were effectively reserved for patrician families, though a handful of highly successful newcomers might make their way to the top. Formal political decision-making was thus reserved for the very few. Factionalism between rival groups at the municipal or provincial level could be bitter and long-lasting, and one faction might, in an escalated conflict, whip up the local public to take up its side.

No self-respecting patrician of the "true freedom" seriously entertained anything remotely resembling democratic government. On the contrary, in the wealthy towns of the west the city militias and guilds lost influence in the Golden Age as rich patricians behaved more and more exclusively, gradually shutting those under them out of power. Though the role of militias and guilds in political appointments remained stronger in the poorer towns of the east it was different in Holland. To be sure, in Hoorn the magistrates still had to be chosen from a section of the citizenry and in Dordrecht from among the guilds, but in most of Holland's towns the magistrates were an almost wholly self-sustaining in-group, only occasionally allowing in wealthy parvenus. Sometimes it required riots before popular grievances were addressed by town rulers, and pro-Orangist, anti-elitist ideology often served as the popular ideological bedrock of local discontent. Violent threats against local magistrates were hardly unknown, and local officials could never entirely discount the possibility that their houses might be plundered by angry residents eager to exact rough justice for a perceived wrong. Town oligarchies, sometimes in rivalry with each other, remained largely in control of local Dutch politics, but it was always prudent for them to rule well enough to prevent public opposition.

The Rise of Johan De Witt

Taken as whole, Holland – and thus the Republic by extension – was led in the period of "true freedom" by an exceptional political talent, Johan de Witt, who became pensionary of Holland in 1653. From the rather anti-Orangist and influential town of Dordrecht, he was the son of a prominent regent who had been briefly imprisoned by Willem II in 1650. From the outset – he was only twenty-seven when appointed to his high position – De Witt demonstrated his abilities. A wide-ranging intellectual and talented mathematician who possessed a thorough grasp of the issues facing the Republic – he later used his skills to calculate better probabilities for paying out state life annuities – De Witt tirelessly employed his office and his political skills to direct both domestic and foreign affairs. Though his personal integrity stood

22   The brothers De Witt, commemorated here in the year of their deaths, came from a town and a family opposing the Oranges. Their father, Jacob, had been a prisoner of Willem II in 1650.

out in his day by his refusal to take gifts beyond the occasional meal, he knew the value of favors in keeping the Republic together. Together with his older brother Cornelis, a high admiralty official and the regent of Putten, he controlled much of the patronage in Holland – and across parts of the Republic. Through this the De Witts built up a vast network of associates who conveyed to them vital news from every corner of the country.

It helped the De Witts that most of the other provinces, partly because of the lack of a *stadhouder*, were badly wracked by internal tensions, forcing them to take all the more account of Holland's leadership in the Republic. In Overijssel, the States could not agree on how to divide the lucrative functions available in the province, and it came close to civil war, with Zwolle and Kampen bombarding the recalcitrant town of Hasselt in 1657 for its refusal to pay taxes to the contested *drost* (bailiff). Here, as elsewhere in the Republic, Johan de Witt was able to serve as intermediary and help defuse the conflict.

Deeply committed to the principle of the provincial sovereignty that so benefited Holland, De Witt was aided by his close and cordial ties to the powerful Bicker–De Graeff clan of Amsterdam, marrying into the family in 1655. In such a formidable coalition, De Witt's position as leader of the Republic soon became unassailable, a position recognized by foreign leaders. Even at the height of his power, though, De Witt had to take account of a powerful undercurrent of Orangist loyalties whose proponents were ready to oppose him whenever the opportunity arose. Even a figure as able as De Witt was unable to undo the persistent factionalism that characterized the Republic's politics.

Trouble with the English

The English had been sometime allies of the Dutch Republic since Elizabethan days, but they had also been trading rivals for a long time, occasionally sparring with the Dutch in Asia and in the Atlantic. Orangist support for the House of Stuart during the English Civil War had also placed tensions on the relationship. But the deepest source of tension lay in Dutch trade primacy. At mid century, the Dutch merchant marine was larger than all of the other European fleets combined, and its entrance into the Spanish colonial markets after the peace of 1648 only further increased its leading position. The fact that the Dutch had a more extensive and efficient network and – in contrast to the English – could sell their products without paying taxes and duties, made Dutch-bought goods cheaper, edging out English skippers even when they traded between England and English North America. English frustration went hand-in-hand with London's rising maritime ambitions, and it was powerfully tempted to take some trade away from the

Dutch. It was this incipient protectionism, first in England and later in France, that would ultimately undermine Dutch commercial supremacy, dependent as it was on free trade.

An additional source of tension was the failed commonwealth between England and the Netherlands, along the lines of the Anglo-Scottish pact of the seventeenth century. The prospect of a close relationship between England and the Republic dawned when Oliver Cromwell, having beheaded Charles I and instituted a Calvinist Commonwealth, sought political union with the Dutch. He did so on the basis of vague expressions of Dutch interest in the past, when Holland had sought an ally against the *stadhouder*. Cromwell's proposal was grandiose: England would cede all of Asia and Africa to Dutch trading interests in exchange for their help in the English military conquest of the Americas. The Dutch, unwilling to be yoked to England in such a risky venture, demurred, and Cromwell, offended, let the English Parliament find ways to reduce the trading dominance of England's chief commercial rival. This resulted in the passage of the Navigation Act of 1651, which determined that goods entering England could only be brought by English ships or by the country of origin. Though the Act cut off only a small portion of total Dutch trade, it was intended to damage the Dutch, and London now aimed at provoking The Hague into open conflict. The Commonwealth Navy and English privateers boarded and seized scores of Dutch ships suspected of breaking the Act. By July of 1652 the English and the Dutch were formally at war.

Neither side was prepared for armed conflict, and it went badly for both, though worse for the Dutch. The Dutch naval presence was more widely distributed than that of the English, and Dutch ships drove the English out of the Baltic and the Mediterranean, seas important for English trade. In the North Sea, however, the English were superior. The Dutch navy, divided into five regional admiralties, lacked a centralized command. Moreover, it suffered from the fact that the Republic had down-sized its navy in the wake of the Westphalian Peace – precisely at a time when Cromwell's navy had been built up to fight the royalists in the civil war. By 1652, England's best ships outclassed in size and armament anything the Republic could bring against them, and the merchant vessels, hastily armed by the Dutch in order to fight the war, were no match for English warships. By June of 1653 the English succeeded in blockading much of the Republic's coast, practically eliminating the trading and fishing so essential for its economy. Hunger and economic collapse generated calls for the return of the Oranges. Under Admiral Maarten Tromp, the Dutch navy sailed out and engaged the Commonwealth Navy in the Battle of Scheveningen in August of 1653. Though the intrepid Tromp was killed by an English sharpshooter and the Dutch lost ten ships, the English fleet was damaged enough that it abandoned its blockade. Even before the Battle of Scheveningen both sides began negotiating over possible peace terms.

The damaging effects on English trade aside, it was in Cromwell's interest to make peace with the anti-Orange States party, now led by De Witt, and prevent them from losing political control over the Republic. Mary Stuart, daughter of the decapitated king and mother to the toddler son of Willem II, resided in The Hague and had assembled a coterie of Stuart and Orangist supporters. It was vital for Cromwell's own regime that this group not be allowed to gain power and spread their influence from their base in Holland. Partly for this reason negotiations continued apace, resulting in the Treaty of Westminster in April of 1654.

Though the peace basically kept things as they were before the outbreak of war, it contained one highly controversial – and initially secret – annex. Without the knowledge of the negotiators of the States-General, two delegates of the States of Holland, at De Witt's instruction, pledged to Cromwell that the young Willem of Orange would never become *stadhouder* in Holland, or hold any high office in the Republic. Most of the other provinces would never have countenanced this proposal, and many delegates from the States-General were outraged when they heard of it. But the measure passed, against the will of the Orangist cities in Holland and the States of Holland, and De Witt coolly defended the Act of Seclusion, as it was called, on the grounds that it did not bind the Republic as a whole but only Holland. In so doing, De Witt and Cromwell dealt a serious blow to the hopes of the Orange–Stuart dynasty, at least for the moment.

De Witt's Foreign Policy

The war with England did not long repress Dutch domination of the seas; to the contrary, the Dutch were free again further to expand their pre-eminent position. To be sure, there were losses. The Kingdom of Portugal, benefiting from an uprising of Portuguese planters in Dutch Brazil, drove the Dutch out of Recife in 1654 – a painful symbolic defeat for the Republic and a serious economic loss to the WIC, whose sugar-driven profits depended on the Brazilian plantations. At the same time, the VOC was successful in taking the western coast of Ceylon from the Portuguese, already weakened by the Kandyan kingdom, by 1658, thus effectively gaining a chokehold over the world cinnamon market. Dutch relations with Rajasimha, king of Kandy, remained tense, however, and in 1664 a long war between the two parties began that ended in a further consolidation of VOC control over southwestern Ceylon.

De Witt's own vision of foreign policy was shaped in part by the experiences of the Anglo-Dutch War. He was not inattentive to what happened at the land borders of the Republic; in the 1650s he tried – without success, it might be added – to intervene in Münster in order to weaken its zealous bishop, who had known territorial designs on Gelderland and Overijssel. But his decided focus was on naval power that would protect the Republic's – and especially Holland's – economic interests. He took an active and personal role in centralizing the Admiralties' command structure. He pushed through the extensive naval construction program for some sixty new warships that supplanted the Republic's obsolescent reliance on armed merchantmen; in the 1660s another sixty would be added. Crucially, Holland and Amsterdam were willing to pay most of the costs – not surprising, given how much their economies depended upon the protection such a force provided.

To promote Dutch commercial and maritime interests De Witt pursued a foreign policy that tried to remain as free from foreign entanglements as possible – entanglements that might bog down the Republic in European territorial conflicts. But this effort at neutrality did not mean that the Dutch refrained from militarily intervening if the Republic's seaborne interests were at stake. De Witt, seeing the Baltic trade, with its grain and wood, as the most important lifeline of the Republic's economy, boldly stepped in to prevent a surging Sweden from taking over the Baltic coast and possibly restricting Dutch traffic there. In November of 1658 a Dutch fleet, after waiting for advantageous winds, successfully attacked an equally powerful Swedish force in the Danish Sound just off Copenhagen, relieving the Danish capital from a siege by driving the Swedish fleet into the Baltic. In restoring a rough balance of power in the Sound between a weaker Denmark and a stronger Sweden it also ensured that the Sound remained open to Dutch shipping.

De Witt also put an end to older conflicts. He made peace with Portugal, controversially conceding the loss of Brazil. And in 1661 he attained a favorable agreement for the Republic with Spain over the contested lands of the Overmaas, in which significant areas of Limburg, including towns such as Heerlen and Valkenburg, were placed under the Republic's control. In conformity with post-1648 religious settlements, the Catholic population retained freedom of worship, and in a few villages Protestants and Catholics were compelled, if rather uncomfortably, to share the same church building.

The Republic's territory, 1661
Spanish Guelders
Northern boundary of the Generality Lands
Boundary of the Republic
Regional boundaries

AMELAND
STAD EN LANDE
Dokkum
Groningen
Leeuwarden
Harlingen
FRIESLAND
Sneek
DRENTHE
Stavoren
Coevorden
Medemblik
Enkhuizen
Alkmaar
Hoorn
Kampen
Zwolle
Haarlem
Harderwijk
OVERIJSSEL
Amsterdam
Deventer
Enschede
Leiden
Zutphen
UTRECHT
The Hague
HOLLAND
GELDERLAND
Gouda
Utrecht
Delft
Arnhem
Den Briel
Rotterdam
Gorinchem
Nijmegen
Dordrecht
'Den Bosch
ZEELAND
STATES-BRABANT
Middelburg
Breda
Gelder
Tilburg
SPANISH
GUELDERS
STATES-FLANDERS
Antwerpen
FLANDERS
PRINCE-BISHOPRIC
OF LIÈGE
BRABANT
Maastricht
STATES-LIMBURG
Brussels
Aachen
LIMBURG
Liège
HAINAUT

10   The Dutch Republic after 1661, including the Generality Lands.
Some parts of the Netherlands, including large sections of the southeast,
remained outside its authority.

The High Water Mark of Dutch Culture

The Republic's continued ascendancy in global trade generated, in the 1650s and 1660s, an unprecedented wealth that easily surpassed the standards of the earlier part of the century, when war had dampened economic activity. The same period marked, at least as measured in hindsight, the high point of Dutch "Golden Age" culture, when many of its most exuberant expressions came into being. The Netherlands had taken a large role in international science, as evidenced in the field of optics. The mathematician and astronomer Christiaan Huygens developed a telescope that could observe and explain the rings around Saturn. And later Antoni van Leeuwenhoek improved the microscope so much that he has been hailed as the father of microbiology. Both of them were internationally active.

In addition to even more splendid canal homes and monumental country estates – before 1648 the prospect of invasion made investment in landed houses seem a bit risky – much of the new artistic impulse went into enhancing the civic pride of the city. The impulse to show off one's own town was expressed in the decision of local regents to pay commissions to artists from their own towns rather than hiring them from elsewhere; indeed, it was civic pride that sustained artistic accomplishment in Holland towns such as Delft or, outside Holland, Middelburg and Utrecht. Naturally, it was Amsterdam that had the most money and the most pretensions, lavishing its public spaces with expensive new buildings. The landmark building of the whole period across the breadth of the Republic was the new Amsterdam town hall, designed by Jacob van Campen and completed in 1665. Unusually large by Dutch standards, Van Campen's perfectly balanced classicism conceived of the town hall as a microcosm of God's creation, and Vondel waxed rhapsodically on the hall being the center of the Republic's great imperium of peace. Nor were the town hall's impressive features merely external; Italian marble floors and impressive paintings by the town's greatest masters were proudly on display.

Such enterprises took place on a smaller scale across the Republic, and encouraged the close collaboration of architecture, painting and other decorative arts to bedazzle the patrons and the citizens. Not all painters benefited from the change in taste; Rembrandt, perhaps the most versatile of the country's painters and continually changing his own style, was written off as a difficult man and an artistic has-been by the 1650s, and his choice at that time for a broad-brush approach ran contrary to the predominant preference for refined detail. He died, in at best modest circumstances, in 1669. Compared to earlier in the century, Dutch paintings – which at the time began to enjoy an international reputation – made use of brighter, more expensive colors and were renowned for their portrayal of light, as seen in the Delft painter Johannes Vermeer. While some painters specialized in

23 The son of tavern owners, Jan Steen's paintings often show his deep familiarity with everyday life. The intent of this painting, though, was to offer warnings of its excesses.

dreamy Italian landscapes for private homes, it was cityscapes and seascapes – the latter the specialty of the Van de Velde family – that were intended for public buildings, to emphasize the greatness of their patrons. As befitted a period without a *stadhouder*, the themes praised the benefits of republican government, a form of government that had manifestly brought so much freedom and so much prosperity to its virtuous inhabitants.

Debating the Contours of Dutch Society

But was the Republic virtuous enough? Outsiders considered the population generally to be well disciplined, especially in the towns. Dutch women dressed chastely and students, well-monitored in their studies, drank less than their German counterparts. Brothels were carefully camouflaged so as to avoid public offense. The Republic's rambunctious discussion culture, though often acrimonious, disciplined people to deal with difference in non-violent ways. The Reformed Church, and to a lesser extent the non-privileged churches, played a role in disciplining the population, but the question at that time remained whether all this was sufficient. The Republic was also a freewheeling society where all manner of ideas spread easily and where people frequently questioned authority, starting with children, whom foreigners considered saucy and impolite. Everyone had a different view of how freedom and order could best be balanced in this highly dynamic society.

The spiritual successors of the Arminians in the town councils, the so-called "flexibles," or libertines, strongly discouraged political challenges to their elite position, and they possessed little enthusiasm for additional moral or theological reforms in society. They did not want to cede too much influence to the pastors of the Reformed Church or to pursue policies that practically would be difficult to enforce, and they frequently resisted the more stringent theological and moral demands of this church. Some

197

among the flexible party, the most outspoken of them the textile manufacturer Pieter de la Court, were anticlerical republicans and principled champions of religious tolerance, vehemently opposed to the return of the *stadhouder* and the political Orangism cherished by many Reformed clergy. A few of them symphathized with antidogmatic groups such as the Collegiants, who espoused a universal Christendom that would transcend all religious difference. At the radical outer edges of this coalition were a handful of political and religious radicals, including, most famously today, Baruch de Spinoza, of whom more will be said later.

Opposing the "flexibles" was the stalwart orthodox wing of the Reformed Church, particularly proponents of the so-called Further Reformation, who were heavily influenced by the English Puritans. Although these "precisianists" were primarily interested in the inward conversion of hearts, they believed that this could only be effected if the government fulfilled its responsibility by imposing biblical norms on society and properly turning the Netherlands into a Second Israel. Transforming Sunday into a rest day, punishing cohabitation and adultery, rooting out "false" religion, and banning theater as a godless "vanity" were among their aims. In pursuing these aims they did, at least in the long run, have an influence on public life; Dutch theater performed risqué Spanish works but was likely less bawdy than elsewhere, and strict laws prohibiting work on Sunday were eventually implemented. The sweeping "precisianist" vision of bringing all of Dutch society into conformity with Reformed doctrine and piety, however, could not be achieved, and Reformed pastors were often frustrated by the unwillingness of local magistrates to implement their demands. Frustration with the lack of spiritual rebirth led small groups of individuals, including Anna Maria van Schurman, to withdraw decisively from sinful society and from a flawed Church into small sects and "conventicles." Van Schurman became a leading figure of the Labadists, one of the more radically separatist groups. For radicals on both sides of the religious divide, the religious and political order of the Republic was a source of deep discontent.

Closer to the ideological center of the Republic, too, political anger could be fiercely expressed. Public debate between the "flexibles" and the "precisianists" mounted in the late 1650s and 1660s, and the theological conflict had much to do with the continuing and intensifying political debate over the place of the young prince of Orange in Republic, and the repercussions his position would have for military and foreign policy.

The Orangist Challenge and a New War

The Restoration of royal government in England under Charles II in 1660 changed the political equation in the Dutch Republic. Charles was the uncle of the prince of Orange, and in order to placate the new monarch it seemed necessary for De Witt to show the king's nephew greater regard. In 1660 the States of Holland took it upon themselves to educate the nine-year-old prince for high, if carefully unspecified, office, with De Witt later personally giving him lessons in the affairs of state. In keeping the boy's future unclear De Witt at the same time hoped to head off within the Republic the hopes of the Orangists, whose aspirations had been rekindled by Charles's support.

Contrary to the desire of Holland and Zeeland, whose maritime interests were best served by good relations with the English, relations with London did not improve, the half-hearted alliance of 1662 notwithstanding. English and Dutch global interests simply competed too much, in East Asia, along the West African coast and in the Americas. The slave trade between Africa and the Caribbean was one such area of competition. English encouragement of the Orangist cause in the Republic, meant to put pressure on De Witt for trade concessions, failed. English attacks on Dutch shipping, in which scores of vessels were lost, occurred with increasing frequency, and in 1664 an English naval force under the duke of York seized New Amsterdam, its governor Stuyvesant unable to offer effective resistance. By 1665, this led to an open declaration of war between the two states.

The new war initially showed the military weaknesses of the Republic. Its naval forces were in far better shape than they had been in 1652, but the English navy too had continued to improve and they remained the largest military fleet, with firepower that could still outshoot the Dutch. The monumental Battle of Lowestoft in June of 1665, considered by some the greatest naval defeat in Dutch history in which the flagship *Eendragt* exploded with nearly all hands lost, showed that the Dutch navy was outgunned and, moreover, insufficiently trained. Moreover, in August of 1666 the English fleet destroyed some 150 merchant ships anchored in the Vlie, burning the nearby town of West-Terschelling in the process. To make matters worse, the bishop of Münster, Christoph Bernhard, invaded the Republic from the east, driving home his old claims to Borculo in eastern Gelderland and meaning to free the region's Catholics from persecution. The armies of the eastern provinces were wholly inadequate to check his advance, and affirmed that the land forces of the Republic, lacking good fortifications, sufficient numbers and effective leadership, were no longer able to carry out their defensive duties.

In the course of 1666, however, the Dutch were able to retake the initiative, albeit with foreign help. The bishop was forced to retreat after the Dutch made use of their alliance treaty with the French in 1662. King Louis XIV sent 6,000 soldiers to drive out the Münsterites, though the behavior of the marauding French soldiers prompted the inhabitants of Gelderland and Overijssel to wonder if they were any better off with the French than with the pillagers from whom they had just been rescued. On sea and against the English the new commanding admiral, Michiel de Ruyter, did enough damage to the English fleet to drive them home for repairs – repairs that the English king, strapped for money, could not afford to pay. New peace negotiations began, and when Charles dragged his feet De Witt ordered his brother Cornelis to undertake a daring raid in June of 1667 against the English fleet, harbored deep along the River Medway, just 50 km east of London. The raid was spectacularly successful, the Dutch sinking three capital ships and hauling the flagship *Royal Charles* back home. This coup sped the signing of the Peace of Breda in July, in which the Dutch pushed only modest demands, such as their insistence that they keep the potential sugar colony of Surinam in exchange for the English keeping New Netherland, which they now called New York. With the English chastened and peace proclaimed, De Witt and the Republic had reached the pinnacle of prestige and power.

A New and Looming Danger

In reality, though, the security of the Republic was already eroding. Louis XIV launched an invasion, to Dutch concern, of the now weakly held Spanish Netherlands, the Dutch now regarding the region as a welcome barrier against a powerful France. De Witt, although not eager to antagonize the French, nevertheless made the Republic signatory to the Triple Alliance of 1668 with England and Sweden as a way to force France to conclude peace with Spain. It also included a secret clause that committed the Republic to attack the French should Louis XIV not make peace. The English king, Charles II, soon shared this secret clause with an outraged Louis, who felt betrayed by the Dutch – still formally his allies. Both Louis and Charles, smarting from the Medway loss, had personal reasons to wreak vengeance on the Republic, just as both of their countries stood to benefit from a weakening of Dutch trading dominance. By the late 1660s, Paris, following London's example, had begun imposing anti-Dutch trade policies, in Paris's case through the introduction of higher import duties, meant to reduce Dutch products in French markets. By the end of

1670 France and Britain had secretly resolved to go to war against the Republic, and garnered further support in the months thereafter from an eager Münster and from the elector-archbishop of Cologne, who also stood to gain territorially from the Dutch. This alliance effectively aimed at little less than the dismemberment of the Republic.

Many Dutch leaders recognized that the land borders of the Republic were vulnerable, and the experience in the east strengthened calls for a powerful captain-general who could offer effective leadership. This went hand-in-hand with the fact that the prince of Orange was nearing adulthood in 1667, heightening the feeling, especially outside Holland, that some important office should now be accorded him. The so-called Eternal Decree of 1667 was a compromise ultimately supported by De Witt to meet these demands; it abolished the stadholderate in Holland and made that position incompatible with captain-generalship in the other provinces. This at the same time made it theoretically possible for Willem to become captain-general in all of the provinces, an unwelcome scenario for De Witt but an eventuality that he thought could be avoided. The calls for his appointment to this position, however, became ever more persistent in subsequent years, including – rather to De Witt's dismay – in cities such as Amsterdam, which suffered from French trading policies and became more interested in an effective army with strong leadership that might serve as a deterrent to further French aggression in the region. In February of 1672 Willem became captain-general for all of the Republic.

Despite this recognition of France as an imminent military threat and a belated strengthening of the land defenses, few in the Republic could anticipate the size of the assault that was about to befall them. Various warning signs appeared in the course of 1671, and the Dutch government in vain sent emissaries to ensure the peace. But De Witt was slow to recognize the possibility of an Anglo-French attack, to be carried out by two states whose political and economic interests he deemed so incompatible as to eliminate the possibility of their forming a united front. It was the fruit of this unlikely match, however, as well as the fury of Orangist sentiment, which De Witt had tried so hard to contain, that would soon topple the pensionary from power, and plunge the Republic into unprecedented crisis.

4
Diminishing Returns and New Hopes, 1672–1795

~

The attack on the Dutch Republic in 1672 signaled, in hindsight, the gradual waning of its fortunes. It became clear that both the French and the English had begun to surpass the Dutch – in the case of the English in economic might as well. For a long time, the decline was relative and not absolute; the Republic remained, until at least the mid eighteenth century, a country of wealth and status. Only as Dutch decline became more apparent at mid-century did the Dutch began to think seriously of reform, and of ways to give energetic redefinition to their national identity. Both the continued decline and the question of how to give form to new hopes would challenge the Republic in its last years.

From the "Year of Disaster" to the Peace of Utrecht, 1672–1713

1672 and Its Effects

The year of 1672 has gone down in Dutch history as the "year of disaster." The massive invasion of that year threatened to destroy the Republic, and in the summer of 1672 many Dutch concluded that they already had been defeated. Contrary to their expectations, though, together with new allies they managed to beat back this very grave threat. But if this *annus horribilis* itself turned out to be less disastrous than many expected, it can nevertheless, in hindsight, be seen as a turning point, after which the Republic's power and prestige gradually diminished. The decline in political and economic power was thus not immediately obvious, but the Republic's changing position, first as a European power and then as an economic force, would become apparent by the early eighteenth century.

Although the omens of 1671 strongly pointed to a French attack, the Dutch were unprepared for both the scale of the attack and the multiple quarters from which it sprang. The English were the first to strike, their warships pouncing on a Dutch merchant convoy off the Isle of Wight in late March of 1672. This was soon followed by formal declarations of war not only by France and then England but also by the Republic's old enemy, the prince-bishop of Münster, who had supported the English in the last war against the Dutch out of territorial ambition and who regarded himself as the protector of the Republic's Catholic population. An additional opponent, the elector of Cologne, was the last to declare war. And it was not only the magnitude of the force against them that dismayed the Dutch, but the rapidity of its advance. Louis XIV had chosen the Rhine as his primary invasion route, and the Dutch garrisons calculated to hold off armies for at least a few weeks now crumbled in a matter of days, some having scarcely fired a shot in defense. The government in The Hague had hastily been mobilizing more soldiers in the months ahead of the attack, but it was too late; the decision to trim the size of the land forces now bore its bitter fruits. On the other hand, Michiel de Ruyter's well-prepared navy kept an Anglo-French fleet from blockading the coast in the Battle of Solebay in early June of 1672.

For the time being, this offered little hope for the Republic. Gelderland and Overijssel were soon overrun and knocked out of the war. The key city of Utrecht, its defenses neglected and its inhabitants fearful, also opened its gates to the French, who proclaimed freedom of worship and held high mass in the great cathedral for the first time in a century. Towns in these regions fell quickly, with neither their garrisons nor their citizens motivated to contest such a formidable enemy. By late June, the

States-General – or the part that could be mustered together – voted to offer terms to the French king, which included the surrender of the Generality Lands. Louis dismissed these terms as too little, and the invasion continued unabated as the French reached the Holland Water Line, a defense system designed to keep Holland and Zeeland safe. A quick French breach of the Water Line in the early days of the war would have been possible, as it was only lightly defended and the flood waters were slow to rise in summer, in part because farmers hostile to the inundation of their fields sabotaged early efforts to do so. Instead, however, the French chose to consolidate their position, leaving it to the English to invade from the west as previously agreed. By early July, though, the Water Line was fully operational, now making it extremely difficult for the French to cross into Holland.

The shock of this sudden and apparently successful invasion had a profound impact on the Dutch population, especially in the populous and urban west, where scores of pamphlets concluded that only gross incompetence or – more likely – treachery could account for the debacle. Public opinion viewed the existing leadership of the Republic as discredited, and sought new guidance. The prince of Orange had already been made captain-general of the army, but now, at the beginning of July, he was recognized by the States of Holland as *stadhouder*. It was a decision that wholly reversed their edict of 1667 to abolish the post altogether. But the public mood left the States little choice. Unruly city militias, rising first in Rotterdam but swelling to include almost all sizeable towns in the unoccupied Republic, gave the authorities no option but to give the new *stadhouder*, Willem III, an uncontested role as military and political leader. Grand Pensionary De Witt, politically finished, resigned his post. But a worse fate soon awaited him, along with his brother Cornelis. The latter, prosecuted and tortured for having conspired to murder the *stadhouder*, and consequently condemned to exile, was being visited by his brother when hundreds of citizens, led by the local militia, surrounded The Hague's Prison Gate on August 20. The brothers were hauled out of the prison and quickly killed by the mob, who then mutilated their bodies, consuming parts of them to exact savage judgment for their supposed treachery.

These grisly political murders have been the focus of a great deal of historical discussion, much of it relating to Willem's possible role in the dispatching of his opponents: he later rewarded several instigators of the murders with public posts. Whatever his role there can be little doubt that he was the chief beneficiary of this violence. Throughout much of the Republic, crowds now demanded the immediate resignation of many magistrates, with the threat that the fate of the De Witts might also overcome them if they did not. In this menacing atmosphere perhaps a third of regents in Holland alone quit their posts in the late summer of 1672. Patricians and other prominent citizens with ties to the *stadhouder* were frequently appointed to replace them.

Gradually, the military fortunes of the Republic improved. Though Willem had no military experience, his determination to seize the offensive and to appoint competent military and political associates had an impact. Groningen managed to beat off a siege by the Münster bishop, and De Ruyter's several victories at sea against the English-dominated fleet helped sour the government in London on continuing the war. The Treaty of Westminster, signed in 1674, ended hostilities between the two countries. French forces in the Low Countries were threatened from the east by new allies of the Republic: Brandenburg and the Holy Roman Emperor. Willem's soldiers, aided by imperial troops, captured Bonn in late 1673, the supply base of the French, forcing them to abandon almost all of the Republic territory that they had captured. In the meantime, the civilian population frequently suffered at the hands of the foreign troops – the pillaging and destruction of towns were not uncommon. Regions where warfare lasted for years suffered particularly, as marauding armies went in search of supplies. The large fortress town of Sittard – then in the duchy of Jülich – suffered from both sides; Dutch troops brought dysentery and death to hundreds of inhabitants, and in 1677 the French razed nearly the whole town, leaving only sixty-eight buildings standing and two monasteries. For those living north of the great rivers, in the secure parts of the Republic, 1672 and its aftermath brought them face to face with war for the first time in nearly a century.

For some, the economic downturn caused by the war was an even greater misfortune. Dutch trade was seriously disrupted by it. Dutch ships were the targets not only of the English navy but – for longer – of French privateers. This hampered commerce both within Europe and with the Dutch colonies. By the end of the decade the economy had improved as war receded, but the great boom of the years before 1672 did not return, as competitors began effectively to challenge Dutch seaborne trade. Some historians have argued that the wars against the English and the French – and the fact that both England and France were closing off their markets to the Dutch – were only contributing factors to a deeper problem: the Dutch economy had stopped growing in the 1660s. Prices began to decline, as did profits in a high-wage economy that was no longer competitive as it once had been. Construction in parts of the Republic came to almost a complete standstill in 1672, but more significant was a long-term decline in real estate prices, an indication that long-term economic growth had definitely come to an end. Rental prices declined by some 40 percent in Leiden between the early 1660s and the early 1680s.

The events of 1672 apparently also triggered a great psychological shock among the population, who became more cautious with their expenditure. Historians have often pointed to the collapse of the country's famous art market in 1672, when – suddenly – paintings could not be sold for any price. The collapse ruined the fortunes of the Delft painter Johannes Vermeer, who was also an art dealer. When he died in 1675, as the result, it was said, of despair over his financial predicament, his widow was forced to ask the magistracy to protect her from creditors she could not pay. More fundamentally for the long run, patrons, even as they began to buy art, ceased to be interested in innovation but preferred the tried and true. No longer paid for the painstaking efforts that contributed to the quality of their work, Dutch artists who continued in the field after 1672 delivered work that is generally considered of a lesser standard than their earlier masterpieces. The number of active artists was also reduced by a quarter in the course of a decade. Thus the country lost ground in the art world in the span of only a few years, even as artists of note continued to produce for the international market into the eighteenth century and even as the Dutch market remained important. Indeed, the artistic move to more classic and conventional painting in the Netherlands of the late seventeenth century was not, at the time, regarded as a step back.

In hindsight, then, 1672 might be seen as the beginning of a long-term decline in Dutch fortunes, though with the rebounding of the Republic's situation directly after the scare and the country's still formidable role on the world stage this could not have been immediately apparent.

Sustaining the Dutch Position Abroad

War also changed the geopolitical position of the Dutch Republic. It now played a pivotal role in a long-lasting anti-French alliance that would persist until the Peace of Utrecht in 1713, and to a hesitant and diminished degree down to the 1750s, when the European alliance system fundamentally shifted once again. This alliance was led, for as long as he lived, by Willem III, who saw it as his life's task to check French power. Willem's vision saw the Republic's future as wedded to the European alliance system, in which its safety was procured through the mutual support of long-standing allies, which included the Holy Roman Empire and, strikingly enough, Spain. Willem's marriage in 1677 to fifteen-year-old

Mary Stuart, niece of the English king and Willem's first cousin, was informed by such strategic considerations; he saw England as an essential element in the anti-French consortium, and was frustrated at the unwillingness of the Stuart kings to join him in this endeavor. Willem's investment in the construction of an anti-French consortium was very different from De Witt's strategy, which had focused on Dutch freedom on the seas and on as few lasting alliances as possible. Willem's strategy arguably placed the Republic's future on a more secure footing, but it was also an expensive option that the Republic was increasingly unable to

24 Michiel de Ruyter's death mask, 1676. His body, embalmed for the long trip home, was placed in a mausoleum in Amsterdam's New Church during an impressive state ceremony.

bear, as shall be discussed below. De Ruyter himself would die in 1676 as the result of battle wounds in the Mediterranean, helping to defend the Spanish against the French. This conflict was not exclusively European in scale; Dutch naval forces, for example, attacked the French in Acadian Canada and Martinique in the Caribbean. Securing Dutch trade abroad remained a crucial consideration in the strategic calculus of the Republic.

Keeping their trading empire was an important aim of the Dutch, but their ability to maintain their global position had peaked. This was true in the crucial case of Baltic trade; in 1650 the Dutch generated 60 percent of the total trade but by 1690 this had been whittled down to 47 percent, as British mercantilist policies especially reduced the Dutch share. With the end of Dutch Brazil and New Amsterdam there would be no large-scale territorial expansion of their empire until early in the nineteenth century. Here, too, competition from the French and the British had made such expansion difficult, and by 1670 they had also squeezed the Dutch out of direct trade with their own colonies. The bankruptcy of the WIC in 1674 before it was refinanced was one indication of declining Dutch fortunes. Nevertheless, Dutch entrepreneurs undertook new and riskier ventures to keep their profit margins intact. The VOC doubled in size from the 1680s to the 1720s, expanding its trade from goods on which it had a monopoly, such as spices and pepper, to increasingly popular items such as coffee and tea, which were widely in use in Dutch households by the early eighteenth century. Research shows that 56 percent had accessories for tea, and 38 percent for coffee, and those percentages would only rise. But profits on these goods were smaller because they were offered on an open market, and the company's shift to a higher-risk strategy occurred precisely at a time when it had less control over shipping among Asian ports. In the course of the eighteenth century, the VOC would become an increasingly top-heavy and inefficient business that could still generate considerable trade volume but with less profit.

Dutch seaborne trade, in Asia, Africa or the Americas, was hardly premised on the ideal of free labor. Slavery was common in early modern societies but it was not without its opponents in the Republic; in the Revd. Jacobus Hondius's *Black Register of a Thousand Sins*, published in 1679, slavery was one of the sins castigated. But it never became a major theme in Dutch preaching, and many Dutch remained convinced, to the extent that they thought about it at all, that many non-Europeans were congenitally incapable of becoming civilized Christians and thus were superbly fitted for a life of servitude. The VOC made use of an existing Asian slave market, buying and selling hundreds of thousands of people in the course of its existence, many of them as house slaves. The Dutch role in slavery, then, was not restricted to the Atlantic.

The only new colonial project of this period was the establishment of a slave-based plantation economy in Surinam. For most of the seventeenth century, the Dutch, particularly merchants from Middelburg, had been engaged in the slave trade. In 1665, the WIC began systematically to bring slaves across the Atlantic, and soon made Curaçao and its bustling free port of Willemstad its center for that trade, from which slaves could be sold to the Spanish in South America. But it was only in 1683 that the Surinam Company, shared jointly by the city of Amsterdam, the WIC and a wealthy nobleman, established what was to become the Netherlands' chief plantation colony along a patch of South American coast the Dutch had recently secured from the English. Refugee Huguenots and Jews each made up part of a rather diverse planter class, which by the early eighteenth century was importing about 2,000 slaves a year. Even by the standards of the day, slavery in Surinam was wretched, as planters – Dutch, English, French and Sephardic Jewish – imposed a violently harsh regime to maintain control over their colony. The labor of those condemned to slavery did pay off for the plantation class and their investors. In the first half of the eighteenth century, Surinam was a prosperous if small-scaled colony, providing the Republic with supplies of coffee and particularly sugar, which was a growth industry in the colony until the 1770s. Similar colonies – Essequibo, Demerara and Berbice – were established on the nearby Guyana Coast. Compared to the rapid expansion of English settlement in these years (including plantation slavery), however, these Dutch colonization efforts were on a very limited scale.

25   Gesina ter Borch painted this 1680 portrait of the six-year-old Hillegonda Louise Schellinger on a fancifully imagined Curaçao, though the toiling African slaves seem real enough.

Internal Political and Theological Tensions

Meanwhile the *stadhouder's* concerns lay closer to home. The crisis of 1672 had afforded him a chance to bend the structures of the Republic in his direction, and to exercise more control over public affairs than his predecessors had been able to. Willem permitted Gelderland, Overijssel and Utrecht, the regions that many wanted punished for so easily capitulating to the French, to be readmitted to the States-General, but only after he ensured that they would be represented by his men. In these provinces even more of the old elites were therefore turned out of office than had been the case in Holland and Zeeland. The *stadhouder* thus solidified his power and his patronage in large parts of the Republic. He now had a much fuller grip on local and regional politics than any of his predecessors had possessed. Nevertheless, Willem's authority was not without substantial limits; the absolutist kings of Europe enjoyed far more power. The great towns of Holland, most notably Amsterdam, were politically and economically powerful enough to pursue a course that deviated from Willem's vision. And the prince of Orange's own power declined as the war continued, as public unhappiness with the increase in taxes needed to pay for the hostilities mounted. The Peace of Nijmegen (1678–1679), which concluded the war with France, was primarily fed by Holland's desire to reignite commerce with France, though Willem harbored misgivings about the terms, which he thought too favorable to Louis. The proper stance toward France – along with the perennial struggle for political influence in many of the Republic's towns – generated new tensions between the *stadhouder* and a significant portion of the country's political elites.

The conflict between *stadhouder* and local elites became evident in high-profile corruption cases, in which some of the prince's men, such as Lodewijk Huygens, the bailiff of Gorinchem, and Jacob van Zuijlen van Nijevelt, the sheriff of Rotterdam, were involved. Both were accused of extortion, the latter fleeing town after this estate was burned down by an angry mob. At the root of both cases, the first in 1675, the latter in 1690, was a resentment of established elites at the high-handed way in which Willem's new appointees conducted themselves, without any apparent regard for local mores and arrangements. Willem in turn protected both of his appointees from the charges. It was one indication of how the tussle for local power could be intensified by Willem's efforts to solidify his control.

Deepening the tensions between the two camps was the re-emergence of theological divisions in the public Church. Since the 1650s two groups had emerged in the Dutch Reformed Church that struggled for control. The followers of Utrecht theologian Gisbertus Voetius were pitted against his German-born colleague Johannes Coccius. Theologically, the dispute centered on how different God's message in the Old Testament was that from that of the New Testament. This question mattered greatly to many Dutch as it determined how one should read the Bible. Concretely, for example, it was partly about whether the Old Testament command to rest on the Sabbath demanded from Christians that they scrupulously cease all work on Sunday. Voetians insisted that this was the case, while Cocceians were more equivocal. These differences quickly became tied to existing divisions in the Reformed Church. Cocceian theology came to stand for a more symbolic and allegorical reading of the Scriptures, a higher estimation of Decartes's controversial ideas, more dialogue with other Protestants and less austerity on lifestyle issues such as theater-going. Voetian theology, on the other hand, was strongly associated with the so-called Further Reformation, with its continuing efforts to boost the spiritual and moral character of society and to vigorously oppose all thought and action, including the radical doubt of Cartesianism, that ran counter to these efforts. Although the theological issues were different, this debate bore resemblance to the old Remonstrant controversy of half a century before. As in 1618, it divided many Cocceian-leaning regents over and against the new *stadhouder*, whose sympathies tended toward the Voetian camp.

It was this internal struggle within the public Church that kept authorities and a good many Calvinists most busy in the late seventeenth and early eighteenth centuries. But there was a new challenge that came out of the older debates over Descartes's legacy, articulated in the 1670s by the philosopher Baruch de Spinoza. Banished for heretical views from his Sephardic Jewish community in Amsterdam as a young adult, Spinoza became the leading light of a small intellectual community of those who in varying degrees had become sceptical of the claims of revealed religion and of the established churches. Spinoza was influenced by the critical philosophy of his day, but he systematically radicalized these insights, including a thoroughgoing critique of the Bible, particularly the Hebrew scriptures. He argued for full freedom to philosophize as one wished, and not to be prevented from doing so by religious groups whose beliefs, he thought, were grounded in ignorance. As an early, if uneven, advocate of democracy, he critiqued the existing political hierarchy. Moreover, and even more controversially from the standpoint of his age, Spinoza rejected the classic dualism between God and nature, seeing the two as having the same substance. Like many philosophers of his day, he sought to bring about unity through a return to simple truths, to be deduced by reason, by which people might lead virtuous lives.

Spinoza was well aware that the publishing of his ideas, so beyond the pale of conventional thought, was risky, even in the relatively easy-going Republic; his associate Adriaan Koerbagh had been arrested for baldly contesting the authority of the Bible and had died in a penal workhouse. Spinoza hesitated before publishing his work, and his *Ethica* – his most extensive and important work – was only published after his death in 1677. The work was widely condemned for its "atheism": a charge, incidentally, that the sometimes rather mystical Spinoza had denied. Even in the Republic, with its fairly relaxed press climate, Spinoza's ideas had crossed the line, and his work, along with those of a few other notorious authors such as the English philosopher Thomas

BENOIT SPINOSA
Né à Amsterdam, l'an 1632. Mort le
21. Février 1677. âgé de 44 ans.

26 Spinoza's controversial ideas and originality of thought were
not worked out in isolation; he cultivated many friendships and
correspondences with leading intellectuals of his day.

Hobbes, was formally suppressed by the authorities. Nevertheless,
intellectuals soon became acquainted with it. Spinoza's work
helped give shape to a significant undercurrent of rationalism and
religious scepticism in the Republic and contributed powerfully
to the international importance of the Netherlands as the center
of an early Enlightenment. Spinoza's circle, among others, also

came to influence the ideas of John Locke, who had been forced to flee from England in the 1680s but advanced his own distinctive notions of tolerance and rational religion after his stay in the Republic.

In the 1690s two new disputes showed how a widening divergence between traditional theological commitments and new philosophical insights could lead to public confrontations. The first and widely disputed case concerned Balthasar Bekker, a Reformed Church clergyman who had an established reputation as both a Cocceian and a Cartesian. In 1691 he published a book that would be translated a few years later into English as *The World Bewitched.* In it, he challenged the conventional understanding that biblical references to the devil, demons, witches and angels pointed to actual entities, suggesting instead that they were used figuratively to accommodate limited human understanding. Bekker's work was widely condemned by the Reformed clergy, even by old supporters, who felt he had gone too far this time. He was accordingly suspended as minister. But his book sold thousands of copies in the Netherlands and was soon translated into other languages, its impact international in scope. It was another example of Dutch influence in the early European Enlightenment. Bekker also had vocal supporters close to home, and the mayors of Amsterdam saw to it that he continued to draw a salary as pastor.

Much less publicly discussed at the time but also reflecting these tensions was the fate of Pierre Bayle, a French Reformed refugee who taught at the *Ecole Illustre* in Rotterdam. Bayle's plea for religious toleration as a way of defusing the conflict between Calvinists and Catholics in his home country was regarded by many of his fellow refugees, and fellow Calvinists, as an abandonment of the Protestant struggle against French Catholic absolutism. He was accordingly stripped of his office in 1693 by town authorities under pressure from the French Reformed exiles and the Reformed Church, which supported them. Bayle, however, would soon play a crucial role in the early Enlightenment, publishing his

Dictionnaire historique et critique in 1697. The *Dictionnaire* was critical of those who claimed to act on reason, particularly those who claimed that religious belief could be built on rational arguments. Bayle, whose comprehension of Dutch was poor, barely interacted with the Dutch discussions, and these were largely omitted from his scholarship. But his work, oriented toward francophone readers, was, in its erudition and skepticism, deeply influential, and proved an inspiration to eighteenth-century Enlightenment philosophers such as Voltaire.

These disputes illustrated not only strong religious but also political divisions in the Republic, but the political leadership on both sides were careful not to let the conflict get out of hand. Indeed, there were new political reasons for promoting religious tolerance at the end of the seventeenth century. After a range of conflicts between the *stadhouder* and his opponents, both parties realized in the 1680s that more could be gained from a less confrontational power-sharing agreement. On a religious level this was apparent when the city council of Amsterdam determined that Voetian and Cocceian pastors be appointed in equal numbers in their town. For the *stadhouder*, being able to demonstrate tolerance toward the country's Catholic inhabitants was important in his effort to solidify his alliance with Catholic but anti-French states of Europe. Domestic religious policies, then, sometimes were related to international diplomacy, and Willem had every reason to make common cause with as many allies as he could.

War with France and England's Glorious Revolution

By 1685 a new conflict with France had quickly reappeared on the horizon. Part of the new tensions pertained to developments in France itself. In that year, Louis XIV fully abrogated the worship rights of the French Protestants, the Huguenots, forcing them to convert or to leave France. Perhaps as many as a third of these refugees – roughly 35,000 people – fled to the Republic in the wake of this persecution. Many, but certainly not all, of these refugees were prosperous and well connected, and they were, at least for a time, often welcomed in the Republic's larger towns. But Louis's decision set the Protestant Republic on its guard; anti-Catholic sentiments brewed in the larger towns, and his decision seemed a grim foreboding of what would occur in a French-dominated Europe. Dutch concerns about the French deepened again in the summer of 1687, when the French king, attempting to restore his own country's economic fortunes, again restricted the French market for Dutch goods, thereby depriving many Dutch merchants of their livelihood. Now even some key regents of Amsterdam, previously reluctant to pursue enmity with France because war both disrupted trade and kept taxes high, determined that the Dutch must stand firm, though for the time being the Republic held off from war with France.

More momentous for the Dutch, as it turned out, were the unfolding events in England. There, the brother of Charles II had ascended the throne in 1685. The new king, James II, was a Catholic, which was enough to cause deep unease among England's Protestant establishment. More dangerously, he cherished close ties with his cousin, the king of France, which deeply worried English leaders and, of course, the *stadhouder* himself. In 1687 some English leaders had already begun to explore the possibility of the *stadhouder* and his wife Mary – the Protestant daughter of the new king – toppling James from the throne. As long as Mary and her husband (who was himself, after all, the grandson of an English king) were next in line to the throne, though, Protestant England might be willing to sit out what amounted to interim Catholic rule. Matters became more urgent, however, when James's new wife gave birth in June of 1688 to a son, who would be raised in the Catholic faith and thus keep the English throne in Catholic hands. This prompted a new group of leading English nobility to seek Willem's assistance.

Sending an army to overthrow his father-in-law entailed enormous risks for Willem. It meant leaving the Netherlands vulnerable to French attack, and failure might very well bring about the end of his own rule, perhaps even the existence of the Republic. But the rewards were even greater, as it could singlehandedly transform England from a possible French ally into a welcome partner in the coalition against France. Taking the Republic's leaders into his confidence, Willem prepared an invasion force, moving with sufficient secrecy to keep his opponents guessing until it was too late. An invasion fleet of 500 ships, much larger than the Spanish Armada that had sailed against England exactly a century earlier, landed 20,000 of Willem's best men on the southwest coast of England in November of 1688. James, hesitant to use his own army lest they desert him, allowed Willem's forces to move on London without any meaningful resistance. By the end of the year, Dutch forces had taken London and occupied it, and in early 1689 the English Parliament had Willem and Mary crowned king and queen, in return granting their English subjects a "bill of rights" that, in hindsight, solidly confirmed constitutional monarchy in Great Britain.

This Glorious Revolution, as it is known in English history, had all in all been an exceedingly well-planned and well-executed venture – an indication, some historians have argued, of just how effectively the Republic could plan and carry out complex military operations at the end of the seventeenth century. And it certainly paid off. In seizing political power in England, a Dutch *stadhouder* had not only enhanced the glory of his dynasty but dramatically changed the balance of power in Europe.

The new rulers were soon challenged by James, however, who invaded Ireland from France in 1689. There in the following year he was defeated at the Battle of the Boyne by Willem, whose Dutch forces played an important part in the victory. That battle not only confirmed English rule in Ireland and secured Protestant settlement on the island, but secured for Willem and Mary an uncontested

27   The presence of Dutch soldiers at the Battle of the Boyne in 1690
show not only how crucial they were in the anti-French coalition but in
sustaining British Protestant domination of Ireland.

status as monarchs in England itself. For the Republic, Willem's
success had other repercussions. It meant another war with France,
a war that would both show the centrality of the Republic in the
coalition against France and reveal its limits as a great power.

Continued Military Conflict

The Nine Years' War (1688–1697) that began as Willem was preparing his invasion was a conflict that pitted France against the
Republic, England, Spain and the Holy Roman Empire. It, too,
was both a European-wide and global conflagration. It ended
largely in a draw, formally brought to an end by the Treaty of
Rijswijk, named after the town just outside The Hague where it
was signed. Of significance to the Republic was a provision that
allowed the States army to be stationed in several towns such as
Ypres and Namur in the Spanish Netherlands, designed to keep

the French out of the Low Countries. It was the beginning of the so-called Barrier, which was to be manned by Dutch garrisons up until the 1780s and which initially cost the southern Netherlands a large percentage of its budget. It underscored the importance of the Dutch in the anti-French alliance by checking Louis's ambitions at the northern border of France.

Willem invested in a strong land force; but the Republic remained at the same time a great naval power. The central importance of shipbuilding in the Republic – for its own use but also as an export product – is illustrated by activities in the Zaan region, just northwest of Amsterdam, where the construction of ships reached its zenith at about the turn of the century. Some 300 sawmills, powered by the wind, enabled between 100 and 150 seagoing ships to be built each year. It was a full-service industry; smiths built anchors on the spot for the ships, and bakers made the biscuits to be eaten on board. Shipbuilding also stimulated the growth of other activities in the region, such as paper-making, providing the basis for early industrialization on the Zaan. It was shipbuilding that first brought the Russian tsar, Peter the Great, briefly to the area in 1697, hoping as he did to learn techniques to be taken back home.

Dutch merchant vessels would continue to play a crucial role in early eighteenth-century trade, and the Republic's navy remained formidable, but at the time of Peter's visit its position was already beginning to deteriorate. By the 1690s, the English navy had begun to move decisively ahead of the Dutch in terms of size and quality, and the French, too, would soon overtake them. The country's shallow waterways and small harbors could not easily accommodate the mammoth men-of-war that were now the standard among their rivals. More generally, the modest population and territory of the Republic were no longer sufficient to compete effectively now that neighboring states had become more centralized and more efficient. Superior finances had kept the Dutch ahead, but this advantage was now slipping away in

London's favor and the vastly more numerous populations of rival states were becoming more decisive for raising taxes, training armies and building fleets.

By the end of the century, then, the Republic, though still an important power on sea and on land, was rapidly being eclipsed in power by its English ally, whose use of Dutch innovations, such as an effective banking structure, was beginning to make its weight felt. Heavily taxed to pay for its defenses, the Dutch Republic desperately needed an extended peace to reduce its costs and restore its trade. This, however, was not to be. A Bourbon and close relative of Louis XIV became king of Spain in 1700, transforming these two old foes into close allies. This had immediate effects for the security of the Republic. French troops moved into the Spanish Netherlands in 1701, and Dutch garrisons manning the forts in the southern Netherlands were forced out. There was no longer any barrier separating French armies from the United Provinces and, moreover, the new government in Brussels undertook anti-Dutch economic measures. Other European powers, such as the Austrian Habsburgs, also felt threatened by the shift in the balance of power. Another war was inevitable.

This time, however, the standard bearer would not stem from the House of Orange. Mary had already died of smallpox in 1694, and her husband, catching pneumonia after a fall from a horse, followed her to the grave in 1702. They left behind no children. With the personal union between England and the Dutch Republic now at an end, and with British power rapidly rising, the United Provinces would quickly become a junior partner in the renewed conflict.

A Second Stadholderless Period

Willem's death dramatically changed the power relations in Dutch politics. Just as they had in 1650, the anti-Orange States faction moved to retake the power and prerogatives that the *stadhouder*

224

had held for the past three decades. Orangist politicians quickly lost their power and positions in many parts of the country. In Holland the shift in power had the least effect, since Willem's power had been weakest there, but even there some of his key allies were swept to the margins. In other provinces, including Overijssel and Gelderland, where Willem's authority had been imposed from above, the vacuum left by his death launched an extensive struggle for power. Historically, the key towns of these provinces, particularly Overijssel, had been the most "democratic" in the Republic. Their guilds were stronger, and citizens' committees in Gelderland were traditionally consulted in the selection of town councils. These prerogatives had been quashed by Willem back in the 1670s, but now the citizens wanted them back. The old guard, Orangist or not, were not prepared to concede these old rights, and confrontations, sometimes violent, erupted. In Nijmegen, for example, the regents appointed by Willem refused to cede power to a powerful group of patrician families that had been excluded from power since 1675. This led to street battles for control of the city hall, in which, in the end, five Orangists were hung from the windows of the building. The unrest continued until The Hague sent the army to restore order in Gelderland in 1708. The conflict between the Orangist and States parties ended in an uneasy truce, but in no place did the pleas for broader representation of 1702 find success; the patricians on both sides had no interest in greater political inclusion.

The Second Stadholderless Period, which was ushered in in Holland and several other provinces, was dominated by an established group of mostly anti-Orangist elites who would resist a wider public influence in politics until the unexpected upheaval of 1747. And with the loss of their leader, the Orangists would have to take consolation in the fact that Johan Willem Friso of Nassau-Dietz, a third cousin of the dead king, was still hereditary *stadhouder* of Friesland and Groningen, and potentially for the rest of the Republic. For the time being, most of the provinces, led by Holland, squarely resisted the return of the stadholderate, which had so limited the power and influence of the anti-Orangist "States Party."⌉

The Republic's leadership, although long wary of Willem's anti-French policies, did not shy away from war against Louis in 1702. French domination would have threatened Dutch commercial interests, and not supporting the English in the war against France also contained risks. The Netherlands was also an important launching pad for the war with France, as evidenced by the arrival of the English duke of Marlborough there in mid 1702. His first military campaign, moving down the Maas Valley from Dutch-controlled Venlo to Liège, was an immediate success, though the plundering of his troops would cause his name – "Malbroek" ("Funny Pants"), as he was known – to be hated for generations by local inhabitants.

For the next ten years, Dutch soldiers would be an important part of Marlborough's army that successfully fought against the French. Much to the initial unease of the Dutch political leadership, who preferred to keep their troops as close to home as possible, the duke led his combined armies to the south of Germany in order to prevent a French attack on Vienna, resulting in the Battle of Blenheim (1704), where allied forces annihilated a large French force. The Dutch also played a crucial role a few years later in Marlborough's important victories at Ramillies and Oudenarde in the southern Netherlands, which effectively eliminated the French threat in the region and opened the way to an Anglo-Dutch administration in Brussels. Dutch soldiers further took an active role in the extremely bloody Battle of Malplaquet (1709), in which some 30,000 casualties fell in a single day at this northern French hamlet. The Dutch portion of the army, led by Johan Willem Friso, suffered more than 8,000 dead and wounded: over half their total number. The battle greatly weakened Dutch forces, and the heavy losses prompted the Allies to seek peace with Louis

XIV, who, already having lost his bid for European domination, was pleased enough to come to terms.

Dutch troop levels – reaching well beyond 100,000 men at their zenith – had never been higher than in the first decade of the eighteenth century. But these numbers were no longer impressive in comparison to the mass armies that the European great powers now managed to mobilize. Although the Dutch had been critical allies of the British (their fleet and army were crucial, for example, in the seizure of Gibraltar) the crucial initial peace talks between the British and the French were conducted without their knowledge. Formal negotiations did take place in the Netherlands, as they had in the past – this time in the city of Utrecht, which had a reputation for being less hostile to the French than the cities of Holland. But the demotion of the Dutch to the level of a second-rate power was confirmed by the character of the negotiations, in which the French emissary Melchior de Polignac remarked to Dutch negotiators that "Nous traiterons sur vous, chez vous, sans vous." France was forced to make a number of important concessions, but the Dutch Republic, as nominal victor, gained little in the Peace of Utrecht. In subsequent negotiations it received modest portions of what is now the province of Limburg, and the re-establishment of the Barrier Treaty. The southern Netherlands passed out of the hands of the Spanish and to the Austrian Habsburgs, who now were to share the defense of the region with eight Dutch garrisons placed along the frontier with France. The Austrian government was to pay for the Dutch troops.

As it turned out, the Treaty of Utrecht and its follow-up agreements would usher in an extended period of peace, the longest in the Republic's history. The Dutch hoped for a peace dividend, but that would prove politically and economically difficult to achieve. Indeed, it has been argued that peace removed a powerful incentive for the country's political elites, always keen to defend their own particular interests, from working together to achieve the reforms that were now demanded.

Political Impasse, Economic Entropy and Cultural Ferment, 1713–1747

Financial Problems

The horrendous condition of the state finances was the most urgent political issue facing the Dutch at the end of the conflict. The war had been financed by loans, and accordingly the public debt of Holland had doubled to nearly 200 million guilders between 1673 and 1713, at increasingly high interest rates to attract the necessary investment. Indeed, encouraging private individuals to grant government loans had become so difficult in the very last years of the war that the government had to offer prize lotteries to investors. The mountain of debt could not be sustained, even with the quick and deep reduction of military expenditures after 1713. The situation was particularly difficult for Holland, which paid well over half of the Republic's expenditures and in practice nearly all of its debt. Up to 60 percent of government revenues had to go to service the debt. In 1715 the States-General ran out of money to pay off their debtors, and resumed payments only after unilaterally reducing the interest with which they reimbursed investors. Provinces such as Friesland and Gelderland also refused in the years after the war to fund their share of the Republic's costs, citing their own hardship. It was not the first time a lesser province had done this, but now Holland itself was in too poor a financial position to cover the debts of the recalcitrant provinces.

Strategically, the necessary belt-tightening put the Dutch at a further disadvantage in international politics. After forty years of taking a leading role in the anti-French coalition, the Republic now tried to pursue a more neutral course, staying out of expensive and dangerous entanglements whenever possible. Yet the Austrians and British expected from the Dutch continued support in containing the French, and the government in The Hague felt obliged to take these commitments seriously enough to avoid alienating London and Vienna. The rising power of Prussia also necessitated a sufficient deterrent force. Prussia had become a neighbor by claiming and taking the counties of Lingen and Moers after its lord, Willem III, had died, and after 1715 it came to rule over parts of the Gelderland *Overkwartier*, situated in the current Netherlands. Even maintaining a deterrent land force against France and Prussia did not solve the Republic's security problem. The vulnerability of the Dutch was perhaps most felt on the high seas, where the Dutch admiralties were less capable than ever of protecting their merchant fleets, and increasingly dependent on the goodwill of their maritime rivals, especially but not exclusively the British.

These problems were recognized, though Dutch elites, still wealthy and resting on the laurels of a great past, were unsure as how to respond to this intractable situation. The crisis of the state finances and its consequences for the future of the Republic became the primary drive of would-be reformers such as Simon van Slingelandt, the long-serving secretary of the Council of State. Van Slingelandt played an important role in reducing the size of the Republic's army and the navy in the years after the war, but such measures were, in his eyes, insufficient: only a more centralized government in The Hague, with the Council of State at its core, would offer the Republic a structure better to collect and allocate resources. He helped bring about the Great Meeting (*Groote Vergadering*) of 1716 and 1717 to discuss the possibilities of such reforms. These discussions led to nothing, except further reductions in the size of the army. The provinces and cities preferred to keep their own prerogatives, and in the absence of public interest in such reform they easily resisted Van Slingelandt's proposals to centralize power. Later, the highly able Van Slingelandt would be promoted to grand pensionary, Holland's highest office, but only after forswearing further efforts to change existing arrangements. Discussions over reform would continue, but local interests also prevented the finding of a compromise that would have had sufficient support.

More broadly put, it might be doubted to what extent those with political or economic influence were inclined to enact reform. Like many others among their fellow citizens with disposable income, the Republic's elites were creditors of the Republic, depending on the income gained from the interest on state debt. From a financial standpoint, the state's high debt was not a problem as long as the government could be counted upon to repay it, and with sufficient interest. But as interest declined, many of Holland's elites sought lucrative jobs in government, from which they might make a good living collecting fees for services.

Joining the small number of political elites – it was no more than a few thousand across the Republic – had always been difficult, but the making of fortunes in the decades of economic growth in the seventeenth century had then offered some possibility for advancing socially and politically. That door of opportunity seemed to have closed in the eighteenth century, as fewer parvenus contended for a place at the table. Additionally, the existing elites themselves were less enterprising than their forebears, and more likely to see public administration as a career and a sinecure – one to be passed down if possible to sons and other relatives. To this end they were not above creating new government positions for the purpose of helping their family. Though no longer making as much money through trade, the country's wealthy continued, as they had in the seventeenth century, to build lavish and increasingly ostentatious summer estates along the quaint River Vecht or in other charming locales. It was this section of the population that could most fully enjoy the benefits of world trade by consuming the luxury goods now readily available on European markets. For the Dutch upper middle class, the financial crisis and relative decline in economic power did not impinge on a very comfortable lifestyle, an indication both of the country's still very considerable wealth and its ability to protect its own interests well.

The Dutch Economy in Global Context

That the Dutch, at least those with a bit of money, continued to consume should not be surprising. On crucial fronts, the Republic, in the generation after the Peace of Utrecht, remained a prosperous country – it could claim the world's highest standard of living throughout the eighteenth century. Its industries, from Delftware to sugar refining, continued to do well, at least for the time being, and Dutch ships brought many of the world's goods to market; its trade in the North Sea, in the Baltic and in European waterways continued at high volume. The VOC continued to generate profits, and in this period became a larger part of the Dutch economy. Until about 1750 it remained a major trader of goods among Asian markets, including Bengal, Ceylon and Batavia, the three parts of the company's holdings that had the right to trade directly with the Republic. The company maintained an active presence in these places; making political alliances; warring against its opponents; and, to some extent, supporting Christian missions and schools. But the company's profit margins, as noted above, had become smaller, in part because of its expensive maintenance of forts in a trading region where it was losing to competitors.

The WIC, restarted in 1674 after its bankruptcy, was chiefly interested in the gold trade along the Gold Coast in West Africa, trading European goods for the gold provided by African kings. It was also active in the slave trade, in which it initially had a monopoly. About 100,000 slaves were sold via its emporium on Curaçao in the century after the Dutch seized it in 1634: about 20 percent of the total number of slaves were brought across the Atlantic by Dutch ships. The Dutch ability to trade in slaves was, however, dependent on the international context. As a part of the treaty that had ended the war, the Spanish had granted the British, and not the Dutch, the *asiento*, the monopoly that provided their South American colonies with slaves, and slave trading declined in importance on the Dutch Caribbean islands after 1716. The focus of the Dutch slave trade then shifted heavily toward the plantations of Surinam;

perhaps 200,000 slaves alone were brought to the Surinam plantations in the course of the eighteenth century. Conditions on Dutch
ships, some three-quarters of which came from the province of
Zeeland, were even more horrendous than on English slavers, and
the Dutch lost on average some 11 percent of its human cargo in
the course of a voyage. Dutch slave-trading was not very profitable, in part because of this high mortality. It has been estimated
that the profit margin was on average no more than 3 percent
per trip to the Indies – and with thirty trips a year the trade, as a
share of total Dutch commerce, was not of enormous economic
importance. Nevertheless, it was a key element in the West Indies
trade on which other business depended, and slaves undoubtedly
reduced the costs of merchants who sold sugar to European con-
sumers. And for a small number of plantation owners and traders,
slavery was sufficiently profitable.

With the loss of the *asiento*, though, Curaçao and St. Eustatius
were forced to reorient their commerce. The WIC further
declined in importance as it was forced to yield ever more to
private traders, Dutch and non-Dutch. With few products of its
own – the slave-manned salt pans of Bonaire and St. Maarten were
its chief marketable industry – it sought new commercial connections. It became a trading network whose ships transported South
American cacao and silver for goods stemming from New York
and other English colonies. The substantial African population on
Curaçao – perhaps two-thirds of the total – worked chiefly not on
the island's few plantations but as sailors or stevedores, sometimes
as slaves and increasingly as freedmen.

All of this economic activity was insufficient, however, to preserve the economic heart of many of the Republic's towns, particularly in Holland, where dynamism had been the strongest
in the seventeenth century. Amsterdam fared better than most
commercially, but it, too, was losing its place as a staple market
to London and Hamburg. Towns such as Leiden and Dordrecht
had already begun to contract in the 1680s, but after 1720

their economic fortunes shrunk dramatically. Now shut out of many markets by mercantilist laws, or unable to compete with cheaper competition, they were forced to watch new competitors from the southern Netherlands, England and parts of western Germany take away much of their business. This had a huge negative impact on textile production and tobacco-processing, classic industrial goods of the Republic's western towns. But the new competition was also evident at sea, when towns such as Enkhuizen and its herring fleets lost out to the Scandinavian competition. The herring fishers' traditional British markets were also now closed by protectionist policies. By the 1750s the Enkhuizen herring fleet was a quarter of what it had been in the heyday of the mid seventeenth century. Similarly, shipbuilding shriveled. This very serious economic downturn led to a sustained period of urban decline in the Dutch Republic that would last until the early nineteenth century. It was worst in the textile towns of Haarlem and Leiden, which lost half of their population between the end of the seventeenth century and the mid eighteenth century. The Netherlands in general and Holland in particular had been the urbanized part of Europe, but now lost this position in both absolute and relative terms, as the cities of rival powers and regions began to grow. Still, in the 1740s annual per capita income remained relatively high in the western provinces compared to those in the east and south. And per capita income remained remarkably stable across the eighteenth century.

The sustained urban decline had far-reaching social and political consequences. It much reduced migration to the great towns of Holland, both by non-Dutch immigrants, particularly Germans and Scandinavians, and from the Dutch countryside. Dutch towns, like their counterparts elsewhere, were cesspools of disease in early modern times, and immigrant absence depressed the population levels. Economic decline also severely reduced the ability of the urban elites to launch either new business enterprises or new civic projects. It generated labor conflicts between business owners eager to maintain a profit and workers seeking to maintain a living wage. And more than ever it set cities and provinces against each other as some attempted to reduce their tax burden because of population loss. In the long run, the Dutch economy would benefit in part from the shift to agriculture that now occurred. As shall be seen the Netherlands remained a wealthy country in part because of its ability to shift its economy.

Declining Intellectual Position

Accordingly, it is not difficult to make the argument, as some historians have, that the loss of urban vitality also reduced the basis for the Republic's role as a European intellectual and cultural center. The development of the universities is illustrative in this respect. In the first half of the eighteenth century, many international students continued to flock to the Netherlands in the range of the studies it had to offer, from theology to medicine. Carl Linnaeus, the Swedish naturalist who would become celebrated for the modern classification of species, traveled like many other Swedes to complete his doctorate in the Republic, in his case at the University of Harderwijk, in 1738. Dutch universities had in the period a particularly good reputation in the empirical sciences such as botany, chemistry and medicine, embodied in the person and work of Herman Boerhaave, who had also received his degree at the "poor man's" university at Harderwijk, but whose international fame was achieved as professor at the University of Leiden in the decades before his retirement in 1729. His fame apparently extended as far as China. Boerhaave, more than anyone else, systematized medicine as a science, established the guidelines for clinical instruction and wrote a textbook that was used for decades across Europe. In the long run, though, the flow of money and ideas toward other centers of Europe hit the Dutch universities hard and, with less to offer, they could not sustain their international position after about the 1740s. They lost ground in particular to the German universities. In absolute terms, too, they became less important; perhaps 3 percent of Dutch young men went to university in 1650; by 1800, this was just 1 percent.

The ultimate decline of the universities did not mean, of course, that the Dutch public sphere was barren and devoid of debate; the role of those institutions in public debate had always been limited anyway. Domestically, though, in a country where perhaps three-quarters of the men and half the women could read, there continued to be a strong basis for the discussion of news and ideas. This continued to feed the Republic's relatively free atmosphere. Voltaire, who resided in the Dutch Republic five times between 1713 and 1743, admired the unpretentiousness of its citizens and the freedoms they enjoyed. He in turn was admired by enlightened Protestants, particularly from the small dissenting churches, who sympathized with his pleas for greater tolerance. Voltaire's ideas could be published in the Republic, so much so that he became frustrated with a host of publishers who cribbed them and neglected to pay him royalties. Voltaire certainly had his enemies, but he benefited from the relative freedom of the Dutch press in publishing ideas that would not be countenanced in most other places.

Nevertheless, as the century wore on, the Dutch publishing climate became less exceptional. The country's press, responsible for nearly half of the books published in Europe between 1650 and 1725, began to decline thereafter as publishers in other countries increased their own market share. Foreign publishers sometimes benefited from a freer atmosphere than had hitherto been the case, and their increased publishing also reflected the fact that many of the newest philosophical and scientific ideas were no longer emanating from the Republic but from other parts of Europe. Here, too, was an indication of the country's relative decline.

Enlightenment, Religion and Tolerance

Compared to the seventeenth century, one could argue that the theological and philosophical battle lines had softened a bit. The radical doubt that the thought of Descartes and Spinoza had facilitated was largely replaced by the rise of empirical science, which valued experimentation over inductive reasoning. This new kind of science, exemplified by Isaac Newton but also by Dutch scientific luminaries such as Boerhaave, was easier to combine with a reverence for nature's God, who in his wise providence had marvelously crafted the laws of creation. Boerhaave was an anti-Spinozist, and spent much of his time reflecting prayerfully on the wonders of creation. Reacting against both Descartes and Spinoza, the physician-philosopher Bernard Nieuwentijt, too, looked to nature for the conformation of religious truths in his highly popular book translated into English as *The Religious Philosopher* (1718). The new science was often an expression of confidence in the order and administration of the universe, and it went hand-in-hand with a new kind of Protestant faith that emerged in the early eighteenth century: less concerned about the formal doctrines of the Church, more concerned with having the right affections toward God and one's neighbor, and, partly through the new science, more trusting in the moral and spiritual capabilities of human beings. This shift could be seen as far away as Dutch Ceylon, where the governor, Gustaaf Willem Baron van Imhoff, changed the curriculum of the Christian seminaries to make room for this new orientation.

In this context, the theological energy of the Voetian–Cocceian controversies wound down, though it continued to define very roughly those who were Orangist in sentiment and those who were not. The new emphasis on virtuous behavior as the mark of a civilized person was characteristic of the concerns of the "coffee house public," the reading middle class. The journal *Hollandsche spectator*, launched by the publicist Justus van Effen in 1731 and inspired by the English "spectatorial" press, scrutinized Dutch society in a moralizing way, from dissecting the house-cleaning habits of housewives to illustrating the pitfalls of excessive eating and drinking. It also celebrated the glories of the country's past and emphasized the value of religious tolerance. In its critical stance toward the declining moral state of the Netherlands this press in the long run served to undermine the natural authority of the standing elite.

The shift in religious sensibilities is most tellingly told in the entangled history of a small German sect, and changing Dutch views toward the slaves of the West Indies. Dutch Calvinists had made few inroads toward converting the slaves of their colonies, and Dutch planters and traders often preferred to think of Africans as congenitally incapable of becoming Christians. The existing notion that being a slave and being a Christian were ultimately incompatible identities served as a disincentive to Christianize slaves. This was very different in the Roman Catholic Church, where slaves were routinely baptized and integrated into the structures of empire and Church; most of Curaçao's slaves and freedmen had become Catholic because of the clandestine work of priests on the island. This situation began to change in 1735, when the Moravians, a small German group that stressed conversion of the heart, arrived in Surinam as missionaries. Although initially met with distrust by the slave-owning population, they made converts within the slave community, and over time a church of slaves emerged in Surinam that operated largely autonomously from the religious structures of the whites. At the same time, the Moravians tried to establish themselves in the Netherlands, and the lord of Zeist offered them a home on his Utrecht estate in 1745. The Moravians' arrival in the Republic was controversial – it undermined the status of the public Church – but they had many sympathizers who appreciated their simplicity and heart-oriented religion. Their permanent settlement was one indication of a shifting religious mentality.

This new – if limited – appreciation for a religion of the heart that could reach even the Africans is best illustrated in the short life of Jacobus Capitein, an African boy captured into slavery at the age of eight and brought to the Republic from the Dutch slave-trading port of Elmina on the west coast of Africa. His

IACOBUS IOANNES ELIZA CAPITEIN, V. D. M. op D'ELMINA.

28 Jacobus Capitein's tenure as clergyman in Elmina was not a success but his translation of the Ten Commandments and Lord's Prayer into his native Fante would be used for his mission work.

master offered him an education, and later Capitein apparently earned a doctorate in theology from the University of Leiden in 1742, in which he argued that being a slave and being a Christian were compatible. He was then sent back as a Reformed chaplain to Elmina. He soon ran into difficulties, however, with both the white population, who were unwilling to be subordinate to him, and the local Africans, who resisted his conversion efforts. The Church in Amsterdam also refused to accept his unorthodox proposals for conversion, and Capitein left the ministry, dying not long afterwards, at the age of thirty.

That Capitein had been able to become a clergyman at all in a white church was a striking occurrence in the eighteenth century, but his fate, and his uniqueness, also illustrate the more the social boundaries that determined life in the Dutch-ruled world. Racism, strongest in colonies such as British North America where whites were most numerous, was arguably less rigorously applied in a context such as the Dutch Caribbean, where whites were a small minority. Nevertheless, Asians and Africans were hardly equal to Europeans either in the India Companies or, in the case of a small number of African slaves and servants, in the Republic itself. Slavery in Surinam and the Guyana coast remained very harsh, even after the government issued regulations on the treatment of slaves, and many Africans opted for escape into the rainforests when they could. Life for Africans on the Caribbean islands was generally milder, where the rights of both freed and enslaved to own property were more fully recognized, but justice was hardly color-blind here either.

There were other boundaries, too, that could suddenly and sharply emerge. Authorities in the Netherlands had prosecuted "sodomy" – widely and variously defined – since at least the fourteenth century, but these prosecutions were by comparative standards infrequently pursued, under both Catholic and Protestant regimes. In 1730, though, concerns about homosexual acts in the ruins of Utrecht's Dom church (its nave destroyed by

239

a tornado in 1674) paved the way for a wave of prosecutions in some locales, after suspects, under torture, revealed networks, real and imagined, of "sodomites." Moral uncertainty about possible divine judgment, stemming from a cattle plague and the attack of the pile worm on the dikes, may have played a background role in the seeking of scapegoats. Whatever the precise reason, some seventy men were publicly executed for sodomy in the early 1730s by strangling, twenty-four in the Groningen village of Zuidhorn alone, where the local bailiff declared he had discovered such a network among his political opponents. Prosecutions would continue intermittently for the rest of the eighteenth century, though no longer with fatal effect.

It should be added that the new tolerance, to the extent that it was embraced at all, also had its religious limits. It was not intended to benefit Spinozists or Deists, though these voices persisted. Masonic lodges, inspired by foreign example, were formally forbidden in Holland when they first appeared in the 1730s, though more for political reasons – fear that secret societies might be Orangist – than for their Enlightenment religious beliefs. They soon, though, became popular among the country's elite. The restrictions on Jews, for example, on whom they could marry or where they could reside, mostly continued; the city of Utrecht did not allow Jews to live there until 1788. This was true not only of the generally more wealthy Sephardic Jews, but also of the Yiddish-speaking Ashkenazi, who through migration from Germany and eastern Europe surpassed the Sephardic in numbers by 1700 and, by the end of the century, accounted for over 90 percent of the Republic's 30,000 Jews.

Catholics, as by far the most substantial minority in the Republic, continued by law to be suppressed. Although they could worship in private and were allowed to live their daily lives unhindered, their numbers continued to decline through the early eighteenth century: the lack of access to priests and the Church's sacraments, as well as to effective charity, had put pressure on Catholics to convert. Moreover, popular Protestant sentiment, among all classes of the population, remained strongly, even viscerally, anti-Catholic – sentiment fed in the 1730s by the expulsion of Protestants from Catholic Austria, who as refugees found shelter in the Republic. When under Protestant control, Catholics were freest in those parts of Limburg that had come under the control of the Republic and of Prussia after the Peace of Utrecht; here, these Protestant governments were bound by treaty to grant full religious freedom to the Catholic Church, which had been dominant in the region. The Limburg town of Venray, by then under Prussian Protestant rule, continued to be a center of Catholicism that ministered to the needs of Brabant Catholics only a few kilometers away, who still could not build their own public chapels and churches. In practice, though, Catholics otherwise often participated in the public life of States-Brabant (for example, in the guild life of Den Bosch), their numbers too large to suppress too rigorously.

That Catholics remained a repressed minority in the Republic as a whole did not mean that they took on a passive role; in the early eighteenth century, in fact, they were faced with a difficult choice in respect to their own Church leadership. The papacy had come to suspect many of the regular priests working secretly in the Netherlands of tending toward heresy; they were probable Jansenists, a theological strain that was popular in the Low Countries and that, among other views, downplayed the value of external conformity to the Church and did not accept papal infallibility. Dutch Catholics also often took a live-and-let-live stance toward the Protestant Republic, and tried to show their Protestant neighbors that Dutch Catholics, too, knew their Bible and could be counted upon to be good citizens. This pragmatic stance did not sit well with either the religious orders in the region or the authorities in Rome, who believed the faith required a more militant stance. These tensions ultimately resulted in a break. In 1723, a couple of hundred priests appointed their own bishop without requesting prior approval of the pope, precipitating a break in the Dutch Catholic Church. Though in the end a large majority of the Catholic laity remained faithful to Rome, Dutch Catholics now had two churches to choose from, and the conflict between the two would color much of Dutch Catholic life for the decades to come. The offshoot – the Old Catholic Church, as it became known – was understandably preferred by the Republic's leaders for its opposition to papal authority, and they offered it a greater measure of tolerance. The dispute also illustrates that Dutch Catholicism was hardly a monolithic bloc, and that it was a "mission" area that was notoriously difficult to steer from above.

Developments in the Southern Netherlands

Dutch Catholic life was shaped to a considerable extent by what happened across the border in the Austrian Netherlands; many of its priests had come from the seminary in Roermond; its popular piety was influenced by the Flemish Catholic Church; and the Dutch Church was, after 1727, directed by a papal nuntius who was seated in Brussels. Though prohibited from traveling to the Republic, he tried as best he could to direct the Dutch Church.

More broadly, the whole Republic had to take account of what was occurring to the south. By mid-century, its agriculture, industry and trade were beginning to rival the Republic's. And, as long had been the case, the Republic was compelled to be concerned about the security situation in the Austrian Netherlands. A new crisis arose in 1740, which would prove to have far-reaching consequences for the Republic's domestic politics. Maria Theresa's ascension as empress of Austria in that year was contested by Prussia and France on the grounds that Salic law forbade the ascension of women, but it was really motivated by a desire to exploit Austrian weakness. The British and Dutch felt obliged, given their long-term alliance, to support Maria Theresa, and the Dutch Republic became involved in hostilities against France when their Barrier fortresses were attacked and overrun by French forces in 1744. For the next several years the armies of the Republic fought with their allies against France in the southern Netherlands, losing key battles in the process. Peace negotiations were already under way by 1746, but French forces, now facing little military opposition, decided to attack key Dutch positions in the south of the Republic in order to discourage them from offering more support to the Austrians and the British. This limited campaign would unintentionally have sweeping effects on the Republic's domestic politics.

Growing Crisis, 1747–1795

The House of Orange Returns to Power

The French invasion of Zeeland in early 1747 seemed to confirm the haplessness of Dutch military policy. It seemed as if 1672 was repeating itself, and that the perceived solution of 1672 – leadership of an Orange *stadhouder* – was required once again. Across the Zeeland towns crowds demanded the return of Orange, a demand to which the anti-Orange authorities quickly had to consent. Faced with town rioting and spreading unrest, all the provinces soon showed their willingness to appoint a *stadhouder*. By May of 1747, all the provinces, for the first time in the history of the Republic, had agreed to appoint the same *stadhouder*.

This clamor for a *stadhouder* dramatically changed Orangist fortunes. Johan Willem Friso had been shut out of the stadholderate in the western provinces upon Willem III's death in 1702, and after he drowned as the result of a ferry accident in 1711 his yet-to-be-born son Willem Karel Hendrik Friso had to take up the mantle of the Orangist cause. From his very modest base at the Frisian court in Leeuwarden, home to his branch of the Orange-Nassau family, the young prince of Orange had been able, by the time he was a young man, to become *stadhouder* in four provinces, including the politically insignificant Drenthe, which still had no representation in the States-General. Overijssel, Utrecht, Zeeland and all-important Holland, however, steadfastly kept him at a distance. His 1734 wedding to Anne, second daughter of the king of Great Britain, George II, indicated that the British regarded him as an important catch. But it was a marriage Holland had done much to prevent, and it hardly changed the dominance of anti-Orangist sentiments among those in power there. Orangist feeling among large sections of the population in the western provinces was substantial, but it was ineffective until the French invasion electrified public opinion against the political status quo.

The popular revolt of 1747 – it has been called the only European revolution of the mid eighteenth century – was about more than dissatisfaction over the course of the war, or merely an expression of love for the House or Orange. It was fed by a widespread frustration over economic decline and rooted in a long-standing political tradition of urban revolt that justified popular uprising if a basic level of accountability on the part of those who ruled was not met. Political in-breeding and the corruption it generated had been observed for decades; in Amsterdam some 3,200 public offices had been created by the mid eighteenth century – many of them, or so it was suspected, as empty sinecures. This situation was now, in this revolutionary moment, regarded as intolerable, particularly by the literate leaders of the revolt, who were inspired by English notions of popular representation and by classical notions of virtuous government. The revolt was Orangist because the *stadhouders* were widely regarded as champions of the people who, once in power, would restore true religion and morality – anti-Catholicism played a role here – and throw the ruling clique out of office, allowing true representatives of the people to take their place. In this sense the Revolution of 1747 and 1748 was an important early articulation of a political vision for a new kind of Republic.

The cause of Orange and that of popular government thus initially seemed to go hand-in-hand, certainly to the terrified political

244

establishment of the country, who, intimidated and threatened in the streets, were anxious to negotiate with the prince to save what they could of their positions. The bloody sack and fall to French forces in September 1747 of Bergen op Zoom – a fortress the Dutch had considered impregnable – brought about another wave of panic. A close advisor of the prince, Willem Bentinck, lord of Rhoon, made use of this panic to arrange that the office of *stadhouder* would now become hereditary. The House of Orange thus attained semi-monarchical status. In the ensuing months, Willem and his advisors moved to assert political control over the provinces and towns.

Abortive Reform

Willem IV – as Willem Karel Hendrik Friso now became known – used the popular unrest to solidify his grip on power, but he was otherwise distinctly disinclined to grant more concessions to the protesters than was absolutely necessary. One popular reform he did support was eliminating the tax farming system, which collected the excise taxes on goods being traded and sold. Popular sentiment deeply resented, particularly in a time of economic decline, these private tax collectors, who won the government bid by promising to collect the most revenues. Unrest broke out first in Groningen in early 1748, when a mob plundered the homes of tax farmers who had seemed insufficiently enthused in celebrating the birth of Willem IV's son. In the course of the year the revolt spread to Holland, where civic militias initially stood by as citizens looted the homes and property of the hated tax collectors. Later, as the looting spread, the militias did intervene, and in Amsterdam they fired on a crowd that extended its plundering to other wealthy homes. Officials there tried and hanged three leaders of the revolt for sedition, including the fish-vendor Marretje Arents, who was dragged to the gallows while calling on the gathered crowd to avenge her. The States of Holland, in accordance

29 Plundering the houses of tax farmers in 1748, including the one owned
by A.M. van Arssen pictured here, did prompt the only real reform offered
by Willem IV: an improved tax system.

with Willem's advice, suspended the tax farming system. Taxes
would now be collected by government officials who, though subjected to stricter rules of accountability, likely cost the taxpayer
more money than the tax farmers.

On the crucial issue of political office, though, those desiring
deep reform were to be disappointed. In 1748 Willem resisted
the earnest entreaties of the Amsterdam *Doelisten*, members of a
citizens' militia who, in addition to opposing the tax farmers, reasserted an old desire to appoint their own leaders instead of having
them appointed by the city mayors, and who demanded that the
positions of public office be opened up. Willem dismissed part
of the city council in favor of new men, many of them wealthy

patricians, but declined to implement structural reforms. In the end, the reformers who sought a measure of democratization failed to implement them anywhere in the Republic. With the coming of peace in 1748, the unrest abated. The revolution of 1747–1748 had only served to return the House of Orange to the center of power. It would in any event generate, as hindsight reveals, a hereditary dynasty that would produce sons and daughters who would rule the Netherlands to the present day.

There were limits to the Orangist triumph, partially stemming from Willem IV's decision to keep the old arrangements of the Republic in place. He, for the most part, ignored the advice of his associate Bentinck, who saw the hereditary office with its regal allure as the first step in the direction of a more centralized and reinvigorated state. The *stadhouder*, however, saw his predecessor, Willem III, as the standard to follow and believed that his newly won position was sufficient to secure the cooperation and loyalty of the country's political class. Perhaps he also sought to avoid the major confrontation that centralizing reform surely would have caused. However, he died unexpectedly in 1751, aged forty, leaving his wife Anne behind to serve as regent for their three-year-old son. Soon thereafter the old States coalition, with its hostility to the domination of the *stadhouder*, reasserted itself. This was particularly evident in Amsterdam, the historic heart of the "true freedom," where Orangists were effectively shut out of local government. In several other Holland towns a similar process took place, thus continuing to challenge the *stadhouder*'s power, particularly at the local level.

Even with Willem's death and the return of this opposition, however, the Orangist regime would continue to hold the lion's share of power in the Republic for the next thirty years. The leading figure of the government was Ludwig Ernst, duke of Brunswick, a former marshal in the Holy Roman Empire and confidant of Willem IV who became captain-general of the Dutch army after the *stadhouder*'s death. Brunswick exercised great influence over the young and hesitant Willem V, first as his tutor; then as his regent after the death of Anne in 1759; and later as an adult, when Brunswick, through a secret contract of his own making, had himself recognized as the *stadhouder*'s chief advisor. Caricatured for his enormous girth and increasingly detested for his outsized influence – he was the target of an assassination attempt in 1771 – Brunswick steadily sought to strengthen his master's control over the Republic. Crucial to the government's staying in power was a very extensive system of patronage, arguably more systematized, more repressive and more venal than the patronage that always had been part of the Republic's political system. The Orangist lock on power was most complete in the provinces where, during the political crisis, they were able to reassert a throttlehold the same regions that Willem III had gained in 1675: Gelderland, Overijssel and Utrecht. But in most parts of the Republic, including Holland, the government's leading authorities, such as the regional bailiffs, could become wealthy by selling offices to reliable persons – frequently from families of note or from the often Orangist officer corps – who could be counted upon to rule the towns and countryside in loyal fashion. This patronage system might be said to have had the virtue of giving the Republic an important measure of political stability. But it obviously generated resentment from opponents outside this patronage network. And in times of crisis, the system, with its ethos of partiality and cronyism, could be vulnerable to the same kind of public anger that had suddenly brought the *stadhouder* to power in 1747.

External Pressures, Internal Decay

Brunswick's military ties to Austria and the House of Orange's marriage connections seemed to solidify the Republic's position standing close to Vienna and London while avoiding war. But the old Anglo-Austrian alliance fell apart in the mid 1750s, as Austria sought an alliance with France against its new adversary Prussia, thus rendering it an ally of Britain's arch-enemy. This put the Republic in a hopeless position: its Barrier fortresses were useless now that France and the Austrian Netherlands had become allies, and geopolitically it was stranded. It understandably chose neutrality in the Seven Years' War, which began among these states in 1756 – despite British appeals, on the basis of earlier treaties, that it join them.

Neutrality, though, is a relative term, and the Dutch did not entirely escape the conflict. At war against the powerful British navy, France had relaxed its mercantilist policy and let Dutch ships trade at French colonial ports so that their goods might safely be transported by a neutral party. The British, provoked by this measure, moved to confiscate Dutch ships on which French "contraband" was found, and in 1758 went further and attacked merchant ships sailing for St. Eustatius and Curaçao. For a time, too, English privateers raided Dutch vessels in the Channel. In Asia British forces, without warning, attacked VOC ships heading to protect their interests in Bengal, and subsequently restricted Dutch economic activity there in a bid to expand Britain's own influence in India. This had consequences for Dutch business in the region, as seen, for example, in the opium trade. For eighty years, the VOC had enjoyed a lucrative monopoly by bringing opium from Bengal to Batavia, where Dutch middlemen further resold the narcotic to buyers in Java and China. Now the British obliged the Dutch to buy the Bengal opium from them at hefty rates. The end of the war in 1763 normalized Anglo-Dutch relations, but the experience illustrates how British military and economic might was squeezing Dutch trade – and how increasingly dependent the Dutch were on British forbearance to keep what they still possessed.

Foreign observers had admired the cleanliness and orderliness of Dutch towns throughout most of the early eighteenth century; by the 1760s some observers, such as the famous man of letters James Boswell, were remarking on the ruinous state of

Dutch towns such as Utrecht, where he had come to study. Delft was described as a dead city, with a good many of its domiciles abandoned. Urban industries continued to decline, losing out to competition from abroad. Technical innovation also seems to have declined dramatically. In the years 1774–1794 only 39 patents were publicly recognized, a small percentage compared to the high water mark of the Republic, 1615–1634, when 262 such patents were granted. Adding to the loss of competitive ability were the still-high public debt and the tangle of seals, stamps and other red tape that hobbled local trade. In this deteriorating context, the options for the working class of the cities were far from ideal. They could apply for poor relief – as they increasingly did – and if they were fortunate they could make appeal as members in standing to a local church. Other charity-seekers had to appeal to the municipality, where the terms of support were worse. By the end of the century, half of Leiden's work force was on poor relief. Another option for the unemployed was to emigrate out of the cities, seeking work in other towns or in the countryside. Local authorities, however, were increasingly insistent that new residents bring letters from their former towns in which they, and not the new place of residence, promised to pay for their upkeep should they become indigent. This obviously did not encourage mobility.

In some cases, the growing poverty led to vagrancy or worse. The specter of homeless and transient young men – especially former soldiers – and the violence they seemed to bring had long troubled early modern Europe, but in the 1760s and 1770s it was felt to have become a problem in the Republic. Beyond its borders, as for example in Limburg, the marauding bands – eventually called *Bokkenrijders* because of the rumors that they flew about the countryside on hell-sent goats – robbed and killed at isolated farmsteads and rectories. It was a plague that came and went, but seemed to reach its climax in the 1770s. Some 375 people were then executed by Limburg authorities for their participation in the raids, although with torture as their interrogation tactic, and with a large bonus as an incentive for convicting as many people as possible, it is impossible to know how many of those executed were truly involved. Such bands were not unknown in the Republic, but now reports of increased vagrancy and rural attacks prompted officials in places such as Alkmaar to move harshly against suspected wrongdoers; in 1768, three people were hanged there on such charges. Fears of rising lawlessness in the countryside thus accompanied the economic decline.

It was not bad economically everywhere, of course. In the Austrian Netherlands, the rise of trade, agriculture and an incipient industrialization, aided by sufficient natural resources and encouraged by the systematically mercantilist policies of the government, promoted growth and new economic prosperity in the southeast corner of the present-day Netherlands. Within the Republic there were also points of light. In a few locales, sometimes at the edges of the Republic, the economy blossomed. The easy availability of iron ore in Gelderland's Achterhoek made possible the first blast furnace there in the 1750s, a sign of incipient industralization. In Vaals, German Lutherans, having found greater freedom of worship in States-Limburg than across the frontier in Catholic Aachen, developed a profitable textile industry that exported its goods across Europe. Schiedam, having lost herring-fishing as a livelihood around 1700, became the center of the hugely expanding *jenever* industry. A somewhat different recipe for what became known as "gin" was soon produced in England, but that barely hindered Schiedam. Its distilleries – 113 of them in 1778 – continued to sell most of its *jenever* abroad, including to West Africa, where it was a cherished trading good. The town enjoyed strong employment and new construction in the late eighteenth century, with scores of windmills erected high above the houses to power the town's chief industry.

Above all it was the agrarian sector that fared best. The population of western Europe, having escaped centuries of plague and enjoying longer periods of peace, began to expand substantially after the mid eighteenth century, driving up the demand for and price of food. It was this need that the Dutch economy now responded to. This was not true for the country's agricultural hinterland, where marginal farms, sandy soil and low agricultural productivity hobbled growth – though it might be added that Drenthe, where farmers mostly subsisted on the rye they sowed for themselves, also saw none of the rising poverty felt in the western towns. Rather, it was the already technically advanced agricultural regions of Holland and Zeeland, as well as the river region in the middle of the Republic and Groningen-Friesland, that did especially well. With their specialized crops, high-quality dairy products and superior animal husbandry, not to mention easy access by water to international markets, these regions became a key motor of the Dutch economy for the coming century.

This positive development could be of little consolation to the impoverished residents of the dilapidated towns, or to the middle-class citizens who, since mid-century, had become disturbed at the depths to which the Republic had sunk. Like their counterparts in other parts of Europe and the Atlantic world, they developed a heightened sense that they shared a national history and identity, which in their case made them all the more painfully aware that their ancestors had lived in a great and glorious commonwealth as they no longer did. Influenced by Enlightenment ideas, they came to believe that the decline could be remedied by a change in human behavior, and much of the late Dutch Enlightenment was focused on how to reverse national decline, which they saw in the first instance as being corrected by the moral regeneration of the nation. Classical republicanism, drawn from Roman antiquity, became a source of inspiration for cultivating better citizens and improving government. Many Dutch, then, believed that the Republic, with moral effort, could be made great again.

Hopes of a Better Future

The way to gain greater collective insight in the late-eighteenth-century Republic, as elsewhere, was to engage in "civil society," in associations of like-minded people, who in civilized and reasoned fashion would discuss a whole range of topics, making appropriate use of the newest scientific and philosophical knowledge. Masonic lodges, which by now had become societies of the well-connected, played a role in this development. Newly established associations, such as Felix Meritis of Amsterdam and the Teyler Societies of Haarlem (both founded in 1778) were exclusive affairs, affordable only to the wealthy, but together they aimed at promoting the public interest through, among other things, support of the arts and the sciences. But the new associations were genuinely popular; many less elevated reading societies joined the fray, discussing the newest knowledge and ways to apply it to the state of the country. Two initiatives aimed specifically at developing a national network to address the country's problems. The "Economic Branch" (*Oeconomische Tak*) of the Holland Society of Sciences in 1778 sought to discover ways to improve the economic situation by establishing chapters across the country – to little avail, it might be added. Of great significance was the establishment in 1784 of the Society for the Common Good (*Maatschappij tot Nut van 't Algemeen*), which was, the churches excepted, the first successful national organization of citizens that the Republic had known. A society of the well-educated Protestant middle class, it believed that a collective commitment to love of the Fatherland, broad-minded Christianity and moral self-restraint was the path to restoring the nation. Its orientation was primarily educational, aiming to reach the working classes, whose natural impulses, it believed, were ill-disciplined, necessitating the need for guidance. The "Nut," as it became known, was emblematic of a wider initiative among the middle classes to "elevate" the unschooled mass of the population, chiefly through education – an initiative that would have a profound impact on nineteenth-century Dutch society.

Learning the importance of wise self-discernment was not only a message aimed at the poor, but something for everyone to work toward, as the popular *History of Miss Sara Burgerhart*, written in 1782 by women authors Betje Wolff and Aagje Deken, illustrates. There has been much historical discussion about the place of women in the late Dutch Enlightenment. On the one hand, women writers and poets were recognized in the public sphere, and it was often conceded that they had been endowed with comparable intellectual and moral capabilities to those of men; yet – if their economic and social circumstances permitted it – their chief role was seen as mother and homemaker, and the professions were in any event closed to them. *Sara Burgerhart*, which took the form of 175 letters written by various protagonists, describes the adventures of a young woman who escapes the clutches of her rigidly religious aunt; braves various dangers; and in the end marries a virtuous man, in the process having attained inner wisdom. The book, written in the first place for young women, was meant as a warning against diversionary entertainments merely dictated by fashion and luxury, echoing a republican concern for the virtue of citizens. These concerns were clearly gendered, but the theme of the morally capable citizen, directed by an inner compass, was one that could find broad resonance among the Dutch middle class at the end of the century.

Historians have long debated the extent to which the agenda of the reform-minded citizenry was politically driven. Much of their program was not explicitly tied to politics at all and seemed more about setting the right moral tone for society than about changing the political order. The Dutch Enlightenment, shaped within a Protestant Republic, bore little of the sharp, politically charged resentment against an all-powerful state and hierarchical Church that was characteristic of the movement in France. Yet the concerns of the late eighteenth century cannot be typified as apolitical. The decline of the Republic might have been experienced as chiefly moral in cause, but its political tensions also informed their views. It is telling that some of the most prominent reformers and leading publicists came from the ranks of the Mennonites and the Remonstrants, dissenting Protestants who, though often wealthy and well-connected, as a rule were shut out of the Republic's power structures. They came to find this exclusion morally and, increasingly, politically unacceptable. Many, though certainly not all, of the leading lights of this period would come to sympathize with the Patriot movement, including Wolff and Deken.

The American Revolution and War with Britain

Within this context events after 1775 conspired further to foment political tensions in the Republic, culminating a decade later in dramatic confrontations. The chief catalyst was the American War of Independence from British rule. Officially the Republic was neutral in the war, but in the course of the conflict Dutch divisions surfaced that were to have far-reaching effects. The *stadhouder*, with his historic ties to Great Britain, had no intention of supporting the American rebels, and indeed was initially asked by the British, though without success, to supply mercenary troops for service in North America. Moreover, many Dutch had an unfavorable view of the revolt, believing it wrong to oppose established authority. Others, sensing business opportunities, thought otherwise. St. Eustatius, in the 1770s at its economic height as a trading center of legal and illegal trade in the Caribbean, soon functioned as the conduit for supplying the Americans with ammunition, this despite a formal British ban. This supply stream was crucial to the rebels, and it is doubtful that without it they could have achieved independence. It was also clearly beneficial economically to the Dutch island, reflected in the famous gun salute that its governor-general offered the rebel ship *Andrew Doria* in November 1776, now seen as the first international recognition of American independence. The trading benefits for the Dutch, however, were considerably wider than to St. Eustatius alone; though rebel munition supplies originated from various ports in Europe, Amsterdam was the chief supply source. Efforts by the *stadhouder*'s government to prevent this trade foundered on the political resistance of the recalcitrant city.

Willingness to help the Americans was motivated by more than material advantage. Dutch republicans critical of the *stadhouder* were pleased that American rebels drew inspiration from the Union of Utrecht, and were excited about their struggle against monarchical rule. They were part of a growing transatlantic movement that believed that it could be justified in overthrowing the established order in order to advance the natural rights of liberty and equality for all citizens. Dutch maritime interests, long chafing in the shadow of British naval predominance, also wished for a British defeat. After the American captain John Paul Jones sailed into the anchorage at Texel in late 1779 with two captured British warships, he was enthusiastically greeted in Amsterdam as a hero. Dutch publications showered interest and praise on the revolution that the Americans had unleashed.

Jones's short stay in the Republic ended when the wily captain sailed away during a storm in order to evade the British ships that were awaiting him off the island. But his stay had angered the British, and London was not to be endlessly humored by the inability of the Dutch government to prevent Dutch merchants actively aiding the American rebels. Written evidence, seized at sea in late 1780, that the city of Amsterdam was exploring a possible trade agreement with the United States brought Britain and the Netherlands to the brink of war. Dutch intentions to join the League of Armed Neutrality, a Russian-led coalition, in order to stop the British from searching and sometimes seizing their vessels – an intrusion and insult that deeply vexed the Dutch public – further contributed to a break in relations. Thus began the Fourth English War in December of 1780.

It was a disaster for the Dutch. Deadlock over defense priorities – the *stadhouder* and Brunswick had thought land defenses paramount, Amsterdam and other maritime interests favored a strong naval policy – had ensured that both were neglected. A decision to build more naval warships in 1779 – the Dutch had only twenty ships of the line at the time – came too late to prevent the British from wreaking havoc on the seas. St. Eustatius was captured and its rich store of goods looted, and the British also seized Dutch posts on the Guyana, Ceylon and Sumatra coasts. The war crippled the trade of both the VOC and WIC, bringing these already weak organizations near to the point of collapse. That it was not worse than it was came from the fact that the Dutch government had asked the French to protect its colonial interests. Most devastating for the Dutch was the fact that the British blockaded the Republic's harbors, making maritime trade exceedingly risky without the military convoys that the navy was scarcely able to mount. An attempt by Admiral Johan Zoutman to escort merchant ships resulted in the Battle of Dogger Bank in August of 1781. Although the Dutch declared victory, the battle was a draw, the Dutch merchantmen returned to Texel and the navy did not again venture out. The result of the British blockade thus brought Dutch maritime trade to a virtual halt. Though in hindsight the war was not as destructive as the Dutch would face during the French Period (1795–1813), it hit the western port towns extremely hard. This can be illustrated by the number of foundlings recorded in Amsterdam; already rising from the average of 30 a year in the 1770s, by the 1780s it had risen to nearly 400 a year. The high prices and low employment caused by the blockade pushed many of the city's poorer inhabitants to the point where they could barely survive.

Clearly, then, the country was in crisis, and some began to believe that only radical political reform could still save it.

The Patriot Movement and Near Civil War

Quit the name!

The course of the war prompted the Baron Joan Derk van der Capellen tot den Pol to write anonymously *To the People of the Netherlands* (*Aan het volk van Nederland*) in 1781. Van der Capellen, for a time a member of the States of Overijssel through the support of Willem V, had learned English and read the work of English political radicals, inspired also by the citizen militias in America that had resisted the regular army of the British king. This minor nobleman now pilloried the *stadhouders* for having usurped the historic rights of the Dutch through corrupt patronage, and blamed Willem V entirely for the deplorable state of affairs. His pamphlet called on the Dutch people to defend their rights against the *stadhouder*.

The baron's call to action was a crucial catalyst in galvanizing a new political movement whose members would soon describe themselves as "the Patriots." They sought to challenge the corrupt institutions of the Republic and, in the first place, to "restore" the civic government of their respective towns. In this sense, they were locally and not nationally focused, more concerned about regaining old local rights than about full-scale political revolution. They launched an active political press in support of their cause, and by 1783, first in Dordrecht and then elsewhere, they were heeding Van der Capellen's call for the organization of new civic militias.

The Patriots' appeal was considerably broader than the regents of the old anti-Orangist factions, and they attracted a large segment of the middle class who had had no say in the governing of their towns or of the Republic. Their participation signaled an important democratization of Dutch politics. From this extensive popular and enthusiastic base, the Patriots were able to demand – and receive – power in key towns of the Republic. They gained more and more votes in the various States and in the States-General. They managed to ban the hated Brunswick from the Republic, and by 1785 their political influence was such that they were able to strip the *stadhouder* of much of his political power. Feeling unsafe in The Hague, Willem V left for the safer environs of Gelderland. The Patriots' movement reached its high point when in August of 1786 some 20,000 militiamen from all over the country paraded in a show of unity in Utrecht and, holding their own democratic elections, sent sixteen of their own to the town council. It was the first election of its kind.

Yet in reality the Patriots' position was hardly secured. They were strongly divided among themselves, particularly on the issue of who exactly should be politically represented, and their focus on local reforms made national unity difficult. Though they tended to be disproportionately drawn from the ranks of dissenters and Catholics, and from provinces such as Overijssel, Utrecht and Holland, they constituted a motley jumble of interests and aims. Moreover, they had to contend with still-strong formidable Orangist opposition, with its bulwarks in Gelderland, Friesland and Zeeland. Orangists furthermore were represented across the Republic, and came not only from the old political establishment but from the better part of the Reformed Church clergy, the small Jewish community (which enjoyed close political and economic ties to the Orange court) and sections of the Dutch lower classes that were historically pro-*stadhouder*. Indeed, one of the Orangists the Patriots loved to hate was the low-born Rotterdam mussel-inspector Catharina Mulder, also known as Kaat Mossel, who in a well-publicized case had helped to lead popular protest against the creation of Patriot militia, in which brawling, arson and looting were the result. The Orangists, no less than the Patriots, then, were a diffuse faction.

In the rather anarchic situation of the mid 1780s, with its street-fighting and military skirmishes between the *stadhouder*'s army and local militias, outright civil war was never far away. Another factor, however, soon broke the impasse: the great powers, in this case Britain and Prussia. The British were keen to push the ever hesitating *stadhouder* to take bold steps to assert his authority and

Het aanhouden van de Princes van Oranje 28 Juny, 1787.

30   The Patriots had good reason to detain Wilhelmina at Goejanverwellesluis, given her intent to reach The Hague and retake power from them. But the action likely hastened their defeat.

make use of his popular support. Such an assertion meant a return to The Hague. It was not he, however, but his wife, Princess Wilhelmina, who undertook the journey. Sister of the Prussian King Friedrich Wilhelm II, of stouter disposition than her husband and long active in seeking to restore Orangist fortunes, it was she who sought out confrontation with the Patriots. Stopped by Patriot pickets at Goejanverwellesluis just east of Gouda late in June of 1787, Wilhelmina used the indignity of her detainment as a person of high birth as the basis for appealing to her brother for help. Demanding "satisfaction" for this deed, the king sent 26,000 soldiers to invade the Netherlands. Patriot militias melted away in the face of this force, and Willem V was fully restored to his office in the fall of 1787.

A New Revolutionary Tide

Orangist vengeance on the now hapless Patriots was not mild. Throughout the country the homes of prominent Patriots, particularly Catholics, were plundered by mobs. All authorities in cities such as Amsterdam were forced to display Orange colors to demonstrate their loyalty. Many Patriots were promptly prosecuted by the authorities, and thousands of them fled to the Austrian Netherlands or France, where they regrouped themselves, hoping and planning for better days. Orangist triumph did not lead to any rejuvenation of the 200-year-old Republic. By this time the *stadhouder* was, in foreign policy at least, little more than a pawn of the British and the Prussians, and proposals for reform, initiated by the grand pensionary, Laurens van de Spiegel, foundered on Willem's lack of interest.

Meanwhile, the danger of revolt and revolution in the region had not dissipated. In the Austrian Netherlands, Emperor Joseph's ambitious reforms had caused a full-scale revolt in 1789. His centralizing policies had alarmed some local elites, and his decree that all monasteries without a public purpose be closed earned him the opposition of traditional Catholics. Towns such as Weert and Roermond fell under a regime seeking an independent Brabant before being recovered by Austrian troops late in 1790. Further south, in France, the Revolution reached a radical phase late in 1792, and it now became the mission of French revolutionary armies to drive all reactionary rulers from power. France thus declared war on Britain, Austria and the Dutch *stadhouder* in February of 1793. From this time on, Dutch Patriots, both in France and in the Republic, made plans for a Republic that could be proclaimed once the *stadhouder* had been driven from office; they were keen to make their own mark and impress on the French that in victory their country should not be treated like a vanquished territory but as a "sister republic." Through the French Revolution many of them had radicalized, and they were no longer interested in merely restoring traditional rights in the old Republic but were driven by architectonic visions of a revolutionary new order.

The chance to implement their new ideas, however, was contingent on the fortunes of the battlefield. For many months, the *stadhouder*'s army fought with the Austrians against the French in the southern Netherlands. In June of 1794, these allies were decisively defeated by the revolutionary army at Fleurus, just south of Brussels. Vienna, long doubtful about the value of a distant Netherlands for an empire that was expanding into southern and eastern Europe, quickly abandoned the southern Netherlands to the French, leaving an invasion path open to the Republic. French armies accordingly took the fortresses of Den Bosch and Maastricht in the fall of 1794. Even then, the French might have been persuaded, under terms advantageous to them, to make peace with the Republic. But in December 1794 a new opportunity came their way: a severe cold spell froze the great rivers, eliminating the natural defense on which the *stadhouder* and his allies had relied. In January 1795, the French swept across the rivers, driving off the smaller forces that had opposed them. On 18 January, accompanied by his sons and eighteen wagons of valuables, Willem V left by boat from Scheveningen for Britain, leaving the seat of government to his foreign and domestic foes.

For decades a strong sense of national pride among Dutch citizens had prompted them to look back to the great achievements of their venerable Republic. It also caused to them to look with concern at its declining fortunes, so evident in recent years and decades, and yearn for national renewal. The political question in 1795 was whether political and economic restoration could be achieved by maintaining past features of that Republic, or whether a whole new blueprint would be necessary.

5
Building a Nation-State, 1795–1870

~

The French invasion ushered in a new regime. Although the Netherlands was, from the outset, a satellite of Paris, Dutch revolutionaries were initially given room to develop a new state. Under Napoleon in particular, this room for the Dutch to arrange their own affairs was gradually diminished. The defeat of Napoleon brought the Oranges to power and resulted – for a time – in the United Kingdom of the Netherlands, which included north and south, not to mention extensive colonial possessions. Belgian revolt, however, put an end to this united kingdom. The Dutch regime, initially autocratic, was transformed into a liberal parliamentary government in 1848. The new freedoms encouraged new groups in Dutch society to become active members of the nation-state. By 1870, when Europe and the world would be struck by new political, social and economic developments, the Dutch had shaped a state and society that were well positioned to take on new challenges.

After 1795, then, Dutch politics and society would be forced to reinvent themselves. Though that process would continue – even intensify – after 1870, the basic contours of the Dutch nation-state, domestically and internationally, would be determined by the 1860s.

French Domination, 1795–1813

Different Revolutionary Outcomes

As the French armies entered Dutch cities in late 1794 and early 1795 the Patriots celebrated their new-found freedoms with the planting of liberty trees. Taking partial inspiration from a tree in Boston under which the Sons of Liberty met to resist British rule in North America, French revolutionaries had planted their own trees to show that freedom was taking root in France. Now Dutch Patriots were doing the same, symbolically emphasizing that the old order was over, and the new had come. Drawing on international inspiration, their use of the liberty tree illustrates again just how much the country's "Batavian Revolution" – so-named to honor the freedom-loving Batavians whom the Dutch regarded as their ancestors – was part and parcel of a broader transatlantic unrest.

What set much of the Netherlands apart from revolutionary activity in America or France was the absence of much violence. Orangists were dismissed from their governmental posts and forced into political retirement, the symbols of the old regime pulled down. But there was very little physical retribution in the velvet revolution that established the new Batavian Republic. The same generally can be said for the whole history of the young Republic, which was characterized by a moderate style that – even when it engaged in acts of repression – was at pains to use restraint. A bourgeois, non-sectarian Christian spirit that emphasized prudent and moderate Enlightenment helped keep the guillotine and the firing squad, used in the French Revolution, away from the Dutch revolutionary experience. Perhaps the confrontations of the 1780s had also lessened Dutch passion for extreme measures.

Nevertheless, it is important to note that 1795 held different fates for different parts of what now constitutes the Dutch kingdom. In August of that year a slave rebellion broke out on Curaçao, in which perhaps 1,000 slaves took up arms to protest the conditions of their servitude. Their leader, Tula, took his inspiration not from events in faraway Holland but from Haiti, where slaves had overthrown the old order. With the hope that – as in France – slavery would be abolished in the Dutch colonies, Tula and his compatriots rebelled. The revolt was soon put down at the cost of 100 slaves killed, and to set an example the authorities crushed all

31 Tula's was for a long time hardly a household name on Curaçao; long dismissed as a rioter and a thief, only in recent years has he been recognized as a freedom fighter.

the bones in Tula's body before they executed him. The Batavians did briefly consider freeing the slaves in their dominions, but most of them feared the collapse of social order in the Caribbean, and the Revolution brought no change in their status. New rules were, however, introduced in the colony, to better regulate the working conditions of slaves so as to prevent a new rising.

In other colonies, the danger to Dutch rule came from other quarters. Britain, afraid that Dutch colonies would fall into the hands of its enemy France – the French did indeed take possession of St. Eustatius in 1795 – secured in the so-called Letters of Kew the formal permission of the deposed *stadhouder*, Willem V, temporarily to take over Dutch colonies. In August of 1795, the British defeated Dutch colonists on the South African Cape at the Battle of Muizenberg, bringing VOC rule to an end after a century and a half. Although Britain briefly transferred the Cape back to Dutch control (1803–1806), this was the beginning of British rule in South Africa. Similarly, the British seized Ceylon in 1796, ending Dutch colonial presence there for good. Malakka, too, was taken. Revolution in Europe had profound consequences for the colonies, not least in the Dutch case.

At home, too, the Dutch paid a price for the political transition. The French, in the Treaty of The Hague (May 1795), not only made the Dutch pay for the costs of liberation (some 100 million guilders) but also forced the Republic to cede States-Flanders and States-Limburg to France. Maastricht's revolutionaries accordingly celebrated the city's formal incorporation into the French Republic: the town's great public square, the Vrijthof, was rechristened La Place de la Liberté to mark the occasion. Other territories, currently in the Netherlands but which had belonged to Austria, such as around the city of Roermond, were also annexed by the French. Some years later France formally annexed the small territories belonging to the Holy Roman Empire, such as Thorn and its former abbey, localities that were already effectively under French control by 1794.

"Revolution" meant something very different in these regions than it did in the Batavian Republic. The years under the Directory (1795–1799) were particularly difficult for the local population. An entirely new governmental structure was immediately imposed and all special privileges annulled, to the confusion and hindrance of many locals. The anticlerical government in Paris quickly abolished the monasteries and abbeys (such as the one in Thorn), sold many Church properties or closed them, prohibited use of the Christian calendar (including the celebration of feast days) and imprisoned priests who did not swear loyalty to the Republic. Most of the Netherlands that then came under direct French rule was heavily Catholic, and these policies forced the Church underground – in some cases literally, as evidenced in the hidden chapels at Geulhem and elsewhere, carved into the marlstone quarries deep under the Limburg countryside. Deeply unpopular, too, was the forced conscription of all unmarried men between twenty and twenty-five years of age into the French army, where the life expectancy of recruits was extremely low.

All this brought parts of Limburg to the edge of rebellion in 1798, though the region mostly avoided the open warfare between peasants and the French government that erupted a short distance away in the Belgian countryside. Napoleon's rule (1799–1814) brought more tranquility, particularly since his Concordat with the papacy in 1801 ended the conflict with the Church. French administrative reforms in the courts and in municipal government also brought a new rational ordering to these regions. These areas, for example, were subject to a Civil Registry years before this was implemented further north. Local administration was better managed, with each village receiving its own mayor, supported by several councillors. The repressive measures against unrest in the countryside also resulted, in the long run, in a more effective police presence that cut down on the brigandage that had been symbolized by the rural crimes of the *Bokkenrijders*.

Within the Batavian Republic itself 1795 witnessed a great swell of enthusiasm for what the future would bring. To be sure, the treaty with the French, with its high financial costs, was rightly seen as injurious to the Republic's future, as it dangerously raised an already high debt level, and rendered the Netherlands less able to help the French financially in the future. A French military presence of 25,000 troops, which the treaty had stipulated the Dutch financially support, made this status further apparent. But French meddling in Dutch domestic affairs was – at least for the time being – rather restrained compared to other republics in the French orbit; France's respect toward a wealthy ally meant to forestall an alienation that would be counter to its interests. In this context, the "Batavians" were largely free to create a state according to their own vision, supported by a very substantial part of the population, whose political expectations, long suppressed by the Oranges and long encouraged by the Patriot press, could now at last be met. The quick formal approval by the Dutch provisional government of its own version of the Declaration of the Rights of Man and the Citizen, that great document of the French Revolution, symbolized the great aspirations of the new republic. Newspapers and journals went into overdrive in their excitement, discussing the preferable course that should be taken.

A Failed Political Process

The Batavians agreed with each other, at least initially, on some key issues. They all were glad to be rid of the House of Orange. Shaped by the Enlightenment and by the emphases of the French Revolution, they stressed equality before the law. This was apparent in the elections that chose representatives for the National Assembly, which first met in March of 1796. All men over the age of twenty were entitled to vote, unless they subsisted on poor relief or held fast to an oath of loyalty to the House of Orange. Religion and class were all cast aside as criteria for determining who could vote, resulting in a strikingly broad electorate by the standards of the late eighteenth century. Obviously there were limits: women, though now often hailed as "citizens" (*burgeressen*), were excluded without serious discussion, and a women's movement demanding political rights, as in the unsuccessful case of France, did not really emerge. But the democratic effects were nevertheless noticeable: over a quarter of the National Assembly were trades- and craftsmen, uncommon vocations for such a body. Some 27 percent of the 126 deputies were Roman Catholic. Though this figure suggests that Catholics, given their numbers in Dutch society, were still somewhat underrepresented, it was a radical reversal of the fortunes they had known in the old Republic, where they had been shut out of public office. Protestant dissenters such as the Mennonites and the Remonstrants were even overrepresented.

The open franchise eventually permitted the first Jews to take seats in the National Assembly, the first time such an admission occurred in Europe. The relative equality of the Assembly was reflected in laws that disestablished the Dutch Reformed Church, treating all denominations, formally at least, as equal before the law. And Jews, in a separate law of September 1796, were granted equal citizenship slightly later than Christians. The end of their status as a foreign nation did not suit all Jews, including religious leaders, who saw their authority threatened. Others, such as one of the first Jewish deputies, Hartog de Hartog Lémon, a progressive foe of the conservative Orangist synagogue in Amsterdam, fought against religious inequality. He noted that Jews were still not allowed in the all-Christian Society for the Common Good (the "Nut"), and he sought to abolish the guilds because their bylaws kept Jews out.

The Revolution generated great expectations for the future, with grand political questions over the best kind of representation and the best kind of constitution for the dawning new age, unleashing a wave of new journals to debate these issues. Practical politics, though, proved disappointing. The National Assembly became deeply divided, irreconcilably so as it proved. It did not help that one of the few statesmen with the political talents and the authority to lead the Assembly, the Rotterdam lawyer Pieter Paulus, died almost immediately after taking on the role of chairman. One coalition – the unitarists, or "revolutionaries" – wanted a strong centralized authority, as inspired by the French revolutionary state. They were arrayed against the federalists, who wished the regions of the old Republic to maintain an important measure of power (those deeply committed to regional power were called "federalists"). "Moderates" were a third group, who leaned toward unitarism but, in their centrist position, could not break through a growing divide and political impasse.

Other crucial and related issues fed the divide. Unitarists saw a strong state as an expression of the people's will, whereas the federalists and moderates preferred representative bodies that could rise above what they saw as mob rule. What made these differences particularly pressing was the issue of the very high level of state debt. Holland had effectively born more than its share of this burden, but unitarists wanted this debt to be assumed by a single, national government. This dynamic has led historians to assert that it was public debt, made worse by the French, that drove the Dutch toward centralization. But this was not the overriding concern of everyone. Whatever the case, it is not surprising that many of the moderates, who wanted to preserve some regional autonomy, came from outside Holland.

Moderates and federalists were most numerous in the Assembly, but all factions were splintered and none of them had a full rein on power. The result of the constitutional deliberations, which finished in January of 1797, was a proposed constitution known as the "Fat Book," which consisted of no fewer than 918 articles. This messy compromise of a constitution was roundly rejected by the voters, many of them concerned that the document did not go far enough. A second National Assembly was forced to start again from scratch, but in the course of 1797 it became clear that they were hopelessly gridlocked.

Radicals in Power

At this point a group of radical unitarists determined that the deadlock had to be ended in order to ensure the further advance of the Revolution. Supported by the French, who preferred an effective republican government with which it could do business, these radicals seized power by force of arms on January 22, 1798. Twenty-eight moderates and federalists were immediately arrested. All opponents, including insufficiently radical unitarists, were excluded from what was now called the Constituent Assembly, enabling the coup leaders to pass their own constitution without opposition. That constitution was then sent for approval to voters, who now had to swear their hostility to federalism before they could vote. The outcome was accordingly lopsided: 154,000 votes for, to just

11,500 against. The result was the country's first written basic law, which, as it turned out, decisively and for good transformed the Netherlands into a unitary state, in which all key decisions would be made by the government in The Hague. A national tax system and educational policy, a uniform legal code, the abolition of the guilds (and thus local privileges), and the consistent separation of Church and state were now enshrined as constitutional principles.

The coup plotters, in granting the country its first and, in key respects, influential constitution, had achieved a quick and remarkable success. They also succeeded in abolishing Holland and all of the formerly "sovereign" states of the Republic in favor of French-style departments, forming a centralized national government that enabled the assumption of existing debt and put government finance on a stable footing. But in other respects they failed. The irony of their effort to save democracy from itself was not lost on the government's critics, who resented the narrow political base on which it attempted to rule the country. Misuse of public office by some leading politicians added to the anger.

To restore a broader base of support for the national Revolution, a second coup, led by General Daendels – who had supported the seizure of power in January – now successfully ousted the increasingly unpopular government in June of 1798. The unitary constitution, though, remained in place. Daendels's coup did not restore popular confidence in the government, with many citizens concluding that the brief experiment in democratic self-rule had been a failure. These citizens, for all of their pessimism, could not know that between 1798 and 1815 the Netherlands would be subject to no fewer than seven different constitutions. Political instability, electoral chicanery and anything but democratic rule would become a mainstay of Dutch public life for some time to come – a far cry from the Batavian dream of 1795. All of these factors, too, would lead to a profound estrangement from the democratic politics so enthusiastically embraced at the beginning of the Revolution.

The constitution of 1798 made a start on crucial reforms, such as standardizing taxation and education. Several reforms failed, however, because they were impracticable or difficult to implement. The Batavian government's efforts to put all churches on an equal footing, its stated policy since 1796, is a good example. Unlike the anticlerical French revolutionaries, the Batavians esteemed churches as institutions, believing in their ability to form virtuous citizens for the Republic. But the Batavians thought that a privileged Church contradicted both true religion and political equality. Consistent with disestablishment, the government sought to cut state support to the Dutch Reformed Church by paying no salaries to all new Reformed clergy. All churches would now have to finance themselves. All Reformed Church property acquired before the Reformation was to be the collective property of all members of the municipality, regardless of faith, with town officials determining its future use. In areas with high Catholic populations, these churches might systematically revert to Catholic use. All of this, however, proved far too ambitious. Property rights were complex and hard to disentangle. But if many Reformed had, in principle, accepted the notion of religious equality, they now openly protested these plans through petitions, and they were shelved. Moreover, Protestant resentment of gains that the "upstart" Catholics had won through the Revolution became an important undercurrent in Dutch politics after 1798, and was one important component of an increasingly powerful trend in Dutch society to "moderate" revolutionary change by rendering it less egalitarian and democratic.

Financial and Economic Difficulties

Neither did the Batavian Revolution bring about the sudden revitalization of the Dutch economy – quite the contrary – though this was less the fault of the government than of the deplorable state of international affairs. As a people allied with France, the

Dutch were drawn into war with Britain and its various allies that – apart from the brief peace of 1802–1803 – lasted from 1795 until 1813. This not only resulted in a loss of colonies, as noted above; the war with Britain finished off what was left of the VOC, and the government was forced to nationalize its "assets" – some 120 million guilders of debt – in 1799. Within a few short years, too, the Dutch navy was effectively eliminated as a military force: the British captured ten of its warships – ships that were to have played a critical role in the French invasion of Ireland – in the disastrous Battle of Camperdown in 1797.

What was left of the fleet at Den Helder, manned by sailors sympathetic to Orange, mutinied and surrendered when a Anglo-Russian force, accompanied by Willem Frederik, son of the *stadhouder*, invaded North Holland in 1799. After Daendels, who was sent to repulse the enemy, was initially defeated, Batavian–French forces effectively rebuffed the invaders at the Battle of Castricum, prompting the Russians and British to re-embark and depart for home. The groundswell of popular support for the House of Orange, on which the invasion had been predicated, did not materialize, and it would be another fourteen years before Willem Frederik was to see his country of birth again. The Netherlands thus remained in the French orbit, compelled to follow Paris in its foreign policy. Even when the Dutch negotiated alongside the French to make peace with the British in the Treaty of Amiens (1802), they were disdainfully treated by Napoleon Bonaparte as a vanquished nation that had no independent voice at the table.

The long years of war were bad news for the Batavian Republic, at least for the western part of the country where the wealth and the bulk of the population lay. (North Holland, the most densely populated region, had at this time 167 people per km², while Drenthe, the least densely populated, had only 15.) The need to raise some 230 million guilders in new taxes after 1795 to meet French demands pinched most people's pockets at precisely a time when maritime trade was generally in decline. In the long run, French manipulation of Dutch financial wealth severely undermined Amsterdam's role as the chief financial center of the world, a claim it had managed to maintain throughout the eighteenth century but that now shifted definitively to London. The debt rose from 455 million guilders in 1795 to over 1.1 billion in 1804. The boom in demand for agricultural products, promoted in part by the war, was good, however, for the inland regions, where the economy and the cities grew modestly during the period of French domination.

For the urbanized west, however, all this meant substantial and sustained decline; seasonal migration to the cities of Holland stopped after 1795, and the cities of Zeeland and Holland would lose 10 percent of their population in the next twenty years, with Amsterdam losing perhaps as much as 20 percent. The Netherlands was still the most urbanized European country in 1800, but it would now lose in absolute and relative terms to its neighbors. Inequalities in wealth, already considerable, widened appreciably in this period. Dependence on poor relief spiked in these years, and churches, faced with their own declining budgets, were not eager to take on new members to benefit from their burdened charity. It mattered financially, incidentally, to which faith one belonged if one became dependent. In Rotterdam in 1798, for example, the poorer congregations of the Catholics and Lutherans, which had many immigrants, could manage to offer only the absolute minimum for subsistence of 30 guilders a year per recipient, while the Reformed and the unaffiliated city poor received more, at 40 guilders. The smaller Walloon and Scottish Reformed churches could afford to pay 100 guilders, the off-shoot Old Catholics a rather generous 150 guilders. In any event, poor relief in the cities was not enough to offset the flight from the western towns and cities.

Napoleonic Reforms

By the dawn of the new century, political changes in the Netherlands were directly orchestrated by the specific political and economic needs of Napoleon Bonaparte. In 1801, to signal to his enemies that the revolutionary period was over and that he was willing to make his peace with the old status quo, Bonaparte encouraged a third coup in The Hague, whose leaders then penned a new constitution. The referendum to approve the constitution was a farce: three-quarters of the nearly 70,000 voters rejected it, but the new government declared victory by claiming that the 330,000 voters who had not voted had thereby given their approval. This constitution of the new "Batavian Commonwealth" was far less democratic in aspiration than the previous one, with much power invested in a twelve-man council, and with new restrictions on the rights of the press and Assembly. But it allowed not only moderates but also Orangists to participate in public life. From his German residence, Oranienstein, the old *stadhouder* released his followers from their vows and recognized the government in The Hague so that in compensation his son might rule the small German principality of Nassau-Orange-Fulda. The changes of 1801 ended the ban on Orangists in public office, thus ushering in the return of many of the country's old ruling class to positions of authority. The time for democratic experimentation was clearly over.

Bonaparte had hoped that the reorganization of the Dutch government through national reconciliation would enable the country once again to become a golden goose by which he might pay for his wars. In this hope he was disappointed – Dutch state finances deteriorated with the resumption of war – and he determined that the country needed a tighter and more effective regime, with a single head more responsive to his own wishes. His choice fell in 1804 upon Rutger Jan Schimmelpenninck, a revolutionary of the moderate party who had represented the Dutch at Amiens and who had gained Napoleon's trust as the Netherlands' ambassador in Paris. Schimmelpenninck's political ideal had long been the United States, and he would have preferred for himself the title of president, but Napoleon insisted on the position of grand

32 Although involved in the Batavian Revolution, Rutger Jan
Schimmelpenninck was never a democratic radical, and his stance fit the
more autocratic temper of the Napoleonic period.

pensionary, with its pretentious reference to the Golden Age. The
electorate were much less excited about the new position and
the new constitution Napoleon had asked Schimmelpenninck to

write; only 4 percent of those eligible to vote did so, most viewing the grand pensionary merely as Paris's proxy.

Yet Schimmelpenninck's government – in the thirteen months that the Emperor Napoleon allowed it to remain in power (1805–1806) – turned out to be singularly productive. Building on the reforms of 1798, the government's greatest and most lasting achievements lay in the fields of education and finances. In respect of education Schimmelpenninck's government was aided by the active presence of reformers from the "Nut," who had long worked for a national educational system. Thanks to these efforts educational reform was more easily achieved in the Netherlands than in surrounding countries. The ideas had been forged into plans in previous Batavian ministries; under Schimmelpenninck these plans were actually implemented.

The School Law of 1806 established for the first time national standards for teachers and for classroom instruction, giving order to what had been a patchwork of private and local educational initiatives. Sectarian education was forbidden, though in practice the new public schools often took on the religious character of the communities in which they were situated. A non-sectarian mandate for the public schools to teach "social and Christian virtues" in a broad and non-offensive way would later cause controversy, as the Dutch increasingly came to disagree with each other over what this meant. But – crucially – a national educational framework had been achieved.

The same was true for taxes. The talented financial secretary was the radical unitarist Alexander Gogel, who made taxes uniform across the country, thus gaining the hostility of the inland regions, where they had been substantially lower than in Holland. He also eliminated the special tax privileges of certain groups such as the guilds. Although regressive taxes on products were now nationally imposed, Gogel also made efforts to tax luxury property at higher rates than necessary property; each home might enjoy two hearths tax-free, for example, but having additional ones meant paying additional taxes. Central to the success of this new tax structure was the creation of a government bureau entrusted with revenue collection. These reforms went hand-in-hand with new standards of public accountability; laws specifically criminalizing the corruption of civil servants already had been made law for the first time in 1804.

None of this was enough for Napoleon to sustain his commitment to this new government. Gogel's tax reforms had been designed to stave off government bankruptcy, and indeed provided it with a stable tax system that would last another half century. But for the time being the government continued to slip deeper into debt; by 1807 this amounted to a whopping 225 percent of annual national income. Schimmelpenninck's descent into blindness, the result of an eye disorder, was another compelling reason for the emperor to replace him with his own brother Louis. Given the logic of Napoleon's evolving dynastic plans, however, it could be argued that Schimmelpenninck's government was bound to be replaced. With the death of the deposed *stadhouder* Willem V in early 1806, Napoleon saw his chance to bind the Netherlands closer to himself. This was a time when the emperor, in dynastic fashion, was placing members of his own family at the head of numerous kingdoms and principalities throughout Europe. Louis was additionally viewed as pliant by his brother, and the emperor certainly expected him to rule his new kingdom in line with French – and familial – interests. But here – once again – Napoleon was to be disappointed.

The First Dutch Monarchy

Thus, in June of 1806, the Netherlands was at a stroke transformed from a republic to a monarchy – permanently, as it turned out. Over this fundamental change the Dutch themselves were barely consulted, let alone offered a choice. Amsterdam – not The Hague – became the formal capital of the new kingdom, and the city hall – that monumental seventeenth-century tribute to republican government – was now put on loan in service of the king, who came to reside there formally. Never ceremonially crowned out of concern for republican opposition (which failed to materialize under the by now politically apathetic Dutch), Louis's own legitimacy was uncertain. Under his rule, the mechanisms of repression were strengthened – police surveillance and inform- ants, already a feature of the Batavian period, were strengthened, as was press censorship. A mandatory travel pass was implemented. At the same time, Louis assiduously sought to win over the hearts of his new subjects. He impressed the Dutch with his sympathiz- ing visits to disaster areas; in 1807 he toured Leiden when its cen- ter was flattened by an accidental gunpowder explosion, and he inspected the great rivers region in 1809, when huge dams of ice had blocked the flow of water to the sea, resulting in the flooding of large tracts of land.

Louis did more. He finally abolished the guilds for good in 1808. He also championed religious equality, particularly for his fellow Catholics, who in some places where they formed the large majority were allowed to take over the medieval churches that had been in Protestant hands. Wholly in line with the view of early- nineteenth-century monarchs that the state should use religion – all religions – to undergird the moral and political order, Louis established a Ministry of Worship in 1808, which would regulate and financially support the country's churches. For the next sixty years, the Dutch government would build churches to this end, primarily for Catholics, who possessed few of their own edifices.

Louis also responded to the Dutch need to project their own national identity. The search for the national character – by means extending from the study of the country's regional dress and customs to the collection of stories – only intensified after Dutch political dreams had been dashed. Around 1800, the politicized myth of the freedom-loving Batavian was replaced by a more culturally minded myth of the seventeenth-century

Golden Age, though references to this great period of Dutch history, too, could also be a locus of cultural resistance to French domination. It is of course true that some cultural aims – such as standardization in 1804 of the language in the Holland-oriented Siegenbeek spelling – very much served the political purposes of a centralized government.

Launching new initiatives was also intended to bring king and country closer together. Under the new king, a patron of the arts and sciences, new royal institutions served also to propel national pride, as well as scholarly and cultural achievement. In this policy the Royal Dutch Academy of Sciences, the Royal Library and the National Art Gallery – later called the Rijksmuseum – were all launched. Louis also stoutly defended Dutch legal customs, resisting his brother's wishes to implement the Napoleonic code in the Netherlands, seeing to it instead that Dutch jurists wrote their own legal code. Though similar in many respects to its French analogue, it differed in crucial respects: for example the Dutch code regarded men and women as equals in cases of divorce, and had greater legal consideration of illegitimate children – an indication, perhaps, of a less patriarchal society.

Because Louis rather contrarily took Dutch interests seriously he ran foul of his brother. His refusal to introduce conscription – that dreaded instrument already imposed in those parts of the Netherlands annexed by France – irritated the emperor, who was desperately in need of more troops. The British invasion of the Zeeland island of Walcheren in 1809 also sowed doubts in Napoleon's mind about his brother's rule. That invasion – with 40,000 men the largest British army on the continent – was potentially a serious threat to Napoleonic rule in Europe. But things went wrong for the British almost from the start, including 4,000 deaths from malarial fevers contracted in mosquito-infested marshes (in contrast to only 100 dead in combat). After four squandered months the British sailed away in defeat. But to

Napoleon, Louis's weak performance during this military threat had been anything but reassuring.

Probably the most serious complaint against Louis, though, was his failure fully to enforce the so-called "Continental System," imposed in November 1806 across Napoleon-dominated Europe to prevent any trade with the arch-enemy Great Britain and so ruin the economy of that island nation. This virtually ended maritime trade in the Netherlands, and led to very severe economic depression that began in 1807 and lasted until peace in 1814. In 1805 nearly 2,400 merchant ships had entered Amsterdam harbor; in 1810 it was a mere 210, and almost none the year after that. Perhaps as much as 80 percent of the Jewish population of Amsterdam, a community heavily involved in trade and commerce, was without work. Louis's apparent leniency toward smuggling and other breaches of the trading embargo created a rift with his brother. Napoleon had had enough by 1809: he annexed the southern regions of the Kingdom of the Netherlands, and a year later incorporated the whole country into France.

Annexed to France

Annexation, incidentally, was not a fate especially reserved for the Dutch. Between 1808 and 1811, Napoleon expanded the boundaries of France proper by directly incorporating portions of Italy (the pontiff, too, was deprived of the Papal States), Spain, Germany and the eastern Adriatic coast as far as present-day Montenegro. The Netherlands was thus only one part of Napoleon's strategy to annex key areas of Europe as a way to exercise better strategic control over his empire.

By this time, the Dutch had lost nearly all of their colonies to British occupation. Already by 1807 the Dutch Caribbean, its trade long disrupted by British naval power, had fallen to this foe. Despite the vigorous military and administrative reforms of the

11   The French Empire in 1811 stretched from the Frisian islands well into the Adriatic; annexation of the Netherlands was only a small part of a larger Napoleonic strategy.

irrepressible General Daendels, their key possession, Java, under-went the same fate in 1811. Though its maritime trade was cut off, the Netherlands itself managed to boost its situation a bit through inland trade with French-dominated Germany, improving the roads and developing a more intensive river traffic. French markets – belatedly – opened to them in 1812.

But at home the regime became even more repressive. Affecting everyone was the implementation of the Civil Registry in the years 1811–1812, which required all inhabitants of the country to have their vital statistics, such as births and deaths, marriage and divorce, recorded by the municipal government. This seems nowadays a natural part of what a state does, and it had been standard within the French Empire, but it was galling to many Dutch that they henceforth had to register where they resided. In line with the demands of the registry, all Dutch were required to possess a surname. While this had been common in the urban and densely populated western parts of the Netherlands, it was less so in the rural east and north. It would take years, even decades, before some Dutch actually used in daily life the surname they had formally acquired.

Some effects of the new measure were, however, immediate. Aided by the Registry, conscription – finally – was implemented in the Netherlands, precipitating unrest, even riots, in some locales. As a result of the conscription, some 15,000 Dutch troops were with Napoleon on his ill-fated march to Moscow in the course of 1812; only 500 made it back home alive. Throughout all of this, French law enforcement, including the secret police, kept a watchful eye on the population, and the whole judicial system was completely conformed to French standards – a change that would remain intact after Napoleon's departure. French rule also brought the metric system to the Netherlands, though the Dutch for a time returned to their old weights once they were rid of the emperor.

The fifteen years after 1798 had brought about unprecedented change in the Netherlands. A centralized government with powerful prerogatives ruled over a people who increasingly saw themselves as citizens not of a locale but of a centralized nation-state. What citizenship meant in practice, however, was unclear; local expressions of citizenship such as the guilds and the militias had been suppressed without anything much to replace them. As Napoleon's power crumbled in late 1813, the future of his legacy soon became a pressing national issue.

Restoration and a United Kingdom, 1813–1830

Creating a Post-Napoleonic Future

Napoleon's defeat at the titanic Battle of Leipzig in October 1813 – where Dutch soldiers, as French citizens, had still fought for their emperor – triggered sudden change across western Europe. France's German allies defected. By November the advance cavalry of the Allied Army, the Russian Cossacks, arrived in the Netherlands, though their behavior toward the frightened citizenry was far less ferocious than their reputation warranted. French forces fled south, leaving behind only a handful of garrisons that in some cases would hold out until May of 1814. Riots broke out against French rule in cities such as Amsterdam and later The Hague. No one knew for sure which force – French, Allied or otherwise – would effectively take power in the near future, and many leading authorities sat on the fence awaiting a decisive outcome.

There were two issues from a Dutch perspective that required a settlement: the first, largely an issue of domestic politics, about who would have authority in the former Dutch Republic, and the second, an international one, about the place of that new government in the European – and global – balance of power. With respect to the first issue the vacuum of power was quickly filled by Willem Frederik, son of the last *stadhouder*, thanks in no small measure to the pivotal role of the country's leading Orangist, Gijsbert Karel van Hogendorp. For years Van Hogendorp had quietly busied himself with outlining a constitutional order centered around the House of Orange. He made contact with Willem Frederik, and when French authority collapsed he announced a provisional government in his name. Willem Frederik's arrival at Scheveningen on November 30, 1813 resulted two days later in his being proclaimed in Amsterdam the "sovereign prince" of the Netherlands. Under what conditions he would rule – and under which title – was left open for the moment. But in most parts of the country the return of the House of Orange was immediately accepted; Hogendorp's promise of the return of the good old days resonated with one part of the population, while others, indifferent, shrugged at just one more change in the political constellation. Estranged from politics, all many likely wanted was a government that would bring better economic times. Crucially for the sake of administrative stability and continuity, many of Napoleon's leading officials, abandoning their old loyalties, stayed at their posts in the service of Orange.

Orangists may quickly have asserted the authority of their prince over much of the Netherlands, but Willem Frederik's future – and indeed the very independence of the country itself – depended on the good will of the anti-Napoleonic coalition – crucially the British, whose strategic and economic interests in the Low Countries were greater than those of the other powers. The British foreign minister, Lord Castlereagh, had cultivated ties with the House of Orange since April of 1813; considered a strategic marriage between the British House of Hanover and the Oranges; and encouraged Willem Frederik to strive for kingship, so as to give leadership to the new state. With Orange firmly in control, the Allies accepted the Netherlands as an independent state in March of 1814.

Less immediately certain was the future of other territories impinging on Dutch sovereignty. London determined in August of 1814 that, in order to make the new state strong, most of the colonies that had been under Dutch rule in 1803 should be returned; they kept the strategic Cape Colony for themselves but returned Java, much to the distress of British experts familiar with the island's priceless riches. The British, who had just prohibited the transatlantic slave trade, did force the Dutch to do the same as a condition for the transfer. The end of the slave trade hit the economies of the Leeward Islands (Saba, St. Eustatius and St. Maarten) hard, though it arguably forced masters to treat their slaves better because they could not so easily be replaced.

Java, as well as Surinam and the Dutch Antilles, was returned in 1816. The Dutch colonial presence for the next century, however, would continue to depend on the benevolence of the British navy, which at a stroke could retake the possessions that London had chosen to grant The Hague.

Also requiring careful attention from the Great Powers was the fate of the former Habsburg Netherlands, which had been ruled by Austria until 1794. It was crucial that present-day Belgium should not fall into French or Prussian hands, particularly – from the British standpoint – the vital harbor of Antwerp. Since Austria did not want the region back, and an independent southern Netherlands was judged too weak to withstand France, the best option seemed a united kingdom under the House of Orange. This was the option for which Willem Frederik himself had lobbied hard among the Great Powers, as it would grant him a territory large enough to justify his kingly ambitions (his further designs on German territory being mostly rebuffed). There was some doubt about whether this union would be supported sufficiently in the Catholic south, or if the state would be strong enough to contain France. For that reason Luxembourg, with its mammoth fortress, though to be ruled by the Oranges, was to be defended by a Prussian garrison and politically placed within the German Confederation rather than the new Netherlandic kingdom. Under these conditions the Allies informally came to support the union of the northern and southern Netherlands under Willem Frederik by the summer of 1814.

Thus the United Kingdom of the Netherlands became one of the buffer states designed by the Congress of Vienna to hem in the French, along with Prussia (with its new Rhineland territories), Baden, Württemberg, Bavaria, Switzerland and Piedmont-Sardinia. The new state was soon and unexpectedly challenged to prove its mettle. Napoleon, having slipped out of exile, retook control in France, and moved north to defeat the British and the Prussians in turn before his foes could unite against him. Just south of Brussels, at Waterloo on June 18, 1815, an army consisting of British, German and Dutch units, commanded by the duke of Wellington, stood ground against Napoleon's advancing army. The Dutch divisions – with about 17,000 soldiers accounting for about one-quarter of Wellington's army – acquitted themselves well, with General David Chassé (distrusted by Wellington for his long service under Napoleon) leading his division to help disperse the French at a critical juncture in the battle. The prince of Orange, wounded in the battle while leading his men, was hailed a hero. The new kingdom had been saved, helping to cement Orange's authority over a single kingdom of north and south, and the battle itself gave the king's subjects a collective memory of their common cause against a great enemy. Indeed, the Dutch would continue to commemorate Waterloo annually until the Second World War.

Victory at Waterloo, however, did not entirely dissolve issues over the new state. In 1814 a new constitution had been written for the northern Netherlands, which gave the sovereign prince

33 Commemorating the Battle of Waterloo, depicted here by Nicolaas Pieneman, might have helped meld a truly united Kingdom of the Netherlands. But bad policy undid this possibility.

wide powers to govern, including the right of decree, and a relatively weak States-General that did possess the right to vote on legislation or to approve and disapprove budgets once a decade. No room for parliamentary debate was allowed. By point of comparison, states such as Prussia or Denmark had no real parliamentary representation until mid-century, but the new States-General had considerably fewer prerogatives than the British Parliament. In some respects it resembled the Parliament created by the Charter of 1814 in France. Neither a parliamentary system nor an absolutist government, this constitutional arrangement would ultimately run aground on its own internal inconsistencies.

For the moment, however, the issue was how to accommodate the constitution to include the south in the new kingdom. A crucial sticking point was the promise of Willem Frederik to enforce full religious freedom throughout his realm. This was a condition imposed by the Allies in one of the so-called Eight Articles, which defined the conditions of the union, in this case to protect the Catholics from the Protestant monarch and thus make the union more palatable to the southerners. But full religious equality was the last thing that some southerners wanted, who preferred a privileged Catholic Church, as had been the case in eighteenth century. To the shock of the king, a majority of the 1,600 prominent "notables" he had charged with representing the south in a vote over the constitution voted "no." Willem Frederik, using an old Napoleonic trick now called the *arithmétique hollandaise* by the Belgians, counted all abstentions and those who had voted "no" on the religious clause as "yes" votes, the latter on the grounds that these objections were moot because the Great Powers had imposed such a demand. It was an important sign of trouble between Orange and his Catholic subjects, though it did not prevent King Willem I from imposing his constitution across his whole realm in August of 1815. Though public enthusiasm for the whole enterprise was lacking, not only in the south but also in the north, the king himself was confident and full of energy.

A New Kingdom

Despite the distinct lack of enthusiasm for the new kingdom contemporary historians reject as finalistic the assertion that the union of north and south was bound to fail. Indeed, as shall be shown, the creation of Belgium in 1830 had to do with an unpredictable constellation of international factors, just as the very creation of the United Kingdom depended on such factors in 1814–1815. Commercial interests in the south saw economic advantages, and southern liberals suspicious of the power of the Catholic Church could appreciate a constitution formally committed to the freedom of all beliefs. Moreover, many supposed that the union would be enforced by the Great Powers, permitting them to accept Willem on the grounds that they could not do otherwise. From both parts of the kingdom there existed a strong sense that the king had a calling to unite, for the first time in centuries, those lands that had once fallen under the dukes of Burgundy and Habsburg royalty.

Willem saw himself as the father of his nation, kindly but firmly attending to the needs of his subjects. His regime was less oppressive than Napoleonic rule had been. Dutch judges now punished less severely, often bypassing the death penalty and other severe punishments dictated by the Napoleonic Code, a legal code that itself was later softened by a thorough overhaul in 1838. But Willem essentially left intact the Napoleonic police regime, which included many spies and informants. Press laws, briefly relaxed, were tightened again by 1818, and those associated with publishing opinions critical of royal policy were often prosecuted. Dissent in the new kingdom was thus actively discouraged.

But Willem's vision did not end with repression. It included, among his many wide interests, attacking the problem of poverty, which had drastically increased prior to his reign. To increase the prosperity of his kingdom the king invested in businesses in economically depressed areas, which often failed and increased government debt. The best-known but not very successful effort to give the poor a new lease on life was the Society of Charity (Maatschappij van Weldadigheid) founded in 1818. Led by General Johannes van den Bosch, the Society established several colonies in Drenthe in what was effectively wilderness. In the course of the next century about 1,400 impoverished families would move to settlements such as Frederiksoord and Wilhelminaoord, where they were offered a small plot of land and, over time, technical schooling. This kind of paternalism, however, did not improve the economic situation of its participants.

It was not until the mid 1820s, though, that Willem developed a strong program for his united kingdom. He meant for it to rank among the Great Powers of Europe and pursued, insofar as he could, a foreign policy that demonstrated its independence vis-à-vis the large continental powers. To this end, he sought both to promote and to integrate the strongest aspects of the economies of both parts, not least the burgeoning industry of the south and the maritime and financial interests of the north. Emblematic per-haps of this active wish to link north and south economically was the creation of the Ghent–Terneuzen canal, initiated in 1823 and finished four years later. One of many new waterways initiated by the "Canal King," as he has been dubbed, this new canal, built across Zeeland-Flanders, linked one of the south's key cities with the Schelde and thus the North Sea. Willem also committed him-self to the expansion of the road system, which promoted trade and furthered economic integration. He encouraged the creation in 1823 of the first Dutch steamship company, founded in Rotterdam but powered by steam engines manufactured in the south.

The linchpin of Willem's creative efforts to integrate the economies of north and south was the Netherlands Trading Society (Nederlandsche Handels-Maatschappij, or NHM), founded in 1824, which sought, in simplified terms, to trans-port southern products on northern ships. Crucial in this calcu-lation were the Dutch East Indies, which would import many of these products, such as textiles, in return for coffee and indigo.

A bloody Javanese rebellion, however, launched in 1825 by Prince Diponegoro, in which some 200,000 people lost their lives, disrupted trade until the Dutch finally took the prince captive in 1830. After that date, the NHM would play a crucial role in the Dutch economy, but by that time the Belgians had broken with the king.

Rising Southern Alienation

The reasons for southern alienation were myriad. Irritations stemmed from the language policies of the king. Although the search for "ancient" and "pure" Dutch was not as intense as the parallel quest was in Germany, standardized use of the Dutch language was an important part of nation-building in the Netherlands of the early nineteenth century. Willem required as of 1823 that Dutch be used for official business in his Flemish provinces, a requirement that angered the elites of these regions, who had been accustomed to using French. A much more serious point of tension were government finances, or more particularly state debt. The new government had wholly assumed the debt of its predecessors: debt that was chiefly held by Holland's bourgeoisie, a key group that Willem, in his rather strong orientation toward Amsterdam, was eager to placate. In effect Willem taxed the south at rates higher than its residents were accustomed to, half of which went to pay off the northern creditors. Some 45 to 50 percent of the revenue was raised in the south, but only 20 to 23 percent was spent there, and too much of that went to benefit the investments of the king's inner circle. What made matters worse – in the eyes of both southerners and northerners – was that the proposed royal budgets, which had to be approved in 1819 and again in 1829, were not financially sound. Willem routinely bypassed the States-General and hid from all public view his very considerable expenditures that came out of the national treasury.

Certainly also important was the fact that Willem's religious policies, as suggested above, drew wrath from Roman Catholics.

Despite formal disestablishment, churches were crucial social institutions, with each denomination zealously guarding its rights to organize poor relief for its own members as it saw fit. Drawing from his experiences as a young man in Germany, the king sought to bring the churches under the direction of the state, in order to prevent religious conflict and in order to give his rule spiritual legitimacy. His own preference was ultimately to unite Catholics and Protestants into a single state Church, but in the meantime he sought to make the various churches extensions of state policy. Willem drew up, soon after becoming king, religious compacts (*reglementen*) with the Reformed, the Lutherans and the Jews respectively – agreements that organized each of their religious bodies under a centralized administration with state supervision. The close relationship of these organizations with the state enhanced the status of each of them, and gave their clergy financial security. This was particularly so in the case of the Reformed Church, to which over half the northern population belonged and which, in its intimate connection to the state, now seemed to have regained its old glory as the "public Church."

But with the Roman Catholics – who in the united kingdom constituted nearly three-quarters of the population – it was very different. Anti-Catholicism was strong among Dutch Protestants. The king's policy of implementing an enlightened Christian curriculum in the schools; of preventing the return of monasteries and restricting religious orders; and of forcing all candidates for the priesthood to follow the state-determined curriculum at the specially created Collegium Philosophicum, which would supplement the academically inferior seminaries, generated much unhappiness among Catholics. They felt that the king was riding roughshod over their religious liberties. A Concordat of 1827, contracted between the pope and the king and designed to resolve these issues, failed to be implemented after the Belgian revolt. Parenthetically, the leading ideological defender of the Catholic cause was not a southerner but Joachim Le Sage ten Broek, son of a Holland clergyman and a convert to Catholicism, who, in vigorously attacking Protestant theology and defending the rights of the Church of Rome, inspired Dutch Catholics to assert themselves more often in public life. In the short run, though, Willem's religious policies undermined support for his kingship among Catholics, especially those in the south, where the Catholic Church had once been privileged.

Finally, the repressive features of Willem's regime, which did not shrink from punishing opponents (including Le Sage) with imprisonment or exile, alienated him from southern liberals. Orangism had been a significant political force in the south among the region's industrial and commercial leaders as well as its professional class, who also embraced the king's measures against the Catholic Church. With repression aimed at several of their own leaders this support, too, began to thin. All these factors fed widespread disaffection, evident in the hundreds of petitions presented to him between 1828 and 1830, to which some 350,000 signatures were affixed, bringing before him a wide range of grievances. It did not help the cause of the king that a recession in the textile industry prompted rising labor unrest in the course of 1830. It was in this context of discontent that the Belgian revolt began. On the evening of August 25, 1830 the singing of "Amour sacré de la patrie" in Auber's opera *La muette de Portici* prompted riots in Brussels, which soon erupted into open rebellion. The Belgian revolt was not an isolated incident on the international stage; the Bourbons had been expelled from the throne in Paris a month before, and soon other rebellions would rise across Europe against the repression of Restorationist regimes.

The Belgians Bolt

The Belgian Revolution took the king by surprise. His army's efforts to retake Brussels failed, though they resulted in hundreds of dead on both sides. Belgian units also seized what is present-day Dutch Limburg, moving as far north as Venlo. With the royal government expelled from much of what had become the new independent state of Belgium, Willem appealed to the Great Powers for help. The Russians and Prussians were willing to send in troops to help the beleaguered Dutch king. Tsar Nicholas I, brother of the Dutch Crown Princess Anna Pavlovna, committed himself to quelling revolution wherever it might occur and promised 60,000 troops. But the French, sensing the possibility of annexing the southern Netherlands, supported the rebels. War among the Great Powers over the fate of the United Kingdom of the Netherlands now seemed a real possibility. Crucial was the stance of the British government, which under Viscount Palmerston determined that the United Kingdom of the Netherlands was – regrettably – a lost cause and that an independent Belgian state must be recognized. Palmerston's position was strengthened by the November Uprising in Poland, which undermined the ability and willingness of the Russians to act militarily in the Low Countries. By the end of 1830, the Great Powers agreed to recognize Belgium as independent.

Consistent with his independent streak and obstinate nature, Willem refused to accept this *fait accompli*. Nor did the Dutch public, which adopted a stridently patriotic mood in the face of Belgian "mutiny," though the motivation lay more in punishing southern disloyalty than in reconciling Belgium to the kingdom. In Jan van Speyk, commander of a gunboat patrolling the waters around Antwerp, the Dutch found their first war hero, when in February 1831 he blew up his vessel rather than let it fall into Belgian hands. Van Speyk was buried with full honors in Amsterdam's New Church, near the resting place of the great Admiral de Ruyter. The Dutch public enthusiastically supported the mobilization of an army of 40,000 soldiers that invaded Belgium in the summer of 1831. The Ten-Day Campaign, as it became known, restored Dutch pride through an unbroken set of victories against weak Belgian forces. But prospects of a war with France – made imminent by the entry

294

of a French army into Belgian territory – were enough to send
the Dutch army back north. Still, the Dutch held on to two key
fortresses deep in Belgian-held territory: the citadel of Antwerp
and the city of Maastricht. The Dutch garrison in Antwerp surrendered after a full-scale attack by a large French force later in 1832,
but the Dutch army steadfastly held on to Maastricht, despite the
hatred of the pro-Belgian citizenry. The proven military prowess
of the Dutch was one factor that prompted the Great Powers to
offer the Dutch a relatively advantageous peace settlement once
Willem finally accepted Belgian independence in 1839. Belgium –
much to the disappointment of the local population – abandoned
eastern Limburg to the Dutch government after financial compensation, Zeeland-Flanders remained Dutch and the eastern part
of the duchy of Luxembourg remained under the Oranges, now as
an independent state.

The Belgian conflict, and the king's refusal throughout the
1830s to come to terms with the new independent state, weakened
the autocratic power of the monarchy. Keeping the army mobilized throughout the 1830s further depleted the treasury, to the
alarm of Dutch elites, and they determined that they must put an
end to Willem's wanton spending after the failure of his Belgian
policy. Out of these concerns the constitution was amended in
1840. The king could no longer issue laws without the approval
of a minister, he could no longer keep public finances secret and
budgetary approval was now to take place every two years instead
of every ten. Willem, unhappy with these restrictions in what
could be interpreted as a vote of no confidence, abdicated in that
year in favor of his son, Willem II.

The Netherlands after Belgian Independence, 1830–1848

The end of the union with the Belgians compelled the Dutch
intelligentsia to think again about the identity of their own

nation. There had long been a robust sense of north Netherlandic nationhood, and now it could take flight again in a new context. Part of the reflection focused on the international value of a small European state. In 1815 the Dutch could imagine that they constituted a great power similar to that of Prussia, but now such pretensions could in no way be sustained. Small-state nationalism now came to the fore, in which the moral virtuousness of the Dutch, particularly their realism and their moderation, were touted as praiseworthy expressions of a venerable people. Along with the commitment to neutrality that the shrunken state felt obliged to adopt came the first hopes that the Dutch could serve as a moral example to other nations, not through feat of arms but through their commitment to the amicable resolution of international conflicts. It was a theme that would find more systematic expression later in the century.

For the time being, the Dutch middle class celebrated their national virtues, such as a practical and sensible religiosity and respect for classicist harmony, in reverence for a past they now recreated. Central to this enterprise was a literary culture that drew romantic inspiration from Dutch history. Hendrik Tollens's poem commemorating Barentsz.'s famous visit to Nova Zembla (1819) was one such example. But it found perhaps most popular and lasting expression after 1830 in the rise of the historical novel. Jacob van Lennep and Geertruida Bosboom-Toussaint, both of whom were influenced by the writings of Sir Walter Scott, were among the leading figures in this genre. Historical focus was often, not surprisingly, on the Golden Age. After 1850 the Catholic man of letters Joseph Alberdingk Thijm would write historical prose focused on a period that better evoked his religious commitments: the Middle Ages. But this age was less appealing to the Protestant dominant culture of the time, which illustrates how difficult it could be for the Dutch to imagine a shared religious past. The regional novel, which explored the unique histories and attributes of various parts of the country, was also widely read.

And along with literature there was an increasing interest in the Dutch language, its dialects and variations, reflecting an interest in the diversity that made up the nation.

Mixed Economic Success

Nation-forming was more than national sentiment, of course, and one of the tasks of the government was to build a sound economic and financial basis for the kingdom. From an economic and financial standpoint Willem I's greatest success lay outside either Belgium or the Netherlands, in the Dutch East Indies. There the new governor-general, Van den Bosch – the same man who had created the Society of Charity – implemented the so-called "cultivation system" in 1830. In this system 20 percent of arable land was to be cultivated with crops mandated by Dutch authorities of the NHM, such as indigo, coffee and sugar. The goods produced were seen as taxes paid for by the Javanese population, so the government did not have to pay for the products. Although, as shall be shown, the cultivation system developed an infamous reputation for the abuses and injustices that it indubitably invited, and though the labor used amounted to involuntary servitude, recent evidence suggests that it increased agricultural productivity in Java sufficiently to feed a sharply rising peasant population.

Whatever its ambiguous social effects on Java, the system's financial fruits for the Dutch government were substantial once the income started pouring in around 1840. Since the NHM was government-run the coffers of the state now quickly filled from the proceeds from East Indian products; at the high point in the 1850s up to half of all government revenue came from the cultivation system. This was welcome news to a government that for decades had struggled against high debt – though it was not until around 1860 that the government was substantially in a financial position to fund large public projects. But Willem's initial aims went beyond making money from taxes, intending to create a neomercantilist system where Dutch parties at home and in the colonies bought from each other. Indeed, private businesses did flourish as a result of the cultivation system. The nascent textile industries in Twente and in North Brabant were protected from British competition by being able to sell as a monopoly their cotton and woolen goods in Java in exchange for the products grown there. And the very substantial rise in trade between the East Indies and the Netherlands fully revived Dutch shipping and shipbuilding; by mid-century the Dutch had the fourth-largest maritime fleet in the world, before its rank would decline again in the face of new international competition. The success of the NHM – and of the Dutch economy as a whole – was now aided by the free trade policies of countries such as Britain, which now opened their markets, particularly the strong agricultural sector, to the Dutch.

Although the cultivation system injected revenue into the Netherlands, it did not immediately improve the lives of the Dutch population, which remained susceptible to multiple threats. Arguably, life for ordinary people in the first half of the nineteenth century was as hard as it had been at any point since the Middle Ages. Life expectancy was about thirty-five years of age, owing in large part to high infant mortality. The poorest classes received little education, and saw few prospects to rise above their station. A very large part of the population was either in poverty or not far from it. At least 10 percent of the population lived – in good times – on charity, and in some sparsely populated areas such as the Veluwe religious or social organizations barely existed at all, with its inhabitants eking out a hardscrabble living on poor sand grounds, the best land being in the hands of a few wealthy landholders. Uncertain labor opportunities in the cities made the lives of the urban working class scarcely any better.

After about 1770 the potato had been intensively cultivated in many parts of the country, as it offered more nourishment per hectare than the traditional grain crops. Its wide use thus reduced hunger. But the carbohydrate-rich though low-protein potato, served in the poorest households with only a bit of vinegar or pepper for taste, was not an unambiguous improvement in the diet if eaten alone, and in places such as eastern Groningen, in the Oldambt, the tubers were eaten three times a day. Undernourishment was in any event a daily experience for many poorer Dutch, with well over half of all household income of the urban poor going on food. The housing of the most impoverished was, judged by bourgeois observers of the mid nineteenth century, often abominable, with large families living together in spaces sometimes no greater than 15 m². Though the dank and filthy cellars of the city speak perhaps most to the contemporary imagination, domiciles in the countryside for landless day-laborers could scarcely be called better, consisting of wretched hovels that barely protected their inhabitants from the elements.

Furthermore, these structural deficiencies do not include the more cyclical or periodic perils to which many Dutch were subject. The population in low-lying areas remained subject to flooding; in 1825, during a powerful storm of unrelenting rain and wind, nearly 400 perished in the northern provinces when sea levels reached the tops of the dikes and caused them to collapse. And in 1859 the 600 inhabitants of Schokland in the middle of the Zuyder Zee – after decades of seeing their island further reduced – were ordered to evacuate after the situation was (erroneously as it turned out) judged to be hopeless. The unpredictable water levels of the country's great rivers periodically threatened residents of the region. Cholera, an Asian import, made its first appearance in the Netherlands in 1832, killing half of the 40,000 people it infected and spreading panic throughout the country. The disease would strike again, most powerfully in 1866, when 23,000 died during an epidemic, most of them among the poor.

In 1845 and 1846 potato blight destroyed the staple on which the most needy depended. Hunger reached new and desperate proportions, combined as it was with other crop failures in the late

1840s, though widespread famine as in the Irish – or Flemish – case was averted. Nevertheless, in those areas where the potato dominated, such as Friesland and Zeeland, malnutrition was severe and the charitable institutions, relying on wealthy farmers whose own income had been swept away, were overwhelmed and unable to assist all those in need. The food crisis, which facilitated the return of cholera, led to such a high mortality rate that deaths exceeded births at the height of the crisis, for the only time in the nineteenth century. An economic downturn in the late 1840s further reduced the prosperity and health of the population; in 1847 some 25 percent of the population of North Holland depended on charity.

At the same time, the Dutch economy and social support systems were robust enough to inhibit emigration; despite a spike in the late 1840s, and despite migration from the border regions to the industrial Ruhr in Germany, the number of Dutch leaving the country remained, in contrast to some parts of western Europe, relatively low in these decades. And with new scientific insights and techniques some problems were reduced. Sanitary measures slowly adopted in the cities, such as the emptying of many city canals, which were little more than open cesspools, helped contain cholera by the 1860s. In 1853 Amsterdam was guaranteed clean water through a pipeline that led from aquifers under the dunes on the North Sea to the city – the first of its kind and a source of excellent drinking water, at least for the wealthier parts of the city to which the pipes ran. And with their introduction steam engines were increasingly used to keep – or to make – Dutch land dry. The greatest achievement in water management of the nineteenth century – and the largest drainage undertaking up to that time – was laying dry the Haarlemmermeer, at 170 km² by far the largest lake in Holland. It was known as a "water wolf" for its voracious appetite for land during storms. Willem I thus resolved in 1837 to eliminate the shallow lake after its floodwaters had again threatened Amsterdam and other towns. After years of preparations and intensive use of four new steam engines, the last water was pumped out in 1852, making way for new farmland.

A More Critical Society

One of the most striking characteristics of the Netherlands in the first half of the nineteenth century is the extensive if fragmented set of philanthropic organizations – several thousand local ones – in addition to the churches. There were important private societies as well, the most important of them being the "Nut," or Society for Public Benefit, which churned out many pamphlets urging the moral improvement of society, and set up institutions by which the population could save money and receive a better education. This society had some 13,000 members in 1830, large for a voluntary association of the time. There were also important religious organizations founded at the beginning of the century supported by the elite, such as the Dutch Missionary and Bible Societies, both directly inspired by foreign example. Each of these organizations promoted a sense of national unity and mission, particularly among literate Protestants. At the same time, there was little left of the corporative organizations – the guilds, the mutual aid societies, the militias – of the old Republic, organizations that had always offered the possibility of political resistance. Seen this way, the autocratic one-man rule of Willem I – a rare case of centralized power in Dutch history – went hand-in-hand with a lack of social and political organizations that might have constituted a more effective check on his power.

Some of the earliest resistance to royal policies in the north came from religious groups whose concerns, though chiefly religious, had political overtones. This did not come, for the time being, from the Catholics. Though their active role in signing the petitions against Willem I's policies had shown their potential, they remained as second-class citizens, underrepresented in the life of the nation, their church structures and social organizations underdeveloped. The transnational Réveil movement, which reached the Netherlands via Switzerland in the early years of Willem I's reign, was more influential. At heart a pietistic Protestant movement that stressed spiritual regeneration and religion of the heart over empty outward conformity to religious precepts, those associated with it were often critical of the Revolution's legacy, particularly with what they perceived as its secular spirit. The poet Bilderdijk, though too mercurial to be defined by any movement, influenced Réveil leaders with his effusive Orangism and, at the same time, his distaste for the new order. The center of the Dutch movement lay in Amsterdam's high bourgeoisie, but the aims had a wide scope: to uplift and reform the nation morally and spiritually through organizations and publications. In time, the most important and influential figure to emerge out of the Réveil was the The Hague aristocrat Guillaume Groen van Prinsterer. Critical of the Dutch Reformed Church for its anything-goes stance with respect to doctrine and its apparent abandonment of the faith entrusted to its fathers, Groen would develop in the 1840s "Anti-Revolutionary" political notions that sought to bring back to the state a proper sense of God's sovereignty and his special blessings to the Dutch nation. How that would translate itself into concrete politics would only become apparent later.

More overtly a challenge to the government in the 1830s was a small group of Calvinist separatists. Though broadly in tune with Réveil concerns, these separatists, coming from the lower and middle classes, were more decided in rejecting existing Church authority as deviating from the old true faith. When Seceders claimed that their own church was the true Reformed Church and refused to seek government recognition for it, royal authorities attempted to hound these Seceders into conformity, forbidding their assemblies, fining or imprisoning their clergy and billeting troops in their homes. This persecution was controversial even at the time, and the new King Willem II put an end to it, though both the religious and economic climate in the Netherlands remained uncomfortable enough for many of these Seceders to leave for Iowa and Michigan in the late 1840s. In hindsight, the Secession (*Afscheiding*) was a sign of things to come: growing religious pluriformity and self-consciousness that rendered the existing religious settlement increasingly problematic. It also illustrated once again how religious unrest in the mid nineteenth century could have ramifications for Dutch politics.

Partly as a consequence of this ferment, new civil society organizations began to emerge around 1840 that more assertively sought to reform society – independently of government policy and occasionally in opposition to it. In this process, the Réveil played an important role in the development of a social Christianity that would improve the lot of those most in need. The Réveil-inspired pastor Ottho Heldring, for example, established a special institution in the countryside to help save "fallen women" from prostitution. The Amsterdam Mennonite Christiaan Pieter von Eeghen established a nursing school and home in 1843 that offered free care to the poor and similar initiatives took place in Rotterdam and elsewhere. They were also involved in the creation of temperance societies and, to the displeasure of the government, anti-slavery societies – both movements, incidentally, inspired by British example, where they had been established earlier. In these efforts other Dutch now pitched in, creating Protestant or more secular societies to further these moral ends. Catholic leaders, though more focused on their own co-religionists, also made important contributions. On Curaçao the first Apostolic Vicar to the island, Martinus Niewindt, worked intensively in the 1840s and 1850s to improve the lot of the almost entirely Catholic slave population, building schools, hospitals and orphanages, despite initial resistance from authorities who opposed the growing influence of the Roman Church. Although diverse in motivation and purpose, these initiatives reflected a new confidence among Dutch citizens, particularly the middle class, that their input mattered.

But social activism, even if it was politically tinged, was not the same thing as possessing and using political rights. In the 1840s, despite the more moderate stance of Willem II, most Dutch citizens continued to lack both the interest and the rights to participate in government – a situation that had not much changed since 1815. Political liberalism, which emphasized the rights of the responsible individual over the power of the state, had become firmly anchored in Belgium as the result of the revolution against the Dutch king, but this was much less the case in the Netherlands itself. Nevertheless, liberalism was a transnational movement of the middle classes, who, mindful of their educational accomplishments and economic importance in a fast-changing Europe, were less likely than before to accept as self-evident the authority of "throne and altar." This was also true in the Netherlands, where liberals in the late 1820s and 1830s, partly in response to the Belgian Revolution, considered how the Dutch constitution might be reconfigured in a modern – that is, liberal – way. The literary journal *De Gids* (*The Guide*), founded in 1837 and rapidly influential among the well-educated bourgeoisie, soon adopted a liberal stance. Next to liberals there was a small but radical political press, written by and for the lower classes, which as well as supporting political change decried the social conditions of the workers. Ideas such as universal suffrage and progressive taxation were discussed: ideas that went much further than most Dutch liberals in the 1840s could countenance.

Leading the political liberals in the Netherlands in the 1840s was Johan Rudolph Thorbecke, professor at Leiden. Reflecting the pattern that much of the political discontent with the status quo came not from Holland but from the more peripheral and less privileged inland provinces, Thorbecke was himself an outsider; he came from Overijssel, and was Lutheran instead of Reformed. After extensive study in Germany he had taught at Ghent, becoming deeply acquainted with international developments in political theory. He was the principal author of the so-called "Nine

Men Proposal" of 1844, parliamentary bills that demanded, among other things, ministerial accountability to Parliament and direct elections to the Second Chamber. Thorbecke and his allies, however, were still crying in the wilderness, at least in the political world of conservative Holland; their bills were not considered in Parliament and he himself lost his parliamentary seat in 1845. The States-General – filled with cautious conservatives in the Second Chamber, who saw Thorbecke's proposals as radical and thus as un-Dutch – not to mention the king's appointees in the First, were not at all inclined to embrace political reform.

A New Dynamism, 1848–1870

The Constitution of 1848 and Its Legacy

Once again, it was international events that would prove decisive for a fundamental political shift in the Netherlands. Political frustration and economic distress combined in early 1848 to usher in a spate of uprisings across Europe. In late February of 1848 revolution broke out again in Paris, causing King Louis Philippe to abdicate and flee within forty-eight hours of its inception. Both the speed and the dramatic effects of the French uprising made an immediate impression on Europe; it stimulated revolt elsewhere and shocked autocratic governments into acquiescence, at least for the moment. Soon western German governments made concessions, and unrest in the Habsburg Empire followed. Willem II's concern was now that the unrest might spread to the Netherlands, although – in contrast to Paris – no serious demonstrations had yet erupted. On March 13, 1848 Willem announced that it was his wish that a new liberal constitution be promulgated; he said that he had gone in the course of a day from being very conservative to very liberal. Recent research has confirmed that Willem's sudden conversion was influenced by blackmail; leading liberals had information about his sexual liaisons with another man, and were willing to leak this information to the press if Willem was not politically obliging. Blackmail or not, the political impulses of this rather amiable man in fact were not very consistent, and for some time he had been afraid of the possibility of revolution. The lessons of history – particularly the suddenness of revolutions – now impressed upon more observers than the king himself that an uprising might be but days away and must be headed off.

With Willem now committed to reform the task soon fell to Thorbecke to write an appropriate constitution. Conveniently the statesman had already written down most of what he wanted in a new constitution, and merely a month later – on April 13 – the king gave his consent to Thorbecke's draft. In many ways the new constitution was a classically liberal document. Freedom of assembly and freedom of the press were guaranteed, and churches could no longer make special claims on the state, or the state on the churches. Government ministers were now accountable not to the king but to Parliament, and those elected to the Second Chamber of Parliament, the chief legislative body, were to be directly chosen by voters. The First Chamber would no longer be appointed by the king, but elected through the provincial States. Changes in the electoral rules caused consternation among the parliamentarians, who only reluctantly approved the constitution, as the complicated indirect elections that had made their own positions possible were now about to disappear.

Thorbecke's constitution was not a democratic one, recent historians emphasize. It rejected popular sovereignty and restricted voting to substantial property holders (who alone, it was reasoned, possessed the financial independence to vote beyond their pocketbooks). This amounted to about 10 percent of the adult male population and about 2.5 percent of all citizens – all told slightly *smaller* than the electorate under the old regime. It has been said that a larger share of the Dutch population was effectively (if not formally) politically represented in 1750 than in 1850. But in his progressive view of history Thorbecke believed that an increasingly prosperous and educated nation would naturally expand the number of voters, and that it was only for the time being that the dictates of good and responsible government demanded a restricted electorate of wise and able men.

From a bird's-eye view, the Dutch "revolution" of 1848 – the word must be used advisedly as unrest remained limited – was also one of the few really successful national transitions to a freer form of government that had been so earnestly sought across Europe in that year. Broadened electorates or new parliamentary forms offered a semblance of change in autocratic France and Prussia, but only in Denmark and Sardinia were there similar outcomes to the Netherlands: that is, the creation of a parliament that functioned as the locus of political power and authority. But it would take many years for the new Parliament to develop its own new rules and procedures, and for all political forces fully to accept the liberal constitution. Moreover, the Dutch colonies did not see improvement in their own representative structures; on the Antilles, as well as in the East Indies, governors appointed by The Hague continued to hold most of the power. Even parliamentary oversight of the colonies remained limited.

Nevertheless, 1848 was decisive for the political and administrative structures of the kingdom. It largely removed the House of Orange from the power equation after nearly 300 years, although, as we shall see in the parliamentary crisis of the 1860s, the new monarch, Willem III, invested as king in 1849, did not immediately accept the new and very substantial limitations on the old royal prerogatives. And it paved the way for other, fundamental administrative reforms. Key was the Municipality Law of 1851, which eliminated the administrative distinction between town and country and divided the country up into municipalities, which were now – for the first time – structured and run according to a uniform code. Another law regulated the relationship between the provinces and central government. In all of this, a new ethos of public transparency and administrative rectitude, in which the cronyism of the old regime that Thorbecke despised was to

34 Willem III's family life was tragic; he lived in enmity with his first wife
and his three sons died. A second marriage and a daughter – Wilhelmina –
gave him some solace in his last years.

have no place, received a new emphasis – even if the actual running of the country's affairs remained in the hands of a relatively
small elite.

New Religious Freedoms and Divisions

Most crucially of all, though, the constitution of 1848 created the space for new social and political groups to assert their own place in Dutch public life. And new claims were not long in coming. Dutch Roman Catholics, long the object of Protestant-led repression and distrust, benefited the most from the new constitution, which was clearer in defending their right to worship, more open toward the establishment of religious orders and less rooted in a Protestant establishment. Leading Dutch Catholics, then, were some of the most enthusiastic supporters of the 1848 constitution, and were instrumental in its passage through Parliament. In the 1850s and 1860s, a Catholic–liberal political alliance seemed a natural coalition in Dutch parliamentary politics. But that slowly began to erode, beginning with, paradoxically, an event that Dutch liberalism had made possible: the return of the Roman Catholic hierarchy to the Netherlands.

Since roughly 1580 and the ascendancy of Protestantism there had been no bishops in the Netherlands, except for those of the small Old Catholic Church, which had broken with Rome in the early eighteenth century. Vicariates and the Holland Mission, once set up to govern a church in a Protestant state, continued to be the organizational forms of the Catholic Church in the Netherlands. Now influential Catholics such as Alberdingk Thijm – himself increasingly active in efforts to revive Catholic cultural life in his country – began to press Parliament and Catholic clergy alike to restore the episcopacy to the Netherlands, to give both substance and symbolic expression to the full legal emancipation of Roman Catholics. By 1852 the Dutch state and the papacy had agreed that the Church was now free to organise itself however it wished, and in early 1853 the Holy See announced that it would create five new sees in the Netherlands, centered around the archbishopric of Utrecht.

The return of the Roman Catholic bishops was important in at least two ways. It transformed the Dutch Catholic Church in the long run by giving it a structure that improved its self-organization, and over time aided Dutch Catholics in their increasing drive to create their own associations. Not all Catholics – particularly among the Dutch laity, who had played an important role in Church life – appreciated the necessary price that was to be paid for this gain, namely a stronger hierarchy in the Church. The bishops would increasingly become the chief voice of Dutch Catholics, and under them the clergy would play a more prominent role in defining the lives of the laity. That did not mean at first that the new Dutch bishops were particularly keen to follow the wishes of Pope Pius IX, whose strongly anti-liberal line, shaped in part by his own harrowing experiences of the 1848 revolution in Rome, went further than their own milder inclinations. But by the 1860s, the Dutch Catholic world, bishops and laity alike, was drawn into the international conflict between the papacy and the anticlerical forces arrayed against it. That conflict intensified doctrinal conformity and social discipline within the Church, and it prompted an ideological response that gravitated against the liberal-dominated nation-state. The bishops did not cause the trend toward greater Catholic militancy and self-assertion, but the new hierarchical structures did facilitate the self-discipline and internal organization of Dutch Catholicism. It was clear by the 1860s that there was a shift within Dutch Catholicism, away from a sympathy for liberalism entertained by some Dutch Catholic elites, and toward a more militant Church, increasingly led by the clergy but with much lay support. This development would set new terms for the way in which Dutch Roman Catholics would participate in public life.

In the second place, news of the return sparked an unprecedented backlash among the country's Protestants. In April of 1853 the Church council of the Utrecht's Reformed Church launched a petition campaign, demanding that the government prevent the bishops' return. Fearing the end of the Protestant nation – even the return of Catholic repression – some 200,000 citizens signed. The "April Movement," as it was called, failed in this aim, though the liberal government that had permitted the return fell, and a new more conservative government tightened the restrictions on public worship without, notably, impeding the return of the bishops. More important in the long run was the fact that Protestants, too, now proved ready to contend for their interests in the public sphere. The rise of prayer and evangelistic meetings throughout the country showed the new zeal of religious communities in concerning themselves with the future of their nation. And changes within the Dutch Reformed Church – then constituting 55 percent of the Dutch population – only encouraged this trend. The Church, released from state oversight in the years after 1848, was forced to reorganize itself, giving more authority to local congregations. This reorganization left it open to various theological factions, which now fought with each other over the desired direction of the Church.

35   Pilgrimage and processions increased in the late nineteenth century as Catholics, such as these in Oostrum Limburg, sought to give renewed form to their faith in a hostile world.

By the 1850s theological modernism, which rejected the super-
natural claims of the Bible in order to bring Christianity into
harmony with emerging scientific norms of the day, had made considerable inroads among the clergy and Protestant elites. These
modernists, however, were now challenged by more orthodox
elements, which were appalled that traditional Christian doctrine
was being cast aside. And much to the dismay of the modernists,
it was the orthodox factions that won the first Church elections
of 1867 – elections that, in allowing all male members to vote,
preceded the universal male franchise for government elections
by half a century. But the fight for the Dutch Reformed Church
remained inconclusive. If the new liberal freedoms had the long-
term effect of promoting unity among Catholics, they had the
opposite effect among Protestants, who became more fragmented
than ever into competing factions. This did not prevent, however,
Protestant groups, particularly orthodox ones, from making their
own claims on the public space, whether in popular revival meetings praying for the spiritual restoration of the country, or in political activity, as evidenced in Parliament by the Anti-Revolutionary
Groen van Prinsterer.

The ferment in Protestant and Roman Catholic circles
increasingly had an impact on Dutch national politics and policy.
Most telling of the early conflicts was the debate surrounding
the School Law of 1857, which specifically permitted citizens
to establish their own private, religious schools – at their own
expense. The minister responsible for the law, Justinus van der
Brugghen, had intended so to accommodate the rising clamor
among the religious for their own schools, but vociferous critics
such as Groen van Prinsterer saw Van der Brugghen's plan as
chiefly confirming the primacy of the vaguely Christian public school, which could not be satisfactory to Roman Catholics,
orthodox Protestants or Jews. Groen's own vision for public
schools to be divided according to religious confession, though,
had no chance of success. The new law raised among Catholics

and Protestants the issue of whether they should remain committed to public schools, or whether they should erect their own private ones. The 1857 law set the stage over time for organized networks of Catholics and orthodox Protestants to found hundreds of their own schools, increasing the interest in state financial support for them. Underscoring this trend, the Dutch Catholic bishops, inspired by Pius IX, came out four-square against public education in 1868, and for the necessity of Catholic schools to educate the faithful.

The emergent militancy of Catholics and various factions of Protestants put considerable pressure on Thorbecke's vision of a society to be characterized by a "Christendom above divisions." Dutch society's religious pluralism had now manifested itself with a passion, and there was no way back. At the same time, the emergence of freethinkers' publications, the burgeoning of deistic Masonic lodges and – with the advent after 1860 of Darwinian science – the rise of agnosticism and atheism stimulated a new secular ethos among some Dutch who no longer saw any value in religious doctrines or institutions. The freedoms created by the new constitutional order, in short, only seemed to encourage citizens to adhere more stoutly than before to their preferred identities, whether religious or secular, conservative or progressive. Social stratification, whose complex structures had always shaped Dutch society, arguably became more pronounced in the last half of the nineteenth century. Expanding on longstanding cleavages, the upper and middle classes in towns such as The Hague used exclusive societies and cultural initiatives to mark their social status as they built up the city's cultural life. Not just anyone could become a patron of newly established botanical gardens or musical societies. The rise of new working men's associations – the forerunners of trade unions – also created a new sense of class solidarity that had not existed before. All of these developments, though, pointed to a growing segmentation of society.

Economic Reorientation

All of these new group identities were fed by a sense, pervasive in the 1850s and 1860s, that change was afoot: that a period of languor had been replaced by the dynamics of the machine and of science, which in turn necessitated a new moral and spiritual energy. The new political situation, as noted above, contributed to this sense of movement. But so, too, did noticeable and important changes in the Dutch economy. Up until 1860, agricultural products had dominated Dutch exports, which kept food prices high in the Netherlands. The Dutch government, deeply in debt, had also refrained from investment in public infrastructure. Private enterprise – not the state – had constructed the country's first railroads: the first laid between Haarlem and Amsterdam in 1839, and only modestly expanded thereafter. But in the 1860s the government played a dominant and active role in the very sizeable extension of the railroad network, made possible by money from the cultivation system on Java. At

36 The first Dutch railway track between Amsterdam and Haarlem of 1839 was not particularly early; the Brussels–Antwerp railroad in more industrial Belgium preceded it by several years.

roughly the same time, the government also expanded the country's telegraph network. Better infrastructure helped incipient industry, including the increasingly important textile factories of Twente in the far east of the country. There, the textile industry had begun to take off in earnest in the 1850s, but it was the arrival of the railroad at Hengelo in 1865 that allowed entrepreneurs to expand their factories across the whole region, and better to transport their goods to markets. Trains also made the transport of coal much cheaper, which was good for homes and factories alike. Dutch trade was also helped by the rise of Prussian industry, as the Prussians were now interested in free waterways on which to ship their goods. As a result, and much to the pleasure of the Dutch government, tolls on the Rhine were finally removed in 1868. Gradually, the Dutch economy became more diversified, and came to benefit more from free trade. Dutch cities, after almost two centuries of stagnation or decline, began to grow again in the 1860s. Real incomes, too, began to rise after mid-century. Dutch women and men, genetically predisposed toward tallness, began to grow in height with better nutrition, the latter having grown some 20 cm on average since the mid-nineteenth century.

Tall

The benefits of free trade also prompted an increasing number of Dutch to question the merits of the cultivation system in the Dutch East Indies. It was not only that Javanese farmers, in their effective state of servitude, were impelled to plant crops of someone else's choosing; it was also that a government monopoly, which largely controlled this lucrative trade, inhibited free enterprise. Manufacturers and some merchants, especially from Amsterdam, where the NHM was seated, had benefited handsomely from the system, but other important firms effectively had been shut out of this neomercantilist arrangement. Economic liberals increasingly believed that it would be better both for the Dutch economy and for the development of the Indies to end this system.

Additionally fueling this growing unhappiness with the cultivation system were moral concerns over the system's exploitative

37 Eduard Douwes Dekker, or Multatuli, was not only a critical writer but a freethinker who broke wholly with religion; he let himself be cremated, at the time an unconventional choice.

qualities – concerns expressed by critics since the 1840s, but that were powerfully stated anew by Eduard Douwes Dekker, a writer who preferred to be known by his nom de plume Multatuli ("I have suffered much"). Dekker had worked as a minor colonial official and had observed abuses first-hand in which Dutch colonial officials did nothing to stop Javanese landowners from demanding far more from the peasantry than their formal contracts allowed. His fictionalized work *Max Havelaar*, heavily based on these experiences and published in 1860, was controversial at the outset but it did have the intended effect of shaking

the Dutch out of their moral complacency over what was tran-
spiring in the East Indies. Concerns about exploitation in the
Indies in the Dutch press and Parliament abounded in the 1860s.
After some years of parliamentary debate, the government ended
the cultivation system in 1870 by opening up the colonies to free
enterprise. Whether the market economy that replaced the cultivation system was much better for the residents of Java has been
a matter of debate.

One of the ironies of the cultivation system is that it made financially possible the end of slavery within Dutch-controlled jurisdictions, as it allowed owners to be compensated – at 300 guilders per
slave in Surinam, 200 per slave on the islands – which they were
forced to manumit. At the end of 1859 involuntary servitude was
already formally abolished in the Dutch East Indies – though in
practice it continued to persist for decades thereafter – and in 1863
emancipation followed in the Dutch Caribbean and in Surinam. In
Surinam some 40,000 slaves were thus freed; on the islands nearly
12,000. On the plantations former slaves were bound to work on
the land for ten years before being free to leave for other employ.
Dutch public debate over slavery had never been very lively, as
it had been in Britain, where strong reform movements had battled important economic interests. In the Dutch public mind, both
slavery and the West Indies seemed to be a rather unimportant
sideshow, and Parliament abolished slavery only a generation after
the British did, following the French, too, by some years.

That is not to say that the Dutch Parliament was indifferent to
what went on in the colonies, or that it was content to leave everything to the market, as government interventions in the country's
infrastructure – noted above –illustrate. To the contrary, liberal
parliamentarians – the most influential if rather diffuse faction in
the 1850s and 1860s – were keen to exercise their new authority
over all national issues that claimed their attention, taking it as
their responsibility to construct a well-ordered state. Their claims
to oversight included policy areas that Dutch political elites had

tried to wall off from them, including the colonies and foreign affairs.

This new parliamentary assertiveness led to crucial showdowns between 1866 and 1868, which tested the principles of Thorbecke's constitutional order. A liberal-led Second Chamber censured the conservative minority government of Count Van Zuylen van Nijevelt for having appointed its own minister of colonies as the new governor-general of the East Indies, thus in effect demanding that the government step down. In a parliamentary system, that should have meant the end of the government. But King Willem III, a moody and mercurial monarch who never had reconciled himself with the liberal constitution, claimed that such appointments were royal prerogative and encouraged the cabinet not to step down, calling instead for new elections. The conflict between government and the new Parliament – again dominated by liberals – recurred again two years later over Parliament's disapproval of the foreign minister, whose budget was twice voted down. After the second vote the king – to his regret – bowed to parliamentary demands and dismissed the cabinet. These showdowns decisively confirmed – some twenty years after the constitutional reforms of 1848 – that the government served at the pleasure of Parliament, not the king.

Achievements and Insecurities

Not only nationally but also locally, government was becoming more proactive. Throughout the last half of the nineteenth century, municipalities, better financed and better organized, steadily took over the task of aiding the poor from the churches, which formally were charged with taking care of their own members. But much of the work to help the poor came from the private sector. New humanitarian initiatives, thought to befit a Christian and civilized nation, expressed themselves on several important fronts. The death penalty, last imposed on the Maastrichter Joannes

Nathan in 1860 for murdering his mother-in-law, was abolished ten years later, the Netherlands being one of the first countries to do so. Prison life, too, would become more humane, or at least be more tightly controlled; new prisons in Arnhem and Breda, built in the 1880s, were dome-shaped panopticons, designed better to monitor prisoners and to discipline and improve their behavior.

In the cities, wealthy and influential citizens undertook efforts to improve the lot of those less fortunate than themselves. Wealthy businessmen established the first public housing corporations in the 1850s, in which low-income families could enjoy decent housing at affordable rents. The Jewish physician Samuel Sarphati, in the quarter-century before his death in 1866, singlehandedly introduced many improvements in the city of Amsterdam, including affordable bakeries for the poor and a rubbish-collection system, to name but a few of his initiatives. Many of these initiatives were also aimed at "elevating" the working classes by teaching them values such as self-discipline that were associated with the bourgeoisie. This was seen, for example, in the cult of the domesticity, perhaps particularly powerful in the Netherlands, which celebrated the home-oriented virtues of the Dutch housewife, such as cleanliness and frugality. Although working-class women were hardly in a position to stay at home and manage the household as a sole task, they increasingly learned to hold in honor these virtues, even if that only meant placing geraniums in the windows of their lowly cellar dwellings, as one historian noted.

Developments seemed be succeeding each other at a rapid pace. The telegraph and trains, the intensification of commerce, the rise of new associations that concerned themselves with everything from animal welfare to skating, the expansion of the press – repeal of the tax on newspapers made possible a press available to all – all created a deeper sense among many Dutch that they were part of a shared, national community. The newly felt communal bonds could be local and regional rather than national, and they could certainly create a sense of connection that was primarily restricted only to the like-minded. But there can be little doubt that a shared sense of Dutch nationhood grew in this period, and the Dutch felt acutely that they were bound up in a shared fate.

That sense of a shared fate was given a fright in 1866, when it briefly appeared that the Netherlands might not survive as an independent nation. The Prussian chancellor, Otto von Bismarck, after having wrested Schleswig-Holstein from Denmark, had gone on to defeat the vaunted Austrian Empire in a matter of weeks. There were deep concerns that Dutch Limburg – which in the 1830s had been made part of the German Confederation to keep it out of Belgian control – might serve as a pretext for new Prussian aggression that could put an end to the Kingdom of the Netherlands, just as it had put an end to the neutral Kingdom of Hanover and other smaller German states. Not only Limburg but the Grand Duchy of Luxembourg, also part of the German Confederation, was a source of worry to the Dutch government. Though not a part of the Netherlands, the duchy was ruled by the House of Orange and Willem III, who had shown himself amenable to the proposal of the French Emperor Napoleon III to sell Luxembourg for 5 million guilders. Prussian hostility to the cession of this strategically placed territory made war a real possibility, and Dutch involvement in this Franco-Prussian conflict had to be avoided at all costs.

In the end, both potential points of conflict were resolved without war, at least for the time being, and at least for the Dutch. Limburg was excluded from the new North German Confederation, and Luxembourg was made a demilitarized, neutral state. But if the Dutch were spared military conflict, the creation of the German Empire in 1871 would confront them with a new and demanding problem of how to defend their borders in the future against such a powerful eastern neighbor.

By 1870, in sum, the Kingdom of the Netherlands had secured for itself a modest but respected place among the nations of Europe. At the beginning of the century little more than a vassal state of France, and under the early kingship of Willem I a kingdom of some size and ambition, the country was by mid-century a small European kingdom whose boundaries were honored by the great European powers, and whose colonial possessions were secured by British acquiescence. Troubled by instability and later by an unusually authoritarian government in the first decades of the century, the country was now governed by a parliamentary system – a form of government still more exception than rule in Europe. Facing economic crisis and deurbanization in the Napoleonic age, the Dutch economy was well positioned by the 1860s to participate again in the world economy, a position that it owed in part to the less-than-voluntary service of the Javanese peasantry. But the period after 1870, with its intense competition in both international and domestic politics, would create new challenges of its own for the Dutch nation-state.

6

Progress and Crisis, 1870–1949

~

The Dutch, fully integrated into a global economy, mostly benefited from the effects of the Second Industrial Revolution. Their
flourishing cultural scene permitted some to talk of a second
"Golden Age." Yet the expansion of these years resulted in both
colonial wars and rising domestic tensions between competing
ideological factions. The Dutch did manage with some difficulty
to avoid direct participation in World War I, and until World War
II maintained a parliamentary system that kept revolution and
dictatorship at bay. Yet the Great Depression of the 1930s, the
Nazi occupation of World War II, and the bloody and traumatic
denouement of decolonization in the 1940s made some wonder if
not progress but chronic crisis would be their perennial destiny.

Expanding Horizons, 1870–1914

Dutch Imperialism

From about 1870 to 1914, the world was carried by a new "wave"
of globalization. Those forces that defined it – free trade, unprecedented technological advances and economic output; the rise
of international networks; and an increasing assertiveness on
the part of the world's Great Powers – also greatly affected the
Netherlands. And nowhere was this more apparent than in the
Dutch relationship with the East Indies.

The beginning of a new, more intensive relationship began in
1870, when the first Dutch steamship passed through the Suez
Canal, which had been opened the year before. Dutch shippers,
like many of their European counterparts, had been skeptical of

322

the new waterway, fearing that its tolls would drive up the prices of their goods. But soon Dutch shipping companies developed regular services through the canal, transporting mail, passengers and cargo. Hundreds of Dutch ships came to pass through Suez in the course of a year, meaning a trip to the Indies no longer lasted several months, but only a few weeks. The new route proved to be a boon for the Netherlands' antiquated shipbuilding industry, which now built fast, modern ships to link Fatherland and colonies. But far more than that, the canal enabled the Dutch to trade, to settle and to fight in the East Indies as they never had before.

Historians regard the period around 1870 as a pivotal shift from an "old" to a "new" imperialism. This shift from the old to the new, in which the European powers sought to expand and protect their colonial position in a politically unstable world, can be seen in the fate of the Gold Coast, a portion of which had been held by the Dutch since the 1630s. With the slave trade long abolished, the Netherlands' only colony in West Africa had been an economic burden. By the late 1860s, the Dutch government proved willing to sell the Gold Coast to the British, but they preferred to link the transfer to two other issues. With the abolition of slavery in Surinam, the Dutch sought new sources of labor to work the plantation. They contracted indentured service from British India, which would result in some 34,000 "Hindustani" laborers moving from British India to the Dutch colony in the decades before World War I (a group later supplemented by nearly as many Javanese). The other issue concerned the future of Sumatra, an Indonesian island situated on the boundary of British and Dutch colonial interests in Asia. After tough negotiations, the British government proved willing to accept new and far-reaching Dutch claims of influence on the island, including recognizing Dutch hegemony over Aceh in northern Sumatra, whose sultan had hitherto been internationally recognized as sovereign. In 1871, these three issues – the transfer of the Gold Coast, the indentured labor agreement and Dutch influence in Sumatra – were settled.

In hindsight, the Sumatra Treaty of that year was the beginning of a dramatic expansion of Dutch colonial power in the Indonesian archipelago. The reasons the Dutch felt themselves justified in pacifying and controlling all of Sumatra were multiple. Dutch interests in the Indies were possibly threatened by an independent Aceh, and by pirates along the new shipping routes to and from the Suez. Following the logic of the new imperialism, the Dutch also feared that other colonial powers might stake out their share of the planet at the cost of the Netherlands. National pride also played a role. Economic interests, from domination of the pepper, tobacco and rubber trade to the discovery of oil, can also be factored in.

In practice, Dutch control over Aceh proved elusive. Efforts to establish it led to a bloody conflict that would last, off and on, for nearly a generation, starting with the first Aceh war in 1873 (launched, incidentally, in part with the support of African troops from the Gold Coast). Perhaps 100,000 people were killed as a result of resisting colonial rule, and the Dutch lost thousands of men, mostly to tropical disease, in pacifying the island. Dutch critics protested colonial policy, and visible excess – notably the massacre at Kuta Reh and surrounding villages, where 1,150 women and children were shot by Dutch troops in 1904 – prompted shock and dismay in Parliament. But like other European publics, the Dutch in the end stood behind their government's colonial policy, accepting the wars that such policies demanded.

Aceh was not, of course, the only Dutch conquest around the turn of the century. After Dutch soldiers were massacred in a surprise attack on Lombok in 1894, the Dutch resolved to "pacify" all the "outer regions" of the archipelago. A vast territory forty times the size of the Netherlands itself, stretching from Aceh in the west to New Guinea in the east, was thus brought under Dutch rule. The Dutch were also prepared to make a show of force in the Caribbean, as in 1908, when The Hague used gunboat diplomacy to impound Venezuelan ships and bring about regime change there after its president had introduced anti-Dutch trade measures.

As colonial rule expanded and solidified, increasing numbers of Dutch civilians made their way to the East Indies. By 1900, nearly 100,000 lived there (about 40 percent of them women), and that number would increase in the 1920s and 1930s. It was never a great number: perhaps no more than 1.5 percent of the Dutch population born in the nineteenth century migrated there. But new opportunities awaited: Christian missions rapidly expanded, as did the colonial administration. And in the newly freed markets of the Indies business and commerce flourished. Companies such as what later became Royal Dutch Shell (1890) got their start there, and businesses established in the Indies were highly successful in the international economy. Although there was no longer a cultural system to generate huge revenues for the national treasury, the Indies' economy remained an important source for Dutch prosperity.

The Indies were, moreover, an important source of inspiration for Dutch scientists, legal scholars and linguists; the Colonial Institute (1910; now the Tropeninstituut) was established to promote research on the Indies useful to Dutch rule. The usefulness of such knowledge was also evident in the work of the scholar and high civil servant Christiaan Snouck Hurgronje, who specialized in Islam and advised the Dutch government on how best to regulate it; the jurist Cornelis van Vollenhoven specialized in Islamic *adat* law and its application in the Indies. But Dutch interest in the Indies was far broader than scholarship alone. The public imagination was captivated by "their" Indies – some 1.5 million people visited the Colonial and Export Exhibition held in Amsterdam in 1883. Literature, the arts and museums were all strongly shaped by Dutch experiences in their Asian colony.

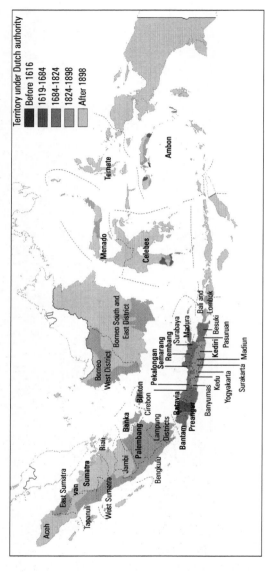

12   Expansion of Dutch colonial authority in the East Indies. In territorial terms, most of this expansion took
     place in the four decades prior to World War I.

Economic Modernization

Dutch energies and imaginations were not directed at the East Indies alone. The decades before World War I saw a boom in the Dutch economy, as it became more deeply integrated into the regional and global economy. The Netherlands' role in maritime shipping benefited from the rise of world trade, and new water channels. The North Sea Canal, which connected Amsterdam to the North Sea, and the New Waterway, which better connected Rotterdam to it, were each finished in the 1870s. Rotterdam in particular became an increasingly important harbor, ever more closely tied to service of the rapidly industrializing Ruhr region in Germany; indeed, German technological know-how from large industrial concerns such as Siemens aided the modernization of the Dutch economy. Holland had always played the dominant role in the Dutch economy, but vital economic centers elsewhere contested that dominance, most notably the textile industry in Twente and in Noord-Brabant, and somewhat later coal-mining in South Limburg. The electro-technical factory of the Philips family, established in Eindhoven in 1892, became an industry leader – first in Europe, later across the world. Industrialization in the Netherlands, which came later than in Britain, Belgium or Germany, focused not on heavy but on light industry and on the processing sector. The country's key industries, ranging from food processing to textiles, were in turn strongly oriented toward the export market. The pattern of processing and exporting, so crucial in the seventeenth century, now repeated itself two centuries later.

The country's relatively modern and efficient agriculture, also benefiting from the expansion of the world economy, remained strong, reducing the pressure to industrialize. Throughout the 1880s, Dutch farmers also suffered from a long-term slump in European agricultural prices that resulted from cheap imports of American and Russian products. But they emerged with higher-quality products and were now better organized, with farming cooperatives and the reliable credit of local savings and loan banks

Urbanization

putting agricultural producers on a more secure footing. Over the long run, though, the move from country to city set in after the 1860s, as commerce and industry increasingly beckoned. In 1880, 40 percent of the Dutch population lived in cities; by 1930, that had climbed to 65 percent. The population of Amsterdam rose from 240,000 in 1860 to 510,000 fifty years later. Rotterdam's growth as a harbor town was even more striking. In 1869, fewer than 120,000 lived there: in 1913, over 460,000.

Indeed, the Dutch population continued to grow at a fast rate. There was, by European standards of the time, little emigration, though the agricultural crisis of the 1880s did for a time prompt many farm families to leave. In the course of the nineteenth century only 140,000 Dutch left for the United States, compared to 5 million Germans, proportionally a much higher percentage. Sufficient economic prospects and social support kept the Dutch from leaving in large numbers.

Striking, too, was the birth rate. After 1880, the number of children began to decline in many parts of northern and western Europe, but that decline was less marked in the Netherlands, to the consternation of the Dutch Neo-Malthusian League, established in 1881 to promote birth control. The existence of tight-knit orthodox Protestant and Catholic communities, with their pro-birth stance, continued to play an important role in the growing number of children. Rising population figures also had to do with rising life expectancy. Better hygiene and stronger public health measures, which sharply reduced infant mortality, boosted life expectancy from thirty-nine years of age in 1870 to fifty-six in 1910. More births and longer lives can be seen in the population statistics. In 1889, the Netherlands had a population of 4.5 million, and by 1930 that had more than doubled to 9.6 million.

The Dutch economy was strong enough to sustain this growth, and to benefit from it. This was evident in the per capita income, which rose from $2,750 (in 1990 dollars) in 1870 to $3,850 in 1914. Dutch gross domestic product (GDP) and labor productivity at the beginning of the twentieth century neared that of Great Britain, and were roughly that of Germany's. After a long period of losing ground economically, the Dutch were gaining traction again.

The School Controversy

This economic history, in hindsight, can be regarded as a success, but it hardly proceeded without serious social and political tensions. Rapid economic and social change intensified debate over two issues: who should have a say in running the country's institutions, and to what extent the government should interfere in social and economic matters. As increasing numbers of citizens mobilized themselves to assert their own vision for society, so, too, their demands on government grew. And Dutch citizens were increasingly empowered to organize themselves and make demands. Not only income but literacy, though at relatively high levels already, rose as well. Access to inexpensive transportation and media opened up a new world of ideas – and a new sense that the future, if contended for, could be much better than the present.

The leading controversy in the Netherlands concerned education, as it did in much of western and central Europe in the decades before World War I. Education mattered enormously for many liberals. The public school was crucial in socializing future generations to become virtuous and productive citizens, and the new demands of a modernizing economy required the necessary improvements in the educational system. Sixty percent of the Dutch work force in the 1860s were effectively unschooled laborers, and Thorbecke's reforms launched in that decade began to address this. But post-Thorbecke liberals saw the need to further this program. Johannes Kappeyne van de Coppello, a prominent jurist and liberal parliamentarian, propounded a "modern worldview" that saw the state's task as ensuring that all citizens, if they proved themselves, could reap the benefits of civilization. Upon becoming interior minister in 1877 Kappeyne acted in this spirit, introducing legislation that compelled all schools to raise their standards. Significant financial help from central government – necessary to improve standards – was made available. Private, religious schools were to be given no government assistance, but they were required by the new law to meet the same higher levels of quality imposed on public schools.

Kappeyne's reforms may seem both logical and sensible, certainly if one keeps in mind that religious schools formed only a small percentage of all schools: orthodox Protestant schools, for example, numbered only 200 out of the total of 3,800 primary schools across the country. But those who sought an affordable religious education for their children saw this legislation not as an advance but as an attack on their religious convictions. And their distrust had everything to with developments in the Catholic and Protestant worlds respectively, and their relationship to the liberals.

Dutch liberals in the late nineteenth century were not as militantly anti-Catholic as they were in other parts of Europe; some monastic houses harassed in Germany and later in France established themselves in the Netherlands, where they could operate unhindered. But many Dutch liberals were committed to the march of science and progress, and were unfriendly to religious forces that might stand in the way – in particular a resurgent Catholic Church. They sympathized with Bismarck's efforts to curb German Catholicism, and they made renewed efforts to enforce the laws banning Catholic processions, which resulted in confrontations and arrests. Dutch Catholics, in turn, had been electrified by the Italian seizure of the Papal States in 1870; indeed, some 3,200 Dutch Catholic *zouaves* (a third of the pope's army) had volunteered in the failed effort to defend the papacy by arms. Because of what had happened in Rome, and because of what was happening to Catholics in places such as Germany,

Dutch Catholics were more assertive in defending their faith at home as well. The Catholic laity now felt strongly that they were part of a titanic worldwide struggle to defend their faith. Holding processions in the face of government opposition was one way to express their religion; arguably, the right to hold processions mattered more to ordinary Catholics than access to their own schools. But to Catholic clerics and politicians, the establishing and defending of Catholic education was the primary task in a country – and a world – where the forces of irreligion threatened to triumph.

A sense of unrest, too, made itself felt in the Dutch Reformed Church, though there the conflict was chiefly internal. The fact that male members could now vote in Church council elections challenged the modernist clergy; no longer could they preach their controversial ideas from the pulpit without finding resistance from new, often orthodox, Church councils. Leading the militant faction of the orthodox party was the clergyman Abraham Kuyper, a convert from modernism. Although mistrusted and feared for his ruthlessness, Kuyper was undoubtedly the most intrepid politician in modern Dutch history; he found the Calvinist daily, *De Standaard*, and established the Calvinist Free University, among other institutions. He believed that Christianity should pervade all areas of life, and that Christian organizations should be established to achieve this end. His insistence that the Church be purified of modernist ideas eventually led to his break with the Dutch Reformed Church in 1886, when he and his associates in Amsterdam were put out of office for refusing to accept into the Church catechumens who had been taught by modernist clergy. Roughly one out of seven members of the Church left with him, a significant split that resulted in the new Reformed Churches in the Netherlands (Gereformeerde Kerken in Nederland). Wholly in line with Kuyper's spirit, this new Church consisted of members whose zest for organization and social engagement would lead them to influence Dutch society to a degree that exceeded their numbers.

But in 1878, when Kappeyne's School Law was passed, the schism had not occurred, and many orthodox Protestants, followers of Kuyper or not, were united in their opposition to the School Law. This expressed itself in the petition drive of 1878, directed at the king, requesting him not to sign the recently passed education law. Over 470,000 Dutch citizens (two-thirds Protestant, one-third Catholic) signed the petition – an astonishing number that reveals just how politically mobilized Dutch society had become. The king was in no position to prevent the law from coming into effect, but the mobilization necessary for the campaign served as an important impulse for further confessional activity, both on the side of the Catholics but particularly on the part of the orthodox Protestants. Under Kuyper's leadership, orthodox Reformed established the Anti-Revolutionaire Partij – with an explicit political program, the country's first modern political party.

The School Law of 1878 and the reactions to it changed politics in the Netherlands. In a narrower sense, it launched a debate – lasting nearly forty years – about whether the government should subsidize religious schools. This debate formed the crux of what has gone into Dutch history as the "School Struggle" (*Schoolstrijd*). Most liberals (and later, social democrats) long resisted such subsidies, because they thought the nation's young should be schooled together regardless of creed. In contrast, most Roman Catholics and orthodox Protestants after 1878 came to regard government financial support for their schools as necessary for parents to educate their children according to their own convictions. The first Catholic–Protestant coalition of 1888–1891 saw to it that religious schools received 30 percent of their operating costs from the government, but the struggle for more subsidies continued. In a broader sense, the "Struggle for the School" after 1878 served as catalyst for the mobilization of Dutch politics and society on religious grounds. The issue gave Catholics and orthodox Protestants, who were already mobilizing themselves to assert their own place in the Dutch public sphere, a focal point in defining who they were, and what they wanted to achieve. For many Dutch, religion became, more than ever, the defining organizing principle of their lives.

Debate over the Right to Vote

As important as religion was in unifying believers in a common cause, it did not resolve other pressing issues on which the Dutch were divided – not by religion, but by convictions shaped by class and gender. One crucial issue was the franchise. Liberals in the late nineteenth century believed that citizens should be encouraged to take responsibility in public life. They passed a law in 1869 making it legal for workers to organize themselves in associations, a law paving the way for the creation of trade unions. But voting for Parliament was another matter. Before the reforms of 1887, which doubled the number of voters, only about 12 percent of all Dutch male citizens were enfranchised. The old premise, held by many European liberals, that financial independence was an essential condition for independent voters, and that enfranchisement should be a gradual process, remained a strongly held conviction in the Netherlands. The mobilization of not only religiously minded members of the public but also socialist ones, encouraged by a now assertive and popular press, made this traditional stance increasingly difficult, however. "The people behind the voters," as Kuyper put it, could no longer be shunted aside as unqualified to speak in politics. But Kuyper's stance was not shared by all Dutch politicians; the Netherlands at the end of the nineteenth century was a country where "aristocratic" and "democratic" factions were arrayed against each other.

Sharp divisions over the franchise became most evident in the early 1890s, when interior minister Johannes Tak van Poortvliet proposed extension of the franchise to male citizens who could read and write. Both the Anti-Revolutionaries and the liberals were split on the issue – resulting in the permanent fragmentation of both groups – and Tak's measure failed. In 1896, a more conservative law nevertheless relaxed the voting requirements, permitting about half of the male citizenry to vote. By time of World War I, rising prosperity enabled about two-thirds of Dutch males to vote under the requirements of the 1896 law. In hindsight, what characterized the expansion of Dutch voting rights for males was indeed the gradual character of its progress, paralleling in this respect the process in Great Britain, and in contrast with France, where under revolutionary pressure extended rights had been granted suddenly. It was development that, in spirit, probably suited most of the country's political leaders, who preferred a disciplined electorate responsive to their direction. But the speed of the enfranchisement remained an important issue, pressed in particular by the growing Social Democratic Workers' Party, who thought they had much to win by giving the poor the vote. Popular demonstrations in support of the universal franchise were common in the years before World War I.

This extension of the franchise in the decades prior to 1914 did not benefit women. Quite the contrary: the franchise extension of 1887 explicitly forbade, for the first time, the right of women to vote. This exclusion came in response to Aletta Jacobs, the country's first woman physician, who in 1882 had attempted to run for Amsterdam City Council. As a champion for women's rights she assailed the conventional norms governing women in the workplace and in the home. One of the first to join the Association for Women's Franchise in 1894, Jacobs fought for the right of women to vote, and in 1911 she went on an extended world tour to promote this cause. The founder of the association, Wilhelmina Drucker, later developed close ties with international socialism in order to promote women's rights. Weaving socialism with feminism was controversial, however, and proponents of suffrage for women were themselves divided over the best political course. The Dutch National Exhibition of Women's Labor, held in 1898 to coincide with the inauguration of the first Dutch Queen Wilhelmina, revealed tensions among the organizers, including the difference between liberal and socialist women over the role of class in their struggle.

There were differences, too, over the very basis on which women should become full citizens: was it because they complemented men, or because they were the same? Support for women's rights was strongest among the left-liberals, social democrats and some Protestants – the first Dutch clergywoman, the Mennonite Anne Zernike, was installed in 1911 – but resistance from the religious parties and conservative liberals prevented a prewar breakthrough on women's right to vote, as had been the case in Scandinavia. Dutch suffragists, reflecting the more restrained character of the Dutch political style, were less overtly combative than some of their counterparts in Britain or the United States.

38 Like many Dutch progressive reformers of the nineteenth century, Aletta Jacobs was inspired by British activists, including some early suffragists whom she met as a young physician.

The Social Question

Perhaps more fundamental than voting rights was another issue: the so-called "social question." The economic boom prompted an emerging group of progressive or "social" liberals to take steps to reduce injustices that had risen as a consequence. Their first serious attempt to use the power of the state to curb market abuses resulted, after more than a decade of emotional debate, in the regulation of the very widespread practice of child labor. An 1874 law forbade children younger than twelve years old to work in factories. Championed by the parliamentarian and social reformer Samuel van Houten, the "Child Law" was a dilution of his original intent and lacked the teeth of enforcement; moreover, young children could still be expected to work in the home and in the fields. Only with the arrival of compulsory education at the turn of the century would child labor effectively be brought to an end.

The initially limited legislation at the national level did not prevent reforms related to the social question from being advanced. In the first place, urban government was increasingly active in improving the living conditions that affected workers, particularly in offering better public utilities such as lighting and sewage, and taking an increasing role in organizing and dispensing poor relief, in which the churches had been progressively unable (or unwilling) to discharge their responsibilities. But Dutch civil society took an ever more active role that at once sought to improve the condition of the working class and to "elevate" it. For many reformers, alcohol was a crucial part of the social question, and a growing one: between 1850 and 1880 Dutch consumption rose from 4 to 7 liters of pure alcohol per capita per annum. In 1880, there was one saloon per 146 inhabitants in Amsterdam, where on average residents each drank 15 liters of distilled liquor per year. This situation was a danger not only to public health but to business, which required a dependable labor force. Reform efforts and increased social discipline among socialists, Catholics and Protestants alike were important reasons why drinking levels sharply declined by the early twentieth century. Another important initiative was the effort to create decent housing in the cities, where a large portion of the population lived in the most unhealthy conditions conceivable, including dark, wet cellars. Private philanthropy and housing cooperatives were launched in the late nineteenth century to correct this problem.

By the late nineteenth century, most groups in society, including those in the Netherlands, recognized the importance of the social question. Pope Leo XIII's encyclical *Rerum novarum* (1891) denounced exploitation of the poor, and Kuyper's "Social Congress" in the same year sounded similar concerns. A parliamentary study into abysmal factory conditions in the late 1880s had also shocked the Dutch public into a more sympathetic stance toward the plight of the workers. The socialist Herman Heijermans's play *Op hoop van zegen* (1900), on the sad lot of fisherfolk, was an immediate success. But the concern of many reformers, liberals and Church leaders was not sympathy alone. The prospect of social upheaval – even of revolution – also worried them. Dutch liberal reforms in the early 1870s had been informed by the specter of the Commune in Paris, in which revolutionaries had seized the city before being crushed with much violence. Holland's own urban masses were also simmering with resentment. Amsterdam's Eel Revolt of 1886, begun when police tried to stop an instance of the popular but cruel game of eel-pulling, was stopped only when the army stepped in, killing twenty-six demonstrators. What might be next? And the teachings of Karl Marx, which preached and predicted proletarian revolution, made more pressing the question: What would the workers do?

Marx had visited The Hague in 1872 to attend the congress of the International Workingmen's Association, the first socialist "international." The Dutch chapter of the Association (like many others) failed to make much headway among workers, however. It was the politically liberal Algemeen Nederlandsch Werkliedenverbond

337

(1871) and its orthodox Protestant offshoot Patrimonium (1876) that initially were more successful in organizing the working class, though neither was strident in defending workers' rights. It was only after 1890 that Dutch labor would become strongly organized, as socialist unions vied with each other and with religious groups for the membership of workers. Each had its distinctive flavor. Important sections of the Catholic Church were uncertain about labor unions, preferring associations that united employers and employees, but over time a Catholic working class was able to assert its own voice, a voice that rejected a revolutionary path while seeking an autonomous course from that of Catholic employers. What became the Protestant-dominant Christian National Trade Union Alliance (1909) was also generally moderate. More confrontational were the socialist unions. The General Dutch Diamond Workers' Alliance (1894), initially established by mostly Jewish workers in Amsterdam, served as an important basis for the creation of a broader Dutch Alliance of Workers' Unions (NVV; 1906). At the radical end was the syndicalist National Workers' Secretariat (1893), which wanted unions, and not the state, to serve as the organizing principle of society.

The earliest champion of a socialist party was not a Marxist but Ferdinand Domela Nieuwenhuis, who established the first socialist party, the Social Democratic Alliance (SDB) as early as 1881. As a spellbinding orator and as a provocateur – Domela was imprisoned in 1887 for *lèse-majesté* in attacking Willem III as an ineffectual "king gorilla" – he had no equal. But his growing preference for ideological anarchism did not meet the needs of a growing movement that saw a strong organization – and parliamentary representation – as the surest way to safeguard worker interests.

It was an offshoot from the SDB, the Social Democratic Workers' Party (SDAP; 1894) that would become by far the most important socialist party. Like its German counterpart, the Sozialdemokratische Partei (whose Erfurt Program of 1891 it emulated), the party was Marxist in ideology and tightly organized, building toward the day of revolution when workers would take all the means of production into their own hands. In practice and over time, though, the Dutch social democrats, like their German (and other west European) counterparts, tended toward revisionism – a belief that key workers' aims could be achieved within the parliamentary order. From this perspective, achieving these specific aims, and not working toward revolution, were the best goals of the movement. But it would be a long time before the social democrats forswore revolution, and a long time before their political adversaries trusted them to work within the system. Between roughly 1900 and 1920 Marxist socialism (espoused by the SDAP and its more radical offshoot, the Social Democratic Party, later the Communists) rapidly achieved wide support from within the working class, coming to represent about a quarter of the electorate. Even as its influence grew, though, the strength of the religious parties and unions would prevent social democracy from attaining the same large vote share as in Germany or the Scandinavian states.

Emblematic of the divide between the socialists and many of their bourgeois rivals was the Railway Strike of 1903. The initial successful strike of workers against the railroads triggered a reaction from a nervous government of Catholics and Anti-Revolutionaries, which made it illegal for public-sector workers, including the railwaymen, to strike. A general strike in response failed, and Kuyper's law was passed. The legacy of the whole affair was one of additional mutual distrust, with both sides preparing for the next crisis. Indeed, the socialist NVV was founded better to coordinate worker action, and the Protestant National Federation of Christian Trade Unions better to counteract these efforts.

A House Divided

Schools, the franchise, and the social question were some of the crucial issues that reflected the growing fissures in Dutch society.

Liberal power had been broken by the newcomers, but there was no single dominant party that could replace them. The Dutch Parliament was split, prior to World War I, between the religious parties of the right and the secular parties of the left, each at best attaining a narrow majority. In 1905 and 1913, the SDAP rejected liberal overtures to form a "bourgeois" government with them, making a majority government impossible. Parliament's condition reflected the divisions of society: Protestant versus Catholic, secular versus Christian, liberal versus socialist, democrats versus elitists, bourgeois versus working class. Regional resentments against the encroachments of a centralizing Holland – expressed strongly in Friesland and in Limburg – added to the tensions. In a fast-changing world where old certainties seemed at risk and where new opportunities seemed particularly bright, the Dutch gravitated toward like-minded citizens to defend and advance their principles and their interests in the nation-state, and also in the wider world. This was not a uniquely Dutch situation. Across Europe and the Americas, citizens banded together by race, religion, gender and class to contend for the public sphere.

The Dutch variation on this transnational pattern is now known as *verzuiling* ("pillarization"), in which Catholic, liberal, orthodox Protestant and socialist "pillars" – quite distinct and separate from each other – held up the roof of the Dutch state. In practice, of course, it was messier. Although they increasingly organized nationally and internationally, the earliest forms of mobilization were local in character, and it sometimes took decades before local struggles became tightly linked with national causes. And the drive toward self-organization was not the same everywhere. Dutch Jews, for example, constituting about 2 percent of the population around 1900, did not assert themselves powerfully as a group, in part perhaps because they thought that a thoroughgoing assimilation, now afforded by Gentile society, offered them better prospects. The Amsterdam diamond-workers, many of them Jews, were organized along non-sectarian lines, for instance. And liberals – who felt that "neutral" organizations ought to appeal to everyone, were ideologically resistant to what they viewed as sectarian or class spirit. Finally, it is important to stress that "pillarization" was a matter of degree; most Dutch continued to read daily newspapers not formally associated with any group, for instance. "Pillarization" thus never completely characterized the contours of Dutch society, but was unevenly applied.

Showing by far the most coherence and most systematic efforts to offer an alternative to a society steeped in Protestantism and dominated by liberal institutions were the Catholics. It was not of course that they were invariably of one mind: the tensions between social progressives and conservatives were perennial. It took years before the Twente priest Herman Schaepman, the leader of the Catholics in Parliament, was able to persuade both the hierarchy and the powerful landowners and "notables" of the Catholic south that a well-organized Catholic party, with heavy lay representation, was in the Church's best interest. The increasing role of the clergy in directing Catholic society also generated some alienation among the laity.

But to the outside world, Catholics formed a single and closed front. They changed the Dutch landscape; 506 churches were consecrated in the fifty years following the return of the bishops in 1853. These often neo-Gothic buildings, many designed by the famous architect Pierre Cuypers, were designed to reassert Catholicism's public presence, whether to the joy of Catholics or to the dismay of Protestants. Sons and daughters of the Church flocked to take vows; if there were only 1,850 sisters in 1853, that number had climbed to 9,280 by 1888. Deep popular piety, held by many Catholics in these years, animated the passion for entering the priesthood, orders or monastic life – paths that also accorded social status and offered professional advancement. Moreover, from the 1880s onward the clergy successfully pressed the faithful to organize themselves separately into Catholic organizations. In so doing, Dutch bishops, like their counterparts in Belgium,

Austria and Switzerland, hoped to protect the laity from modern influences that they saw as detrimental to the Catholic faith and to lay obedience to the Church. Many laity in turn saw Catholic organizations as a way to assert their own agenda, which they increasingly did in the course of the twentieth century.

Orthodox Protestants were much less cohesive, divided as they were across denominations and theological camps. But thanks to Kuyper and the Anti-Revolutionary Party he founded, political Protestantism as a distinct movement was stronger in the Netherlands than anywhere else in Europe. And building on a longer tradition of civic participation, orthodox Protestants were enormously productive in establishing schools and social organizations of all kinds. The socialists were less organized still than the Protestants; they did not have their own schools, but over time they developed their own network of clubs. It was certainly not the case that religious groups were the only ones to develop a strong identity. The *openbaren* – those who sent their children to public schools – could form tight communities that set themselves off against those who went to religious schools, and Freemasons – who flourished in this period – offered many men (and only men) a distinctive community.

These divisions were deep and enduring because they were based on serious differences as to what Dutch society should be like – there was a clash of principles, as Domela Nieuwenhuis and Kuyper recognized. But the Netherlands was not an armed camp that threatened to erupt into civil war. The rule of law was respected, public administration trusted, the tone of the press relatively restrained. Indeed, for all the democratization and difference of conviction, the Dutch population was content to leave many issues in the hands of Dutch political and social elites. Compared to the great conflicts between clerical and anticlerical parties in Roman Catholic countries, and the battle lines between capitalists and socialists in many others, Dutch tensions seemed mild. With the absence of really large cities the Dutch bourgeoisie were less worried about "the masses" than their French or German counterparts. And gradually a new modus vivendi emerged, in which these ideological differences became accepted as the new normal. In a country now consisting of only minorities, some give-and-take was accepted as necessary.

And most, if not all, Dutch were bound together by a sense of shared nationhood. They spoke a common language that was increasingly standardized in education; they were subjects of the same sovereign; and they were joined by, as they imagined it, a common history and a shared cultural heritage. Standing for the Netherlands' place in the world, including colonial expansion, also served to bind the Dutch together, as such processes also took place among other publics. For example, the British war against the Boers (1899–1902) angered the Dutch public, who felt an ethnic kinship with the Afrikaners. Some 140,000 signed an indignant protest addressed to the British people. This keen sense of nationhood was more than passions focused abroad, though; the Dutch reveled in national success wherever it might be attained.

A Second Golden Age

The period from 1890 to 1914 may have been fraught with divisions, but it was also a period of lasting achievement. For all the divisions, this was true in the political domain, though more might have been achieved with greater consensus. The state became more and more important in the lives of the citizens. A fairer tax code was made possible through the introduction of the income tax. Mandatory schooling and accident insurance were introduced by the Nicolaas Pierson Cabinet (1897–1901), a left-liberal government that was particularly activist in extending the role of the state. It also introduced a far-reaching Housing Law (1901) that, besides regulating housing, made it possible for the government to support housing corporations financially in the construction of decent dwellings for low-income tenants. Later on, laws improving the financial support of the poor, the sick and invalids were introduced. At the local and regional level, more was done to improve the lives of the lower classes. The State Mines in Limburg, in close cooperation with the Catholic Church, sought to offer workers decent pay and housing. In Amsterdam, radical liberals such as Willem Treub brought gas, water, electricity and telephones under public control, and the social democratic commissioner Floor Wibaut launched an extensive program of municipal housing for the working class. Through better understanding of disease, public health officials started programs to reduce or eradicate illnesses such as malaria, which had plagued the country's soggy countryside. These initiatives added an important measure of security and welfare to a large portion of the public.

In the Netherlands, as elsewhere in Europe, education took giant strides during this period. The illiteracy rate declined to no more than 10 percent by 1900, two-thirds lower than it had been at the beginning of the nineteenth century, and roughly equal to levels in other parts of northern Europe. Hundreds of libraries established by the "Nut" and new reading societies stimulated reading. Teachers with diplomas tripled in the last half of the nineteenth century. Most striking, at least in international comparisons, were the successes in higher education. The Hogere Burgerschool (HBS), initiated in the 1860s and soon allowing female students, served, among other things, as the basis for high-quality scientific research. The Netherlands' success in producing Nobel laureates was at its high mark in the first decade of the twentieth century: five scientists – Van 't Hoff, Kamerlingh Onnes, Lorentz, Zeeman and Van der Waals – were so honored, four in physics, one in chemistry. All had backgrounds, in one way or another, in the HBS system. Other Dutch scientists, too, made their mark on international science; Hugo de Vries, the botanist and geneticist, linked the recently discovered mutation of genes to the theory of evolution. And Dutch universities also competed with the best in Europe. The dynamics of the new education, along with high investment, meant that the Netherlands scored at

344

the high end educationally compared to other European countries in the early twentieth century, before it began falling again as the consequence of declining financial support.

Dutch literature and poetry also enjoyed a second Golden Age, but owing to the language attracted less international notice, as was clearly the case in art. The so-called Hague School, defined by painters such as Jozef Israëls and later Anton Mauve and Hendrik Willem Mesdag, were very widely praised as a group of painters that rivaled the French Impressionists, though now they are held in lower esteem. Vincent van Gogh, now considered by far the greatest Dutch artist of the period, was himself a one-time student of his cousin-in-law Mauve, though he received little appreciation during his tortured life, which culminated in his suicide at age thirty-seven. Later on, Amsterdam would harbor a school of

39   Though Vincent van Gogh's fame rests chiefly on work created in France, a quarter of his total extant production, such as this *Wheat Field*, came from his earlier sojourn in Nuenen.

notable impressionist painters, most famously George Hendrik Breitner, himself a one-time colleague of Van Gogh but no fan of his work.

The Netherlands, both as picturesque preindustrial landscape and as seat of the Golden Age, led foreign artists, including hundreds of Americans, to spend time in there soaking up all things Dutch. The Dutch themselves reveled in their seventeenth-century heritage; all manner of buildings were constructed in the style of the Holland Renaissance, a "neo" style that resurrected the gabled look of the seventeenth century and was proclaimed the new national style. The architect Cuypers attempted to express this new style in the monumental Rijksmuseum building, finished in 1885, though critics, including King Willem III, castigated its Gothic aspects as too Catholic. The new museum was a fitting showcase for Rembrandt, now more than ever elevated to the status of national muse, but other Golden Age figures, such as the poet Vondel and the admiral De Ruyter, also enjoyed a similar *Nachleben*.

For all this celebration of art and culture, modern Dutch artists did not always find the ethos in the Netherlands very encouraging to their path-breaking aesthetic expressions. Van Gogh would move to France for the last four years of his life (1886–1890), where most of his masterpieces were created, and later leading figures such as Theo van Doesburg and Piet Mondriaan would find artistic life more compelling elsewhere. The Dutch art market remained small, and only later would the German-born Helene Kröller-Müller, wife of a prominent businessman, play a decisive role in improving the situation through the building of an insuperable private collection. Other forms of artistic expression, such as classical music, would eventually generate composers and conductors of some note, but only slowly, after the German composer Johannes Brahms had declared (in 1884) that he would go back to Amsterdam for good food and drink but not for its musical talent.

Aside from high artistic expression many forms of popular culture took off, perhaps most notably in recreational and professional sports imported from Britain. The first cycling club began in 1871, and what later became the mass organization Algemeen Nederlandsche Wielrijders Bond (ANWB) started in 1883. Personal fitness, social discipline, the improvement of transport and the stimulation of tourism were all aims of the ANWB. Soon bicycles became an integral part of the social landscape. Soccer made its entry into Dutch life at roughly the same time. The Haarlemsche Voetbalclub, the first of its sort, started in 1879, and the Netherlands would become one of the handful of countries that established the now dominant professional football association, the Fédération International de Football Association (FIFA), in 1904. Skating had long been a quintessential pastime of the Dutch, but now new standards of ambition were set. The first effective organization of the 'Eleven Cities Tour' (*Elfstedentocht*) took place in 1909, offering a gruelling 200 km ice-skating race through the Frisian countryside – a tradition that has since been held in winters with a sufficiently hard freeze (a total of fifteen times in the twentieth century).

Dutch Peace Policy

Confident of their own achievements, and committed to addressing serious social issues, the Dutch determined to shine their light overseas as well. They directed most of these efforts to the colonies in the East, and launched the so-called Ethical Policy (*Ethische Politiek*) in the early years of the twentieth century, fueled by the conviction, widespread in the West at that time, that white Christian civilization carried a moral burden to help the less developed peoples in their colonies. These efforts were mostly aimed at helping the people of Java, where the population had expanded enormously and where poverty reigned. The Dutch government invested much more money than it had in public works, in improving agriculture (including irrigation as a central focal point), in public health and in education. These policies brought about improvements, though the limited budget available to the colonial government meant that the measures were not adequate to address the needs of so large a population (some 30 million at the beginning of the new century). In 1910 the larger cities were governed by elected councils, the first limited opportunity for Indonesians to have a direct say in their own affairs. During World War I the colonial government in the East Indies would take important first steps in the creation of representative government in the form of a People's Council (*Volksraad*), but the Council itself remained advisory in nature. Anything approaching real self-rule was brushed off by most Dutch as something for the distant future.

International law offered another place for the Dutch to make their mark. The legal scholar Tobias Asser, scion of a prominent family of Jewish jurists, played a central role in the creation of international agreements on private and family law, and on civil trials. For these efforts he was awarded the Nobel Peace Prize in 1911. Through Asser's efforts the Netherlands had become a center of international law, and its scrupulous neutrality made it a natural place for the countries of the world to meet to discuss their commitment to it. In conjunction with Tsar Nicholas II's desire to organize an international gathering to promote peace, the Dutch government convened The Hague Peace Conference in 1899, and a second one in 1907. These conferences established the rules of modern war – no aerial bombing or chemical warfare, for instance – and set up a court for the voluntary arbitration of disputes (mandatory arbitration, supported by most countries, was vetoed by Germany). The result was the establishment of the Permanent Court of Arbitration housed in The Hague's Peace Palace, a splendid edifice completed in 1913 and largely paid for by the American industrialist Andrew Carnegie.

The conferences' failure, of course, became manifest at the outbreak of World War I. But some of their concerns were later further codified by the Geneva Conventions, and the Permanent Court of International Justice was ensconced in the Peace Palace in 1922. The prominence of the Dutch role prompted the jurist Van Vollenhoven to envisage a "calling" for the Netherlands in creating and leading an international military force that would check unlawful aggression. The Dutch government quickly dismissed this risky and unlikely proposal, though a variant on it would later be adopted by the United Nations. But that dismissal did not alter the country's emerging reputation as a principled proponent of international law, a stance that the country, small and dependent on trade, had every reason to embrace.

War, Peace, Depression, 1914–1940

A Precarious Neutrality

The Dutch government declared neutrality upon the outbreak of World War I in August 1914, supported by all the parties, including the SDAP, which, like all social democratic parties in western Europe of the time, chose to align itself with whichever course its own national government took. The Dutch military situation was precarious. Since the early nineteenth century Dutch control of its colonies depended on British good will; Dutch government support for the Boers in their fight against the British was impossible. And after 1870 it was Germany, not France, that posed the greatest threat of land invasion. Armed neutrality was the only possible course between two power blocs, neither of which it could afford to alienate. The Dutch developed a two-fold strategy: build an impregnable fortress system through the use of water (most notably the Holland Water Line) and possess a mobile force that could punish the invader. German calculations were crucial, however. The German military's original Schlieffen Plan envisaged no full-scale invasion of the Netherlands – its aim was Paris – but it did intend to invade Dutch Limburg, which lay on the way to the French capital. This would have forced not only

349

Belgium but also the Netherlands into war. But a revision made by Chief of General Staff, Helmuth von Moltke, left Limburg out of the plan, as he thought that it would divert resources from a quick seizure of the Liège fortresses, the gateway into France. And so the Netherlands managed to avoid invasion in 1914 and, as it turned out, for the rest of the war.

Although the Dutch were spared the desolation and death that their southern neighbors experienced under the German invasion, they were nevertheless confronted with a serious problem within the first weeks of the war: the serious influx of Belgian refugees into the country. The steady move westward of the front lines, which by October had reached the city of Antwerp, prompted perhaps a million Belgians, mostly civilians but also tens of thousands of soldiers, to seek shelter over the frontier, swamping local authorities with the temporary care of this population. Most returned to Belgium within weeks or a few months, but some 100,000 remained. Over time, work was found for most of these

40   The 322-kilometer-long "death wire" along the Dutch–Belgian border, seen here, appalled many Dutch. But The Hague saw the wire as proof that the Germans respected its neutrality.

within the Netherlands, but 20,000, unable to fend for themselves, or considered undesirable or too dangerous to be released, remained in camps until the war's end. Soldiers, too, remained interned. Meanwhile, German military authorities constructed an electric fence along the Dutch–Belgian frontier, a fence that cost hundreds – perhaps thousands – of Belgians their lives. This "death wire" had a powerful impact on the Dutch imagination, underscoring their uneasy sense of being a peaceful island surrounded by a dangerous world.

The influx of refugees may have represented a dramatic confrontation with the miseries of the conflict; the longer-term impact of the war threatened Dutch lives and property on the open seas, and threatened to undo the very neutrality that the Dutch sought to preserve. Once war was declared none of the belligerents had much interest in punctiliously respecting the neutrality of those who stayed outside the conflict. From its very beginning in August 1914, each side pressed its advantage in The Hague, hoping to benefit from a Dutch tilt in its own direction. At the same time, neither the Allies nor the Central Powers – or more specifically the Netherlands' neighbors Britain and Germany – had much motivation to end Dutch neutrality; indeed, there were crucial reasons to respect it. For the British, it was important not to drive the Netherlands into German arms and thus precipitate a German military and naval presence on the Dutch coast; for the Germans, the Netherlands (as well as neutral Denmark) provided a useful "funnel," allowing Germany to obtain foreign goods that had otherwise been closed to it by British blockade.

One crucial challenge, then, for the Dutch government was to maintain its lifeline to its global trading partners and colonies while assuring the British that such trade would not benefit the Germans. This led to the creation of the Netherlands Overseas Trust Company (NOT) in November 1914. The Dutch government was bound by treaty to free trade with Germany, and could not negotiate with the British government to end this trade without breaking the agreement. The NOT was thus created as a private agency, led by business executives, who, in line with British demands, "voluntarily" restricted their own imports so that they would not be sent to Germany. Though in practice a breach of the free trade treaty, the Germans accepted the NOT because Dutch trade on the seas was good for the Dutch economy and this in turn was good for German–Dutch agricultural trade. They moreover benefited from the fact that Dutch smugglers energetically broke restrictions on this trade by sneaking Dutch farm products across the German border. For two years these arrangements helped the Dutch economy; through the end of 1916, Dutch agriculture, industry and even shipping, dangerous as it could be, prospered.

Though the government formally played no role in the NOT, they were in effect deeply involved, and state control over the economy massively grew, just as it did in the countries at war. The Dutch confessional parties and some liberals, preferring private initiative over state controls, helped see to it that the scores of boards charged with managing all products, from poultry to peas, were formally private. Whatever the form, the effect was the same: an increasingly regulated economy in which the government intruded ever more into the economic and social spheres. World War I also prompted both more efficiency in Dutch business and at the same time more cooperation with government.

Yet the history of the NOT, and other organizations designed to regulate trade, was one full of perils. The NOT's effectiveness declined as the war dragged on. It did not help that the Dutch government, and leading businessmen in charge of international trade, were often bitterly at loggerheads with each other about the best course to take. Both the wartime cabinet of P. W. A. Cort van der Linden and the NOT itself were rife with these divisions. The Germans, the British and later the Americans each, at various moments in the war, found reasons to bully the Dutch into terms that would decisively favor each of them. Dutch ships were subject to British searches and occasional confiscation of goods – or worse, ran into British mines in the North Sea. Britain also once cut the telegraph service to the Dutch East Indies, to remind the Dutch that their empire depended on British goodwill. And German submarine attacks on commercial vessels – a policy that had nearly caused the United States to enter the conflict in 1915 and that brought them to declare war in 1917 – also afflicted the Dutch, who were in no position to threaten military retaliation.

Cause célèbre for the Dutch was the March 1916 sinking by a German submarine of a passenger steamer, the SS *Tubantia*, a ship that had been on its regular route to South America. Miraculously, no one lost their lives, but the clear identity of the ship prompted an outcry in the Netherlands, generating considerable anti-German sentiment. German-spread rumors of an impending British invasion of the Netherlands helped hush the outcry. The government's effort to keep Dutch opinion neutral enough to avoid the appearance of taking sides was proving a difficult task. Some population groups, including orthodox Protestants and conservative liberals, sympathized with Germany, while Catholics often did with their Belgian and French co-religionists. To the embarrassment of the government, the mass daily *De Telegraaf* was overtly pro-Allied. Maritime-oriented business interests favored the Allies, while Rhine-oriented ones tended to favor the Germans.

And neutrality as a balancing act became more difficult from 1917 onward, as the Germans became more demanding in their desperate struggle, and as the United States entered the war on the Allies' side. All Dutch ships in American ports were requisitioned in March of 1918 – the silver lining being that some Dutch skippers made a handsome profit in the forced service of the Americans. As a result of the new Allied determination to deny Germany any goods, the overseas trade of the Netherlands slid to dramatic lows; by 1918, the port of Rotterdam received only a tenth of the volume of transport it had seen in 1913. In the end, some 300 Dutch ships were sunk as the result of the war, mostly by submarines, despite the Dutch arranging with the Germans for a special travel corridor through the sea zones that Berlin had declared forbidden for shipping.

If the war brought the Dutch into an increasingly difficult economic position, it also had an unexpected – and for many welcome – effect on Dutch politics. The war pressured Dutch politicians to overcome their political differences for the sake of the nation's interests. Politics was thus "pacified" in a double sense. In the first place, Premier Cort van der Linden determined to accept two longstanding demands: the vote for all, as called for by the political left, and full subsidies to religious schools, long the key aim of the political right. These issues would likely have been settled in the coming years, but the war and Cort saw to it that in 1917 both aims were passed by near unanimity in Parliament, as both right and left engaged in a supreme act of political horse-trading. Two years later, in 1919, women were also granted the right to vote, a breakthrough that, with a public preoccupied with other concerns, was achieved with little discussion. Universal suffrage found no corollary in the colonies; democratic representation on the Antilles would have to wait until after World War II.

The pacification of 1917, as it is commonly called, was soon accompanied by new social legislation, such as the introduction of the eight-hour day (and forty-five-hour week) in 1919, which attempted to pacify workers in an increasingly restive time. The Netherlands did not entirely escape the social radicalization precipitated by the war, though. The so-called Potato Riot in Amsterdam in 1917, which highlighted food shortages among the worker population, was followed by a period of heightened worker unrest punctuated by wildcat strikes – a pattern evident throughout war-weary Europe. The government responded, again parallel to labor legislation in other European countries, by introducing unemployment benefits and an eight-hour day.

The Allied victory in November 1918 briefly brought new uncertainties, however. Inspired by the revolution in Germany that toppled the Kaiser, SDAP leader Pieter Jelles Troelstra publicly proclaimed that the proletarian revolution would also sweep the old order away in the Netherlands. For a couple of days, this seemed a real possibility. No one knew how many of the social democratic working class would respond to his call at such a moment of crisis, and the liberal mayor of Rotterdam handed over control of his city to the socialists in anticipation of the revolution. But Troelstra – himself anything but a steadfast revolutionary – had little support within his own party, and fledgling communist groups that did rise up were too small to pose serious danger. Moreover, massive public support by bourgeois groups for the queen quickly banished any thought of revolution. Troelstra's ill-considered action damaged the rather moderate SDAP's chances to bridge the political chasm with the other parties for the next twenty years.

A longer-lasting concern focused on the victorious Allies, who found the Netherlands' neutral stance unsympathetic in a war in which they themselves had paid such a high price. It did not help that the abdicated Kaiser Wilhelm II had found shelter in the Netherlands, thus evading the punishment that the Allies had hoped to impose on him. In particular, the Belgians were keen to annex Zeeland-Flanders and Limburg at the expense of the Dutch. Dutch diplomacy, led by the intrepid foreign minister, Herman van Karnebeek, was ably undertaken in London and Paris to ward off Belgian claims and restore the Dutch to the good graces of France and Britain. The Netherlands became a charter member of the League of Nations, though its experiences in the war made the government cautious to avoid any international entanglements.

The Roaring Twenties

Dutch neutrality during World War I was once thought to have spared it from the modernizing tendencies of the interwar period that so clearly affected the belligerent nations, whether Germany or the United States. That view has been modified by historians in recent years, who have stressed that Dutch society, from literature to religion and politics, deeply imbibed the sense of crisis and inevitable change that defined modernism during this period. For example, Van Doesburg and his journal *De Stijl*, haunted like so many other European artists by the war, launched a search for ultimate truth and harmony behind the forms of life, to be achieved through the highest degree of abstraction. This sense was not restricted to art; Dutch connections with the wider world, long intensive, grew only more so during this period. Emblematic of this development, perhaps, was the creation of the Koninklijke Luchtvaartmaatschappij (KLM) in 1919, which ran regularly scheduled services, first to London, then later, in what for that time was the longest regular service in the world, to Batavia (Jakarta) in the Dutch Indies. Rapidly expanding, KLM became the third largest airline in the world by the 1930s. It is just one indication that Dutch society during this period was hardly mired in isolated traditionalism.

The period's conservative reputation is to a large extent drawn from the politics of the 1920s and 1930s, when the confessional parties dominated Dutch politics as in no period before or since. Between 1918 and 1939, the Catholic and orthodox Protestant parties ruled alone, except for a period in the mid 1930s, when liberals were asked to join them. The Catholics delivered, in Charles Ruijs de Beerenbrouck, their first prime minister in 1918, though their Protestant allies, numerically inferior to them but better connected and with stronger leadership, would take the lead in the coalitions. Indeed, as in a number of other European countries, the Dutch state, dominated by the religious parties, played a role in strengthening these ties through policies that supported subcultural autonomy through subsidies. One sees this in the total share of religious schools: 38 percent of the total in 1910, 45 percent in 1920 and some 62 percent in 1930, further rising to a high of about 75 percent in 1945.

The 1920s revealed more clearly, from a statistical viewpoint a trend that had been apparent since the 1880s: that the Netherlands was characterized as a country with a very high percentage of active churchgoers, and a very high percentage of people formally professing no religion at all. Catholics busied themselves in the construction of the "rich Roman life," which touched on many areas of their existence. Over 80 percent of them went to weekly mass. Orthodox Protestants showed similar activity and commitment. At the same time, by 1930, after a decade in which many Protestants and Jews in particular abandoned formal religious affiliation, the number of those marked as having no religion approached 15 percent, at that time the highest of any country in Europe. The absence of a state Church, which kept formal membership high in other European countries, and the politicization of religion, along with a marked tendency toward dechristianization in many parts of Europe after World War I, all played a role in this development.

41   A Catholic Goat-Breeding Association (Veghel, 1919). Though rare, later critics specifically cited Catholic goat-breeding clubs as *the* example of just absurdly how far pillarization might go.

The predominance of the confessional parties made itself felt in public and private life, though it might be said that the Dutch state was not as intrusive as it could be in democracies with stronger statist traditions, such as Sweden. The most far-reaching moral program of the confessional parties had already come before World War I. The 1911 law increased the punishment for conducting abortions, forbade the open sale of contraceptives, more strictly regulated pornography, and made brothels and pimping (but not prostitution as such) illegal. It also forbade homosexual relations between an adult and a person under twenty-one years of age (for heterosexuals the age of consent remained at sixteen years). Gambling, too, was prohibited. A later law (in 1932) to muzzle "malicious blasphemy" was employed by prosecutors five times before the last case in 1966.

These changes to the law, though many, were not by European standards of the day particularly strict (homosexuality as such, for example, was not criminalized), but it confirmed that the Netherlands was a country governed by a public Christian morality that set the social standard for everyone's behavior. And it obviously had direct effects for women considering abortions and for some homosexuals, of whom over 5,000, mostly men, were prosecuted under the law during the sixty years in which it was in effect. A majority were convicted. But beyond these measures the confessional parties seemed primarily interested in creating public space – and increasingly state financial support – for their own religious organizations. Clientelism, one effect of "pillarization" in Belgium, was less dominant in the Netherlands, where the operation of the state was less influenced by religious or ideological groups. Even so, the country's religious groups exercised better social control over their members than many states could. And indeed, the Dutch population showed remarkable social discipline during this period, as revealed, for example, in uncommonly low crime rates.

Building a community of this sort was not opposed to modernity. Liberals, social democrats and confessionals were often strongly imbued with a technocratic bent, interested in the further mastery of nature to improve security and bolster the standard of living. Engineers played a leading role in modernizing Dutch society as they saw fit, reordering the landscape and creating new villages and neighborhoods on the basis of the newest scientific insights. The country underwent a substantial improvement in its infrastructure; electrification of the rail network, begun in 1908, was substantially extended from the 1920s until the process was largely completed in the 1950s. Great water projects were themselves an expression of ambitious vision evident in the first years of the twentieth century, which saw the modernization of infrastructure and a more efficient use of land deemed so essential for the Netherlands' future. An *Afsluitdijk*, or causeway, spanning the north of the Zuyder Zee, had been planned since the 1880s, advocated by liberal politician Cornelis Lely and the influential association the Zuiderzeevereniging. The 1916 floods that washed over large parts of North Holland provided an important political impulse, and the political decision to block off the country's internal "South Sea" from the North Sea was made in 1918. In 1927, the work on a 32 km barrier was begun, and was completed five years later. A motorized causeway now connected Friesland with North Holland.

The effects of building this barrier against the sea were not only benevolent. The water south of the causeway became brackish in time, putting an end to the region's fishing culture and to the livelihood of many of its fishermen – an outcome long foreseen by the government, which offered modest help to the struggling fishing villages along the old Zuyder Zee. The new lowlands also initially created new breeding grounds for malaria-carrying mosquitoes. This thus worsened a persistent public health problem that Dutch medical officials had long attempted to eliminate, but that was only effectively combated after World War II by the extensive use of the pesticide DDT.

At the same time, the project enabled the Dutch to begin on – by far and away – the most extensive land reclamation project in

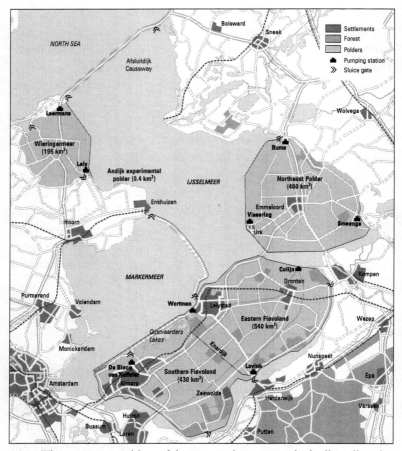

13   The great new polders of the twentieth century, which all in all took
forty years to create, greatly surpassed in size and ambition any earlier
project the Dutch had undertaken.

their history: a project that, it has been calculated, finally allowed
the Dutch to claim more land from the water as they had lost to
it through the centuries. The first effort to polder in the Zuyder
Zee was the Wieringermeer project, resulting in a 300 km² parcel
of empty brown expanse once taken from the sea. By 1934 the

360

new land had been sufficiently desalinated for agricultural use. Preparatory work for the Northeast Polder began in 1936 and was completed in 1942, in the middle of World War II. All in all, this massive project gained 1,650 km² from the sea.

The 1920s, as in many parts of western Europe, were years of plenty, with substantial rises in income. The Dutch economy, having avoided a wartime footing, was ready to compete in peacetime, and fared better even than regions such as Scandinavia, which had also managed to stay out of the Great War. Gross national product grew at some five percent per year between 1923 and 1929. Products from the East Indies – coffee, oil, tin, tobacco, sugar and rubber – were in high demand; by 1938, 14 percent of Dutch national income stemmed from there. In the Caribbean, Curaçao's economy – which largely had subsisted in the export of straw hats – was transformed after 1918 by the creation of a

42   Dutch bicycle companies such as Gazelle, thriving after the advent of the pneumatic tire in 1888, depended on the Dutch East Indies both for rubber and for sales.

Shell-built oil refinery and storage base. Shell's extraction of oil in Venezuela required a deep-water port that did not exist there but did at Willemstad, which now became one of the leading oil harbors in the world. On nearby Aruba, too, a refinery was built. Full employment was assured, though whites remained in control of the economy. Industry enjoyed a growth spurt in the Netherlands proper as well, signaled already in 1918 by the completion of the great steel furnaces at IJmuiden, the Hoogovens complex. By 1930 in North Brabant, some 50 percent of the working population labored in factories, as opposed to only 28 percent on the farm. Industrialization was important to the Netherlands because it sustained its strongly growing population. Rising real wages and full employment also helped keep social unrest to a minimum.

Though politically the country remained placid, the new "modern" way of life, which included dancing and cinema-going, made some authorities (and many public commentators) uneasy. Mayors were charged with maintaining public order locally and they could intervene, when they thought it necessary, in the recreational activities of citizens. The Calvinist mayor of Amsterdam tried, initially with modest success, to curtail dancing in his city, and authorities were alert to films that challenged the moral and especially the political order; Russian-made movies were particularly suspect. Sport, too, to the displeasure of some, had become a mass spectacle. Dutch officials were successful in bringing the IXth Olympiad to Amsterdam in the summer of 1928. Funding, though, had to be secured from private sources after most of the religious parties in Parliament, which had little appreciation for such a vanity fair of ancient pagan pedigree, refused to co-finance the project. Direct appeals to the Dutch public, however, quickly raised far more than the sum requested – an investment rewarded, incidentally, by the Dutch attaining a respectable eighth-place finish at the games.

It was perhaps a fitting response from a public that had grown increasingly passionate about not only their own local football clubs but also a whole range of recreational athletic associations.

362

Between 1870 and 1940, the Dutch brought into being some 15,000 local sports clubs. Dancing, movie-going, sports, the increasing mobility of the population by bicycle or automobile – these were all tell-tale indications that the Dutch society of the interwar years was not exclusively defined by order and discipline, religious or otherwise, but was eager to participate in new cultural trends and find pleasure in leisure.

Economic Crisis and Political Radicalization

It was turn out that 1928 would be the last good year for the world economy, and the emergence of the Great Depression was to have a lasting effect on the Netherlands. A particular problem was that much of the Dutch economy depended on foreign trade, and then precisely in a time when the leading nations of the world economy were increasingly seeking to protect their own national markets. The resulting decline in international business, which both triggered and exacerbated the global depression, necessarily hit the Dutch hard. This trend became particularly evident in the course of the 1930s, when the Netherlands' most important trading partner, Germany, especially after Hitler's seizure of power, sought to become economically self-sufficient. Dutch–German trade withered by two-thirds. It did not help that Hendrikus Colijn, former director of what became Royal Dutch Shell and prime minister throughout much of the 1930s, pursued an austerity policy that vainly tried to maintain a balanced budget. That meant hardship for hundreds of thousands of Dutch who were dependent on the government for support during this difficult period. Colijn also resisted pressure to take the Netherlands off the gold standard. Only in September of 1936, after the other remaining defenders of the gold standard had been forced to abandon their stance, did the Dutch, too, devalue their currency, the guilder. It immediately dropped 20 percent in value, making Dutch products more exportable.

The Dutch managed to survive economically through the Depression in part because their trade links were diverse enough to persist, even if it did mean dumping their agricultural products at extremely low prices, as they did on the British market after Germany shut itself off from Dutch goods. The size of the agricultural sector, where underemployment was a greater problem, and the creation of public works projects kept the unemployed statistics lower than they were in Germany or the United States, where unemployment levels rose to between 25 and 30 percent of the total workforce. Still, the formal rate was alarming enough; at its worst, in the winter of 1935–1936, it reached 18 percent. In the wake of the devaluation of the guilder, the Dutch economy slowly improved in the late 1930s.

As elsewhere, the deep economic crisis in the Netherlands fed the growth of radical parties, on both the far right and the far left. Like other parts of Europe where liberal democracy was most deeply entrenched – Scandinavia, Switzerland, Belgium and the British Isles – these parties remained relatively small, certainly much smaller than Germany, where they together represented over half the electorate in 1932. On the radical left in the Netherlands were several small Trotskyite parties, who opposed both Stalin and the "bourgeois" character of the far larger, reformist SDAP. Their best-known figure, Henk Sneevliet, was internationally well connected and had helped Mao Zedong found the Chinese Communist Party in the early 1920s. Larger than any of these fragmented groups was the Communist Party itself, which reached a prewar high of 4 seats (out of 100) in the parliamentary elections of 1933. Though hardly a threat to the system, its presence could seem outsized, in part because of the loudly confrontational style of its leading politicians and because, in a few places, as in the capital Amsterdam, it was a real political force with which to contend.

The radical left's support of illegal actions against the authorities also made them feared opponents. Activists supported, for example, a bloodless mutiny on board the Dutch light cruiser the *Zeven Provinciën* in early 1933, whose enlisted men, in support of an on-shore strike, were protesting a second round of substantial pay cuts. The Dutch authorities were determined to stamp out the revolt, and ordered warships and planes to intercept the renegade ship. As a warning shot, one of the warplanes unintentionally dropped a bomb on the cruiser's bridge, killing many of the mutiny's leadership. The crew surrendered, and those involved were sentenced to long terms in prison. To much of the Dutch public, the mutiny seemed to illustrate just how serious the radical threat was.

Literally and emotionally closer to home for most Dutch citizens was the unrest in July of 1934, triggered again by government cuts: in this case a 16 percent reduction in unemployment benefits – benefits that were already no more than half the average wage of a worker. The most violent of the confrontations took place in the Jordaan district of Amsterdam, now picturesque but then one of the city's poorest districts and one with a large communist electorate. The riot, in which the demonstrators threw bricks and tiles at the police, soon proved too much for local law enforcement, and premier Colijn, himself an old military man, sent in the army to quell the protests. Order was restored only after several days, during which six people died, and scores were arrested. It would prove the high point of political unrest within the Netherlands proper during the 1930s, but many Dutch, observing the political polarization and violence taking place throughout Europe and fearful of communist insurrection, could only wonder where it would all end.

But it is not the radical left that has captured the attention of recent historians but rather the radical right, in particular the rise of the Nationaal Socialistische Beweging (NSB). It was not the only Dutch fascist party; many tiny groups emerged out of the right-wing criticism of parliamentary democracy in the 1920s, or out of a right-wing agrarian movement that opposed the perceived domination of the big cities in the western part of the country. The NSB, launched in 1931, was headed by Anton Mussert, an engineer who once had achieved national fame by successfully organizing public resistance to a proposed waterway treaty with Belgium. The unprepossessing Mussert was a rather unlikely leader, having little of the charisma or passion that characterized Europe's most famous fascist strongmen. The NSB was not – initially – openly anti-Semitic, and its ethos was noticeably bourgeois and less militaristic than the German Nazis, although it must be said that its efforts to create a parallel uniformed organization to the Nazi Brownshirts were blocked by Dutch law. In any event, these apparently mitigating features cannot belie the fact that the radical aims of the party were to overturn the political and social order, seeking the establishment of an authoritarian state that would forcibly recreate a national community along fascist lines. The NSB was able to appeal to a relatively wide section of the population, especially the middle classes, and its membership shot up after 1933. In the election for the provincial States, the first in which it participated, the NSB secured 8 percent of the vote, securing many votes in well-to-do neighborhoods, but also scoring well in areas of rural unrest and in the larger cities.

The elections of 1935 were simultaneously the high water mark of the Dutch National Socialists, and the point from which their fortunes would slowly wane until the German invasion in 1940. The electorate remained loyal to the traditional Christian and social democratic parties, denying the NSB additional inroads. Some churches, including the Dutch Catholic Church, took a hard line against the NSB, declaring party membership incompatible with being a faithful believer, and the fascist share of the vote accordingly fell in places where initially it had been fairly strong, as in Limburg province. The further radicalization of the party after 1936 – due in part to the increasing influence of the Nazis on the Dutch national socialists, in part to the growing influence of its more radical wing – further alienated some voters. The introduction of anti-Semitism into the party program likely diminished its appeal; although anti-Jewish feeling in the Netherlands was hardly absent it had not been a point of political action. Mussert's own shortcomings as a leader also may have inhibited a sustained fascist surge; even within his own party he faced hostility. In any event, by the late 1930s the NSB lay beyond the pale of political respectability. Though tens of thousands of Dutch joined the peacetime NSB, its members often felt themselves to be a beleaguered minority, dismissed by mainstream politics and held in contempt by their fellow citizens.

Thus the Dutch parliamentary system survived these challenges to liberal democracy without too much difficulty. And in some ways the unity of the country was further solidified by an increasingly important role for the House of Orange. Queen Wilhelmina had taken the throne as a young woman in 1898, but her popularity as a constitutional monarch rose in the 1930s, as the Dutch sought solace for global uncertainty under the aegis of her dynasty. But none of this prevented a sense of crisis from pervading the country's leading political circles. Though the Dutch support for democracy would increase in the late 1930s as the threat to it became more pronounced, the embrace of it had not been always warm. Premier Colijn himself, who believed in decisive leadership, was no enthusiast for the endless dithering he saw as a chronic malady of the parliamentary system and, after initially rejecting Mussolini's idolatry of the state, he began to see merit in more authoritarian arrangements. But he was no fascist or anti-Semite, and in any event undertook no steps to change the Dutch political system or to subvert democracy. The government did restrict demonstrations to prevent political polarization and keep public peace, and civil servants were forbidden from being members of an extremist party, a measure first directed at the communists and later at the national socialists.

In the Dutch colonies, where full civil liberties were typically extended only to those of European descent, the government could be much tougher on political challengers. The Dutch government of the period showed that it had little appetite for meeting the demands of the rising nationalist movements there. The anticolonial activist Anton de Kom, closely associated with the communists and other leftists, was closely watched, and he was forced into exile in the Netherlands after his presence in his homeland of Surinam had triggered unrest. Repression was worse in the East Indies. The limited concessions to self-rule made earlier (see above) were not further expanded, as the British did in India. The rise of a nationalist movement in the 1920s, soon led by the magnetic figure Sukarno, was taken seriously by Dutch authorities as an immediate threat to the public order but not seriously enough to recognize that the movement indicated growing popular opposition to their rule. Sukarno was arrested in 1929 and spent much of the next decade in detention. The 1933 revolt on the *Zeven Provinciën* – primarily carried out by Indonesian crewmen – served as an additional incentive to take a tough stance against threats to public order, even as the Dutch government preferred to frame the rebellion as the work of leftist agitators and not of the "natives," lest the lesson be imparted that the Indonesians were capable of leading a revolt themselves.

Early governors-general of the interwar period, who were appointed by The Hague, understood the need for change and undertook further to improve the economic and educational situation of the population and gradually to increase their say in local affairs. The nationalists were given some room to operate in the public sphere. But these rather modest concessions failed, caught as they were between a radicalizing nationalist movement on the one hand and the Dutch government on the other, which – supported by most of the Dutch population in the Indies – resisted making any meaningful concessions. Just how long the old arrangements could have lasted without the coming Japanese invasion is impossible to say, but the turmoil of the 1940s would leave the Dutch badly surprised by the extent of opposition to their rule.

Catastrophe and Crisis, 1940–1949

Invasion

The Dutch were also largely unprepared for the new threat on their eastern border. To be sure, senior military personnel were alert to the German threat early, and Dutch political leaders were aware that Nazi Germany was a menacing power that at the very least needed to be placated. Local officials, for instance, sometimes sought to prevent artistic expressions of opposition to Hitler, on the grounds that such a law prohibited offending "a friendly head of state." And the influx of mainly Jewish refugees from Germany – especially following the Kristallnacht of November 1938 – for whom the Dutch government reluctantly made some provision, also starkly revealed to them the brutality of the regime. But as was the case with the public in other western European countries, the Dutch were long reluctant to recognize the potential consequences of a Nazi rearmament.

By 1940, the Dutch had a modern but very small air force, supplied by its own Fokker aircraft industry, but no effective air defense system. They possessed almost no tanks, and a limited amount of artillery, much of which dated from the nineteenth century. Efforts to correct this in the late 1930s came too late, and suffered from the fact that the Dutch arms industry was weakly developed and dependent on foreign suppliers who prioritized sales to their own governments. Commitment to neutrality – not only by the Dutch but even more by the Belgians – prevented the implementation of well-wrought plans that would more effectively coordinate Dutch military strategy with the Allies. The Dutch military command did, though, secretly draw up plans with them, should invasion ever come. Dutch intelligence about German military intentions was good, but it foundered in part on the unwillingness of some political and military leaders to trust its credibility, and the Germans for their part possessed an excellent knowledge of the Dutch defenses. Most important of all for the fate of the Netherlands, Hitler had determined in the winter of 1939–1940 that – in contrast to the modified Schlieffen Plan of World War I – the Netherlands must be invaded so as to secure its airfields and to foil any later invasions by the British.

Given Hitler's quick victory over France in the spring of 1940, it seems doubtful that a better prepared and equipped Dutch defense would have altered the ultimate outcome of the Nazi invasion, which began on May 10, 1940 and culminated in a general Dutch capitulation only five days later. German forces simply had too many men, too many armored vehicles and too many planes for a Dutch defense to succeed. The British were unwilling to expend any of their forces on Holland, and the limited French forces sent to the country did little good. In this respect the Dutch may have underestimated the military odds that were stacked against them. In any event the Dutch high command was surprised by the speed of the German advance, and the relative ease with which the invaders seized the Grebbeberg, a crucial defense line in the central part of the country.

But Dutch resistance could be tough in places; the Afsluitdijk causeway's path into Holland was effectively protected by a modern defense system. And in a couple of ways their short-lived defense had far-reaching results. Dutch forces prevented German paratroopers from capturing the queen and the government, allowing them to flee to England by ship on May 13, 1940. And Dutch units situated on the southern approaches to Rotterdam prevented German ground forces from taking the port, prompting the German high command to order the bombing of the city on May 14. Tragically, the bombing could have been avoided; the Dutch, faced with a fast deteriorating situation across the country, had already told the Germans they were willing to capitulate, but a failure to communicate this in time to German warplanes sealed the doom of Rotterdam. Its city center was destroyed, with the loss of more than 800 lives.

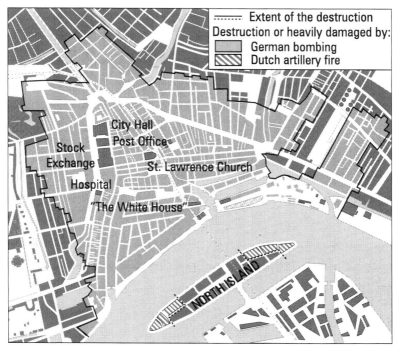

14 The bombing of Rotterdam in 1940 gutted the center of the old town. Dutch planners used the catastrophe to reshape Rotterdam into the modern city they thought it ought to be.

Three days later the medieval town of Middelburg, then being held by the French, was destroyed by fire. By that time, the Dutch capitulation had been signed.

The Early Occupation Regime

In contrast to other western European countries under Nazi control, where military rule was put into place (as in Belgium) or where native governments were permitted to continue under Nazi supervision (Denmark), the Netherlands was placed under a Nazi civilian administration, headed by the Austrian Arthur

Seyss-Inquart. This meant that the whole government apparatus of the Netherlands was now put under his command. Seyss-Inquart saw to it that Mussert and the NSB were denied a central role in government, although the Germans would appoint Dutch national socialist mayors, police chiefs, institutional directors and newspaper editors: positions they would often use for private gain. Regarding the Dutch as fellow Aryans with important economic and cultural ties to Germany, the Nazis were particularly keen to reshape the Netherlands in the national socialist mold. To guide the Dutch along this path a particularly rigorous and visionary administration was required, and this was the task with which Seyss-Inquart was entrusted. Some of the specific contours of the Dutch occupation – including the high number of Dutch Jews who perished in the Holocaust – found their roots in the particularly assertive character of Seyss-Inquart's government.

43 A NSB "hedge speech" celebrating "liberation" at the NSB rally in Lunteren on June 22, 1940. It was perhaps their grandest moment; German authorities largely shut them out of power.

Initially, however, there was little evidence of the brutal occupation that it would become. Dutch prisoners of war were soon released. German soldiers generally behaved correctly toward the population, and Seyss-Inquart went out of his way to seem accommodating. The Dutch, for their part, were willing to accept the new situation out of necessity; it seemed evident enough to them that the Germans were near to total victory. Real systematic resistance to the occupation was slow in coming; indeed, German soldiers stationed in the Netherlands early in the occupation remarked upon the lack of Dutch opposition to their presence. Most Dutch in fact thought that acts of violence aimed against the occupation were an exercise in irresponsibility; most also lived in a moral world in which a getting-along stance seemed the most reasonable way forward for all involved. Many Dutch were thrilled with the creation of the Netherlands' Union in the summer of 1940, which sought to renew Dutch society by breaking through the old religious and ideological divisions. Some 800,000 people joined the Union as a patriotic alternative to the national socialists, who were widely despised as traitors or opportunists. The NSB would get no further than just over 100,000 members, despite the perks of membership.

Being in the German orbit also had its benefits. If Germany had shut them out during the 1930s, the Reich was now extremely anxious to have access to Dutch products and services. Soon Dutch firms were doing excellent business with the German war economy, even where this violated an initial Dutch commitment not to aid and abet the enemy. Unemployment, initially high after the invasion, soon rapidly declined. The Dutch economy boomed through the first half of the occupation. The Germans introduced a few necessary reforms, including the introduction of mandatory health insurance in 1941, which was motivated primarily by the desire to put Dutch workers on the same cost scale as German workers, who had paid such insurance for decades. And the population continued to eat well until the end of 1944, although the healthier diet of less fat determined by rationing prompted the Dutch to complain about the lack of taste in their food.

But the terms of occupation became increasingly harsh as the war dragged on. After 1941 Germany increasingly used the Netherlands as a source of material wealth on which it could draw without offering anything substantial in return. Dutch products were purchased with marks that themselves had little value. As a result, it has been estimated that the Dutch standard of living declined by some 54 percent between 1938 and 1944, even as the Dutch economy continued to produce at the same level. German plunder of the economy substantially impoverished the country.

The Shoa

The harshness of the occupation was, of course, most manifestly and catastrophically experienced by the Jews living in the Netherlands – some 140,000 in 1940, of which over half lived in Amsterdam. The gradual but inexorable drive to isolate them from the rest of Dutch society was already evident in late 1940, when Seyss-Inquart decreed that they were to be dismissed from the civil service. The first violence occurred in February 1941. In response to altercations between Jewish residents on one side, and Dutch national socialists and German police on the other, the German authorities decided to round up several hundred Jewish men, who were transported to their deaths in Mauthausen. This outrage, observed by many non-Jewish residents in Amsterdam, prompted communists to call for an immediate general strike, which they were already planning. For two days the strike continued before it was put down violently by German troops, with nine deaths and many more seriously wounded. This strike, with its demonstrated solidarity for the plight of the Jews, was unique in Nazi-occupied Europe, and it was not repeated.

By May of 1941 the German authorities had determined that the Netherlands, in order to shape the country according to the

German vision, must be "cleansed" of Jews, and the process of incrementally denying Jews access to any part in Dutch society continued apace. Control over the Jewish population was greatly facilitated by the creation of a new identity card system, devised by a Dutch functionary, and based on a new centralized registration system that clearly identified those with three or four Jewish grandparents and was nearly impossible to falsify. In addition to growing restrictions on their movements, Dutch Jews were obligated to deposit their savings and their property in organizations that effectively confiscated them for use by German authorities. All of this occurred with little violence, and with little organized resistance. The so-called Jewish Council of Amsterdam, called into existence by the Germans after the strike of 1941, was used to pressure the Jewish community into submissive compliance, with the threat of worse to follow should they resist. And the Council did advise Jewish residents to cooperate. This accommodating stance, which in effect further facilitated the destruction of Dutch Jewry, has long been criticized; elsewhere, as with the Jewish community in Enschede, in the eastern part of the country, Jewish leaders advised those in their charge to go underground, resulting in much higher survival rates. But the option of going into hiding required careful planning, trustworthy contacts and the nerve to risk the consequences of capture. All in all, nearly 30,000 of the country's 140,000 Jews went underground, with about three-quarters of these surviving the war.

For those who did not try or manage to escape, the statistics were far grimmer. Something more than 5,000 of the more than the 107,000 Jews deported to the east survived the war. From July of 1942 to September of 1944 ninety-three different transports left the Netherlands for the east from the transit camp of Westerbork in the province of Drenthe, where most residents tried as best they could, mostly without success, to stay off the list of those marked for departure with the next train. The great majority of Dutch Jews were sent to Auschwitz, but during the course of 1943 many were

44 Internees at Westerbork Internment Camp. Unlike in Eastern Europe,
the Germans avoided displays of brutality in the deportations but the
effects were no less murderous.

also transported to the extermination camp of Sobibor (where only
a handful survived). Theresiënstadt and Bergen-Belsen were also
destinations. Anne Frank, daughter of a German-Jewish family
who moved to the Netherlands to escape the Nazis and whose
family had gone underground in 1942, was discovered in August
of 1944 and deported on the last train to Auschwitz. She died in
Bergen-Belsen, some weeks before the liberation of the camp. Her
father, the sole survivor in the family, would later publish the diary
she had written from her hiding place.

Thousands of Dutch took very high risks to assist Jews during
the war. Various churches publicly protested, beginning in 1940,
against the discriminatory measures imposed upon the Jews. But
statistically, few Dutch took an active role to assist them. Dutch
police and civil servants carried out Nazi policy, though enthusiasm
for it was usually restricted to Dutch national socialists and fellow
travelers. Indifference or anti-Semitic feelings doubtless further
inhibited some Dutch from helping the Jews, though recent historical research suggests that, in a world rife with rumors and with

little reliable information, few Dutch were in a position to know with any certainty what was happening to the deported Jews. In any event, by the time that the Dutch resistance fully got under way in the course of 1943, most of the country's Jews were already dead. In the fall of 1943 Amsterdam was declared "Jew-free."

Nazification Efforts and Repression

The rest of the population experienced Seyss-Inquart's increasing efforts to Nazify public life. As time went on, Dutch mayors faced a difficult trade-off: stay on and carry out the odious decrees of the German authorities, or step aside and have a national socialist or fellow traveler be appointed instead. The Dutch press, monitored from the beginning by the German authorities, had ever less room to determine the content of their own newspapers and journals. Many editors decided to cease publication; some leading newspapers stayed in print and were effectively Nazified. As the occupation deepened, Seyss-Inquart also left little room for the extensive civil society that had characterized the country. The Netherlands' Union was forbidden at the end of 1941 for, among other reasons, its refusal expressly to support the war against the Soviet Union. Many civic and professional organizations were banned, and their members invited instead to participate in Nazi-controlled associations. Labor unions, for example, were banned in favor of the Dutch Labor Front, and physicians were forced to join a Nazi-run "chamber." Most of these efforts were failures – Dutch physicians preferred to renounce their professional status over joining the Nazi organization – and these ham-fisted efforts only increased resentment against the regime.

What most galvanized Dutch resistance to Nazi occupation were the Nazis' increasingly desperate efforts to exploit Dutch labor through forcible conscription to Germany. Ultimately some 250,000 Dutch worked in German factories, far fewer than the Germans hoped to utilize. A decree ordering former Dutch

377

soldiers to report, as prisoners of war, in order to be used as labor helped to prompt new unrest and nationwide strikes in the spring of 1943, which the SS quelled through the killing of 175 demonstrators. The unrest showed the popularity of resistance to the Nazi regime, and the willingness of the population to help young men elude the German draft. As many as 300,000 men went underground in an attempt to avoid the call, spawning extensive networks of those who determined to help them. Resistance was also evident in a by now very active and varied clandestine press, expressing a whole range of views, from communist to Calvinist. No country under German occupation saw more underground publications than the Netherlands, a sign perhaps of a highly literate culture that continued to believe in the power of the written word. Meanwhile, the brutal character of the regime was increasingly shaped by the SS, led in the Netherlands by another Austrian, Hanns Albin Rauter.

Developments in the Colonies

For nearly two years, the Dutch living in the East Indies had been spared the effects of occupation. But their turn was coming. In the wake of the Japanese decision to move against Britain and the United States in late 1941, the Dutch East Indies, with its bountiful oil fields, also became a target. The Japanese soon captured northern and eastern parts of the Indies, and a Japanese invasion fleet moved against Java at the end of February 1942. It was blocked only by a modest task force of Allied ships headed by the Dutch Rear Admiral Karel Doorman. In the Battle of the Java Sea and subsequent engagements the Allies lost nearly all their ships. The absence of Allied cooperation and of air reconnaissance, as well as a better-armed Japanese fleet, led to the lopsided result. Doorman himself went down with his cruiser. After a week of intense fighting the Royal Dutch Indian Army on Java, better trained to maintain order in the colony than to withstand the

378

attack of a professional army, surrendered. In subsequent weeks, the Japanese would occupy nearly all of the Dutch East Indies, with the exception of the southern coast of New Guinea. This, in addition to Surinam and the Antilles, which had become American protectorates, was all that remained of the Dutch Empire.

The Japanese occupation would prove a disaster for the Indonesian population. Japanese authorities brushed aside Indonesian nationalist aspirations until later in the war, after the tide had turned against Japan. Millions of Indonesian men were conscripted for labor in exceedingly harsh conditions, under which hundreds of thousands died. Japanese efforts to secure rice stores for their armed forces led to widespread famine in many portions of Java toward the end of the war, from which many more died. The European population captured by the Japanese also suffered serious privations. Japanese control of the Indies was premised on the complete removal of Dutch colonial influences, and that meant the internment of all Europeans. Soldiers suffered a particularly hard fate, many of them assigned to the completion of the infamous Burma Railway, where some 2,500 Dutch subjects died. The roughly 100,000 civilians interned lived in camps that separated men from women and children. Conditions varied considerably across the camps, but all came under a tighter military regime in 1944. Some 16 percent of the civilians held in Javanese camps died in the course of the war, most in the last year of captivity that ended after the Japanese capitulation in August of 1945.

The Last Months of War

Liberation in the Netherlands itself came almost a year earlier, at least in those southern regions of the country that Allied armies were able to reach in the late summer of 1944. The first Allied units entered the southeastern province of Limburg in early September, days after the "Mad Tuesday" of September 5, 1944, when thousands of Dutch national socialists scrambled to Germany in anticipation of the Allied advance. In reality, the Allied supply lines were overstretched and they were not in a position to reclaim the whole country. Matters were made much worse by the failure of Operation Market Garden, a British-spearheaded effort that began on September 17 to seize bridges across the Dutch rivers up to Arnhem and from there move into the heart of the Ruhr. British and Polish paratroopers faced many adversities in this failed attack, most significantly the presence around Arnhem of German panzer formations, whose importance had been dismissed by British intelligence.

The failure of Market Garden dashed Allied hopes for victory before Christmas; it also placed much of the Dutch population in a dire predicament. Large parts of the southeastern Netherlands had been freed from the Nazis, but the front line ran straight across the country. The fighting in Zeeland for control of the Scheldt River (and the port of Antwerp) was particularly miserable for the local population; portions of the province were inundated as the Allies – after weeks of fighting – secured the river. Worse for those north of the front was the German decision to block food supplies to the Netherlands in retaliation for a rail strike that began during Operation Market Garden. The embargo was partly lifted later, but the bringing in of food via barges became impossible in the exceptionally frosty winter of 1944–1945. The disruption of distribution networks and destruction of infrastructure were also the results of German efforts to defend themselves against the Allied invasion. Available food was drastically curtailed from October 1944 onward and declined until the liberation; by April 1945 bread rations were less than a fifth of the normal amount and not nearly enough to keep body and soul together. Inhabitants of the western cities were particularly, if not exclusively, hard hit, and walks into the countryside in search of food were common. It is estimated that 58,000 Dutch died of famine-related causes in the infamous "Hunger Winter," which preceded the liberation led by Canadian forces – most of them in the urban west. These included thousands of psychiatric patients. In the very last days of the war the German authorities, in an unusual step, allowed Allied aircraft to parachute food to the starving Dutch population, though this came too late for many.

A "Resurgent Netherlands"

German forces in the Netherlands formally capitulated on May 5, 1945, leaving the country one of the most materially devastated in Europe. Nearly 250,000 Dutch, or nearly 3 percent of the population, had lost their lives during the war, and much of the country's infrastructure was wrecked, as evidenced in the inundation of new polders such as the Wieringermeer, and in the destruction of bridges and railroads. The Allies were enthusiastically welcomed, just as collaborators were rounded up and subjected to rough justice. Women identified as having relations with Germans were publicly shorn of their hair, and many thousands were confined to camps where conditions were initially harsh. Those suspected of collaboration were occasionally liquidated, though the numbers were proportionately far lower than in countries such as France and Italy. Some 150,000 were at least briefly arrested for crimes associated with the occupation, though less than 10 percent of them were eventually tried. High-visibility national socialists such as Mussert, and leading German authorities such as Rauter, were ultimately tried and executed by the Dutch government (Seyss-Inquart was tried and hanged by the Allies at Nuremberg). Forty-two people in all were executed by the Dutch state. As the passion for vengeance that had come with the liberation abated, the sentences meted out were milder, or were commuted (more than three-quarters of all death sentences were never carried out). That mildness was not necessarily tantamount to justice; Dutch Jews and others whose property had been confiscated during the war did not always find Dutch courts on their side – courts that tended to find a middle way between the old and the new owners of the property.

A more pressing political issue was how to reconstitute the government now that the Germans were gone. The London government-in-exile under Queen Wilhelmina, intimately tied to the Allied cause, enjoyed wide support. But the Dutch were divided on whether the war should serve as the basis for a political compact that was different from the prewar situation. Resistance groups – themselves a very disparate group from communists to Calvinists – had their own ambitions for *herrijzend Nederland* – resurgent Netherlands – as did the queen herself, who hoped for a greater measure of royal power at the cost of the Parliament. Moderately progressive politicians – chiefly liberals, Protestant moderates and social democrats – hoped for a "breakthrough" (*Doorbraak*) in which the old "pillarized" political system would be swept aside by a new political configuration in which religion would no longer be the source of political difference. In this way they hoped, as they saw it, to purify both religion and politics, and create a new sense of national unity. At first, this desire radically to reconfigure Dutch politics seemed to have widespread support. The Netherlands' Union, the wartime organization that cherished some of the same ambitions to break out of the prewar mold, had been immensely popular, and many political and social elites seemed sympathetic to the call to political, social and moral renewal. The chief political vehicle for this new vision was the Labor Party, founded in 1946 in the merger of the social democrats, left-liberals and progressive Christian Democrats.

The envisioned political "renewal" was not an immediate success, however. The national elections of 1946 – the first held since 1937 – reflected the wish of the population to return to the world that they had known. Most voters opted for their prewar loyalties, and the Christian parties again won a majority at the polls. The Labor Party received fewer votes than the old parties that had merged into it, in part because of the short-lived success of the Communist Party, which – for its role in the resistance and its ties to the Soviet ally – won more than 10 percent of the vote. Nevertheless, Dutch politics after the war would be very different from the situation in the 1930s. The bridge between the Christian parties – in particular the Catholics – and the social democrats had already been forged in the late 1930s, and the path now lay open for an enduring "Roman–Red" coalition that, with the partial cooperation of liberals and Protestants, would endure until 1958. Though socialists and Catholics would remain in principle at loggerheads as to whether the state should directly intervene in economy and society or merely facilitate the work of private groups, together they charted a course that would lead to an ever closer relationship between government and its social partners. And it was the beginning of the further construction of the welfare state. In 1947, the Dutch government introduced a state pension for those elderly in need – a "temporary" measure that would, in hindsight, set the stage for further national legislation in the 1950s and especially the 1960s.

The Indonesian War for Independence

Even though many were disappointed in the electoral results, the restoration of the old political order within the Netherlands had gone off without much of a hitch. That could hardly be said for the restoration of Dutch rule in the East Indies. At the time of the Japanese surrender in the late summer of 1945, the Dutch had virtually no troops in the archipelago, and for the next year were dependent on reluctant British, Indian and Australian forces to enforce their claims. The nationalist nemesis of the Dutch authorities, Sukarno, had meanwhile declared independence for the Republic of Indonesia. Many Dutch, including those in high government positions, had no real idea of just how strong the support for independence was in most parts of Indonesia, and only a small number of them, such as communists and missionaries with strong ties to the Indonesian churches, sympathized with the nationalists. Furthermore, Sukarno's cooperation with the hated Japanese, as well as the fact that several thousand Dutch civilians were killed by roving groups of young nationalists, made Dutch public opinion even more hostile to nationalist aspirations. In the course of 1946 Dutch soldiers were mobilized and sent to the islands to reassert Dutch authority, culminating in a maximum strength of 140,000 troops at the end of 1948. Their increased presence generated a rise in violent confrontations. At the same time, it seemed that some kind of compromise might be within reach. The Dutch government was now willing to grant far-reaching autonomy to the colony, and Sukarno and many other key nationalists were willing to countenance a transition period – in which effective power on the islands would be shared, according to region, between the Dutch and the nationalists – toward a "sovereign" but centralized United States of Indonesia. An accord was then drafted between the parties at the mountain town of Linggadjati in the fall of 1946.

Key Dutch politicians at home, however, balked at this formula, and Parliament demanded the agreement be changed to create a tighter union with the Netherlands. The Republic's leaders refused, and tensions rapidly increased. Guerrilla attacks by nationalists resumed, which were countered by the Dutch military, which was not above engaging in the systematic and summary execution of thousands of local residents thought to be in cahoots with the rebels. In July of 1947 the Dutch government launched a "police action" (in effect a full-scale military operation) against the Republic, partly in order to reclaim economically important areas that could offset Dutch military expenses. This was followed up by a second "action" in December of 1948, in which the Republic's base on Java was overrun. Though the Dutch were, on the field, the victors in these military engagements, they had too few troops to maintain control over a countryside that had turned against them, and were faced at best with a bloody and inconclusive guerrilla war.

384

45   A Dutch tank division moves through Tangoel in eastern Java during
the First Police Action in July 1947. Superior equipment only drove the
Indonesian nationalists into guerrilla warfare.

Meanwhile, the United Nations Security Council called for the
Dutch to cease their military actions, and the Americans threatened to end military assistance to the Dutch if they did not make
arrangements for independence. By late 1948 they had come to
see the anti-communist Sukarno as a more reliable option for
Indonesia's future than a small colonial power. The Dutch began
to negotiate Indonesian independence, and on December 27,
1949 the Netherlands formally ceded sovereignty. Some 6,000
Dutch soldiers had lost their lives in the conflict, as had several
thousand European civilians. Indonesian casualties may have been
as high as 150,000 dead. Independence also meant the departure
of tens of thousands of Europeans and those of mixed race from
Indonesia. In all these respects the forced end of Dutch colonial
rule resembled the rather violent and traumatic pattern that characterized the French departure from Indo-China and Algeria.

Reorientation

The struggle over Indonesia came at a bad time economically for the Netherlands. As in other parts of western Europe, the country's economic infrastructure, though damaged, had largely survived the war, and by 1947 economic production was at prewar levels and ascending rapidly. But the Netherlands seriously lacked hard currency with which to pay for imports, in part because the Dutch East Indies, as a result of the conflict, were costing The Hague more money than it brought in. Economic recovery, then, was slower than the Dutch government had hoped for. The introduction of the Marshall Plan in 1948, which injected over $12 billion into the western European economy to prime the pump, was thus of importance to the Netherlands. About $1 billion went to the Dutch, mostly in the form of grants that essentially offered the Dutch American products for free. The Plan hastened Dutch economic recovery, and it diminished the hardship for a population where the basic necessities of life could not wholly be taken for granted. Marshall assistance also introduced American notions of "efficiency" and partially changed the practices and the ethos of Dutch business culture. And it had the effect of increasingly bringing the Dutch into the American orbit: the US government used the aid to push the Dutch not only into relinquishing Indonesia but also into sending a contingent of troops to support the American war effort in Korea during the early 1950s.

The increased Dutch reliance on the United States also had other grounds. Naturally enough many Dutch now questioned the viability of the country's longstanding neutrality; not only the experience with Hitlerian aggression but also the rising specter of Stalin's Russia saw to that. As in historically neutral countries such as the United States itself, the lessons of World War II and the meaning of increasing Soviet domination in eastern Europe were not immediately apparent at war's end. But this would gradually change in the next couple of years. In the Netherlands, the Communist coup in Czechoslovakia in February of 1948 confirmed its worst fears over Stalin's intentions, and the Dutch public were prepared to build a common defense against a common threat. In the spring of 1949 the Netherlands became signatory to the North Atlantic Treaty Organization (NATO), effectively tying its future to the United States and its other western European allies. The Dutch government, smarting from American support for Indonesian independence, briefly hesitated, but ultimately concluded that they had no choice but to join. Neutrality was now dead as a principle of Dutch foreign policy, though as an ideal it would be resurrected by later critics of NATO.

The year 1949, then, could be seen as the end of an era: the cession of Indonesia, and the end of neutrality. The creation of the Council of Europe in that same year also signaled a new future, although which contours a new Europe might take lay as yet entirely open. The Dutch had regained their independence, but to many it seemed the beginning of a new period in world history, a period in which they, stripped of their chief colony, would have to surrender every pretension of going it alone. That future now lay largely in the hands of the Americans and their fellow Europeans. But whether it would be a better world – that was as yet by no means certain.

7

A Progressive Beacon to the World, 1949–2017

~

Contrary to widespread expectation, the Dutch economy made a stellar performance in the quarter century after World War II. One effect was the transformation of Dutch society, which, more secure than ever, consciously jettisoned traditional constraints. The country became known for its early embrace of progressive stances. Yet the Dutch suffered economic hard times in the 1970s and 1980s, prompting a gradual reduction of what had been a generous welfare state. After the booming 1990s, the Dutch in the new century faced new global challenges that made them, once again, more insecure about what the future held in store for them.

Cold War and Reconstruction in the 1950s

A Somber Recovery

With the recognition of Indonesian independence, the Dutch could more fully turn their attention to the reconstruction of the Netherlands. As elsewhere in western Europe, the economy was already clearly in the ascendant by the late 1940s. By 1950 the national government was able to balance its budget, and in that year the per capita GDP exceeded that of 1929. And although even then the economic prospects seemed good for the country, no one could know that the Dutch were just entering into an extended period of spectacular economic growth that – before it ended around the time of the Oil Crisis of 1973 – would transform the country beyond recognition. The ensuing quarter century would bring unimagined prosperity and social security to nearly everyone, and it would alter the political and cultural outlook of the population, in part setting into motion the progressive policies that would prompt international attention.

But to many ordinary citizens it was not yet clear in the immediate postwar years that the great crises of the past were entirely behind them. It would take until 1950 before the scarcities that had plagued the population after the war were effectively alleviated. And even then, poverty and underemployment never seemed very far away. Leading figures in society also articulated a deep concern that the young, morally damaged by the war, were showing signs of a nihilism that threatened to envelop society. That the Dutch retained an abiding sense of crisis was evident in polls taken in 1950. Over 40 percent of the population expected a third world war to break out within the next ten years. Nearly a third of the population expressed a desire to emigrate in 1948; only Britons surpassed them on this score in a European survey taken that year. The high birth rates that immediately followed the war informed a government policy that, throughout the 1950s, actively encouraged emigration, helping private organizations to coordinate successful emigration and subsidizing the departure of those deemed "dispensable" to the Dutch economy. Many émigrés required no such encouragement; the period from the late 1940s to the early 1960s witnessed, in real and relative terms, the largest exodus of people from the Netherlands in its modern history. Over 400,000 Dutch subjects – in a population of roughly 10 million in 1950 – left the country between 1946 and 1963. Nearly two-thirds of them went either to Australia or to Canada, with most of the rest emigrating to New Zealand, South Africa or the United States. The chances for a better life in far-flung parts of the globe, for themselves or for their children, appeared to these émigrés substantially better than in a country where economic opportunity seemed so bleak.

46 Dutch passengers leave for far-flung Australia by ship. Emigrating just prior to affordable air travel meant heartbreak, as family members counted on long-term or permanent separation.

That great misfortune could strike at any time seemed to be confirmed by the great floods of early February 1953, which struck the vulnerable islands of South Holland and Zeeland especially mercilessly. For decades the dikes guarding the coasts had been neglected in order to save money: defense spending during World War I and austerity policies during the Depression had reduced funding for dike repair. At the same time, the government had known since the late 1930s of the seriousness of the problem, and in 1950 the first of a planned series of projects had been launched to strengthen the water defense system. But tackling the problem was expensive and time-consuming, and many areas would have to wait, even in locales where the water repeatedly sloshed over the dikes. In parts of Zeeland, where such conditions occurred, the local population had learned to live with such apparently minor nuisances for years, and dike authorities, hopelessly fragmented in scores of rather insular local boards, were often unaware of the new reports that stressed the urgency of the problem.

It would take a combination of spring tides and an exceptionally heavy northwesterly storm to cause the catastrophe that began to unfold in the early morning of February 1. The water, driven by the wind into the estuaries and rivers, inflicted the most damage on the weaker levees positioned away from the coasts, and breached the dikes at seventy different points. In some of the threatened locales authorities and radio operators were able to warn residents, who managed to flee or seek refuge upstairs in their own homes; in others, the inhabitants were tragically surprised by the swiftly rising water. In a few unfortunate villages, a wall of water crushed all structures in its path: often the poorly constructed working-class dwellings positioned at the edge of the villages. In England and in Flanders the storm took a toll too, but the Netherlands bore the brunt of its ferocity; there the disaster would claim over 1,800 lives. Livestock in the affected areas were devastated, and hundreds of square kilometers from North Brabant to Rotterdam flooded, in the worst cases for the better

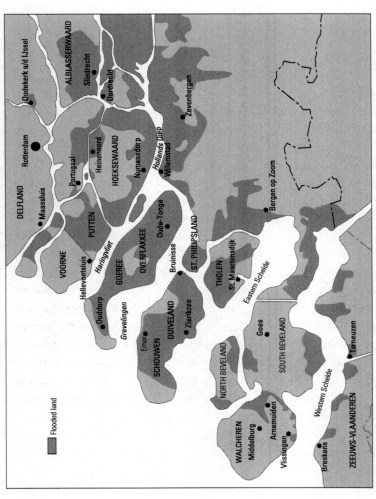

15 The floods of 1953 were the last great water disaster, as more investments and technologies were applied. River floods in the 1990s demonstrated continuing vulnerabilities, though.

part of a year. It might have been worse still; the dikes protecting additional vulnerable polders in mainland Holland had held, though by the slimmest of margins. As it was, the storm brought about destruction the country could ill afford.

The disaster further galvanized public opinion and government action in support of a vast project to eliminate the threat from the sea once and for all. Water policy was centralized, and a new Delta Plan was proposed that set out not only to raise dike levels according to the newest scientific insights but to block key estuaries with dams and sluices, thus keeping the inland coasts protected. Though the first important projects were finished in the late 1950s, the last project, a retaining wall protecting the Frisian city of Harlingen, was completed only in 2010. The signature achievement of the Delta Plan was the five-mile-long storm barrier across the Eastern Schelde, which took nearly a decade to build and which allowed the sea, except in bad weather, to flow under the barrier – a feature required to preserve local marine life in the estuary. Completed in 1986 at the cost of a hefty 8 billion guilders ($4 billion), the barrier combined an age-old search for protection with state-of-the-art environmental technologies. For the first time in Dutch history, the danger of flooding was no longer a perennial concern to residents of low-lying areas. But local flooding – now chiefly caused by the country's rivers – would keep the country alert to the necessity of effective water management, and the anticipation of climate change and rising seas would later compel the Dutch to reconsider whether their defenses would continue to be sufficient.

National Unity and Political Divisions

A commitment to community, to self-discipline and to hard work seemed in the 1950s the surest way to rebuild the country and stave off further misfortune. This recipe included a sustained loyalty to the subcultural communities, religious or political, in which one was raised. The Dutch electorate, in the first postwar elections of 1946, had chosen to return a Parliament that closely resembled its prewar representation, and they would continue to do so well into the 1960s. This stable electoral pattern, which continued to deliver the Catholic and Protestant parties a collective majority at the polls, reflected people's widespread commitment to their respective communities. The Dutch state continued to leave much of the initiative to civil society organizations, subsidizing their efforts with few demands in return.

If ever there were a period when "pillarization" – in which the various subcultural pillars together held up the roof of the Dutch state – could be said to have characterized organizational life in the Netherlands, it was the 1950s, when an influx of new subsidies and trained professionals helped subcultural organizations reach their maximum extent. Though evident among orthodox Protestants, and to a lesser extent among socialists, this was most obviously the case among the Roman Catholics. Under their wily political leader, Carl Romme, they witnessed the high tide of their influence and power in the two decades following World War II, when the Catholic People's Party (KVP) dwarfed their once dominant Protestant counterparts not only in size but in significance. Noting both their high birth rates and the fact that Catholics already constituted 40 per cent of the population, Romme anticipated a day when Catholics would constitute a majority in the Netherlands. A century after the return of the episcopacy – celebrated with great fanfare by Dutch Catholics in 1953 – this once despised and dismissed minority seemed well positioned to keep – even expand – their lock on power. Though disappointed by a lack of evident spirituality among Dutch Catholics, the Polish priest and future pontiff Karol Wojtyła was struck on a 1947 visit by their strong sense of unity and their organizational drive to maintain it.

If the persistence and extension of the pillarized communities was one hallmark feature of the immediate postwar period, then the concentrated effort at political compromise and consensus was another. Like some other parts of reconstruction Europe, the postwar Netherlands was characterized by attempts to transcend old ideological shibboleths. The war had generated a particularly strong sense of national solidarity and of the need to create common cause through active democratic citizenship, regardless of one's own particular convictions. This impulse was evident in the broad coalitions with overwhelming majorities in Parliament, which from 1946 to 1958 invariably included the Labor Party and the KVP (which together represented nearly two-thirds of the electorate), but also some combination of the two larger Protestant parties and the liberals, who in 1948 had joined together in the Popular Party for Freedom and Democracy (VVD). Led during most of these years by the austere but much beloved Willem Drees (1948–1958), the country's first socialist premier, the "Roman–Red" coalitions, in the 1920s considered highly improbable, functioned well in a context where harmonious labor relations, coordinated economic policy and a high level of political trust were widely considered indispensable for both economic growth and social stability. The new impulse collectively to build a secure future for the population could in terms of legislation be most clearly seen in a state pension offered to the elderly, provisionally in 1947 and for good in 1956. Efforts collectively to determine wages and benefits were aided by new semi-governmental organizations such as the Labor Foundation (Stichting van de Arbeid) or (over time more important) the Social-Economic Council (Sociaal-Economische Raad), which sought to advise the government on the basis of its permanent consultations with labor unions, employers and relevant experts. One important result of this consensual approach to labor issues was a collective commitment throughout the 1950s to keeping real wages low in order to improve the country's export balance, a policy achieved with the acquiescence of the labor unions, and with a minimum of strikes or other forms of protest.

Depicting the Netherlands as a consensus-oriented society remains the dominant portrait for the period from the late 1940s to the mid 1960s. And yet historians in the last quarter century have periodically challenged this depiction. Serious political conflict was seldom very far away. To begin with, some Dutch, of course, were not considered part of that consensus. This was most clearly the case with the Communist Party of the Netherlands (CPN), whose political fortunes declined with the deepening of the cold war. They reached a low point in November 1956, when – in reaction to Dutch communists' support of the Soviet invasion of Hungary – angry and violent mobs besieged their Amsterdam party headquarters for several nights running. Although the CPN were not proscribed as their counterparts were in the Federal Republic of Germany, the broadcasting rights of the party were curtailed, as were those of its members in joining the civil service. Anti-communism remained a strong current in Dutch politics through the end of the 1960s.

Less dramatically, political tensions also manifested themselves within the big tent consensus. Increasingly, the liberals and socialists would prove inveterate foes over the size and role of the state; after the liberal VVD left the coalition in 1952, it would take over forty years before the VVD and the Labor Party entered into another government with each other. More fundamentally, however, was the continuing conflict between the proponents of the *Doorbraak* and those who opposed it – that is, between those groups who saw religious divisions as an unfortunate and outmoded partition of society, and those who defended the importance and value of religion in ordering it. It was an issue that divided more orthodox from more liberal Protestants, and which pitted the socially progressive (and at the same time anti-Catholic) leadership of the Dutch Reformed Church against the Church of Rome; in the late 1940s the Protestant churches still cautioned the government against lifting the restrictions on public Catholic processions as a threat to Dutch freedoms.

Most significantly, this political divide led to perennial tensions between the leading partners of the "Roman–Red" coalition – a tension between socialists and Christian Democrats that also marked politics in the surrounding countries of Belgium and West Germany. Lying at the heart of the conflict were not only seriously different views of the state and how great a role it should take in directing the economy, but different views on how politics should be organized. Since the Labor Party's inception the socialists had tried to make electoral inroads with religious voters; the strategy achieved only very modest results but was enough to present a long-term threat to Catholic political interests. Partly in response, the Catholic bishops issued a pastoral letter in 1954, either forbidding or strongly discouraging the faithful from joining socialist organizations. This pastoral letter (or *mandement*) was just one episode in a difficult Catholic–socialist relationship that would prove even more difficult in the course of the next several decades. The letter, incidentally, would prove to be the last statement of the Dutch bishops to demand of their flocks that they commit themselves to Catholic political and social unity. Progressive Catholics and more pragmatically minded KVP politicians viewed the *mandement* as an unwelcome and untimely act of isolationism, and the issuance of the letter also masked deep differences within the Dutch episcopacy itself, between those who supported the pillarized lines articulated in the letter, and those who preferred an approach that gave lay Catholics more room to make such choices for themselves.

Conservative and Progressive Currents

The internal divisions among the Dutch bishops in the mid 1950s can serve to challenge another widely held view of the decade: that it was implacably conservative. It is true that most Dutch voters, informed as they were by years of crisis and war, did not stray much from their traditional allegiances and that a strong sense of community prevailed, illustrated in part by high church attendance rates in the 1950s. Perhaps half of the population attended church weekly, high percentages by the standards of northern Europe at that time. Moreover, many political and religious leaders remained deeply wary of the dangers such as "massification" that they saw as accompanying modern life. An example is the way that Dutch policy-makers initially organized settlement in the new polderlands reclaimed from the Netherlands' inland sea, the IJsselmeer, from the late 1930s to the 1960s. Farmers chosen for homesteads in the new Flevoland region in the late 1940s were strictly selected for their reliability in order to ensure the moral and social cohesion of the new community.

In political terms, Dutch leaders had little to worry about: the population was hardly restive; indeed, political activism was anything but the norm. Women in particular seldom discussed political issues, a 1956 poll found. As in some parts of Europe (such as France) the legal and professional status of women was not high. Only in 1956 were married women legally empowered to manage their own affairs, or to keep their civil service positions in the event that they married – and only then under the stipulation of Parliament that the husband formally remain the head of the household. Children born out of wedlock were relatively rare, though it is less clear whether this was due to a characteristic Dutch prudishness – as suggested in Bert Haanstra's droll 1963 film classic *Alleman* (*Everyman*) – or to relatively good access to reproductive information, as has recently been suggested.

Some writers and artists sought to free themselves from the stultifying ethos in which they found themselves. Perhaps most notable in this respect were a handful of Dutch artists who linked up with kindred spirits beyond the confining borders of the Netherlands: the COBRA group (standing for Copenhagen, Brussels, Amsterdam), which included Karel Appel, and a group of Flemish-Dutch poets inspired by them, who collectively became known as the Fiftiers (Vijftigers). All of them sought consciously to break through the established aesthetic patterns, attempting to express a more immediate experience than they felt convention allowed.

The traditionalism of the country could also be measured by the fact that neither the Dutch people nor the Dutch government were willing, even in the 1950s, to abandon their claims to global empire. Even after the recognition by the Dutch of the independence of Indonesia in 1949, the Netherlands' sustained colonial ambitions were not primarily focused on the Caribbean, where their most substantial holdings now lay. There the Statute for the Kingdom of the Netherlands (1954) transformed Surinam and the six islands of the Dutch Antilles into integral parts of the kingdom, formally equal in status to the Netherlands itself, and permitted unrestricted travel of all its citizens throughout the kingdom. But Dutch attention continued to be directed – as it long had been – to the East. After 1949, this focus was narrowed to the Dutch-administered western half of the island of New Guinea, a California-sized expanse of "swamps, rocks and malaria" (as one detractor of Dutch colonial policy called it) that was home to only 320,000 inhabitants in 1955. As successor state to the Dutch East Indies the Indonesian government laid claim to Irian Jaya, as they called the territory – a claim that led to an escalating conflict with the Dutch, who insisted that their civilizing mission to the Papuans must continue. It might be more accurate to say that the Dutch only seriously began to offer extensive assistance to the Papuans after 1949. Spearheading Dutch policy for the colony after 1952 was foreign minister Joseph Luns, a conservative on colonial affairs who saw the possession of New Guinea as the last base for a strategic Dutch presence in the Far East. Only the communists – for ideological reasons – and business and religious groups – who saw their long-term relations with Indonesia jeopardized – offered sustained criticism of government policy.

Dutch resistance to negotiation and Indonesian willingness to tighten the screws – which included the seizing and nationalizing

399

of Dutch property in Indonesia and ultimately the breaking of diplomatic ties with The Hague – led the countries to the brink of war in 1960. The Dutch sent their only aircraft carrier to the region to show they meant business, and Papuan and Indonesian military units clashed with each other in isolated jungle engagements. The unappealing prospect of another guerrilla war helped bring about a shift in the Dutch position. In 1962, after belated efforts by the Dutch to secure a compromise solution at the United Nations failed, and after Washington – again – put pressure on the Dutch to relent, the cabinet agreed to turn over West Papua to Jakarta after a brief interim period of UN administration. The final Dutch retreat from their last Asian colony was neither very bloody nor particularly traumatic, but it revealed that the old colonial commitments died hard, even in a case where the interests of white settlers, such as had been the case in Algeria, Kenya or Java, was not an issue.

But a portrait of the postwar Netherlands as a bedrock of traditionalism is incomplete and one-sided. The Dutch in the 1950s thought of themselves as modern people, polls suggested – more modern than any other public save the Americans. It was a country that embraced the newest technologies, from the upgrading of Schiphol Airport to substantial expansion of the great international harbor of Rotterdam. The great Delta projects and the expansion of industry at the steel complex in IJmuiden also contributed to the modern ethos of the country. The visible advances in the industrial and commercial sectors of the economy gave the Dutch anything but the feeling that they were stuck in the past. Everywhere, modernist architecture impacted the landscape.

The consciously modern outlook on life was informed by the development of a strongly internationalist orientation that consciously sought a new role for the Dutch in the world. This was evident in Dutch foreign policy, which remained firmly in the hands of diplomats and a small political elite, led for nearly two decades (1952–1971) by the controversial but popular Luns. But

47   Minister of Foreign Affairs for almost twenty years, the debonair
Joseph Luns became the country's most popular politician because he avidly
defended the Dutch national interest.

it was also evident through the growing public interest in the
wider world in which, as World War II had painfully revealed,
the Netherlands was inevitably caught up. One early sign of this
shift was evident in the Dutch Reformed Church, which had
been rather exclusively focused on national affairs but which
now became strongly oriented toward global ecumenism. The
first assembly of the World Council of Churches, consisting of
Protestant and Orthodox churches, was held in Amsterdam in
1948, and the Council's first Secretary-General, the Dutchman
Willem Visser 't Hooft, was to head the organization for nearly

two decades. Through the World Council issues of development aid, decolonization, and war and peace were soon advanced, which would change the agenda of the Protestant churches.

Like many west Europeans in the early 1950s, most Dutch were soon convinced that the future of the continent, and of their country, could not be guaranteed without intensive European cooperation. This sentiment was expressed in two much publicized local referenda held in 1952 at the behest of the European Movement in the Netherlands. The towns selected for the referenda, Bolsward and Delft, were chosen because their electoral patterns most closely approached the national average. In these places the voters were asked if they supported the creation of a constitutional, democratic European government, to which they overwhelmingly responded "yes" (93 percent in Delft, nearly 97 percent in Bolsward). Only the communists and some Calvinists, who partially boycotted the plebiscites, dissented. Within a few years Dutch public enthusiasm for Europe faded, as the soon-to-be-constituted European Economic Community, with its rather inaccessible discussions over economic policy, failed to sustain much élan. The European political community and constitution for which the people of Bolsward and Delft thought they were voting turned out to be a process of decades, not months or years. In the long run, too, the Dutch maintained something of the northern European skepticism toward Europe, regarding their German and southern European partners with a certain moral aloofness. The European federalist Hendrik Brugmans complained in 1961 about the Dutch fancying themselves "on the balcony of Europe." But unlike the Norwegians or the British, the Swedes or the Danes, the Dutch public did not doubt the importance of Europe for their country's peace and prosperity. They realized early on that their fate stood or fell with that of continental Europe. Polls showed that the Dutch consistently were, at least in theory, the most pro-European public in the Community; for decades, starting in the

1960s, support for the European project would typically remain at about 80 percent.

Europe and NATO Policy

The Dutch government more or less shared these European commitments. It had already been an early signatory (1944) to the Benelux customs agreement with Belgium and Luxembourg, which was expanded in subsequent years. But some Dutch politicians had their concerns. The most important Euroskeptic in the Netherlands of the 1950s was the socialist premier Drees, who worried that Dutch national interests and sovereignty would be undermined by such supranational bodies as the European Coal and Steel Community (1951). In the face of popular enthusiasm for Europe he kept his reservations behind closed doors. Luns, similarly, was no ardent Europeanist. To counteract them, however, there were a small number of strongly pro-European parliamentarians and government ministers who defined the European policies of their parties, and who succeeded in setting the public tone in discussions about Europe.

But what characterized Dutch European politics in the early years was neither its skepticism nor its idealism but a pragmatic, critically constructive approach that accepted intensive European cooperation as necessary but bargained hard for the national interest. Even economic cooperation within the so-called Benelux region, first conceived during the war, was achieved slowly, with the Dutch only cautiously willing to expand such arrangements elsewhere. Dutch European politics was specifically characterized by an emphasis on economic cooperation; the efforts of Jan Willem Beyen – from 1952 to 1956 foreign minister alongside Luns – helped rescue European cooperation after the failure of the French to pass the European Defence Community by proposing to restrict European cooperation for the time being to economic affairs. A modified form of this plan, presented by the

Benelux countries through Belgian minister Paul-Henri Spaak in 1955, became the basis for the European Economic Community signed in Rome in March of 1957.

Important, too, was the legacy of Sicco Mansholt who, as the first European Commissioner for Agriculture, extended substantial subsidies to European farmers – a continuation of national policies he had implemented as minister in the Netherlands. The primacy of economics went hand-in-hand with a policy that sought to keep the tariff walls around Europe as low as possible, and to prevent Franco-German hegemony in the Community. To this end, Luns steadfastly resisted French aspirations to take political leadership of Europe, and equally steadfastly championed British membership in Europe – an aim that, owing to De Gaulle's opposition, would find fulfillment only in 1973.

The pro-British stance of the Dutch had much to do with the wider Atlanticism of the Dutch government. European cooperation, the Dutch government held, needed to be anchored in the alliance with the British and the Americans. For this reason, in part, the Dutch staunchly supported American leadership of NATO. They sent over 5,000 combat troops to assist American-led UN forces during the Korean War. They backed the Americans in sensitive issues such as NATO membership for West Germany. They came to coordinate their once independent nuclear research with the United States, and in the late 1950s the government acceded to the stationing of American-controlled, tactical nuclear weapons on Dutch soil. Political opposition to these policies was minimal, and the importance of making common cause with the United States was widely considered important. It is not entirely coincidental that the elite Bilderberg Group, launched at Arnhem in 1954 with Prince Bernhard as key sponsor, was initiated there to counter the specter of European anti-Americanism.

None of this meant that the Dutch were without criticisms of the United States – criticisms often exacerbated by colonial issues. The decision by the American government to supply Indonesia with weapons in 1958 prompted some cabinet members impetuously – and briefly – to put Dutch NATO membership into question, and the refusal of Luns to send, at American request, a contingent of Dutch troops to Vietnam in 1963 can be seen as retribution for US New Guinea policy. By the 1960s, however, the Dutch had developed solid credentials as one of the most "loyal" allies in the Atlantic alliance, with relatively high expenditures devoted to defense. In the long run, their Atlanticism was reflected in the fact that Dutch candidates filled the position of NATO secretary-general far more frequently than those of any other single country, a record helped, incidentally, by the unprecedentedly long tenure of Luns in that post (1971–1984).

Among the Dutch public, too, there was criticism of the alliance with the United States, not only from the communists but also from the members of the small Pacifist Socialist Party, established in 1957, who championed a "Third Way" between the USA and the USSR. Many intellectuals retained more subtle criticisms of the USA and the Atlantic alliance. But the broad support for American leadership was nevertheless dominant, and this support for the United States was probably strengthened by the enthusiasm of the Dutch, in the 1950s and 1960s, for all things American, from marketing techniques, to social scientific theory, to pop music and American literature, the last of which, in prewar years, Dutch critics had barely acknowledged. By the late 1950s, Dutch museums such as the Stedelijk Museum Amsterdam, under its influential director Willem Sandberg, were playing an active role in introducing modern American art to European publics. American public diplomacy, concerned with the strengthening cold war ties with European allies, helped encourage these trends. The Dutch regarded the United States as an ultramodern society, and for that reason consciously emulated, perhaps more than their continental neighbors, the insights and practices of their most important ally. Learning English, more than in many parts of continental Europe, became an important educational aim.

But the new internationalist focus of the Dutch in the 1950s and 1960s was not only directed toward Europe and America but toward the emerging nations of the Third World. Already in the early 1950s Dutch politicians and political parties expressed the need for the Dutch to offer development aid, though for most of the next decade government help would be directed at Dutch colonies. By 1956, however, a wider Dutch commitment to the world was commenced with the founding of Novib, a development organization committed to, as its founders said, helping the world, which had helped the Dutch during the 1953 disaster. Interestingly, it was trouble in a French colony, rather than in their own, that helped develop an abiding Dutch concern for suffering in the world. In 1959, a television special, "Save a Child," which portrayed Algerian refugee children, generated huge viewer interest and, for the time, an unprecedented response: some 2 million guilders. "Save a Child" showed for the first time in the Netherlands the power of television to shape public opinion and action, a phenomenon that would repeat itself in the 1960s, a decade in which the number of televisions in use expanded from roughly 1 to 3 million units. The massacre of black demonstrators by South African police at Sharpeville in 1960 was also an important watershed that prompted many Dutch, who had felt a sense of kinship with the Afrikaners, to become more critical of Apartheid.

Sudden Good Fortune in the 1960s

Prosperity and Social Security for Everyone

These shifts in perceptions about the wider world went hand-in-hand with the transformations of daily life, evident by around 1960. The country was changing rapidly in ways that were already undermining old social relations and old commitments. Nowhere was economic modernization more apparent than in the move from the countryside to the cities. Some 20 percent of the working population earned a livelihood on the land in 1947; by 1956 this was a mere 13 percent, and it continued to decrease as the agrarian sector came to rely more on mechanization and as the internationalization of the agricultural market demanded production on a larger scale. Urbanization increased. By the late 1950s planners began to draw up the first blueprints for the controlled growth of the expanding Randstad, the crescent-shaped urban conglomeration in the west of the country that encompassed Rotterdam, The Hague, Amsterdam, and the towns and villages in between. It was through the move to the cities, not emigration, that the Dutch found new forms of employment: necessary, given the sharp rise in population, which grew from 10 million in 1950 to some 13 million by 1970. A new wave of industrialization and the rapid expansion of Rotterdam harbor, as well as growing public and service sectors, kept unemployment very low throughout the 1950s and 1960s.

However grim the early 1950s looked, they turned out to be the beginning of the most sustained boom in modern Dutch history; from that time until the early 1970s the Dutch GDP grew at a rate of 4.5 to 5 percent per year, a development roughly parallel with other economies in western Europe. Helping the Dutch economy was the new and highly profitable exploitation of natural gas reserves in the province of Groningen from the late 1950s onward. The Slochteren gas fields not only transformed the way the Dutch heated their homes and turned the country into an international energy supplier, but provided a crucial source of government income, indispensable, as it turned out, for funding the country's increasingly generous social welfare provisions. Indeed, the availability of such large natural gas reserves helped generate a mentality, both inside and outside government, that the growth of government services had been effectively and securely financed – a mentality that would only die hard in the rising financial problems of the late 1970s and early 1980s.

These developments provided the basis for a noticeably better standard of living, though it was only in the early 1960s that the government – no longer able to suppress wages in a market of virtually no unemployment – had to abandon a primary strategy for keeping the Dutch economy competitive. Between 1959 and 1962 real wages rose at an average of 7 percent per year; in the few years thereafter that rate doubled. Increased productivity led to the proclamation of the free Saturday in 1960, following the American model of a standard Monday-to-Friday working week that had been introduced across the Atlantic in 1954. The advent of the weekend would transform private life in the Netherlands, opening the way for a wave of recreational possibilities. And, unlike the Americans, but like other western Europeans, the Dutch would use further gains in productivity to finance extensive holiday periods for employees. Some well-to-do Dutch began to book holidays in the Antilles, which rapidly developed into a vacation paradise after 1960, not least for visitors from nearby North America.

And as was the case everywhere that the postwar economic boom held sway, access to consumer goods dramatically increased; whereas only 3 percent of Dutch households possessed a refrigerator in 1957, some 55 percent did in 1967. A similar though somewhat less dramatic expansion in automobile ownership gave many Dutch a mobility that had hitherto been unthinkable. Some problems remained; the Netherlands continued to struggle with a chronic housing shortage, as the population continued to grow strongly, and as people gradually demanded more square meters per capita. Dutch housing corporations, charged by the government with building affordable social housing for those of lower and modest income, built hundreds of thousands of units, but it was not enough to stave off the demands of a rapidly increasing population.

Other forms of consumption also emerged at this time: Dutch teenagers and young adults now had enough discretionary income to generate their own youth culture centered around rock 'n' roll. The new consumerism among all age groups was also evident, for example, in a sharp rise in alcohol consumption between 1960 and 1975 – from 2.6 l to 8.9 l of pure alcohol per capita drunk annually. Alcohol use revealed not only a rise in discretionary spending but a noticeable cultural shift away from the stringent social norms that had so effectively disciplined the Dutch population since alcohol had been signaled as a problem a century earlier. And there were even more important changes afoot. The introduction of the contraceptive pill in the Netherlands in 1962 would quickly change Dutch sexual practices and views, both inside and outside marriage.

Prosperity brought other changes as well, including a vastly increased access to education, which now became affordable to families of few or modest means. The number of students at Dutch universities and the higher technical schools (*hogescholen*) more than quintupled in the period from 1950 to 1965. In the early 1960s the Dutch Parliament passed far-reaching educational reform that stressed social inclusion and made it mandatory for everyone, at government expense, to undertake secondary education. The educational revolution not only raised the vocational and professional level of the workforce but democratized the social ethos, reducing the hierarchical distance between the young and those who had exercised authority over them. Further underscoring a sense of individual independence from family, Church and social network was the landmark General Assistance Law, passed in 1963, which guaranteed a minimum income to all Dutch citizens. The law showed the increased financial strength of the state. With the treasury full, politicians, having hewn to a careful pay-as-you-go vision of welfare provision, now saw new possibilities for offering the citizenry an unprecedented measure of security. These developments confirmed a new ideological commitment among the country's dominant Christian democratic parties: that it was the state after all, and not charity or private initiative, that should determine the contours of social solidarity.

Political and Religious Fermentation

The startling and important shift in opinion among the Christian Democrats on this point was indicative of a broader reflection among Dutch political and religious leaders – one that would help facilitate the far-reaching cultural changes of the 1960s. For many of them, the old ideological oppositions had come to seem stale and unproductive in a space-age world, the moral and ideological gate-keeping onerous. Individuals, they increasingly felt, should be given the responsibility to make life choices for themselves. The younger professionals who were now coming to run Dutch institutions were furthermore far more imbued by the standards of their professions than by the ideological or religious commitments to which they were still formally tied.

Changes to the countries' pillarized institutions were not long in coming. They came earliest in those parts of Dutch society where pillarized arrangements were weakest: among the socialists and the liberal Protestants, many of whose organizations were quickly cut off from a sponsoring subculture or were merged into other ones. And the change in mentality was deepest in the Netherlands' religious communities – a change that would prove crucial, given the preponderance of these groups in Dutch society. Eighteen clergymen from the two largest Protestant churches (the Dutch Reformed Church and the Reformed Churches in the Netherlands) issued a statement in 1961 that called for ecclesiastical unity, an appeal that would trigger the beginnings of a decades-long merger process. Many orthodox Protestant schools widened their theology to become more inclusive, and for the first time the large Protestant parties began to take an interest in the possibility of union with the Catholic KVP.

But the sea-change was most profound in Roman Catholic circles. Fed by the excitement of the *Aggiornamento* emanating from Rome and optimistic about the prospects of a more open Catholicism in the modern world, Dutch Catholic leaders rapidly liberalized their stance. In the early 1960s a series of Catholic radio and television programs that discussed intimate sexual questions without much moral theology had a cathartic effect among Dutch Catholics; the televised sanctioning of artificial birth control (within marriage) by an influential Dutch bishop in 1963 confirmed to a broader audience that the Catholic world had irrevocably altered. Liturgical innovations changed the face of Catholic worship. And in 1965 the Dutch bishops formally dropped their exacting demand that Catholics remain faithful to Catholic organizations, helping to precipitate a crisis in many of these organizations – not least in the KVP. Only in respect of education did the bishops insist on Catholic institutions. Recent research suggests that the tempo of reform may have had the effect of amplifying Catholics' alienation from the Church; in any event, mass attendance halved from the mid 1960s to the mid 1970s, and continued to decline sharply thereafter. Free to develop their own lifestyles in the new contexts of a generous welfare state and a prosperous consumer society, the Dutch cut themselves off from the old bonds that many of them came to reject as coercive or irrelevant.

The Challenge to Traditional Authority

It was in this liberalizing climate that new challenges to authority and established norms could thrive, however dismaying these challenges were to considerable parts of the populace and the political establishment. They were apparent in the popularity of offshore and illegal "pirate" stations, which broadcast the new music, but also increasingly in the mainstream Dutch media. Journalists adopted an impudent style while questioning those in authority and were increasingly daring in their programming; the first naked breasts could be seen on Dutch television in 1967. Most emblematic of these challenges, however, was the group Provo, active in Amsterdam between 1965 and 1967 and soon to become the Netherlands' fabled contribution to a developing global counterculture.

As a group, Provo was minuscule, consisting of no more than a handful of activists, and its central figure, Roel van Duyn, who drew many of his ideas from anarchist writers, possessed no illusions about changing the world. But the Provos – who mockingly took their name from a social scientific term for rebellious youth – were resolutely determined to provoke authority, and through their uncanny sense of publicity were uncommonly successful in drawing attention to themselves. Their unauthorized "happenings" on Amsterdam's Spui, for which they attracted considerable audiences, as well as their cleverly rumored intentions, such as slipping LSD into the water given to police horses, made the group the *bête noire* of the still rather authoritarian Amsterdam police, whose heavy-handed responses only served to enhance the fame of the quick-thinking Provos. Their so-called White Plans, written partly tongue-in-cheek, also revealed them to be romantic reformers; the White Bicycle Plan, never implemented, proposed to do away with automobiles altogether in the city center and replace them with free municipal bicycles. Though associated in the public mind with a growing chaos in Amsterdam, the Provos, much to their disgust, could also count on the sympathy of many middle-class Dutch who were drawn to their unbridled sense of freedom and their criticism of the status quo. Several years after Provo proclaimed its own death in 1967, Van Duyn would help found the Gnomes (*Kabouters*), a countercultural movement that sought, as did many hippies elsewhere, to return to a more simple, organic way of life. In 1970, the *Kabouters* won five out of forty-five seats on the Amsterdam city council, though they soon fragmented and faded.

The Provos and the Gnomes were symbolically important but just two elements that helped solidify Amsterdam's reputation as a countercultural capital starting in the late 1960s and early 1970s. The rise of a dynamic youth club circuit and the arrival of many young tourists who could sleep on the Dam in the warm summers of the late 1960s contributed to this atmosphere. Homosexuals found the relaxed climate in Amsterdam congenial at a time when the rest of the country remained less welcoming. As a center for the arts, too, Amsterdam became an important site for artistic innovation and protest; in 1969 a group of artists staged a sit-in in front of Rembrandt's *Night Watch* to resist government cultural policies, one of many actions that would characterize the artistic world in the coming years. In general, though not always, Amsterdam authorities responded with restraint, including a forbearance toward cannabis use from 1969 on.

New forms of expression were hardly restricted to Amsterdam; two important Dutch reform movements with a broader geographical base were rooted in groups that historically had been quiescent in Dutch society: the Catholic laity and women. For the former group this was evident in the creation of the Pastoral Council of the Dutch Catholic Church, which held session in the hamlet of Noordwijkerhout from 1968 to 1970. In seeking a concrete response to the reforms of the Second Vatican Council (1962–1965) the Dutch bishops called in 1965 for a council within their own Church province, in which laity were given a considerable voice. Council delegates freely discussed controversial issues, often challenging the teachings of the Church, and ultimately voting to abolish mandatory celibacy for priests. Lacking canonical status and the power to enact its reforms, the Pastoral Council in the end served primarily to highlight the stark difference between the educated Dutch Catholic laity and the Roman Curia, not only over sexual ethics but over the very nature of the Church. Perhaps the boldest embodiment of liberal Catholicism in the world Church in this period, the Pastoral Council also precipitated the efforts of Rome to restore traditional authority and teaching to the Dutch Church province, leading to a set of bitter confrontations and considerable disillusionment among Dutch Catholics in the 1970s. This conflict, along with the continued slide into indifference among the laity, would dampen enthusiasm for the Dutch visit of Pope John Paul

II in 1985, when turnout was much lower than typified this pontiff's international trips.

At nearly the same time, Dutch feminists reasserted their voices in the public sphere. Women's groups had played an important part in Dutch civil society through the 1960s but, perhaps more than was the case in Scandinavia, these groups accepted the notion that men and women had different roles to play and that women's work was properly in the home. This began to change in the 1960s, as women's journals in particular began to challenge the middle-class norms and habits of their readers. Translating this cultural shift into political action came late to the Netherlands in comparison to Britain and the USA. But come it did. In 1967 the ennui of the woman as housewife and mother was expressed in a highly influential article by Joke Kool-Smit, whose social and intellectual horizons, she felt, were confined by these roles. A year later she helped establish the Man–Woman Society (Man-Vrouw-Maatschappij; MVM). A feminist organization that focused in its initial phase on the equal participation of women and men in the movement, it argued that the sexes should more equally share the responsibilities at work and at home. As would be the case with the euthanasia movement, MVM's leadership was politically savvy, well connected and temperate in tone, qualities that smoothed their access to government and helped pave the way toward the creation of government "emancipation" policy in the mid 1970s.

In time, though, MVM would be drawn to a more radical line advocated by the Netherlands' most famous feminist group, Dolle Mina ("Mad Mina"), named after the *fin-de-siècle* activist Wilhelmina Drucker. In particular it was the protest methods of these socialist feminists that first drew public attention to them in 1970: occupying an all-male college; disrupting a pageant contest; its female participants painting "Boss of my own belly" ("Baas in eigen buik") on their stomachs as a call for the legalization of abortion. Increasingly fragmented, Dolle Mina's primary significance lay not in the achievement of policy but in drawing

48 Dolle Mina activists pictured here were very effective in drawing media attention to their cause through a playful style that at the same time obscured their ambitious social agenda.

attention to feminist issues and in helping set a more militant tone to the Dutch feminist movement into the 1980s.

These developments illustrate strong trends in the Netherlands during the 1960s and 1970s – arguably stronger than elsewhere. The first was a principled rejection of authority. The 1971 census was the last one ever held; hostility to government intrusion ensured that it would never again be held, the government shifting to other, less controversial forms of data-gathering. Notably, too, the mandatory salute in the Dutch military was abolished in the 1970s, much to the unhappiness of the higher ranks. The second was a shift toward "post-material values," which placed quality-of-life issues over a traditional bread-and-butter agenda. In a country with a high level of social security and an increasingly skeptical view of the traditional sources of moral authority, new social and political agendas were seized upon with great enthusiasm. *The Limits to Growth*, issued by the Club of Rome in 1972 and warning of the dire consequences of exhausting the planet's resources, was read particularly widely in the Netherlands, with a quarter of a million copies sold. Over time, new organizations such as Greenpeace and Amnesty International would find uncommon levels of support in the Netherlands, and Dutch civil society would in subsequent decades continue to be characterized by relatively high membership of such bodies.

Political Polarization and Economic Stagnation in the 1970s

A Different Kind of Politics in a Different Kind of Society

This cultural fermentation took place within a political constellation that was also rapidly changing. In 1967 the religious parties lost their majority in Parliament, and by 1972 the KVP – the bulwark of Dutch Christian democracy – would retain few more than half the seats that it had held in 1963. A merger with the two leading Protestant parties (which faced their own challenges) seemed the most hopeful course, though it would take a decade before Protestants and Catholics, progressives and conservatives, would be able to agree on the terms of a new ecumenical party, the Christian Democratic Appeal. Meanwhile the Labor Party, under the influence of the New Left – a Dutch movement that drew much of its inspiration from similar movements elsewhere – took a hostile line toward cooperation with what was seen as a waffling and unreliable political Catholicism, a stance strengthened by the socialist hope that the days of Christian Democracy were numbered. Until 1971, the liberals and the Christian democrats together had had enough deputies to form a stable government. But after the elections of that year, forming coalitions in a polarized political field became more difficult. The rise in the 1960s of new, upstart parties added to the number of small parties already enjoying representation in Parliament. The upstarts included not only new parties on the left – radical ex-Christian democrats and progressive liberals – but also those on the right – disaffected social democrats and the Farmer's Party, which with its anti-establishmentarian stance generated a considerable number of votes in Amsterdam in the 1967 elections.

Polemics and unstable coalitions, at least by the previous phlegmatic standards of Dutch public life, would be visible from the early 1970s to the early 1980s. This also became evident in the country's long-placid labor market, where the number of strikes noticeably increased in the 1970s, most emblematically in the ENKA-Glanzstoff factory in Breda in late 1972, where soon-to-be-laid off workers occupied – successfully – the synthetic fibers factory in order to obtain a more generous redundancy policy. Such labor unrest was not merely a reflection of a more assertive political culture, but was chiefly precipitated by a shift in the Dutch (and western European) economy, in which industrial jobs were increasingly making way for a rising service sector. In this respect, shifts in the Dutch economy paralleled those in surrounding countries and, if high in relative historical terms, Dutch strike activity in the 1970s remained lower than in most other European countries – certainly than Belgium, Britain or France.

None of this growing political uncertainty, however, could gainsay the fact that Dutch society had transformed itself in the space of a few short years. The further expansion of the welfare state – largely implemented not by the socialists but by the liberals and Christian democrats – significantly extended disability benefits and increasingly focused on the "well-being" of the population. This emphasis on a healthy psyche fit well into a society that would have one of the highest percentages of mental health workers (and patients) per capita in the world. The increasingly decisive rejection of what were perceived as the moral and religious straitjackets of the past went hand-in-hand with an emphasis on the emancipation of the self, though this trend was more muted in the countryside and small towns than in the great cities.

Increasingly, the government was inclined to cede more room to the citizen: the country's strict spatial planning laws, instituted in the mid 1960s, made considerable provision for citizen response – a provision promptly used by many citizens to contest new urban projects, many of which threatened to destroy the old neighborhoods in which they resided. After university students demanded more input into school affairs in 1969, the government passed a reform bill that gave them a greater say in university administration than virtually anywhere else in Europe. The restrictions on homosexual activity were lifted – the age of consensual sex was lowered from twenty-one to sixteen, as it already was for heterosexual relations – and gay groups were formally recognized and, like many groups in those years, given generous subsidies. The relatively quick acceptance of a gay public presence may have been rooted in the Dutch pillarized practice of extending autonomy to minorities, but it was also sustained by a society whose new views on sexuality had consciously moved beyond traditional moral standards.

Apparently emblematic of the Netherlands' process of self-liberation was its rapidly professionalizing soccer, with many teams enjoying a golden age in the 1970s – a time when the Oranje national team, spearheaded for most of the period by the legendary Amsterdam player Johan Cruyff, fought their way to the finals in the World Cups of 1974 and 1978. The practice of "total football" – in which players constantly switched playing position – enchanted the world, and seemed to underline for some analysts the free and creative nature of modern Dutch society. This could be seen in other fields as well, such as in design and architecture, where Dutch innovation enjoyed an international reputation.

More self-evidently tied to the liberalization of Dutch society was its shifting drugs policy, particularly with regard to cannabis. Here a combination of motives – a respect for the "spiritual freedom" of drug use (as one government report put it); a subscription to the scientific insight that "soft" drugs were less dangerous physically than "hard" drugs; and, perhaps above all, a concern that the growing presence of drugs might be creating an unmanageable law enforcement problem – prompted Dutch authorities to move toward the <u>decriminalization of soft</u> drugs. As a signatory to the Single Convention of New York (1961), which defined cannabis as an illegal narcotic, the Dutch government formally retained the penalties on cannabis but drew up prosecutorial guidelines that effectively allowed for the possession of the drug in small amounts – up to 30 grams, according to the modified Opium Law of 1976. Authorities tolerated the activities of appointed "house dealers" in clubs, and the first "coffee shop" in which the drug was discreetly sold opened in 1972, though the real growth of the commercially oriented "coffee shops" emerged in the 1980s. Throughout the 1970s and 1980s the government accordingly did little to interdict the cannabis trade. The 1976 revisions, however, did increase the sanctions, particularly on the dealing of "hard" drugs. The focus in these years was on the sharply rising use of heroin, largely facilitated by global Chinese networks, and the wave of addictions it engendered made the center of Amsterdam a visible and sometimes rather grim battleground between police and a rising tide of criminality. Interestingly, the change in the Dutch drugs policy generated, for the time being, relatively little public heat; conservatives contented themselves with supporting a pragmatic line. In any event, subsequent decades showed that Dutch drug-use and addiction rates were typically at or below the European average.

What did generate an enormous amount of public debate and anguish in the 1970s was a reappraisal of World War II. It was in this new context, far removed from privation, violence and tyranny that the Dutch could collectively look back at the legacy of the war with critical reflection, looking beyond the image of the Netherlands as the brave and virtuous resister of Nazi brutality. The ensuing discussion turned out to be more emotional, more charged with the memory of the war, than many had imagined. Already in the late 1960s the Jewish historian Jacques Presser had made waves with his heart-wrenching account of the demise of

Dutch Jews, and the less-than-heroic role their Dutch compatriots had played in this tragedy. This growing sense of national complicity and guilt would come to haunt further discussions, evidenced in the heated debate of 1972 over the proposed pardon of three last German war criminals held by the Dutch in a Breda prison. In that year groups representing the Resistance and the victims of the war successfully pressured Parliament and the government to keep the three incarcerated; in this way the Dutch might yet make amends for its wartime sins of omission. The two surviving members of the "Breda Three" were released only in 1989, both dying within months of their release.

In the meantime, Dutch memory of the war shifted decisively away from the theme of resistance and collaboration to the centrality of the Holocaust. The writers and Holocaust victims Etty Hillesum and Anne Frank – whose diary initially received far more attention in the United States than in the Netherlands – helped define this new focus, as did a longstanding government effort to compensate the victims of the war for their suffering. Consciously mindful of Dutch failings under Nazi occupation, this civil religion, at its height in the 1980s and 1990s, aimed at steeling the population to resist all forms of anti-Semitism and discrimination. It also formed the basis of the Dutch public ethos in these decades: resolutely anti-racist and determined to show solidarity with all victims of unequal treatment. This sentiment was also reflected by Article 1 of the amended Dutch Constitution of 1983, which flatly forbade discrimination on all grounds.

In practice, of course, this mission proved difficult to implement consistently. By 1983, in fact, the Dutch were forced to confront the fact that they had become a nation of immigrants. Rock-bottom unemployment rates had compelled Dutch employers to look farther afield for labor in the 1960s. Initially, most "guest workers" (the Dutch term *gastarbeider* is nearly identical to its German equivalent) came from southern Europe, but as they returned home new markets were sought in the impoverished interiors of Turkey and Morocco. By the first half of the 1970s the citizens of these two countries together constituted nearly two-thirds of the Netherlands' 100,000 registered foreign workers. As in other western European countries, the initial assumption had been that these "guests" would return to their country of origin, but out of practicality and principle the Dutch government resisted implementing a policy of sending them back. Subsidies to immigrant organizations, and the policy of allowing families to emigrate to the Netherlands in order to be reunited with their menfolk, helped anchor these and other immigrant groups to life in the Netherlands.

Most political parties and other leading institutions emphasized the importance of accepting the new immigrants and their ways of life. Not everyone concurred, however; in the Rotterdam area during the early 1970s two violent altercations broke out, as Dutch residents attacked the houses of Turkish immigrants. Less dramatically, the 1970s and 1980s witnessed the initial signs of "white flight" from neighborhoods increasingly populated by immigrants, and a nativist party – still small and politically stigmatized – first found representation in the Dutch Parliament in 1982. The new Center Party, as this anti-immigrant party called itself, did its best to remain a vocal and vociferous critic of the new immigration, but memories of World War II and a public resolve to reject racism ensured, for the time being at least, that the media and mainstream politics would keep this group at arm's length.

Growing Polarization and Economic Stagnation

In the 1970s and 1980s, Dutch attention to ethnic minorities was neither directed at Muslims more specifically nor at guest workers more generally. Rather, it was two postcolonial populations that would lay the greatest claim on Dutch interest. In one case – the Moluccans – it was through dramatic and violent confrontations: one conflict of several in a society where the tensions had become grimmer than they had been in the 1960s and early 1970s.

The 13,000 Moluccans who, in 1950, had reluctantly been relocated to the Netherlands after Indonesian independence still faced an undetermined future a quarter century later; stateless, poorly housed in former concentration camps, and lacking the training and education to participate successfully in Dutch society, many still aspired to return to their homeland, an aspiration that the Dutch government initially supported. Hostile to the Indonesian regime, the Moluccans could not, however, return; resentful of Dutch passivity to their plight, a portion of this community came to support a more radical approach that would compel the government in The Hague to take a more proactive stance. Following an international pattern that saw a sharp rise of terrorist activity in many European countries, a small number took up arms, most notably in the hijacking of two trains: once in 1975, in which three hostages were killed, and once again in 1977, when another two were. In both cases the standoffs, which lasted weeks, drew international media attention. The latter confrontation ended particularly violently, with 15,000 bullets fired by Dutch marines into the train, killing most of the hostage-takers. As a response to these expressions of violent protest, the government made additional efforts to improve the educational and economic situation of the Moluccan-Dutch community, rejecting the temptation to mobilize the Dutch public into a war against terror.

Of greater impact to Dutch society, particularly the western cities, was the mass exodus of Surinamese to the Netherlands in the 1970s. Political ferment in the Dutch Caribbean had prompted Dutch officials to develop a new tack in ruling the region. The most dramatic event that helped precipitate this change was the serious riots on the island of Curaçao in May of 1969, in which two people were killed and two neighborhoods of the capital, Willemstad, largely burned to the ground. A strike against the reduction of wages at the Shell refinery had been the initial expression of this unrest, an unrest that was seated in the considerable economic inequality between the black and white sections of the population. Subsequent elections in the regional legislature returned a majority that asserted equal rights for blacks in the Antilles. The Dutch government, increasingly embarrassed by the charge that they were behaving like colonial masters – the role of the army in quelling the 1969 riots had been dubious – and anxious to avoid future confrontations, attempted to take a more conciliatory tone and adopt more financially generous policies.

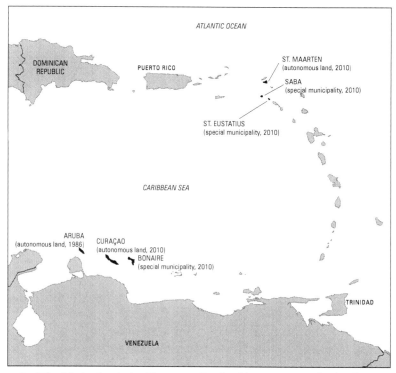

16   The Netherlands Antilles were dissolved in 2010, as each island went it alone. Frictions between The Hague and the islands over governance and finances did not go away, though.

Over time, that would lead to administrative reforms within the six islands of the Netherlands Antilles, whose inhabitants continued to opt for Dutch rule, with each island opting by 2010 for its own administration, either as a "land" of the Kingdom or as a special municipality.

In Surinam it was different. The socialist-led government of Joop den Uyl, committed on principle to ending the unequal yoke of imperialism, determined in 1973 to support the (bare) majority of the Surinamese in their choice for independence. The new state was proclaimed at the end of 1975. Already high before independence, the flow of people from the former colony to the Netherlands was facilitated by a measure that guaranteed an unrestricted right to settlement in the Netherlands until 1980. Roughly 300,000 Surinamese, or nearly half of Surinam's population, relocated to the Netherlands in the 1970s: an astonishingly high percentage relative to any other postcolonial migration. Once in the Netherlands, Surinam's disparate population groups – the Javanese, the "Hindustanis" and the Creoles – would all fare differently in Dutch society, though the initial reaction of many Dutch was to focus on the crime that the migration had engendered. The Dutch managed in the 1970s and 1980s to avoid large-scale, violent confrontations like the kind evident in London's Brixton neighborhood, but racial tensions and irritations were hardly absent.

The ethnic tensions of the 1970s coincided with other sharp ideological confrontations in Dutch society, which contrasted with the more restrained politics of previous decades. Serving to intensify the confrontation was a serious downturn in the Dutch economy that first manifested itself in the early 1970s and came to an end with a clear resurgence of the Dutch economy in the late 1980s. In the fallout of the Yom Kippur War in 1973, the Dutch, along with the Americans, were punished by the oil-producing Arab states for their purported support of Israel, prompting the government to proclaim energy-saving measures.

Through the oil boycott and rise in energy prices can be seen the beginning of the Netherlands' economic hard times; the Dutch faced more longstanding structural problems – structural problems, incidentally, that did not differ all that much from other western European countries. The Dutch economy had performed well in the immediate postwar period, in part because wages were relatively low, but by the 1970s prosperity and high taxation had made Dutch labor relatively expensive. All this would signal the end of some of the Netherlands' classic industries, such as the once substantial textile branch and shipbuilding, a sector that had already struggled in the immediate postwar period to compete internationally. The Limburg mines, too, closed in the mid 1970s, generating long-term unemployment in the area and social decay. Dutch businesses were forced to find alternatives to the high labor costs, increasingly through a greater dependence on technology. Partly as a result of this, unemployment began to rise, ultimately reaching some 13.5 percent in the early 1980s. At the same time, government expenditure continued to grow. In the halcyon days of the 1960s rising government expenditures paralleled rising government income, but they continued to rise in the 1970s as the economy soured, exceeding 60 percent of GDP by 1981. Emblematic of the country's generous – and expensive – welfare state was the Disability Law of 1967, initially intended for 175,000 recipients – a figure reaching nearly a million before the reforms of the 1990s, and comprising some 13 percent of the workforce. Employers found putting workers into the disability system easier than firing them, and the wide parameters for defining disability – uniquely, the law stipulated that the disabling condition did not have to be work-related – made it difficult for physicians to draw sharp lines. Through such programs social spending alone accounted for a third of national income, reducing Dutch economic competitiveness. Dutch politicians were slow to recognize the problem, as fixing it would require painful and unpopular steps.

Achieving political consensus on the economy was not made any easier by political polarization of the period. With a weakened Christian Democracy, the antagonism between a rising liberalism, caustic critics of what they saw as the excesses of the welfare state, and the more powerful social democrats, reached new heights. Moral issues, too, played a role, most notably abortion. Abortion was prohibited by law, and historically Dutch abortion rates had been low. But in the 1960s, calls for liberalization of abortion laws heard in the western world also impacted Dutch views on the issue. Abortion clinics were established in the early 1970s and condoned by the authorities. The Christian Democrats, the chief guardians of traditional sexual morality, were willing to legalize abortions during the first trimester, but not the second. The difference between the Christian Democratic Minister of Justice, Andries van Agt, and the socialist-led government of Den Uyl turned into a serious row in 1976 when Van Agt tried to shut down a clinic engaging in second-trimester abortions, an effort that failed when hundreds of abortion activists occupied the clinic themselves. Ultimately a compromise bill that resulted in a fairly liberal abortion law ended most of the debate after its passage in 1981.

The occupation of the abortion clinic illustrates what made Dutch politics particularly dynamic and sometimes volatile in the 1970s and 1980s: an exceptionally broad support, by international comparison, for "the new social movements" that typically focused on human rights, the environment and peace issues. But in the Netherlands it was also evident in groups such as the Dutch Association for Voluntary Euthanasia, which in the space of a few years managed to build up a membership of over 100,000, in absolute numbers far larger than any international counterpart. In line with the Dutch tradition of state support for private initiative, many – but not all – of these groups were substantially subsidized by the government. For a time, at least, the locus of politics seemed to shift from political parties and Parliament to the new pressure groups, some of which believed that the Netherlands might serve as a "guide land" to usher in a better world.

That notion of being a beacon to the world was not new – it had been propagated in the early twentieth century – but now that sentiment had been democratized into influential political movements. That such movements, from the standpoint of traditional political circles, made governing more difficult is most evident in the powerful anti-cruise missile campaign that began in 1979, when NATO plans to station forty-eight intermediate-range missiles became known. The communists and the Christian-led peace movement, reactivated in their successful opposition to the development of the neutron bomb in the late 1970s, played a leading role in organizing widespread opposition to this plan. For six years the government delayed decision over their placement. Though placement enjoyed the support of many liberals and Christian Democrats, who were then mostly in power, a majority of the population opposed stationing and were represented by a powerful peace movement that in 1983 generated the largest demonstration in Dutch history: some 550,000 people protested in The Hague against the cruise missiles. By 1985 the government felt secure enough to give NATO qualified approval for the stationing, though in the end the missiles were not placed: the subsequent winding down of the cold war had made such plans moot.

Though sometimes militant, most of the new social activism was not violent, and the Netherlands did not witness the home-grown terrorism of the extreme left as West Germany or Italy did. Many Dutch left-wing radicals sympathized with, and occasionally actively supported, the violent campaign of the Red Army Faction, but they did not think that such methods were appropriate in the Dutch context. Nevertheless, politically motivated street violence and bombings were not unknown in the Netherlands during the 1980s. The most spectacular confrontation took place in Amsterdam on April 30, 1980 when Queen Juliana abdicated in favor of her daughter Beatrix. The House of

49   Amsterdam riots during the installation of Queen Beatrix in April 1980 were the zenith of postwar street violence. A decade later such confrontations would have been unthinkable.

Orange had recently weathered the crisis of 1976, when it became apparent that Juliana's husband, Prince Bernhard, had accepted bribes from the Lockheed corporation in exchange for influencing military contracts.

Beatrix's installation as queen, though, was the occasion for protest rather than the cause of it, which focused on the lack of affordable housing – a cause taken up by the city's extensive squatter movement. Relations between the squatters and the authorities had already been tense in the months and weeks leading up to the royal ceremony, but miscommunication and the presence of both large numbers of police on the one hand and squatters and anarchists on the other helped to precipitate a huge disturbance that nearly derailed the ceremony and caused hundreds of injuries on both sides. In the early 1980s, violent confrontations between the police and the squatters would continue, even as local authorities made more effort to meet some of the protesters' demands. Nor was violence restricted to this issue; small left-wing terror groups also emerged. From 1985 to 1987, for instance, some thirty Shell stations and other businesses would be firebombed by the radical antiracist group RaRa as a way to pressure Dutch-based corporations into dissociating from Apartheid South Africa.

Neoliberalism in the 1980s and 1990s

Trimming the State

By the mid 1980s, however, a new mood had settled over the country, as both ideological ideals and rifts lessened. The sober side of the Dutch seemed to have returned. Perhaps a new sense of limits on what state and society could likely achieve played a role in a pragmatic stance where ideology was increasingly downplayed. Religious adherence, which initially had inspired a good deal of participation in the new social movements, clearly had become a much smaller public and private presence by the 1980s, and it was in this decade that the churches realized how marginal they had become. Increasingly the Dutch population, following trends manifest elsewhere, came to embrace a neo-liberal vision of the market, with a greater interest in "efficient" management models, not least in the realm of politics and government. In particular, the Labor Party in the course of the 1980s abandoned its leftist ideological course in favor of policies that were seen as more market-friendly, and let go of its polarization strategy in the face of a Christian Democracy that, at least for the time being, had stabilized its losses and reasserted its control over the center of Dutch politics.

The most important indication of a more pragmatic political ethos was the so-called Wassenaar Accord of November 1982: a one-page statement of principles in which unions pledged to moderate wage demands in exchange for a employer promise to maintain or hire more (part-time) workers. The period of polarization that had also affected labor relations in the 1970s thus came to an end. In any event, the Accord is thought to have substantially improved the long-term performance of the Dutch economy; employment rose, as Dutch companies took on the risk of hiring more employees and as their global competitiveness increased. By the late 1980s the agreement had more than proven itself. Placid labor relations and the commitment to balanced outcome would be dubbed "the polder model" by the 1990s, attracting foreign observers impressed with the Netherlands' economic success. The Social-Economic Council, the formal advisory organ established in 1950, once again, as it had in its initial years, served as an effective forum for negotiating the interests of employers, employees and the state. At the same time, the government, led by the longest-serving premier in Dutch history, the Christian Democrat Ruud Lubbers (1982–1994), attempted, with success, gradually to implement across-the-board cuts to government programs. By the end of Lubbers's tenure, government expediture as a percentage of GDP had declined – a trend that would continue under his successor.

Strong protests arose against the government's plan to make cuts in the public sector. But these protests soon gave way to a pragmatic stance, in which most of the interested parties sought to save as many of the government's extensive programs as reason seemed to dictate. In political circles, fervent or principled discussion on the merits of the welfare state typically gave way to a managerial mindset that eschewed ideology and demanded efficiency, with the government setting new, stricter benchmarks for the recipients of public monies. Initially, this "no-nonsense" stance, as it was called at that time, was motivated less by a convinced, free market "neo-liberal" ideology – despite the fact that much of the new managerialism was inspired by American examples – and more by a desire to keep the state solvent, maintain programs and restore the economy.

Only in the 1990s, as the economy continued to grow, did Dutch policy reflect an ideological enthusiasm for the market.

Privatization of state concerns began, starting with the splitting up and privatization of the government-run Post, Telegraph and Telephone in the late 1980s, and followed by the privatization of the Dutch Railroads (Nederlandse Spoorwegen) in the mid 1990s. The Dutch housing corporations – which as a non-profit sector held an internationally unprecedented 35 percent of the country's total housing stock – were granted financial independence and full ownership of their properties in 1995, though government directives continued to determine in large degree the policies of these corporations. On a similar tack, the government abandoned the television monopoly it had given to Dutch public broadcasting in 1989, allowing commercial broadcasters such as RTL to compete in Dutch markets. It was a decision that, along with the rise of cable television, sharply reduced Dutch public television's market share.

Underlying this whole shift was a new government insistence that citizens shoulder a greater share of the burden. From the end of the World War II to the end of the 1970s, the Dutch government had stressed in its communication with the public its commitment to new programs; in the 1980s and 1990s the government systematically asked that citizens themselves bear a greater responsibility for their own lives. It was a recognition of its own weakness; the government no longer possessed the means to regulate and direct society as some had hoped it would in the 1960s and 1970s. In practice, however, the state remained an important factor in regulating society and in subsidizing the private sector.

Economic Developments

Somber prognostications over the future at the beginning of the 1980s – shaped by high unemployment and the dangers of the nuclear arms race – gave way to a more optimistic mood by the late 1980s. The cold war was coming to an end, and the Dutch economy would show robust growth figures from the late

1980s until the end of the century, a brief dip in 1993–1994 notwithstanding. The incomes of the Dutch rose roughly a quarter in the course of the 1990s, and consumerism expressed itself more loudly than it had before. If the Dutch, historically, had avoided conspicuous consumption as an expression of bad morals or taste, those days were largely gone. The quality of Dutch housing, which for many decades had stressed quantity over quality, began to improve after 1985, and with increasing demand the purchase price of homes began a sharp and sustained trend upward. Strict zoning regulations determined which municipalities were permitted to grow, and the city that clearly showed the greatest growth was Almere, situated in the new and empty polders of Flevoland, recognized as a province in 1986 and an area initially earmarked exclusively for agricultural production. The first houses in the new town were completed in 1976, and by the early twenty-first century Almere had become one of the country's ten largest cities, with a population approaching 200,000. Almere proved highly attractive to residents of nearby Amsterdam, where affordable housing remained in short supply, especially for families. Early settlers in Flevoland often thought of themselves as pioneers, having moved from the old world to a new frontier.

The economy flourished a the country maintaining its role as the international transporter of goods. As in the past, its success as a transporter went hand-in-hand with its successful production of processed goods. The Netherlands was one of the largest food exporters in the world (from cheeses and tomatoes to fish and flowers) and possessed a specialized, high-tech industrial base. Natural gas exports (supplying up to 30 percent of the European Union's needs) and effective financial policies also aided in its prosperity. High productivity continued to characterize the Dutch economy, and the Dutch led the world in efforts to "automate" the economy through labor-saving efforts. Productivity was undermined, though, by the rising importance of the less productive service sector, and by the fact that relatively few Dutch worked at all.

432

Early pensions and easy access to disability benefits were some of the reasons, but another factor was that Dutch women with children often chose to work part-time, encouraged by employment arrangements that made such work attractive. Dutch women, like the (Western) Germans but unlike their Scandinavian counterparts, did not tend to see full-time work as the measure of emancipation, emphasizing instead their freedom of choice, which often resulted in their taking on part-time work if they were mothers. In any event, for a long time the government did little to make daycare for children an affordable option.

In general, the Dutch thrived in the international, globalizing economy. To be sure there were setbacks, as in the aeronautical sector. Their Fokker Aircraft Industries, established in 1919 and in its earlier years the world's largest plane manufacturer, went bankrupt in 1996, unable to compete with Boeing and Airbus. Royal Dutch Airlines came under the control of Air France in 2004, though operationally it continued to work autonomously. The new economies of scale could be damaging to Dutch economic interests, and to Dutch pride. Nevertheless, polls revealed that a large majority of Dutch continued to see an open, global economy as good for their own country. In the 1990s they also remained convinced proponents of the further integration of Europe, at a crucial juncture more enthusiastic than the larger European states. In the last half of 1991 the Dutch government, as the chair of the European Community, proposed changes to the treaty that would result in the European Union – changes that would give the European Commission authority to act in the fields of justice, the police, foreign affairs and security matters, and thus centralize the new union. It was part of a longer-term Dutch strategy that sought to reduce the power of the larger states by strengthening the Commission's prerogatives, rather than leaving them to intergovernmental negotiation, where the larger states could more effectively assert their will. France, Britain and other countries, however, resisted the Dutch proposal, and these areas

50   Dutch ministers sign the Maastricht Treaty, 1992. Dutch media then were more critical of the failure of a Dutch-led plan for political union than of treaty provisions that led to the euro.

were kept out of the treaty and left fully to the prerogatives of the individual states. Dutch failure notwithstanding, the Treaty of Maastricht, signed in February of 1992 and prepared in part by the Dutch government, was an important further step toward greater political union, and to a common currency that would result in the euro a decade later. As a result, too, the European Union formally came into existence a year later, even though criticism and resistance to the new treaty were considerable – if not yet in the Netherlands itself.

Growing Unease over the Nation's Future, 1995–2017

Worries over National Identity

Dutch foreign interests were not only aimed at the European Union, of course. With the end of the cold war, the Netherlands substantially increased its commitment to peace missions from three before the end of the cold war (including the UN-mandated participation in the Korean War) to seven in the 1990s alone. The most traumatic – and tragic – of these missions occurred in the former Yugoslav republic of Bosnia-Herzegovina. In 1994, a battalion of Dutch soldiers was sent to guard the UN-designated "safe haven" of Srebrenica, a Muslim enclave in eastern Bosnia. "Dutchbat," as this unit was called, was in no way prepared to stop Bosnian–Serbian aggression if it should occur. Unable to mount a successful defense with a small command that included too many support personnel and too little ammunition, it was shakily led. Promised air support, which the Dutch desperately sought in the days before the Serbians penetrated the enclave, did not materialize. The will to stand with the Muslims was perhaps further undermined by poor relations with the very residents Dutchbat was supposed to protect. As a result, the hapless battalion stood by as Muslim men were separated from their kinfolk and soon executed by the Serbians, up to 8,000 men in all.

The defense of the enclave had been badly planned and badly executed, with disastrous results. The debacle prompted much soul-searching within the Netherlands. It seemed to some observers an example of the country's moral cowardice, permitting genocide to occur even as the Dutch had sworn, with the memory of World War II, not to let that happen again. For others, it was the end of the illusion that the Dutch, as a country historically committed to international law, could bring peace to the world, and prompted many Dutch to look inward. In any event, the political consequences for prime minister Wim Kok's government were minimal. A government-sponsored study, years in the making and some 6,000 pages long, was mild in its judgments but prompted the Kok administration, in 2002 – a month before slated elections – to step down, as a symbolic sign that it took responsibility for the Dutch role at Srebrenica.

Dutch reflection over Srebrenica was part of a wider discussion in the 1990s over national identity. In the immediate postwar period of liberation and reconstruction, nationhood had been a strongly felt and common commitment among the Dutch. After the 1950s, they were foremost among the peoples of Europe to distance themselves from anything that might resemble nationalism. Now discussions over national identity returned after a long hiatus, fed by growing concerns about Europe – the relative role of the Netherlands in the Union declined as new states joined – and about the effects of globalization, not least immigration. In the Netherlands' western cities migrants together formed a large percentage of the population; in 1995, some 36 percent of the population of Rotterdam was "*allochtoon*" – of non-Dutch origin – prompting increasing unease among much of the city's "native" population. Former guest workers had succeeded in drawing their families to the Netherlands, and the numbers of asylum seekers reached their height in the 1990s, both in the Netherlands and elsewhere.

In the 1980s and 1990s, the new ethnic and religious minorities were given extensive subsidies to establish their own institutions in the name of multiculturalism, with the implicit expectation that these organizations would serve – in the long run – to "emancipate" newcomers into becoming the kind of people that the modern Dutch themselves had become. Doubts among Dutch elites over this policy developed very slowly over the course of the 1990s, however. Concerns were raised as to whether some groups were really becoming more emancipated, and whether Dutch culture was strong enough to absorb these demographic changes and cultural challenges. In 1991 the parliamentary leader of the Dutch liberals, Frits Bolkestein, argued that migrants must no longer be encouraged to maintain their old identities; that Dutch values included principles that should never be surrendered; and that civilizations that embraced these values, such as tolerance, were superior to those that rejected them. In the early 1990s, these remarks were highly controversial among a political elite that continued to support multicultural policies, including

51   Migration transformed western cities such as Rotterdam where annual
events like the Summer Carnival literally changed its rhythms. The effects
of migration remained hotly contested.

significant cultural autonomy, undergirded by government subsidies, for the country's ethnic minorities. Bolkestein also generated notoriety for his critical stance toward Islam. For the
time being, little seemed to change in the Netherlands' political
climate; the progressive ethos that assailed racism or anything
that resembled it remained largely in place, with many Dutch
highly critical of other European countries less enlightened on
this front.

   In hindsight, however, Bolkestein's remarks were the writing on the wall. The government sharply curtailed the potential
for immigrants and asylum seekers to enter the country in the
late 1990s, and the media, which had assiduously avoided nam-
ing the ethnicity of criminal suspects, began to do so. In a highly
influential opinion piece in 2000, the Dutch publicist and social
democrat Paul Scheffer decried the effects of multiculturalism,

437

calling for a greater measure of assimilation – a call that seemed, to some at least, most clearly directed at the country's Muslims, then roughly 5 percent of the population, but a much larger percentage of the population in the bigger western cities) His essay was one more landmark in a process that would prompt nearly all Dutch political parties to eschew multiculturalism in the early twenty-first century.

At the same time, the 1990s were the high water mark of Dutch libertarianism, a trend confirmed – and strengthened – by the dramatic loss sustained by the Christian Democrats in the 1994 elections. For the first time since 1918, no Christian party was represented in the cabinet. This does not mean that the Netherlands was a country where everything was possible, as Jonathan Blank's film *Sex, Drugs and Democracy* (1994) seemed to suggest. In respect of the country's drug policies, in fact, Dutch permissiveness declined in some respects under the socialist-liberal cabinets of Kok. The increasing importance of the Netherlands as a base for the transnational, organized drug trade led to stiffer enforcement of drug laws. To placate neighboring states, the amount of hashish tolerated was reduced from 30 g to 5 g per person per "coffee shop" visit, and the number of coffee shops was reduced from around 1,500 in 1991 to roughly 575 a quarter of a century later. Local councils were often eager to streamline their number in order to avoid the nuisance they brought, a nuisance protested by locals in some Dutch cities who opposed the number of drugs tourists in their neighborhoods. Nevertheless, the government's commitment to seeing drug use first as a health issue and second as a matter of law enforcement was continued across the board.

Libertarian legislation was more clearly embedded in other areas that affected the personal sphere, although it must be added that another motive – the Dutch preference for regulating practices over outlawing them – also prompted policy-makers to support some of the new legislation. Confirming the country's gay-friendly climate, marriage between two people of the same sex was legalized in 2000 – making the Netherlands the first state in the world to do so. In the same year, the government repealed the prohibition of brothels on the books since 1911, hoping – wrongly as it turned out – that the full legalization of prostitution would significantly reduce the coercive features of the sex trade. And in 2001, Parliament approved legislation that formally codified euthanasia as a legal practice, some fifteen years after Dutch courts had effectively given physicians legal protections to engage in the practice. Although most requests for euthanasia continued to be rejected by doctors, many Dutch erroneously believed that the right to die had now been achieved. In 2001, Dutch physicians euthanized 3,800 patients at their own request, either through direct intervention or assisted suicide: 2.7 percent of all deaths in that year. The number of euthanasia cases then declined, only to rise again in recent years, reaching 4.5 percent of all deaths in 2016.

A large majority of the Dutch population supported abortion rights, gay marriage and legalized euthanasia, and in subsequent years these achievements, as they were routinely touted, were increasingly seen as reflecting core secular values that the Dutch must not surrender to a surging Islamic or religious threat. That many felt a tension between their support of tolerant Dutch values and solidarity with their Muslim fellow citizens was just one indication of a society that had become more insistent on conformity to its collective social norms.

Similarly, the embrace of libertarian values could go hand-in-hand with a more punitive public culture that also began to emerge. Tolerance for criminality had begun to decline in the 1980s. Reflecting international trends, the incarceration rate in the Netherlands rose from 35 per 100,000 in 1975 to 134 per 100,000 in 2005, before it would start to dip again as crime dropped. No longer was the Netherlands an international front-runner in keeping the convicted out of prison – quite the contrary in fact. Nor was a new culture of accountability restricted

439

to prison policy. At the turn of the century, two local disasters – a firework explosion in the city center of Enschede and a café fire in the historic village of Volendam, each with significant loss of life – led the Dutch to demand that local authorities strictly enforce their codes. It was a decided rejection of the forbearance policies that had allowed Dutch officials to enforce their own rules flexibly. Litigation, too, increased in Dutch courts. All this – along with the increasing pressures on newcomers to conform to the Dutch way of life – signaled a new strictness that sought to counteract some of the adaptable, conflict-avoiding attitudes of the recent past.

A Surge of Populist Politics

By the turn of the new century, this growing climate of stringency and rising suspicion would have political consequences. Since the decline of polarization in the early 1980s, Dutch politics had become rather technocratic, with little ideological difference among the parties. Ultimately, this created conditions for populist resentments to be expressed. The first politician to exploit this vulnerability successfully was the entrepreneur and publicist Pim Fortuyn, an erstwhile Marxist academic who moved steadily to the right in the course of the 1990s. An overt homosexual, Fortuyn stood in defense of progressive Dutch virtues, condemning Islam as a "backward culture" and excoriating the ruling "leftist Church" for its desultory response to real people's problems. Many voters were drawn to Fortuyn because they felt he dared to say what they had long thought. Nine days before the general election of May 2002, Fortuyn was gunned down by an animal rights activist who regarded him as a political danger to the country. In the wake of his murder his newly created party sprang from 0 to 26 out of 150 seats, easily the most meteoric rise in Dutch parliamentary history. Lacking cohesion and discipline, Fortuyn's party soon imploded, but his legacy persisted. Politicians of the

52   Pim Fortuyn gets three pies in the face, two months before his
assassination in May 2002. He generated vehement opposition, but his
political legacy changed Dutch politics for good.

traditional parties became more uncertain, and tried with not very
successful results to reconnect with the voters.

Political violence did not remain restricted to Fortuyn's murder. In November of 2004 the iconoclastic film-maker Theo van
Gogh – a relative of the celebrated painter – who had made a career
from provocation, was murdered in Amsterdam by a Muslim radical, in retaliation for a short film he had produced on Islam and its
negative consequences for women. The Dutch had imagined that
their country was free of the violence that could generate political
murder, but now two cases had followed each other in dismaying succession. The murder of Van Gogh intensified a sustained
debate in the Netherlands that also took place elsewhere: between
those who saw Islam and the potential for Islamization as one
of the chief threats to Dutch society (including high-profile

441

liberal politicians such as Geert Wilders and one-time Van Gogh associate Ayaan Hirsi Ali), and those who did not. These often heated discussions over the place of Muslims in Dutch society were largely conducted without them. As newcomers, and often of modest means, they frequently lacked effective representation in public life, and the rest of the Dutch did not consider their participation essential to the debate. The appointment of Ahmed Aboutaleb, born in the Rif mountains of Morocco, as mayor of Rotterdam in 2009 symbolically demonstrated that people with backgrounds such as his could break through to the top, but it did not really change the tenor of the debate.

It was not only over Islam that Dutch debate could become vociferous, and the Dutch populace did not hesitate in applying their extensive use of the internet and social media to weigh in, often with a measure of vitriol. Sometimes the political effects of the new political climate were dramatic; in a 2005 referendum nearly 62 percent of the electorate voted against the European "constitution," a stunning break with the past that was as much a vote against the Dutch establishment as it was against an ever-expanding Europe over which they felt they had no say. In this new climate, tolerance of other perspectives was no longer cherished as a Dutch virtue. In more positive terms, it brought new energy into the public sphere. If commentators thought Dutch politics all but dead in the 1990s, they certainly did not think that was still the case after the dawning of the new century.

The new politics, however, was exciting because it was more unpredictable than the old. Paralleling developments in other countries, the Dutch electorate for the most part had little party loyalty left, and the parties themselves, boasting few members (only one in forty voters held a party membership) struggled to connect with society. In particular, citizens with relatively little education had few ties with the political system and low expectations of what it could do for them. The outlook on life between more highly and less highly educated Dutch differed significantly in the early twenty-first century, the latter being much more pessimistic about the future. This is perhaps not surprising, given that their lives on average were seven years shorter than those with more diplomas. The tension between native Dutch and newcomers seemed to grow in significance as well. As elsewhere in Europe, many ethnic Dutch began to fear that both their culture and livelihoods were under threat from outsiders.

That Dutch politics could take a hitherto unthinkable turn was evidenced in the elections of 2010, when Wilders, campaigning on the danger of Islam to the West, won a sixth of the seats in Parliament, a significant victory. Up until then, traditional Dutch politics had held this self-styled populist at arm's length, rejecting his proposed anti-Islamic proposals (including a prohibition of the Koran) as either contrary to law, distasteful or dangerous. The liberals and the Christian Democrats (the latter had been much reduced in the elections) resolved, however, that a coalition government consisting wholly of themselves and tolerated by Wilders in Parliament was preferable to a grand coalition with other parties. Though this arrangement lasted only a year-and-a-half and embraced few of Wilders's proposals, it might be said to have signaled an important break with traditional Dutch politics, with greater room in recent years for a populist style – and more room for a skeptical, even hostile, stance toward Islam and toward migration. A growing unwillingness to accommodate the religious obligations of Muslims (or Jews) was evident in 2011–2012, when a law banning ritual slaughter sailed through the Second Chamber but failed to pass the States-General only after the Senate decided the law want too far in restricting religious freedom.

As in many other parts of Europe, populism in the Netherlands led to political polarization and sharper public contention. Sometimes the distrust had social effects; younger people from ethnic minorities systematically experienced discrimination on the job market, making their full participation in Dutch society more difficult. In the private sphere, though, the Dutch seemed to long more for a time when everyone would treat each other civilly. Unlike any other European public, the Dutch identified rudeness as the number one problem that the country faced for most years of the new century. Articulating dismay at the impatience and thoughtlessness of their fellow citizens, the Dutch seemed more insistent than before on the creation or enforcement of rules that would more effectively guide behavior. In recent years, a growing majority could be found in favor of the prohibition of firework use at private parties during the New Year's celebration, preferring a safer and quieter start to the new calendar. Perhaps all of this was a sign that the Dutch were less willing than before to put up with the nuisance caused by other people.

Economic Recession and the European Crisis

After the great expansion of the economy in the 1990s, the Netherlands experienced slow growth in the first years of the new century. Then, starting in 2004, the economy began to grow again, reaching its peak in 2007. Real estate prices, which had leveled along with the economy, began to rise again sharply, driven by the availability of mortgages with easy lending terms that were predicated on the continued rise of real estate values.

The worldwide financial crisis of late 2008 also hit the Netherlands. One of its most internationally visible banks, ABN-Amro, had just been split and sold in three parts, one to the Belgian bank Fortis. In the wake of the banking crisis, Fortis was unable to meet its obligations and sold ABN to the Dutch government for almost 17 billion euros, effectively nationalizing it. Despite this intervention, the Dutch banking sector was in crisis, which quickly had effects on the availability of mortgages. Between the summer of 2008 and the summer of 2013, when housing prices began rising again, Dutch homes lost roughly 20 percent of their value, and the more expensive ones in particular lost much more. The number of underwater mortgages, where the balance on the mortgage exceeded the market value of the home, rose substantially, forcing some owners to sell and further glut a market with an oversupply of homes. Over the long run, the poor economy affected jobs. Dutch unemployment had long been quite low, by European as well as national standards, and at the beginning of the crisis it had reached a low point of 3.7 percent. It was not until the fall of 2011 that unemployment seriously began to surge, to reach its peak of nearly 9 percent in early 2014 before gradually dropping to 5.3 percent by early 2017. The Great Recession, as it has been called, generally affected the Netherlands somewhat later than other countries, such as the United States; and in some cases, such as that of unemployment, the country recovered later than in the United States.

The sustained economic recession also had significant effects on policy. In the first place, the deepening economic crisis of southern European countries, made worse by their participation in the euro, became manifest by early 2010, and it soon became clear that northern European countries, in one way or another, would have to write off the bad debts that they had directly or indirectly incurred by investing in these countries. Like Germany and Finland, the Netherlands, under liberal premier Mark Rutte, took a hard line toward Greece in particular, insisting that a plan be developed where the debts be paid back. In this stance Rutte had the general support of the Dutch public, which was in little mood to accommodate what it regarded as the profligacy of the Mediterranean states. The Dutch also showed little enthusiasm for a more centralized European policy that would make the euro more durable. If Euroskepticism had reached unprecedented levels during the 2005 referendum, the European crisis surrounding the euro and the Greek debt crisis precipitated even more alienation from the European project. Fears of unrestricted migration from eastern Europe, which proved for the most part unfounded, further diminished Dutch enthusiasm for the European Union. Wilders's calls notwithstanding, Dutch departure from the

Union, as debated in Great Britain, was never a serious political option in The Hague, but a sense of solidarity with southern or eastern Europe was clearly at low ebb. The Dutch referendum on the EU–Ukraine Association Agreement, brought forward by anti-EU groups in April 2016 and resulting in a "no" vote on the treaty, was another indication of just how eroded confidence in Europe was in the Netherlands. The general elections of March 2017 denied Wilders' bid to head the country's largest party – the uncertain effects of Brexit may have reduced his chances – and set the stage for the country's traditionally pro-European parties to share power. But both the victorious liberals and Christian Democrats, competing with Wilders for voters, remained tepid on Europe, emphasizing instead the need for a strong national identity.

The economic recession also put great pressure on the government purse, which was faced with declining revenues. Rather than opting for a Keynesian policy that favored deficit spending (and that would have fallen foul of Brussels's criteria restricting deficit size), the Dutch government stoutly preferred austerity, inducing substantial cuts in the national budget. This affected most areas of expenditure except education; reduced defense spending, for example, was one area where the government hoped to make significant savings. Lower government expenditures also precipitated important reforms. The most far-reaching of these was the decentralization of social policy in 2015, in which municipalities and local providers became responsible for taking care of the vulnerable. Since it was assumed that local agencies could be far more efficient than national government this allowed The Hague to cut its social services budget by two billion euros. It must be said, though, that this reform went hand-in-hand with a new theme that had entered Dutch politics and found wide support among the mainstream parties: the "participation society."

Since the 1990s, the Dutch government had tried in various ways to increase the percentage of citizens working, such as by

inducing women (of whom those with children had often preferred to work part-time) to work more hours; by making it
harder for people to receive disability allowance; and, in more
recent years, by gradually raising the retirement age to 67. The
new liberal-socialist government (an unusual combination of a
right-wing and left-wing party in coalition) expanded in 2013
the notion of "participation" to stress that the individual and her
direct environment, and not the national state, were responsible
for her own life. The welfare state as such would then have to
make way for citizens organizing their own affairs, including
their own care, and only calling in professionals when absolutely necessary. It was this shift in government policy, more
radical than any earlier reforms, that was now entrusted to local
government bodies to implement. All of this was an effort of
government to induce society to take over tasks that the government no longer could or would deliver, and to restore "individual responsibility" to its rightful place. It remained unclear
what the effects of this substantial shift in policy would mean
for society, and whether its networks of support were sufficient
to meet the new demands being made. The Dutch involvement
in volunteer work and membership in civil society organizations remained among the highest in the world, and gave some
hope that this policy might succeed, but these volunteers and
organizations did not perfectly match the real needs of many
Dutch citizens.

An Uncertain World

Meanwhile, it did become increasingly evident to the Dutch
that the world around them had become anything but safer.
The Russians' annexation of the Crimea in the winter of 2014
and their subsequent clandestine forays into other parts of the
Ukraine made the Dutch think harder than at any point since
the cold war about collective security on the eastern boundaries

of Europe. Nothing made them think about this harder than the crash on July 17, 2014 of Malaysian Air Flight 17, when it was likely misidentified and shot down by a Russian separatist missile while it was flying over the eastern Ukraine on the way from Amsterdam to Kuala Lampur. All 298 aboard died, including 193 Dutch citizens. In an impressive series of ceremonies the Dutch mourned with the survivors, but a sense of anger and helplessness at the situation continued, as it became likely that the culprits would never be brought to justice.

The two Islamic terrorist attacks in Paris in the course of 2015 and the Brussels bombings of March 2016 had a far greater impact on Dutch feelings of insecurity. This growing unease was sometimes paired with the sudden rise in refugees seeking asylum in the Netherlands, which neared some 60,000 people in 2015: most of them Syrian, most of them Muslim. Compared to refugee numbers in the 1990s and with the much larger influx into Germany or Sweden, these figures, in relative or absolute terms, were not especially high, and many Dutch volunteers welcomed refugees to the country. But at the same time, the number was a record for a single year, and the influx initially appeared unlimited. Anxiety about the possible presence of Islamic terrorists among the refugees cooled Dutch enthusiasm for taking in any more, as did concerns about whether they would successfully be "integrated" into society. Uncertainty abounded among the refugees too, as to their future fate, and the number to whom the Dutch could and would permit entry in the future. It was small comfort that Dutch uncertainty was hardly unique in a Union struggling to attain any measure of coherence or consensus in the implementation of refugee policy.

The first years of the twenty-first century thus found the Dutch in a worried frame of mind: not just about Islam and Europe, but about the social cohesion of the country, about a basic lack of respect between people, about the wide divide between the more highly and less well educated, between those with more wealth

and those with less, between natives and newcomers, and about
the ability of the Dutch (and Europe) to compete in the long run
with new economic forces such as India and China. For the time
being, however, the Netherlands remained a country much as it
had been before: it was one of the strongest economies in Europe
and the world, with an educated, productive work force and a
reasonably effective and reliable public administration. It was a
country still characterized by relative social tranquility; with little
violent crime; and sustained by one of the most extensive citizen
participation networks in the world, itself an important sign of the
trust that the Dutch continued to maintain in their own society.
Though the Dutch have become more pessimistic about the quality of public life and about future global prospects, they remain
supremely content about their own private lives, and they consistently rank in international polls as among the happiest people
in the world. But it was precisely this concern – that it might all
be taken from them – that made the Dutch chronically uncertain
about the future of their country.

EPILOGUE

The fact that the Netherlands is situated at the estuary of key European rivers has shaped its history for 2,000 years. Since Roman days, if not before, it has accordingly been an area that has beckoned trade along the Rhine and its other great rivers, as well as, of course, the North Sea. Since at least the fourteenth century this has made what is now the Netherlands an important partner in international trade. In the course of the sixteenth century increasingly intense ties with Asia, Africa and the Americas greatly impacted Dutch society, shaping its economy, its international affairs, even its domestic politics. It meant, too, that the Netherlands became a culturally open country: sometimes, particularly during its "Golden Ages," exercising greater influence abroad; at other times being open to outside influences, but in any event frequently interacting with its wider environment. Though the Netherlands has had its pockets of isolation – relatively remote farming areas or insular fishing villages – the Dutch, generally speaking, could not afford to be inattentive to the shifting dynamics around them.

From this perspective, the sweep of the history of the Netherlands, as suggested in the Introduction, is about the Dutch ability historically to respond quickly to changing conditions that included both considerable dangers and opportunities. The physical environment, at least in the west, the north and along the rivers, required some of the first settlers to take account of the water, and it is no stretch to say that the inhabitants of the Netherlands have been working now for some 2,500 years to prevent flooding while at the same time turning water into a benevolent force.

Along the coast the low-lying land also required in places a more specialized economy, that itself had to respond to a globalizing world, thrusting the Dutch into a cycle of innovation. Though this process of adaptation and innovation reached its pinnacle in relative terms during the period from roughly 1590 to 1670 (see Chapter 3), in the long run the Dutch remained an economic power of significance. Their creation of a prosperous and independent nation-state in the nineteenth and twentieth centuries was also the result of their being able to adapt to new political and economic conditions. The result, by and large, has been a society that has been an economic powerhouse far beyond its size and, at least at some points in its history, a leading technological innovator and cultural beacon to others. Frequently at the center of globalization, the Dutch often proved themselves effective at responding to new challenges.

None of these claims about adaptation and innovation should be romanticized. The Dutch struggle against the water entailed almost as much loss as gain until the arrival of the steam engine. Although they have often benefited economically from peace on land and on sea, their entrepreneurial successes, driven by their keen sense of new opportunity, historically depended on their use of force against rivals, whether among themselves, the Hanseatic League, the Spanish king or the peoples of the Indonesian archipelago. Others frequently paid a large price for Dutch profit-taking. Nor were Dutch successes equally shared within their own borders; unskilled migrants working in Amsterdam or slaves toiling on the Antilles are obvious examples of how Dutch dynamism could be exploitative. It might be added to all of this that Dutch successes, for the most part, were not exclusively of their own doing, but were enabled by external forces as well. Dutch innovations, economic or artistic, were not hermetically sealed national achievements autonomously attained apart from wider European and global dynamics of interaction; indeed, the openness of the Dutch to ideas from abroad was also crucial for their own creativity. Overlords and allies also played their part. Burgundian and Habsburg rule encouraged the region's economic rise and political development, and in the last centuries British and later American geopolitical dominance provided the contours for Dutch political freedom, economic prosperity and cultural achievement.

Yet for all its shadow sides and limitations, the ability of the Dutch to adapt to changing circumstances has historically depended on a recurring feature of Dutch society itself that requires particular emphasis: its fractured and pluralistic character, one with a profound impact on Dutch society and politics. From early medieval times the accumulation of power in the hands of one person or a very few was not possible. The Netherlands lay at the outer edge of Rome's expansion, straddling the boundary between the Roman and non-Roman worlds. As a result of the disintegration of the Carolingian Empire in the ninth century, the Netherlands (like much of western Europe) became a patchwork of different jurisdictions, a splintered political situation only partially overcome by Burgundian and Habsburg efforts. The relative weakness of the landowning nobility and the Church as temporal powers, as well as the rise of many modestly sized towns and cities with their rising economic and political power, additionally made it harder to centralize authority – and easier for local freedoms to develop. The Dutch Republic was a continuation of this pattern in early modern times when the heads of other states, such as France, Prussia and the Scandinavian kingdoms, were able to assert absolute rule. The advent of the unitary state, Napoleonic rule and the creation of the Kingdom of the Netherlands in the early nineteenth century eliminated some decentralized features such as the central role of the towns for good, but the rise of a fissiparous politics and wide-ranging civil society that re-emerged in the course of the nineteenth century reasserted the country's pluralistic character and diffuse power structures. In this way new spaces were created for competing groups to contest each other in the public arena. This they did, choosing to do so – for the most part – within the rule of law, creating the stable basis for a modern democracy.

Socially and economically, difference among the Dutch themselves was sizeable and a perennial point of contention, but bridged by a fairly wide middle comprising people of at least some means. Politically and religiously, the Netherlands was a country made up partially or wholly of minorities, with no single province, city or group able to assert its will alone. In particular, the religious diversity of the Netherlands was determined not only by the very different histories of its different regions, but by immigration: Calvinists, Jews, Lutherans and Catholics in the early modern period; later on migrants from Europe and further afield: Christian, Muslim, Hindu and a range of other faiths; mixing with a population that in the course of the last century increasingly came to profess no religious affiliation. It has been said that the Netherlands is the most religiously or philosophically diverse society per square kilometer in the world, a testimony to the challenges the Dutch faced in regulating this wide-ranging pluralism.

This fractured and pluralist nature of Dutch society relates to a recurring theme of Dutch history: its ostensible toler-ance. It is often supposed that this tolerance has much to do with the Netherlands as a trading emporium – that is, that the Dutch accepted difference in order to make money, or that, in a more elevated way, their frequent trading contacts with different peoples made them aware of other ways of thinking and doing, and thus sensitized them to difference. But if this interpretation is, to a large extent, true, it has received too much weight. The extent to which the Dutch were tolerant – that is, forbearing of ideas and people noxious to them – lay more in the fact that the power differential between them was often not all that great. Political and social interactions require a recognition of the limits of one's own power, and of the imperative of making prudent arrangements that astutely assess the complex power relationships between competing forces. This has accounted for

453

the relative degree of cooperation seen in Dutch society and its relatively restrained politics throughout much of its history, as well as a greater reluctance to force strict religious or ideological conformity on everyone. Out of this experience a widespread commitment to accept difference arose.

Here, too, there is no point in overstating the case. As this book reveals time and again, Dutch history has been full of turbulence, violence and repression that were in turn responses to the fractious nature of its society and its politics. Revolution, rebellion and riots were all indications that throughout the centuries not all stakeholders have felt properly represented or had their vital concerns addressed. Tolerance by its very nature was hierarchical and discriminatory: an uneven interaction between those who tolerated and were tolerated, between those who held more power and those who had less. Cooperation for the sake of civil peace or to advance trade was often anything but true embrace or mutual affection. Persistent structures based on class and gender kept Dutch society stratified. Dutch interactions overseas saw little of the restraint practiced at home. Seen this way, Dutch history is not a model for anything but another cautionary tale on the difficulties of negotiating difference, a permutation of a wider human narrative that will find its expression in any honest history, national or otherwise.

Yet because relatively many Dutch had at least some share of power and prosperity, because geography and shared human nemeses required a practical unity of purpose among them, because the diversity of conviction among them demanded some acceptance of difference, because the requirements of commerce and the social order instructed them on the need to live and let live, the history of the Netherlands is the history of an adaptable people who, more often than not, shaped a society conducive to human flourishing. In this respect, the historical ability of the Dutch to live together, despite many trying episodes, is particularly instructive in an age of polarization where this aim seems less and less achievable, or even desirable.

SUGGESTIONS FOR FURTHER READING

Most works on Dutch history are in Dutch, not surprisingly. There is a modest amount that does appear in English, some of which is listed below for the benefit of the anglophone reader. For a more extensive bibliography that also indicates the Dutch-language sources I utilized in the translated version of this book please see James C. Kennedy, *Een beknopte geschiedenis van Nederland* (Amsterdam: Prometheus, 2017). The list below is hardly exhaustive, but gives a good impression of the work available in English.

The books below also indirectly indicate which parts of Dutch history historians using the English language find most interesting. The Golden Age, of course, receives extensive attention, dwarfing interests in other parts of Dutch history. Dutch colonial history across the centuries also gets a fair amount of attention, and the twentieth century draws historians interested either in the World Wars or in the Nazi occupation of the Netherlands. Furthermore, Dutch economic historians have been more assiduous in presenting their part of history than other Dutch historians, as is also evident in this overview.

General Works

Paul Arblaster, *A History of the Low Countries* (Basingstoke: Palgrave Macmillan, 2006)

Jan Bank, Gijsbert van Es and Piet de Rooy, *In Short, the Netherlands: Everything You Always Wanted to Know about Dutch History* (Wormer: Inmerc, 2005)

Herman Beliën and Monique van Hoogstraten, *Dutch History in a Nutshell* (Amsterdam: Prometheus, 2016)

Klaas van Berkel and Leonie de Goei (eds.), The International Relevance of Dutch History. *Low Countries Historical Review*, 125.2–3 (2010)

J. C. H. Blom, Renate Fuks-Mansfeld and Ivo Schöffer (eds.), *The History of the Jews in the Netherlands* (Oxford: Oxford University Press, 2002)

J. C. H. Blom and E. Lamberts (eds.), *History of the Low Countries*, trans. James C. Kennedy (New York: Berghahn, 2006)

Douwe Fokkema and Frans Grijzenhout (eds.), *Dutch Culture in a European Perspective, Vol. V: Accounting for the Past: 1650–2000* (Assen and Basingstoke: Royal Van Gorcum/Palgrave Macmillan, 2004)

Marjolein 't Hart, Joost Jonker and Jan Luiten van Zanden (eds.), *A Financial History of the Netherlands* (Cambridge: Cambridge University Press, 1997)

Jonathan Israel and Reinier Salverda (eds.), *Dutch Jewry: Its History and Secular Culture (1500–2000)* (Leiden: Brill, 2002)

J. A. Kossmann-Putto and E. H. Kossmann, *The Low Countries: History of the Northern and Southern Netherlands*, trans. J. Fenoulhet (Rekkem: Ons Erfdeel, 1997)

Hans Krabbendam, Cornelis A. van Minnen and Giles Scott-Smith (eds.), *Four Centuries of Dutch–American Relations, 1609–2009* (Amsterdam: Boom, 2009)

A. Lambert, *The Making of the Dutch Landscape* (London and New York: Seminar Press, 1985)

Frits van Oostrom, *A Key to Dutch History: The Cultural Canon of the Netherlands* (Amsterdam: Amsterdam University Press, 2007)

Peter Rietbergen, *A Short History of the Netherlands: From Pre-History to the Present Day*, 10th edn (Amersfoort: Bekking & Blitz, 2014)

Herman Selderhuis (ed.), *Handbook of Dutch Church History* (Göttingen: Vandenhoeck & Ruprecht, 2015)

Russell Shorto, *Amsterdam: A History of the World's Most Liberal City* (New York: Doubleday, 2013)

Lee Soltow and Jan Luiten van Zanden, *Income and Wealth Inequality in the Netherlands, 16th–20th Century* (Amsterdam: Het Spinhuis, 1998)

Harm Stevens, *Shades of Orange: A History of the Royal House of the Netherlands*, trans. Lynne Richards (Amsterdam and Zwolle: Rijksmuseum/Waanders, 2001)

Gerardus Petrus van de Ven, *Man-Made Lowlands: History of Water Management and Land Reclamation in the Netherlands*, 4th rev. edn (Utrecht: Matrijs, 2004)

Jacob Vossestein, *The Dutch and Their Delta: Living below Sea Level* (The Hague: XPat Media, 2011)

H. van der Wee and E. Cauwenberghe (eds.), *Productivity of Land and Agricultural Innovation in the Low Countries* (Leuven: Leuven University Press, 1978)

Friso Wielenga, *A History of the Netherlands: From the Sixteenth Century to the Present Day*, trans. Lynne Richards (London: Bloomsbury, 2015)

Chapter 1 From the Margins to the Mainstream: Dutch History to 1384

Bernard S. Bachrach, *Charlemagne's Early Campaigns (768–777): A Diplomatic and Military Analysis* (Leiden: Brill, 2013)

Bas van Bavel, *Manors and Markets: Economy and Society in the Low Countries, 500–1600* (Oxford: Oxford University Press, 2010)

Marc Boone and Martha Howell, *The Power of Space in Late Medieval and Early Modern Europe: The Cities of Italy, Northern France and the Low Countries* (Turnhout: Brepols, 2013)

Roel Brandt and Jan Slofstra (eds.), *Roman and Native in the Low Countries: Spheres of Interaction* (Oxford: BAR, 1983)

Ton Derks, *Gods, Temples and Ritual Practices: The Transformation of Religious Ideas and Values in Roman Gaul*, Amsterdam Archaeological Studies, 2 (Amsterdam: Amsterdam University Press, 1998)

Ludo J. R. Milis, *Religion, Culture, and Mentalities in the Medieval Low Countries: Selected Essays* (Turnhout: Brepols, 2005)

David Nicholas, *Medieval Flanders* (London: Longman, 1992)

N. Royman and F. Theuws (eds.), *Images of the Past: Studies of Ancient Societies in Northwestern Europe*, Studies in Prae- and Protohistory, 7 (Amsterdam: Instituut voor Pre- en Protohistorische Archeologie Albert Egges van Giffen, 1991)

Walter Simons, *Cities of Ladies: Beguine Communities in the Medieval Low Countries, 1200–1565* (Philadelphia: University of Pennsylvania Press, 2001)

Joanna Story, *Charlemagne: Empire and Society* (Manchester: Manchester University Press, 2005)

Tacitus, *Histories* (London: Penguin, 2009)

Adriaan Verhulst, *The Rise of Cities in North-West Europe* (Cambridge: Cambridge University Press, 1999)

W. J. H. Willems, *Romans and Batavians: Regional Developments at the Imperial Frontier* (Amersfoort: ROB, 1984)

Annemarieke Willemsen and Hanneke Kik (eds.), *Golden Middle Ages in Europe: New Research into Early-Medieval Communities and Identities. Proceedings of the Second "Dorestad Congress" Held at the National Museum of Antiquities Leiden, The Netherlands 2–5 July, 2014* (Turnhout: Brepols, 2015)

Ian Wood, *The Merovingian Kingdoms, 450–751* (London: Longman, 1994)

Greg Woolf, *Becoming Roman: The Origins of Provincial Civilization in Gaul* (Cambridge: Cambridge University Press, 1998)

Chapter 2 Rise of the Northern Netherlands, 1384–1588

C. A. J. Armstrong, *England, France and Burgundy in the Fifteenth Century* (London: Hambledon Press, 1983)

Wim Blockmans and Walter Prevenier, *The Promised Lands: The Low Countries under Burgundian Rule, 1369–1530*, trans. Elizabeth Fackelman (Philadelphia: University of Pennsylvania Press, 1999)

Marco van der Hoeven (ed.), *Exercise of Arms: Warfare in the Netherlands, 1568–1648* (Leiden: Brill, 1997)

Johan Huizinga, *The Autumn of the Middle Ages*, trans. R. J. Payton and U. Mammitzsch (Chicago: University of Chicago Press, 1996)

Jonathan Israel, *The Dutch Republic: Its Rise, Greatness and Fall, 1477–1806* (Oxford: Oxford University Press, 1995)

Lisa Jardine, *The Awful End of Prince William the Silent: The First Assassination of a Head of State with a Handgun* (New York: Harper, 2005)

Benjamin J. Kaplan, *Calvinists and Libertines: Confession and Community in Utrecht, 1578–1620* (Oxford: Clarendon Press, 1995)

Helmut Georg Koenigsberger, *Monarchies, States Generals and Parliaments: The Netherlands in the Fifteenth and Sixteenth Centuries* (Cambridge: Cambridge University Press, 2001)

Henk van Nierop, *The Nobility of Holland: From Knights to Regents, 1300–1650* (Cambridge: Cambridge University Press, 1993)

Treason in Holland: War, Terror and the Law in the Dutch Revolt (Princeton: Princeton University Press, 2009)

Gerard Nijsten, *In the Shadow of Burgundy: The Court of Guelders in the Late Middle Ages,* trans. Tanis Guest (Cambridge: Cambridge University Press, 2004)

Frits van Oostrom, *Court and Culture: Dutch Literature 1350–1450* (Berkeley and Los Angeles: University of California Press, 1992)

Geoffrey Parker, *The Army of Flanders and the Spanish Road, 1567–1659: The Logistics of Victory and Defeat in the Low Countries* (Cambridge: Cambridge University Press, 1990)

The Dutch Revolt (London: Pelican, 1985)

Judith Pollmann, *Catholic Identity and the Revolt of the Netherlands, 1520–1635* (Oxford: Oxford University Press, 2011)

Walter Prevenier and Wim Blockmans, *The Burgundian Netherlands* (Cambridge: Cambridge University Press, 1986)

Wybren Scheepsma, *Medieval Religious Women in the Low Countries: The "Modern Devotion," the Canonesses of Windesheim and Their Writings,* trans. David F. Johnson (Woodbridge: Boydell, 2004)

Werner Scheltjens, *Dutch Deltas: Emergence, Functions and Structure of the Low Countries' Maritime Transport System, ca. 1300–1850* (Leiden: Brill, 2015)

Frits Scholden, Joanna Woodall and Dulcia Meijders (eds.), *Art and Migration: Netherlandish Artists on the Move, 1400–1750* (Leiden: Brill, 2014)

Robert Stein and Judith Pollmann (eds.), *Networks, Regions and Nations: Shaping Identities in the Low Countries, 1300–1650* (Leiden: Brill, 2010)

K. W. Swart, *William of Orange and the Revolt of the Netherlands, 1572–84*, with introductory chapters by Alastair Duke and Jonathan I. Israel; trans. J. C. Grayson (Aldershot: Ashgate, 2003)

James D. Tracy, *The Founding of the Dutch Republic: War, Finance and Politics in Holland, 1572–1588* (Oxford: Oxford University Press, 2008)

    Holland under Habsburg Rule, 1506–1566: The Formation of a Body Politic (Berkeley: University of California Press, 1990)

Jan de Vries and Ad van der Woude, *The First Modern Economy: Success, Failure and Perseverance of the Dutch Economy, 1500–1815* (Cambridge: Cambridge University Press, 1997)

C. J. Zuijderduijn, *Medieval Capital Markets: Markets for Renten, State Formation and Private Investment in Holland (1300–1550)* (Leiden: Brill, 2009)

Chapter 3 A Young Republic's Golden Age, 1588–1672

Svetlana Alpers, *The Art of Describing: Dutch Art in the Seventeenth Century* (Chicago: University of Chicago Press, 1984)

Klaas van Berkel, Albert van Helden and Lodewijk Palm (eds.), *A History of Science in the Netherlands: Survey, Themes and Reference* (Leiden: Brill, 1999)

Charles R. Boxer, *The Dutch Seaborne Empire, 1600–1800* (London: Hutchinson, 1977)

Jaap R. Bruijn, Ronald Prud'homme van Reine and Rolof van Hövell tot Westerflier (eds.), *De Ruyter: Dutch Admiral* (Rotterdam: Karwansaray Publishers, 2011)

H. J. Cook, *Matters of Exchange: Commerce, Medicine and Science in the Dutch Golden Age* (New Haven: Yale University Press, 2007)

Mike Dash, *Batavia's Graveyard: The True Story of the Mad Heretic who Led History's Bloodiest Mutiny* (London: Weidenfeld & Nicolson, 2002)

Karel Davids and Jan Lucassen (eds.), *A Miracle Mirrored: The Dutch Republic in European Perspective* (Cambridge: Cambridge University Press, 1995)

Karel Davids and Leo Noordegraaf (eds.), *The Dutch Economy in the Golden Age: Nine Studies* (Amsterdam: Het Nederlandsch Economisch-Historisch Archief, 1993)

A. T. van Deursen, *Plain Lives in a Golden Age: Popular Culture, Religion and Society in Seventeenth-Century Holland* (Cambridge: Cambridge University Press, 1991)

Willem Frijhoff and Marijke Spies (eds.), *Dutch Culture in European Perspective, Vol. I: 1650: Hard-Won Unity* (Assen and Basingstoke: Royal Van Gorcum/Palgrave Macmillan, 2004)

Oscar Gelderblom (ed.), *The Political Economy of the Dutch Republic* (Aldershot: Ashgate, 2009)

Anne Goldgar, *Tulipmania: Money, Honor and Knowledge in the Dutch Golden Age* (Chicago: University of Chicago Press, 2007)

Craig E. Harline, *Pamphlets, Painting and Political Culture in the Early Dutch Republic* (Dordrecht: Martinus Nijhoff, 1987)

Daniëlle van den Heuvel, *Women and Entrepreneurship: Female Traders in the Northern Netherlands, c. 1580–1815* (Amsterdam: Aksant, 2007)

Jonathan Israel, *Dutch Primacy in World Trade, 1585–1740* (Oxford: Oxford University Press, 1989)

Martine van Ittersum, *Profit and Principle: Hugo Grotius, Natural Rights Theories and the Rise of Dutch Power in the East Indies, 1595–1615* (Leiden: Brill, 2006)

Jaap Jacobs, *New Netherland: A Dutch Colony in Seventeenth-Century America* (Leiden: Brill, 2005)

Benjamin Kaplan (ed.), *Catholic Communities in Protestant States: Britain and the Netherlands, c. 1570–1720* (Manchester: Manchester University Press, 2009)

Els Kloek, Nicole Teeuwen and Marijke Huisman (eds.), *An International Debate on Women in Seventeenth-Century Holland, England and Italy* (Hilversum: Verloren, 1994)

Randall Lesaffer (ed.), *The Twelve Years Truce (1609): Peace, Truce and Law in the Low Countries at the Turn of the 17th Century* (Leiden: Brill, 2014)

Thomas Maissen and Maarten Prak (eds.), *The Republican Alternative: The Netherlands and Switzerland Compared* (Amsterdam: Amsterdam University Press, 2008)

Anne E. C. McCants, *Civic Care in a Golden Age: Orphan Care in Early Modern Amsterdam* (Urbana: University of Illinois Press, 1997)

Olaf van Nimwegen, *The Dutch Army and the Military Revolutions, 1588–1688*, trans. Andrew May (Woodbridge: Boydell, 2010)

Paul Otto, *The Dutch–Munsee Encounter in America: The Struggle for Sovereignty in the Hudson Valley* (New York: Berghahn, 2006)

Willie F. Page, *The Dutch Triangle: The Netherlands and the Atlantic Slave Trade, 1621–1664* (New York: Garland, 1997)

Charles H. Parker, *The Reformation of Community: Social Welfare and Calvinist Charity in Holland, 1572–1620* (Cambridge: Cambridge University Press, 1998)

R. Po-Chia-Hsia and Henk van Nierop (eds.), *Calvinism and Religious Toleration in the Dutch Golden Age* (Cambridge: Cambridge University Press, 2002)

Johannes M. Postma, *The Dutch in the Atlantic Slave Trade, 1600–1815* (Cambridge: Cambridge University Press, 1990)

Johannes Postma and Victor Enthoven (eds.), *Riches from Atlantic Commerce: Dutch Transatlantic Trade and Shipping, 1585–1817* (Leiden: Brill, 2003)

Maarten Prak, *The Dutch Republic in the Seventeenth Century* (Cambridge: Cambridge University Press, 2005)

Catharina Lis, Jan Lucassen and Hugo Soly, *Craft Guilds in the Early Modern Low Countries: Work, Power and Representation* (Aldershot: Ashgate, 2006)

J. Leslie Price, *Dutch Culture in a Golden Age* (London: Reaktion Books, 2011)

Michel Reinders, *Printed Pandemonium: Popular Print and Politics in the Netherlands, 1650–1672* (Leiden: Brill, 2013)

H. Rowen, *Johan de Witt, Statesman of the "True Freedom"* (Cambridge: Cambridge University Press, 1986)

Simon Schama, *The Embarrassment of Riches: An Interpretation of Dutch Culture in the Golden Age* (New York: Knopf, 1987)

Heinz Schilling, *Religion, Political Culture and the Emergence of Early Modern Society: Essays in German and Dutch History* (Leiden: Brill, 1992)

Benjamin Schmidt, *Innocence Abroad: The Dutch Imagination and the New World, 1570–1670* (Cambridge: Cambridge University Press, 2001)

Eric Jan Sluijter, *Seductress of Sight: Studies in Dutch Art of the Golden Age*, trans. Jennifer Kilian (Zwolle: Waanders, 2000)

Theo Verbeek, *Descartes and the Dutch: Early Reactions to Cartesian Philosophy* (Carbondale: Southern Illinois University Press, 1992)

Mariët Westermann, *A Worldly Art: The Dutch Republic, 1585–1718* (New Haven: Yale University Press, 2005)

Arthur Weststeijn, *Commercial Republicanism in the Dutch Golden Age: The Political Thought of Johan and Pieter de la Court* (Leiden: Brill, 2012)

Jan Luijten van Zanden, *The Rise and Decline of Holland's Economy: Merchant Capitalism and the Labour Market* (Manchester and New York: Manchester University Press, 1993)

Kees Zandvliet (ed.), *The Dutch Encounter with Asia, 1600–1950* (Zwolle and Amsterdam: Waanders/Rijksmuseum, 2002)

Chapter 4 Diminishing Returns and New Hopes, 1672–1795

C. Berkvens-Stevelinck, Jonathan Israel and G. H. M. Posthumus-Meyjes (eds.), *The Emergence of Tolerance in the Dutch Republic* (Leiden: Brill, 1997)

Paul Brusse and Wijnand W. Mijnhardt, *Towards a New Template for Dutch History: De-Urbanization and the Balance between City and Countryside* (Zwolle: Waanders, 2011)

Wiep van Bunge (ed.), *The Early Enlightenment in the Dutch Republic, 1650–1750* (Leiden: Brill, 2003)

Alice C. Carter, *The Dutch Republic in Europe in the Seven Years' War* (London: Macmillan, 1971)

Ann Coenen, *Carriers of Growth? International Trade and Economic Development in the Austrian Netherlands* (Leiden: Brill, 2014)

Karel Davids, *The Rise and Decline of Dutch Technological Leadership: Economy and Culture in the Netherlands*, 2 vols. (Leiden: Brill, 2007)

Joris van Eijnatten, *Liberty and Concord in the United Provinces: Religious Toleration and the Public in the Eighteenth-Century Netherlands* (Leiden: Brill, 2003)

Pieter Emmer, *The Dutch in the Atlantic Economy, 1580–1880: Trade, Slavery and Emancipation* (Aldershot: Ashgate, 1998)

Andrew Fix, *Fallen Angels: Balthasar Bekker, Spirit Belief and Confessionalism in the Seventeenth Century Dutch Republic* (Dordrecht: Kluwer, 1999)

Willem Frijhoff, *Embodied Belief: Ten Essays on Religious Culture in Dutch History* (Hilversum: Verloren, 2002)

Lynn Hunt, Margaret C. Jacob and Wijnand Mijnhardt, *The Book that Changed Europe: Picart and Bernard's "Religious Ceremonies of the World"* (Cambridge: Harvard University Press, 2010)

Jonathan Israel, *Radical Enlightenment: Philosophy and the Making of Modernity* (Oxford: Oxford University Press, 2001)

Margaret C. Jacob and Wijnand W. Mijnhardt (eds.), *The Dutch Republic in the Eighteenth Century: Decline, Enlightenment and Revolution* (Ithaca, NY and London: Cornell University Press, 1992)

Lisa Jardine, *Going Dutch: How England Plundered Holland's Glory* (London: Harper, 2008)

Benjamin J. Kaplan, *Cunegonde's Kidnapping: A Story of Religious Conflict in the Age of Enlightenment* (New Haven: Yale University Press, 2014)

David van der Linden, *Experiencing Exile: Huguenot Refugees in the Dutch Republic, 1680–1700* (Farnham: Ashgate, 2015)

Esther Mijers and David Onnekink (eds.), *Redefining William III: The Impact of the King-Stadholder in International Context* (Aldershot: Ashgate, 2007)

Chris Nierstrasz, *In the Shadow of the Company: The Dutch East India Company and Its Servants in the Period of Its Decline, 1740–1796*, ed. Rosemary Robson-McKillop (Leiden: Brill, 2012)

David Ormrod, *The Rise of Commercial Empires: England and the Netherlands in the Age of Mercantilism, 1650–1770* (Cambridge: Cambridge University Press, 2003)

George Satterfield, *Princes, Posts and Partisans: The Army of Louis XIV and Partisan Warfare in the Netherlands (1673–1678)* (Leiden: Brill, 2003)

Simon Schama, *Patriots and Liberators: Revolution in the Netherlands, 1780–1813* (New York: Knopf, 1977)

Wayne P. TeBrake, *Regents and Rebels: The Revolutionary World of an Eighteenth-Century Dutch City* (Oxford: Oxford University Press, 1989)

William Temple, *Observations upon the United Provinces of the Netherlands*, reprinted with introduction by G. N. Clark (Cambridge: Cambridge University Press, 2011)

Wyger Velema, *Republicans: Essays on Eighteenth-Century Dutch Political Thought* (Leiden: Brill, 2007)

M. Wielema, *The March of the Libertines: Spinozists and the Dutch Reformed Church (1660–1750)* (Hilversum: Verloren, 2004)

Chapter 5 Building a Nation-State, 1795–1870

Katherine B. Aaslestad and Johan Joor (eds.), *Revisiting Napoleon's Continental System: Local, Regional and European Experiences* (Basingstoke: Palgrave Macmillan, 2015)

David Bos, *Servants of the Kingdom: Professionalization among Ministers of the Nineteenth-Century Netherlands Reformed Church*, trans. David McKay (Leiden: Brill, 2010)

Hugh Dunthorne and Michael Wintle (eds.), *The Historical Imagination in Nineteenth-Century Britain and the Low Countries* (Leiden: Brill, 2013)

C. Fasseur, *The Politics of Colonial Exploitation: Java, the Dutch and the Cultivation System* (Ithaca, NY: Cornell University Press, 1992)

J. S. Fishman, *Diplomacy and Revolution: The London Conference of 1830 and the Belgian Revolt* (Amsterdam: CHEV, 1988)

Alan Forrest, *Great Battles: Waterloo* (Oxford: Oxford University Press, 2015)

Joost Kloek and Wijnand Mijnhardt (eds.), *Dutch Culture in a European Perspective, Vol. II: 1800: Blueprints for a National Community* (Assen and Basingstoke: Royal Van Gorcum/ Palgrave Macmillan, 2004)

E. H. Kossmann, *The Low Countries, 1780–1940* (Oxford: Oxford University Press, 1978)

J. Mokyr, *Industrialization in the Low Countries, 1795–1850* (New Haven: Yale University Press, 1976)

Bob Moore and Henk van Nierop (eds.), *Colonial Empires Compared: Britain and the Netherlands, 1750–1850* (Aldershot: Ashgate, 2003)

Joris Oddens, Mart Rutjes and Erik Jacobs (eds.), *The Political Culture of the Sister Republics, 1794–1806: France, the Netherlands, Switzerland and Italy* (Amsterdam: Amsterdam University Press, 2015)

Gert Oostindie (ed.), *Fifty Years Later: Antislavery, Capitalism and Modernity in the Dutch Orbit* (Leiden: KITLV, 1995)

Piet de Rooy, *A Tiny Spot on the Earth: The Political Culture of the Netherlands in the Nineteenth and Twentieth Century* (Amsterdam: Amsterdam University Press, 2015)

John Halsey Wood, Jr., *Going Dutch in the Modern Age: Abraham Kuyper's Struggle for a Free Church in the Nineteenth-Century Netherlands* (Oxford: Oxford University Press, 2013)

Jan Luiten van Zanden and Arthur van Riel, *The Structures of Inheritance: The Dutch Economy in the Nineteenth Century* (Princeton: Princeton University Press, 2004)

Chapter 6 Progress and Crisis, 1870–1949

Gerard Aalbers, *Nazi Looting: The Plunder of Dutch Jewry during the Second World War* (Oxford: Berg, 2004)

Maartje Abbenhuis, *The Art of Staying Neutral: The Netherlands in the First World War* (Amsterdam: Amsterdam University Press, 2006)

Herman Amersfoort and Piet Kamphuis (eds.), *May 1940: The Battle for the Netherlands*, trans. Fiona Nauta (Leiden: Brill, 2010)

Jan Bank and Martine van Buuren (eds.), *Dutch Culture in a European Perspective, Vol. III: 1900: The Age of Bourgeois Culture* (Assen and Basingstoke: Royal Van Gorcum/Palgrave Macmillan, 2004)

James D. Bratt, *Abraham Kuyper: Modern Calvinist, Christian Democrat* (Grand Rapids: Eerdmans, 2013)

Jaap Cohen, *The Cohen Book: The History of a Dutch Jewish Family from the 17th to the 20th Century*, trans. and annot. Sam Herman (Amsterdam: Manesseh ben Israel Instituut, 2016)

Robert Cribb, *Gangsters and Revolutionaries: The Jakarta People's Militias and the Indonesian Revolution, 1945–1949* (North Sydney: Allen & Unwin/Asian Studies Association of Australia, 1991)

Robert Cribb (ed.), *The Late Colonial State in Asia: Political and Economic Foundations of the Netherlands Indies, 1880–1942* (Leiden: KITLV, 1994)

Jeroen Dewulf, *Spirit of Resistance: Dutch Clandestine Literature during the Nazi Occupation* (Rochester, NY: Camden House, 2010)

Ewout Frankema and Frans Buelens (eds.), *Colonial Exploitation and Economic Development: The Belgian Congo and the Netherlands Indies Compared* (London: Routledge, 2013)

Cornelia Fuykschot, *Hunger in Holland: Life during the Nazi Occupation* (New York: Prometheus, 1988)

Annemieke Galema, Barbara Henkes and Henk te Velde (eds.), *Images of the Nation: Different Meanings of Dutchness, 1870–1940* (Amsterdam and Atlanta: Rodopi, 1993)

Frances Gouda, *Dutch Culture Overseas: Colonial Practice in the Netherlands-Indies, 1900–1942* (Amsterdam: Amsterdam University Press, 1995)

Francisca de Haan, *Gender and the Politics of Office Work in the Netherlands, 1860–1940* (Amsterdam: Amsterdam University Press, 1998)

John Hiemstra, *Worldviews in the Air: The Struggle to Create a Pluralist Broadcasting System in the Netherlands* (Lanham: University Press of America, 1997)

Gerhard Hirschfeld, *Nazi Rule and Dutch Collaboration: The Netherlands under German Occupation*, trans. Louise Willmot (Oxford: Berg, 1988)

Don Kalb, *Expanding Class: Power and Everyday Politics in Industrial Communities. The Netherlands, 1850–1950* (Durham, NC: Duke University Press, 1997)

Wim Klinkert, *Defending Neutrality: The Netherlands Prepares for War,*
1900–1925 (Leiden: Brill, 2013)

Robert van der Laarse, *A Nation of Notables: Class, Politics, and Religion*
in the Netherlands in the Nineteenth Century (Salford: European
Studies Research Institute, University of Salford, 1999)

Susan Legêne and Janneke van Dijk (eds.), *The Netherlands East*
Indies at the Tropenmuseum: A Colonial History (Amsterdam: KIT
Publishers, 2011)

Bart Luttikhuis and A. Dirk Moses (eds.), *Colonial Counterinsurgency*
and Mass Violence: The Dutch Empire in Indonesia
(London: Routledge, Taylor and Francis Group, 2014)

Bob Moore, *Victims and Survivors: The Nazi Persecution of the Jews in*
the Netherlands, 1941–1945 (London: Arnold, 1997)

Ryan K. Noppen, *Blue Skies, Orange Wings: The Global Reach of*
Dutch Aviation in War and Peace, 1914–1945 (Grand Rapids:
Eerdmans, 2016)

Jacob Presser, *Ashes in the Wind: The Destruction of Dutch Jewry*
(Detroit: Wayne State University Press, 1968)

Marloes Schoonheim, *Mixing Ovaries and Rosaries: Catholic Religion*
and Reproduction in the Netherlands, 1870–1970 (Amsterdam:
Aksant, 2005)

David Sweetman, *Van Gogh: His Life and His Art* (New York: Crown,
1990)

Hubert P. van Tuyll van Serooskerken, *The Netherlands and World War*
I: Espionage, Diplomacy and Survival (Leiden: Brill, 2001)

Augustus J. Veenendaal, *Railways in the Netherlands: A Brief History,*
1834–1994 (Stanford: Stanford University Press, 2001)

Michael Wintle, *An Economic and Social History of the Netherlands,*
1800–1920 (Cambridge: Cambridge University Press, 2000)

Susanne Wolf, *Guarded Neutrality: Diplomacy and Internment in the*
Netherlands during the First World War (Leiden: Brill, 2013)

Chapter 7 A Progressive Beacon to the World, 1949–2017

Herman Bakvis, *Catholic Power in the Netherlands* (Kingston and
Montreal: McGill-Queen's University Press, 1981)

Ulbe Bosma, *Post-Colonial Immigrants and Identity Formations in the Netherlands* (Amsterdam: Amsterdam University Press, 2012)

Peter de Brock and Peter Zwaal, *The History of Amstel Brouwerij since 1870* (Amsterdam: Bas Lubberhuizen, 2010)

Ian Buruma, *Murder in Amsterdam: Liberal Europe, Islam and the Limits of Tolerance* (New York: Penguin, 2006)

Beatrice de Graaf, Ben de Jong and Wies Platje (eds.), *Battleground Western Europe: Intelligence Operations in Germany and the Netherlands in the Twentieth Century* (Apeldoorn: Het Spinhuis, 2007)

Jan Willem Honig and Norbert Both, *Srebrenica: Record of a War Crime* (London: Penguin, 1996)

Pete Jordan, *In the City of Bikes: The Story of the Amsterdam Cyclist* (New York, Harper, 2013)

Frank J. Lechner, *The Netherlands: Globalization and National Identity* (New York and London: Routledge, 2008)

William Mallinson, *From Neutrality to Commitment: Dutch Foreign Policy, NATO and European Integration* (London: I.B. Tauris, 2010)

Geert Oostindie (ed.), *Dutch Colonialism, Migration and Cultural Heritage* (Leiden: Brill, 2008)

Gert Oostindie, *Postcolonial Netherlands: Sixty-Five Years of Forgetting, Commemorating, Silencing,* trans. Annabel Howland (Amsterdam: Amsterdam University Press, 2011)

Eric Sengers (ed.), *The Dutch and Their Gods: Secularization and Transformation of Religion in the Netherlands since 1950* (Hilversum: Verloren, 2005)

Stephen Small, *Living History: The Legacy of Slavery in the Netherlands* (Amsterdam and The Hague: Ninsee/Amrit, 2012)

Kees Schuyt and Ed Taverne (eds.), *Dutch Culture in a European Perspective, Vol. IV: 1950: Prosperity and Welfare,* trans. Language Centre, University of Groningen (Assen and Basingstoke: Royal Van Gorcum/Palgrave Macmillan, 2004)

William Z. Shetter, *The Netherlands in Perspective: The Dutch Way of Organizing a Society and Its Setting* (Utrecht: Nederlands Centrum Buitenlander, 2002)

Mienke Simon Thomas, *Dutch Design: A History* (London: Reaktion Books, 2008)

Joris J. C. Voorhoeve, *Peace, Profits and Principles: A Study of Dutch Foreign Policy* (Leiden: Martinus Nijhoff, 1985)

Herman Vuijsje, *The Politically Correct Netherlands since the 1960s*, trans. and annot. Mark T. Hooker (Westport: Greenwood Press, 2000)

David Winner, *Brilliant Orange: The Neurotic Genius of Dutch Football* (London: Bloomsbury, 2000)

Jan Luiten van Zanden, *The Economic History of the Netherlands, 1914–1995: A Small Open Economy in the "Long" Twentieth Century* (London: Routledge, 1988)

INDEX

474

Made in the USA
Lexington, KY
18 September 2017